ALL ABOUT AUSSIES

Dusty and Thistle, a golden cross that created a tremendous influence on the breed. Photo by Phil Wildhagen.

JUST A STOCKDOG STORY
by Gary Bogy

Do you remember when I was just a little tyke,
and you bought that hot new colt named Ike.
He was the color of new fallen snow,
I ran right down to say hello.
Then he kicked a mighty blow,
he nearly hit me, but I ducked low.

I got mad and heeled him hard,
we fought all over the yard.
And when the storm's end was near,
you were pullin' on my ear.
Then I knew I done wrong,
and sang out a sad song.

You said it would be all right,
it was just a kid fight.
Back then you were just a boss,
to a young pup and a green broke hoss.
We made the rounds the three of us,
gathered stock and lots of dust.

That was how it all began,
we all became working friends.
Remember that steer we penned out West,
his horns were longer than the rest.
He was aiming to run me thru,
if it had not been for Ike and you.

Dropped a loop around his neck,
then I really gave him heck.
Then you met that darned old girl,
left me and Ike in a swirl.
We could not find you for a while,
then you brought her home with a smile.

She was really neat,
I loved to lay there by her feet.
One day we got a place of our own,
you and her called it a home.
You remember that brindle bull named Prince,
he had you pinned against the fence.

I told him to let you go and bit him very hard,
he must have kicked me from the yard.
Now I found a place to rest,
like those mountain meadows out West.
But the flowers here stay year-round,
and nobody ever mentions a dog pound.

All the animals here are friends,
it's the way it should have always been.
I sure missed you there at first,
and knew it could not have been worse.
They say it never, never ends,
and I keep making more good friends.

I wanted you to know I am okay,
And I hope to see you here someday.

All About Aussies
Third Edition

The Australian Shepherd from A to Z

Jeanne Joy Hartnagle-Taylor

Alpine
Blue Ribbon Books
Loveland, Colorado

ALL ABOUT AUSSIES

Copyright © 2009, 2005, 1996 by Jeanne Joy Hartnagle-Taylor

All rights reserved. No part of this book may be used or reproduced in any manner whatsoever, including electronic media, internet, or newsletters, without written permission from the publisher, except in the case of brief quotations embodied in critical reviews. For permission, write to Alpine Publications, Inc., P. O. Box 7027, Loveland, CO 80537

ISBN 10: 1-57779-074-X
ISBN 13: 978-1-57779-074-7

Library of Congress Cataloging in Publication Data

Hartnagle-Taylor, Jeanne Joy, 1955-
All About Aussies: the Australian shepherd from A to Z / Jeanne Joy Hartnagle-Taylor
3rd ed.
p. cm.
Includes bibliographical references and index.
ISBN 1-57779-074-X
1. Australian shepherd dog. I. Title

SF429.A79H38 2005
636.737--dc22
2005041069

The information contained in this book is complete and accurate to the best of our knowledge. All recommendations are made without guarantee on the part of the author or Alpine Publications, Inc. The author and publisher disclaim any liability with the use of this information. Readers are advised to consult with their veterinarian before following medical advice given herein.

For the sake of simplicity, the terms " he" or "she" are sometimes used to identify an animal or person. These are used in the generic sense only. No discrimination of any kind is intended toward either sex.

Many manufacturers secure trademark rights for their products. When Alpine Publications is aware of a trademark claim, we identify the product name by using initial capital letters.

Cover Design: Laura Newport
Cover Photo: Courtesy of Marilyn and Bill Hahn
Editing: Dianne Borneman
Text Design and Layout: Dianne Borneman, Shadow Canyon Graphics

Printed in the United States of America.

Contents

Introduction ix
Foreword xi

CHAPTER 1: THOSE LITTLE BLUE DOGS 1
Early Origins of the Breed • Modern Aussies • Breed Clubs and Registries

CHAPTER 2: AMAZING AUSSIES AND CANINE CAREERS 9
Sports • Canine Careers: Service Dogs

CHAPTER 3: THE STANDARD OF EXCELLENCE 17
The Ideal • General Appearance • Character/Temperament • Head • Teeth • Eyes • Ears • Neck, Topline, Body • Forequarters • Hindquarters • Coat • Color • Gait • Size, Proportion, Substance • Other Disqualifications

CHAPTER 4: THE STANDARD IN MOTION 41
Symmetrical Gaits • Asymmetrical Gaits • Analyzing Structure • The View Going and Coming • Stride versus Size

CHAPTER 5: FINDING THE RIGHT AUSSIE 51
How to Find the Right Breeder • The Right Aussie for You • Aussie Profile • Get It In Writing

CHAPTER 6: YOUR NEW AUSSIE 61
The Homecoming • Puppy-Proof Your Home • Crates • The First Night Away from Mother • Crate Training • House Training • Socialization and Training • Leash Training • Finding the Right Puppy Class • Preventative Care • The New Adult Aussie

CHAPTER 7: RESPONSIBILITIES OF OWNING AN AUSSIE 71
Urban and Suburban Aussies • The Working Owner • Identify Your Dog • Controlling Reproduction • Aussies and the Law

CHAPTER 8: KIDS AND AUSSIES 81
The Aussie and Your Newborn Baby • Infants to Preschoolers • Aussies and the Kindergarten-Age Child • School-Age Children and Dogs • Aussies for Pre-Adolescents and Adolescents

CHAPTER 9: NO PLACE LIKE HOME 89
Yards and Runs • Dogs Houses and Kennels

CHAPTER 10: KEEPING UP APPEARANCES 95
The Australian Shepherd Coat • Grooming Table Training • Routine Grooming Care • Brushing • Bathing • Dry Cleaning

CHAPTER 11: NUTRITION 105
Basic Nutrients • Diet • How To Find the Right Diet • Supplementation • Methods of Feeding • Quantities to Feed • The Importance of Good Nutrition

CHAPTER 12: HEALTH CARE 119
Vaccinations and Infectious Diseases • Viral and Bacterial Diseases • Lyme Disease • Autoimmune Problems • Signs of Illness • Treating Stomach Upsets and Diarrhea • Common Antibiotics • Protozoal Intestinal Infections • Worms (Internal Parasites) • External Parasites

CHAPTER 13: EMERGENCY FIRST AID 135
First-Aid Procedures

CHAPTER 14: THE AGING AUSSIE 153
Management • Special Diets • Grooming • Housing • Exercise • Working the Aging Aussie • Traveling • Saying Good-Bye • Grief

CHAPTER 15: TRAVELING WITH YOUR AUSSIE 159
Travel Training • Travel Carriers • Other Essential Items for Travel • Health Requirements • Accommodations • Travel By Vehicle • Travel By Air • Travel By Ship • Travel By Bus or Train • Lost Dogs • When Your Dog Can't Go

CHAPTER 16: PRACTICAL TRAINING FOR YOUR AUSSIE 167
Rewards and Corrections • Training Tools • Teaching the Commands • Correcting Problem Behaviors

CHAPTER 17: FUN ACTIVITIES FOR YOU AND YOUR AUSSIE 175
Canine Good Citizen Test • Frisbee • Tracking • Agility • Other Activities

CHAPTER 18: BORN TO WORK 189
Herding Instincts • Evaluating a Litter • Introduction to Livestock • Play Training • Teaching Basic Commands

CHAPTER 19: TRAINING THE STOCK DOG 201
The Training Enclosure • Selecting Livestock for Training • First Lessons on Stock • Directional Commands • Driving • Cross Driving • Penning • Sorting (Shedding) • Look Back • Whistle Commands • Team Work • Herding/Stock-Dog Trials

CHAPTER 20: PERFORMANCE CONDITIONING 221
How to Condition Your Dog • Overtraining and Injury • Stress and Your Aussie • Care of the Feet • Water and Food • Summer Exercise for Your Aussie • Winter Exercise for Your Aussie

CHAPTER 21: THE DOG SHOW GAME 229
Conformation • How Championships Are Attained • Junior Showmanship • Obedience Trials • Entering a Show

CHAPTER 22: SHOW BUSINESS 239
Look Like a Winner • Grooming To Win • Be Prepared • In the Ring • The Art of Winning and Losing

CHAPTER 23: PICTURE PERFECT 247
Cameras • Before Shooting • Common Errors • Taking Better Photos • Advertising Shots

CHAPTER 24: GENETICS OF THE AUSTRALIAN SHEPHERD 255
Fundamental Principles of Genetics • Using Genetics in a Breeding Program • Eliminating Heritable Defects • Some Traits of Known or Probable Inheritance

CHAPTER 25: THE MATING GAME   281
Breeding Concepts • Pedigrees • Breed Standard • Setting Goals • The Brood Bitch • The Stud Dog • What You Should Know Before You Breed Aussies • Genetic Defects • Fundamental Genetics, Aussie Color Breeding, and White • Breeding For the Wrong Reasons • Developing a Bloodline of Distinction

CHAPTER 26: THE BIRDS AND THE BEES   293
The Brood Bitch • The Estrous Cycle • False Pregnancy (Pseudo-Pregnancy) • Vaginal Smears to Determine When to Breed • Mammary Glands • The Stud Dog • Reproductive Soundness • When To Breed • The Mating • Conception • Diseases of the Reproductive Tract

CHAPTER 27: THE MATERNITY WARD   309
Management • Whelping Box • Preparing for the Birth • Parturition • Whelping Problems • Care of the New Mother • Milk Supply • Eclampsia • Mastitis • The Bitch's Temperament

CHAPTER 28: THE NURSERY   325
Caring for the Newborn • Vital Signs • Examination of the Litter • Culling • Tail Docking and Dewclaws • Toenails • Raising Orphan and Foster Puppies • Bowel Movements and Urine • Puppy Ailments • Puppy Septicemia and Peritonitis • Recommended Vaccination and Worming Schedules • Handling During the First Twenty-One Days

CHAPTER 29: RAISING PUPPIES   337
Maturity • Selecting the Perfect Puppy

CHAPTER 30: ALL ABOUT MINIATURE AUSSIES   349
History • Little Blue Dogs • Character and Temperament • Buyer Beware! • Finding the Perfect Individual • Judging the Breed • Breeding Mini Aussies • Health Issues and Genetic Disorders Concerning Minis • ASCA and USASA Official Stance Concerning Mini and Toy Aussies • Miniature Aussie Registries

Appendix A: Sources of Information   357
Appendix B: Titles Your Dog Can Earn   359
Bibliography   361
Index   362
About the Author   367

This book is dedicated to the little man in my life and co-author,

TYLER JUSTIN TAYLOR

Introduction

Aussies have always been a part of my life. When my memory recalls childhood playmates, names like Daisy, Red, Blue, and Badger come to mind. These dogs were adoring companions to my sisters, brothers, and me. We discovered the world together.

Daisy helped Carol Ann, a baby at the time, learn how to walk. Daisy patiently tolerated Carol grabbing fists full of hair to pull herself up and take her first steps. Daisy endlessly retrieved toys that Carol hurled out of her playpen and returned them. And on many occasions, she would gently take hold of the toddler's small hand to lead her back toward the house when she strayed too far. Now, I have the ultimate pleasure of watching ancestors of our early Aussies help raise my own little boy.

It seemed that Aussies could do anything, and do it better than anybody else. It was mysterious how they always seemed to know what to do — and without any special training. When it was time to gather the sheep from the pastures, my father would send Jinx to bring them home. She would disappear into the horizon until she had gathered every ewe and lamb and brought them down the lane along the creek.

The loyalty was unmatched. Little Goody, Jinx's littermate, had a life filled with many incredible stories about her devoted work, with privation and hardship many times her sole reward from a thoughtless shepherd. When the sheepherder who was working her at the time had a stroke, Goody lay by him for three days to keep the buzzards away until help arrived.

The love affair with Aussies led my parents across the country in search of other Aussies. At that time, there was a growing interest in the breed, but only a handful of people breeding them. It was from that simple beginning that the foundation for the breed was laid. From there, the modern Aussie evolved. Since the first edition of *All About Aussies* was written, a multitude of changes have taken place in the breed and in the dog world, and it became necessary to update the book in its entirety.

I want to thank Betty Jo McKinney for superb publishing; Dianne Borneman for caring; Trish Thornwald for her illustrations; Christine Renna for her stockdog illustrations and for unselfishly lending a helping hand; Ann de Chant, Mike Ryan, and my parents for historical research; my family for a 100 percent commitment to excellence and for always being there for me; my best friend and husband for buying that little black Aussie (little did I know that he would change my life forever); and to the Lord Jesus for making it all possible.

— *Jeanne Joy Hartnagle-Taylor*

Three generations of the Hartnagle family.

Foreword

Few people, if any, are more qualified to bring you the Australian Shepherd as Jeanne Joy Hartnagle-Taylor. Breeder, trainer, competitor, judge, educator, and instructor; her well-rounded background has long established her credibility as an author on the subject of the Aussie. Even more extraordinary than her keen ability to impart information about this breed we know and love, is her depth of knowledge and true understanding of the breed itself.

The first edition of *All About Aussies* was an endeavor to write the quintessential book on the breed. As the very first breed book ever written, it provided an expansive look at the truly wonderful world of the Australian Shepherd, while gaining a prestigious nomination as "Dog Writer of the Year" (from the Dog Writers Association of America), for the author, Jeanne Joy.

Although that original manuscript stands on it's own merit as the most informative and encompassing book of it's kind, Jeanne Joy felt compelled to update the original manuscript, adding even more current material and following-up with new information especially in the areas of the history and origin. Long-time and novice breeders alike, will have a special appreciation for the updated "Spider Web." All readers will enjoy the variety of never-before-published pictures, as well.

Anyone who has owned an Aussie is familiar with the heroism and intelligence of these great dogs. Saving a child from an oncoming car, to the exploits of Topaz, an Aussie who led a herd of mother cows to safety in a spring blizzard, to Kentucky Badger, saving the life of his horse thrown master — we can all identify with the extreme loyalty and courage that characterizes the Australian Shepherd.

These are but a few odes to the glorious history of a truly unique breed. When growing up, these stories became quite commonplace, even to the extent of sounding almost fictional. However, they were indeed true and only reaffirmed the commitment I have to the Aussie to this day. My family's devotion to this magnificent breed and Jeanne Joy's straightforward approach to showing and trialing our favorite dogs, certainly led to an appreciation for raising and showing Australian Shepherds in my own right. Older sister Jeanne Joy led the way by garnering some of the top show honors as well as kudos in the working trial arenas across the country. She has gone on to become one of the foremost and respected experts on the breed and I am truly proud of her unwavering desire to continually search and share information with those who can never learn enough about their beloved Australian Shepherds.

Please sit back and enjoy, as I have, this delightful compilation of facts, accounts, recollections, and perhaps just a few fantasies, contained in *All About Aussies*. I can imagine it will only serve to increase your appreciation for a breed that has always been dear to your heart, the Australian Shepherd.

— *Carol Ann Hartnagle Madsen*

Jay Sisler with Sisler's Shorty (Keno ex Blue Star) on the left and littermate brother Sisler's Stub on the right.

Chapter 1

THOSE LITTLE BLUE DOGS

EARLY ORIGINS OF THE BREED

THE AUSTRALIAN SHEPHERD WAS ESTABLISHED in a time period when ranches were measured in sections (square miles) not acres. For the most part, the breed was founded with dogs that arrived in the Western United States from Spain between 1940 and 1970. Millions of sheep were being grazed on the vast rangelands. Due to an acute labor shortage around World War II, hundreds of Basque sheepherders in Spain were recruited to the American West to tend the flocks. They came under a three-year contract with the Western Range Association. They also brought their sheepdogs which were tools of the trade. As the "little blue dogs" began showing up in fairly significant numbers, they started being noticed. In a few decades they went from relative anonymity to mainstream popularity.

The Aussie name came about when certain Basque herders traveled to Australia hoping to secure work on the large sheep stations. When they arrived, they found out that the Australian method of sheep husbandry was far different from their native system of shepherding with the seasonal migration. Sheep were raised on permanent pastures and didn't require trailing between summer and winter ranges, so the herders took jobs caring for sheep on cargo ships destined for the United States. As the dogs arrived in America with the boatloads of sheep, they were referred to as "Australian Shepherds."

The life of these shepherds was comfortless and full of hardship. The dogs, too, were hardy individuals, toughened by exposure, and they proved to be adaptable. These dogs were capable of herding sheep over the western ranges and protecting the flocks from the predators. They possessed an intense herding ability with an avid devotion to their masters. Aussies were tractable to a remarkable degree but had sufficient independence and common sense to take care of themselves in almost any situation. These qualities were highly sought by the sheepmen of other countries.

These early Aussies were unafraid. They were sensible and dependable. They had stamina and power to move large numbers of sheep on open-range, could stand up to an obstinate ram, and were fearless of a charging bull, yet kind to lambs.

Up on the Gore Range Ranch, known as the IK Bar, which is where the Vail Ski Resort now operates is where my father's uncle ranched (base elevation at 8,120). In the early springtime, the cattle loved to graze on the lush meadows. The meadow grass was to become hay for winter feed, so they would have to push the cattle up the steep mountains (now ski runs) with the vertical rise of 3,450 feet in elevation to the summit at 11,570 feet in elevation to take advantage of the high

George Washington Bush, founder of Centralia, Washington, is pictured with an Australian Shepherd in about 1893. Courtesy Oregon Historical Society.

Note the strong similarity between the Aussie pictured with George Washington Bush and this one photographed by Patsy Carson (1982).

mountain grasses. If they didn't do this before ten o'clock in the morning when it got hot, the cattle would balk and become next to impossible to move.

At that time, Daddy was working Rover, a black 'bob tail,' as they were also referred to back then, and two of Emmett Nottingham's Border Collies. They were excellent dogs, but when push came to shove, they did not have the sand (stamina and power) to keep going when the going got really tough. Rover had the staying power (endurance) to keep going, even when the others were done and could not.

Aussies had the intelligence to think and didn't have to be told every move, but were willing to listen and wanted to please. The early ranchers were not dog trainers. The Aussie's keen intelligence and natural working abilities enabled him to learn as he went along doing the actual work. They were not taught in formal training situations as they are today.

The herding and guarding instincts were important to the early ranchers. The western ranges were relatively wild. Bears and coyotes were commonly encountered and the dogs could be depended on to watch over their charges as well as herd them to safety in an unexpected storm.

BREEDS THAT SHARE A COMMON ANCESTRY

There is a similarity between the Australian Shepherd and the Pyrenean Shepherd, also known as the Berger de Pyrenees, that has been developed as a breed in France since 1926, but it is not a replica; because the Standard, which was written for the Berger in 1926, placed all types of

The elegant Blue Spice of Flintridge (By Harper's Old Smokey out of Smeadra's Blue Mistingo) the main foundation female of the Flintridge line and major contributor to the modern Australian Shepherd. Courtesy Dr. Heard.

This portrait taken in 1899 is pictured at 12,000 feet above Salt Lake City, Utah, where relatives of Charles E. Watson grazed their sheep. There are three Aussies in the photograph. Donated by Janiece A. Wilson.

Pyrenean Shepherds into two categories (smooth and rough faced). Certain traits (including copper trim) were faulted and thus eliminated. Consequently the diversity of the Pyrenean Shepherds comparable to early Australian Shepherds was greatly reduced.

The type of Basque sheepdog that is found in certain remote regions of the Pyrenees mountains and as pictured on page 186 in *The Atlas of Dog Breeds of the World*, a blue merle with tan markings or copper trim, resemble the little blue dogs who were first identified with the sheep on the ranges of the western United States.

In Australia, the German Coolie or Koolie, a breed that closely resembles Australian Shepherds in type and temperament, is believed to be the Welsh Heeler or Old Welsh Bobtail. It is thought that these Welsh Sheepdogs are also descendants of the Basque-Celtic sheepdogs that migrated with the ancient Iberians (northern Spain) to the British Isles.

In the adjoining regions of Germany, not far from the French Pyrenees, exists the German Tiger dog, one of a numerous variety of the Old German Shepherd (Altdeutscher Schaeferhund) reminiscent of some of the early working lines of Australian Shepherds and considered to be one of the breeds contributing to the Koolie of Australia.

The key in common to all these dogs that accompanied the sheep is the sheep industry and the Spanish Merino. The Spanish Merino was especially known for its heavy fleece and very fine wool. The Merinos were bred in Spain. The Saxony Merinos were a breed of sheep taken from Spain to Saxony Germany in the 1700s.

In 1928, William Gibson (Elaine Hartnagle's father), a Wyoming rancher, had "bob-tailed" Aussies. Here he is pictured with "BOB," acquired from the Vasquez Basque sheepherders in Walden, Colorado.

Modern Aussies

The breed was founded on Australian Shepherds who were proven by hard continuous ranch work in real working situations where they learned how to handle themselves in varied terrains under diverse conditions. They were tough enough to turn a charging mother cow, yet gentle enough to nudge a lamb with their nose to get it moving along.

Aussies became popular through their participation in livestock exhibits, fairs, rodeos and horse and dog shows, where they performed tricks and put on herding and agility demonstrations. Audiences marvel at the uncanny ability of the 'little blue dogs.'

Jay Sisler of Emmett, Idaho, was the first to introduce the Australian Shepherd to the American public with his trick-dogs as they performed at rodeos throughout the United States and Canada during the late 40s and into the 1960s. Jay's Aussies appeared in several films, including Disney's *Stub–The Greatest Cowdog in the West* and *Run Appaloosa Run*.

Sisler's Shorty and his littermate brother, Stubby, were products of the mating between Blue Star and the red male, Keeno. Shorty figures prominently in the ancestry of many present-day Aussies. His most famous son is undoubtedly Wood's Jay, the foundation sire of Fletcher Wood's legendary bloodline. A daughter of Jay, Nettesheim's Twinkles, became the dam of Heard's Cactus of Flintridge.

Juanita Ely bought Feo, a little blue merle male who had come from Spain with a Basque herder who worked for the Warren Livestock Company in Wyoming. When bred to Ely's Blue (Heavron's Bob ex Young's Bitchie) produced Hartnagle's Jinx and Goody (Goodie). Under the original registry system for Australian Shepherds, Goody later became known as Wood's Blue Shadow. Through a stroke of fate, Goody (AKA Blue Shadow) became one of the most important foundation matrons in Dr. Heard's Flintridge bloodlines, Hartnagle's Las Rocosa Aussies and Fletcher Wood's line.

Hartnagle's Badger (Christiansen's Buster ex Ely's Blue), 1954–1969, pictured with the author (right) and her sister Christine.

Swain Finch and his wife Sarah in front of their log house, Custer County, Nebraska. Photographed from "Great American Plains, A Pictoral History." Reprinted by permission from Solomon D. Butcher Collection, Nebraska State Historical Society.

When Smedra's Blue Mistingo (out of a granddaughter of Blue Shadow) sired by Wood's Dandy, a dog that the Merino family brought from Spain, was mated to Harper's Old Smokey, the cross produced Heard's Blue Spice of Flintridge, Heard's Salt, and Heard's Chili, the foundation of the famous Flintridge bloodline. Two of the most celebrated sires to come from Dr. Heard's Flintridge line were Champion Wildhagen's Dutchman of Flintridge and Champion Fieldmaster of Flintridge.

Hartnagle's Badger (1954 - 1969), a son of Ely's Blue, was the first of many sires to contribute to the well-known Hartnagle's Las Rocosa family of Australian Shepherds. Champion Las Rocosa Shiloh was one of the most influential sires of the Hartnagle line and appears frequently in the pedigrees of present-day Aussies. One of Shiloh's most famous daughters, Champion Las Rocosa Leslie CSD, produced Hall of Fame Sire Las Rocosa Lester, who was bred to Las Rocosa Christophene OTD-c to produce multiple Hall of Fame producers.

Of the foundation breeders who were active in the 50s and 60s, the Mistrettas developed a distinct line of dogs in the Pacific Northwest based on the excellence of Champion Mistretta's Ballou Pirate. While there are many bloodlines (too numerous to mention) that have played a role in the growth of the Australian Shepherd, Lois George's Red Rustler and Copper Canyon Caligari, Farrington's Buster Ivory and the Twin Oaks dogs were major contributors to the development of the breed.

BREED CLUBS AND REGISTRIES

During the fifties there was a small but growing fancy throughout the western United States. A network of letters supplied the basis for an association. In the fall of 1957, a small group of fanciers established the Australian Shepherd Club of America (ASCA). The National Stock Dog Registry (a division of IESR), became the official registry for Australian Shepherds.

In March 1972, ASCA began to manage its own registry. At that time, ASCA offered a show and obedience program where members could gain Conformation championships and obedience and tracking titles. In 1974, a stock dog program was introduced to preserve and promote the natural herding ability of the breed.

Perhaps the greatest step in standardizing the breed's development and retaining correct breed type and character was the compilation of the ASCA Breed Standard. A committee was formed in 1975 that included some of the nation's most prominent breeders, stockmen, judges, and veterinarians, with input from other canine experts to ensure anatomical and physiological accuracy. Rough drafts were reviewed and critiqued by respected authorities on canine anatomy and gait with input from ASCA affiliate clubs throughout the country. The general membership gave its unanimous approval, and the present Breed Standard became effective January 1977.

In 1990, the United States Australian Shepherd Association (USASA) was established as the parent club to represent the Australian Shepherd to the American Kennel Club (AKC) with the sole purpose of receiving AKC recognition. The AKC is the largest all-breed registry in the U.S. In 1991, the breed standard was modified and adopted, and the breed was accepted for AKC registration. In 1993, Aussies became eligible for full competitive privileges when they were accepted into the Herding Group.

In addition to Agility, Conformation, Herding, Junior Showmanship, Obedience, Rally and Tracking programs, the AKC offers the Canine Good Citizen program. The AKC publishes *The Complete Dog Book*, and *The Gazette*.

ASCA is the original parent club and largest single-breed registry in North America. It publishes the *Aussie Times*, dedicated to Australian Shepherds. It offers Agility, conformation, Junior Showmanship, Obedience, Stock dog (Herding), and Tracking programs in which Aussies can earn titles.

The Canadian Kennel Club (CKC) is the official all-breed registry in Canada. It sponsors programs for Conformation, Herding, Obedience, Junior Showmanship, and Tracking. The CKC publishes a monthly and annual magazine titled *Dogs in Canada*.

The United Kennel Club (UKC) is the second largest and oldest multi-breed registry in the U.S. It sponsors programs in Agility, Conformation, Junior Showmanship, and Obedience. It publishes *Bloodlines*, a monthly journal.

Many Aussies are currently dual-registered in both AKC and ASCA. In order to compete in AKC's programs, the Aussie must be registered with the AKC. On the other hand, anyone wanting to compete in ASCA's programs must be ASCA registered. However, owners of Aussies not registered with one or the other association, can apply with that association for a Limited Exhibition Privilege (LEP) for their Aussie.

Left to right: Heard's Blue Spice of Flintridge (Harper's Old Smokey ex Smedra's Blue Mistingo), Heard's Chili of Flintridge (Harper's Old Smokey ex Heard's Blue Spice of Flintridge), Heard's Salt of Flintridge (Harper's Old Smokey ex Heard's Blue Spice of Flintridge). Foundation dogs of the Weldon T. Heard DVM's Flintridge line. Courtesy Hartnagle.

Jacque Garvin handling WTCh. Justus Birch in the Junior Showmanship competition. Courtesy Marti Parrish.

Chapter 2

AMAZING AUSSIES AND CANINE CAREERS

SPORTS

Agility Dogs

AGILITY IS ONE OF THE MOST POPULAR performance events for Aussies. It is an exciting spectator sport and even more exciting for competitors. Agility is an extension of obedience. Agility obstacle courses closely resemble equestrian grand prix courses that include assorted jumps and hurdles (tire, high, and broad jumps), tunnels (open and collapsed), A-frames, weave poles (weave hoops), seesaws (teeter-totters), ramps (dog walks and sway bridges), and a pause box. Agility is a timed event that tests the training and athletic abilities of Aussies. Competitors are faulted for each failure to negotiate any obstacle correctly and are disqualified for failure to complete the course.

Military and law-enforcement agencies have employed Agility in their dog training for many years. Service dogs crawl through tunnels, jump through window frames or over different obstacles, scale walls, traverse debris, and cross creeks, among other tasks. Agility training also mentally and physically prepares Aussies for all types of work and play, including ranch and farm work.

Hyksos sailing over Flyball hurdles. Courtesy Anne Martin.

Conformation Shows

Theoretically, the purpose of Conformation shows is to improve the purebred Australian Shepherd. Aussies are eligible to compete at hundreds of shows where championship points are awarded. In fact, these shows stimulate interest in more attractive and sound purebred Aussies and have brought public attention to the merits of the well-bred registered Australian Shepherd.

Canadian Conformation and Flyball Champion, Touchstone One Day Will Come, CD (Ch. Blue Isle Peacemaker of Auriga ex Touchstone's One For The Money) eagerly anticipates catching the ball. Courtesy Lisa Cameron.

Lou Mack and World Champion, Scooter, taking a thirteen-foot leap in the air to catch a Frisbee disc. Courtesy Lou McCammon.

Besides providing an absorbing hobby to hundreds of Aussie fanciers and breeders, dog shows present the dog-loving public with the opportunity to view a number of events in which the Aussie is the star.

For the serious breeder, a dog show serves both as a showcase for the results of his efforts and skills and as a measuring stick for the merits of his Aussies as compared to those of other owners.

Flyball

Flyball is an excellent sport of speed and agility for Aussies. It is an exciting event that attracts enthusiastic crowds. Aussies work in teams of four dogs each, and two teams compete against each other. Each dog runs a relay race over a series of hurdles (small jumps), then hits a pedal or lever with his paw to trigger the flyball box, which tosses a tennis ball up in the air. Once the Aussie catches the ball, he runs back over the hurdles, where the next dog is waiting his turn. The height of the hurdles is based on the smallest member of the team. If one of the team members misses a hurdle or fails to retrieve the ball, he must repeat his turn. The first team to finish is the winner. Obedience clubs often organize Flyball teams.

Frisbee

Aussies excel at Frisbee. It is a fun sport for both the owner and the Aussie. Frisbee fetching is a perfect activity for the backyard or park and is an excellent way to provide exercise and entertainment. It is an exciting event and a major crowd pleaser. Local, regional, and national Frisbee disc-catching competitions are held throughout North America.

Herding/Stock-Dog Trials

The purpose of Herding trials is to encourage the breeding and training of better herding dogs. As a sport, Herding/Stock-dog trials have become enormously popular, providing interest and excitement for participants and spectators.

For those who enjoy dogs and have an interest in sports, a Herding trial is a fascinating demonstration of Aussies competing under varied conditions. Unlike a conformation show, where perfection of physical conformation is emphasized, the Herding trial focuses on excellence of performance.

Herding trials are highly competitive and require handling experience even at the started or beginner's level. Herding tests demonstrate each Aussie's willingness to herd. Each association offers Herding/Stock-dog titles and Herding or Working Trial Championships.

Obedience

Every aspect of dog training utilizes some form of Obedience. While the beauty in the conformation ring offers fascination to spectators, Obedience trials are a showcase for Aussies trained to work in unison with their handlers and to obey commands. Australian Shepherds are among the nation's top Obedience competitors. In all-breed competitions, Aussies are often the High-In-Trial winners. Obedience trials display Australian Shepherds as man's ultimate companion and helpmate. Obedience competitions measure the Aussie's skill while performing certain routines in a prescribed manner. Obedience competitions further test the Aussie's ability to perform reliably in public and among other dogs.

Aussies can earn the Obedience titles of Companion Dog (CD), Companion Dog Excellent (CDX), Utility Dog (UD), Utility Dog Excellent (UDX), and Obedience Championship (OC) in competition under the rules and regulations of each association.

Tracking

Aussies excel in Tracking. Tracking stems back to the hunting instincts to trail game. In real working situations, Aussies must track missing livestock. Tracking training is interesting for Aussies and a good way for both dog and handler to get exercise.

Tracking tests judge the Aussie's ability to work different terrain and climatic conditions. Owners learn to trust the Aussie's natural abilities, while the Aussie learns to rely on scent discrimination and the ability to work independently. Aussies can earn two different Tracking titles, Tracking Dog (TD) and Tracking Dog Excellent (TDX).

"While not famous retrievers, 'The Bean' has a good bird sense, does well in the water, and has a soft mouth. In addition to numerous duck retrievals, The Bean has several Canadian geese to his credit as well."
Don Delise, owner and trainer.

Scent Hurdle Racing

While similar to Flyball, Scent Hurdle Racing is more difficult and requires more skill and training. Aussies learn to jump and retrieve in Open Obedience classes and to discriminate scents in Utility classes. Teams of four dogs go over four hurdles, but instead of retrieving a ball, each dog must pick out the dumbbell marked with his handler's scent and return with it. The dumbbell marked with the owner's scent is also marked with a number corresponding to the number worn by the dog. Aussies run relays with two teams competing simultaneously. One dog is released at a time, and when he returns and crosses the finish line, the next dog is released. The first team to finish is the winner. Most Scent Hurdle Racing is organized through Obedience clubs across North America.

Other Fun Sports for Aussies

Hiking and Biking

Hiking and biking are wonderful ways for outdoor enthusiasts to spend time with their Aussies. The Aussie can carry his own lightweight backpack. Custom-designed backpacks are available exclusively for dogs. Sporting-goods stores and sled-dog outfitters are good outlets for such specialty items.

Hunting

Many Aussies are natural hunters and retrievers. They have an excellent sense of smell and will readily retrieve and hand deliver birds or small game for their owners.

Jogging

Aussies are wonderful jogging companions. They benefit greatly from the exercise and companionship.

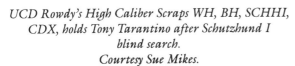

UCD Rowdy's High Caliber Scraps WH, BH, SCHHI, CDX, holds Tony Tarantino after Schutzhund I blind search.
Courtesy Sue Mikes.

Winter Fun. Justus Moxee and Sue Grigsby skijoring down the Old Cascade Highway.
Courtesy Marti Parrish.

Schutzhund

Schutzhund originated in Germany with German Shepherds. It is a complete method of training that includes Obedience, Tracking, and Protection. There are three levels of skill where Aussies can earn titles—Schutzhund I, II, and III. Endurance and temperament tests measure temperament, structure, and stamina.

Sledding

While Husky-type breeds have been known to excel in sledding sports, Aussies also participate successfully in all-breed sled races. Because of their intelligence and trainability, Aussies make good lead dogs in a team. Sled racing is physically demanding and requires sound structure.

Jay Sisler entertained audiences throughout North America with extraordinary performances by his Aussies. Here, Jay skips the rope for Silver to jump, with John at the anchor. Courtesy Vicky Rand.

Skijoring

Skiing with Aussies is popular for those involved in winter sports. Whether pulling a sled or a skier, Aussies enjoy spending time with their owners, and both benefit from the exercise. Skijoring requires sound conformation and proper conditioning.

Doing Tricks

Aussies are natural "hams" and love to entertain, and these attributes are accompanied by the dogs' excellent ability to learn tricks. In addition, their balance enables them to perform certain stunts with ease. Rodeo clowns have trained Aussies to jump through hoops, walk on their hind legs, and run a cloverleaf pattern around barrels (barrel racing) to amuse audiences from Madison Square Garden to the Calgary Stampede.

CANINE CAREERS: SERVICE DOGS

Service dogs must possess sound conformation, they must be trainable, and they must have courage. While they must obey, they also need to display intelligent disobedience by refusing to lead their master into danger. Service dogs search for human scent, plant and animal scents, drugs, gunpowder, and other explosives.

Canine Detectives (Four-Footed Cops)

Aussies can determine if accelerants are present at the scene of a fire. They also can distinguish undeclared and potentially dangerous agricultural products. Narcotic and bomb detection are other areas where Aussies assist law-enforcement agencies.

Guide Dogs For the Blind

Aussies are gaining popularity as seeing-eye dogs. While many Aussies are not well-suited for this work, the overall physical soundness, size, and disposition of some are ideal. Guide dogs must be friendly, even-tempered, hardy enough to work in all weather, small enough to fit under a bus or train seat, yet large enough to pull their master out of danger.

Certain characteristics enable select Aussies to do well as guide dogs. They adapt easily to new situations and demonstrate reliability, they learn and retain new concepts easily, and they are intelligent and can work through challenging situations in order to steer their partners clear of danger. Aussies naturally check back with their partner and gently touch their leg to let them know that everything is okay.

Hearing Dogs

Aussies can easily learn to alert deaf owners and those with hearing impairments to the sounds of a ringing telephone, an alarm clock, a smoke alarm, a baby's cry, the doorbell, a security buzzer, sirens, and many other sounds, such as the owner dropping keys or a wallet. The medium-size Aussie is ideal for hearing work. Hearing dogs must be intelligent, attentive to their master, and willing to please.

Search and Rescue

Aussies are good at picking up human scent in the air and on land. The moderate-size Aussie has the agility and endurance necessary to negotiate the disaster rubble, timber, brush, and boulders that are common in avalanches and earthquakes. Aussies are hardy and energetic and can go places where giant breeds cannot fit. Their coat affords protection in severe weather, and they have enough common sense to take care of themselves in almost any situation.

Cross T's Mr. Innocent (Trueluc Toby ex Hughes Flash of Silver) herding an elephant. Courtesy Annie Furnish.

Stock Dogs

Aussiess are highly valued in livestock districts. In fact, the Aussie is one of the best all-around farm and ranch breeds. Aussies take naturally to working with stock, almost without being taught.

Therapy Dogs

Many Aussies and their owners are bringing joy to aged, ill, and handicapped citizens by visiting residents of nursing homes, convalescent centers, and hospitals. Only experienced handlers with stable, friendly Aussies should undertake this work. Therapy dogs must accept erratic behavior along with considerable attention and petting.

Wheelchair Assistants

Like other jobs that involve working with the handicapped, these Aussies must be adaptable, intelligent, trainable, willing, and sound. A wheelchair assistant helps his owner in many ways, such as retrieving a newspaper or letters from the mailbox, picking up a dropped item (keys, pencils, and other personal items) that his owner cannot reach from the wheelchair, turning a light switch on or off with his nose or paws, or opening or closing a door. Aussies can also detect smoke or fires and alert their owner to many unsafe conditions.

A Breed Standard ideal reflecting beauty and utilitarian function. Ch. Las Rocosa Little Wolf, STD-CD, third-generation Hall-of-Fame sire.

Chapter 3

THE STANDARD OF EXCELLENCE

CURRENTLY, THERE ARE TWO BREED STANDARDS recognized for Aussies. The Australian Shepherd Club of America (ASCA), the Canadian Kennel Club (CKC), and the United Kennel Club (UKC) adhere to the ASCA Breed Standard, while the American Kennel Club is guided by the AKC Breed Standard.

THE IDEAL

The Australian Shepherd is a performance breed. Conformation and temperament affect each Aussie's ability to perform. The Aussie that does not have sound structure will never realize his full potential, nor will he function effectively as a working dog.

The Breed Standard describes the characteristics that enable the Australian Shepherd to accomplish his work with the greatest amount of ease. An Aussie with poor structure will have to work harder and will be less athletic and more prone to injury than one with ideal structure. While the original purpose of the breed was as a herder and guardian, the qualities that enabled him to perform those skills also have allowed him to adapt and excel in other arenas.

The Breed Standard is the model toward which all Australian Shepherd breeders strive. Written by people who knew the dogs firsthand in the environment where they were originally developed, the Breed Standard is the blueprint for judges to evaluate against. The philosophy underlying the manner in which such a document should be written was best described by Dr. Robert Kline, DVM:

> Contrary to the beliefs of many, such a standard is not a textbook but rather an outline describing structure, breed characteristics, color, size, uses, etc. put down in as precise and accurate a manner as possible. In order to perfect such a document without in fact ending up with a textbook the size of a physician's anatomy book, it is predisposed that the people using such a standard have a working knowledge of animal traits, vocabulary, and methods used by the industry to enable them to understand and interpret said standard so as to make it a usable instrument. For those not so familiar with these things and wanting to use the standard, such persons owe it to themselves to seek out knowledgeable breeders and judges, texts, etc. to avail themselves of such knowledge. For accuracy's sake, it precludes a standard to be written for the beginner or novice.

Newcomers to the breed may have a difficult time comprehending the basis on which a judge evaluates each dog. The Australian Shepherd Breed Standard describes an ideal Australian Shepherd in terms familiar to individuals who understand canine terminology, and it assumes a basic knowledge of anatomy and gait. It is not a detailed layout, nor is it a breeding manual for the novice, but it provides guidelines within which breeders can work without compromising with popular fads.

Any characteristic that deviates from the ideal described is faulted according to the degree of deviation. Points that significantly deviate from

This photo shows the dog lunging forward to convince this steer to move away.

This second photo illustrates how the head and neck work in conjunction with the entire body to keep the Aussie away from flying hooves and horns.

breed character or soundness are faulted. Characteristics that entirely detract from both soundness and/or breed character are disqualifications.

Most references to measurements compare one part to another, and all parts to the whole individual Aussie, rather than by specific numerical increments. By doing so, slight variations in size of respective segments are allowed when comparing several Aussies that differ in overall size. This also emphasizes the importance of each part being in proportion to one another, therefore maintaining balance and symmetry.

GENERAL APPEARANCE

ASCA

The Australian Shepherd is a well-balanced dog of medium size and bone. He is attentive and animated, showing strength and stamina, combined with unusual agility. Slightly longer than tall, he has a coat of moderate length and coarseness with coloring that offers variety and individuality in each specimen. An identifying characteristic is the natural or docked bobtail. In each sex, masculinity or femininity is well-defined.

AKC

The Australian Shepherd is an intelligent working dog of strong herding and guarding instincts. He is a loyal companion and has the stamina to work all day. He is well-balanced, slightly longer than tall, of medium size and bone, with coloring that offers variety and individuality. He is attentive and animated, lithe and agile, solid and muscular without cloddishness. He has a coat of moderate length and coarseness. He has a docked or natural bobbed tail.

DISCUSSION

Several words, "medium," "moderate," and "balanced," describe what to look for in a well-proportioned individual. Reading further, you get the impression that an ideal Aussie has neither one outstanding feature nor any glaring faults that would detract from the total picture of symmetry. An ideal specimen will stand out in harmonious balance at rest or while in motion. He blends from one point to another. The Australian Shepherd should convey the impression at a glance that he is capable of enduring long periods of active duty as a working stock dog, which is attributed to his strength and stamina. He is light on his feet. As a genuine athlete, he is agile. He has a lithe sense of power, never cumbersome nor carrying extra timber.

Variety and individuality in color are unique features of Aussies. The variance in tail length accommodates the different lengths that occur naturally at birth. The longer natural bobtail (not to exceed four inches) should *never* be penalized over a shorter natural bobbed or docked tail.

Although never coarse or menacing, the male's boldness and virile strength are easy to distinguish from his distinctly feminine counterpart, who possesses structural equality and a definite strength of character.

CHARACTER/TEMPERAMENT

ASCA: Character

The Australian Shepherd is intelligent, primarily a working dog of strong herding and guardian instincts. He is an exceptional companion. He is versatile and easily trained, performing his assigned tasks with great style and enthusiasm. He is reserved with strangers but does not exhibit shyness. Although an aggressive, authoritative worker, viciousness toward people or animals is intolerable.

AKC: Temperament

The Australian Shepherd is an intelligent, active dog with an even disposition; he is good-natured, seldom quarrelsome. He may be somewhat reserved in initial meetings. **Faults:** Any display of shyness, fear, or aggression is to be severely penalized. (Temperament is further defined in the first two sentences under General Appearance).

DISCUSSION

The temperament or disposition of the Australian Shepherd is equally important to all other aspects in the Breed Standard. A bright look in his eyes shows the Australian Shepherd's intelligence. The Aussie is intuitive and was bred to think and be able to make decisions regarding his charges when his master was unable to. The Aussie is an adoring and energetic companion. He is highly devoted and attentive toward his master and is eager to respond to his master's every wish. He is quick to learn and easy to train. The look of questioning curiosity can become the look of eagles when this dog is at work.

The Australian Shepherd may be reserved and watchful with strangers or in a new environment, but he is not timid or shy. The Aussie is deliberate as a guardian due to his heritage as a herder and protector of livestock. Due to his innate guardian instincts, he is naturally territorial. Viciousness (savage attacks) or unreliable temperament are undesirable traits because they detract significantly from the Aussie's ability to perform either as a trustworthy companion or a dependable working dog.

Time and again he displays great courage when handling formidable livestock. While he can be tenacious with difficult livestock, he can turn right around and handle gentle livestock with great care.

HEAD

ASCA

Clean-cut, strong, dry, and in proportion to the body. The top skull is flat to slightly rounded, its length and width each equal to the length of the muzzle, which is in balance and proportioned to the rest of the head. The muzzle tapers slightly to a rounded tip. The stop is moderate but well-defined.

AKC

The head is clean-cut, strong, and dry. Overall size should be in proportion to the body. The muzzle is equal in length or slightly shorter than the back skull. Viewed from the side the topline of the back skull and muzzle form parallel planes, divided by a moderate, well-defined stop. The muzzle tapers little from base to nose and is rounded at the tip. **Skull:** Top flat to slightly domed. It may show a slight occipital protuberance. Length and width are equal. Moderate, well-defined stop. Muzzle tapers little from base to nose and is rounded at the tip.

DISCUSSION

Perhaps no other single factor sets the Australian Shepherd apart from other breeds and contributes as strongly to breed character as does the head. This feature also distinguishes major bloodlines within the breed. A good head is a mark of quality. It provides a clue as to the overall quality of the rest of the individual. Variations in expression and makeup (head structure, ear set, eye placement, etc.) are slight between bloodlines and are therefore acceptable, providing that the variation is characteristic of the breed.

The head houses the brain, dentition, ears, eyes, and nose (sinus chambers). Its framework protects these structures and minimizes the effects of blows and injury to the special senses: sight, hearing, scent, and the brain. The formation of the sinus chambers adds structural stability to the frame without adding much extra weight, which is important in respiration. These chambers lend moderate width to the head, which is necessary for muscle attachment without altering the correct contour.

"Clean-cut" is a term meaning that the head is clearly outlined, well formed, trim, and neat; free from extra or loose skin, pads of fat, pendulous lips (flews), and/or visible haws (third eyelid). The lips must be snug and not hang below the line of mouth. The skin should fit well around the eye to form a tight, protective covering. This helps prevent debris (dirt, briars, seeds, brush, twigs) from making direct contact with the eyeballs. Loose-fitting lips are more subject to rips and tears while working if caught up and can interfere with "gripping."

While it may appear that the topline of the muzzle and topskull lie on parallel planes, close examination reveals this to be untypical. Due to the slight tapering of the muzzle, these two features are set slightly obliquely (especially if the skull is slightly domed as described by AKC), unlike breeds such as setters and pointers which also sport square, blunt muzzles, abrupt stops, and a prominent brow.

(continued)

The head is equidistant from the width of the backskull to the length of the backskull to the length of the muzzle. The aforementioned dimensions emphasize balance, symmetry, and moderation typical of the Australian Shepherd as a whole. These proportions, plus a moderate but well-defined stop, contribute to the relationship of the bones of the head that are sufficiently thick and have adequate muscles to absorb concussion. The ridge (sagittal crest) on the top of the skull allows for the attachment of muscles used for biting. It further affords protection from a blow on the head.

Left:
The sagittal crest (the ridge on the top of the skull) and the zygomatic arch (the bones below the eyes) and the position of the bottom jaw in relation to the top jaw in conjunction with the length of the muzzle, which equals the width and length of the topskull, define the shape of the Aussie's head. Photo by Wayne Rogers.

Hartnagle's Hud, a male of outstanding head type. The eyes are well protected by the moderate, but well-defined head structure and stop. Note the almond-shaped eyes and ideal ear set.

TEETH

ASCA

A full complement of strong, white teeth meet in a scissors bite. An even bite is a fault. Teeth broken or missing by accident are not penalized.
Disqualifications: Undershot bite; overshot bites.

AKC

A full complement of strong, white teeth should meet in a scissors bite or may meet in a level bite.
Disqualifications: Undershot; overshot greater than one-eighth of an inch. Loss of contact caused by short center incisors in an otherwise correct bite shall not be judged undershot. Teeth broken or missing by accident shall not be penalized.

DISCUSSION

The head structure of the typical Australian Shepherd depends on correct underlying skeletal features, including the entire jaw assembly. This is reflected most noticeably in the profile of the muzzle. The correct scissors bite augments the slightly tapered muzzle as called for in the Breed Standard. To the viewer, teeth can also serve as a window to the quality of the bone within the individual. If the teeth appear strong and well textured, there is reason to believe that internal bones are also as sound.

A full set of permanent adult teeth comprises forty-two teeth—twenty-two in the lower jaw, or mandible (six molars, eight premolars, two canines, six incisors), and twenty in the upper jaw, or maxilla (two fewer molars).

The scissors bite is anatomically correct and indicative of a sound jaw assembly. It is the relationship and alignment of the canine and premolar teeth that accurately reveals the bite. In the scissors bite, the lower canine tooth fits between the upper, outermost incisor and the upper canine tooth. The premolars interjoin with the upper premolars behind their corresponding lower counterparts.

The incisors alone do not accurately reveal the "bite," because repositioning can occur from trauma caused by working accident or other problem. Exhibitors have been known to have the incisors cosmetically altered to "improve" the bite for show purposes. The scissors bite lends substance and support to the face and dentition.

The scissors bite enables the Australian Shepherd to move in and "grip" livestock with a pinching effect and be able to withstand the impact if he is kicked while working. The scissors bite is also necessary for removing burrs and the like from foot pads and the coat. The role that the scissors bite plays in reproduction is incalculable. During birth, the female must be able to effectively sever the umbilical cord of each puppy whelped.

In an undershot bite (prognathism), a disqualification, you observe the abnormal interplay between the lower canine tooth and the upper, outermost incisor and upper canine teeth. Depending upon the degree of the undershot bite, the forward shift of the lower (mandible) creates a space between the upper and lower premolar cusp tips. Again, depending upon the degree of shift, the first lower premolar may be hidden behind the upper canine tooth.

(continued)

An undershot jaw leaves the mandible more prone to injury because it is less protected. The mandible is more vulnerable because it attaches to the head in one place only; therefore, the force cannot be dispersed when the mandible is subjected to trauma. On the other hand, an overshot assembly leaves the upper teeth more exposed to trauma.

An even (level) bite exhibits to a lesser degree the undershot bite (prognathism). The even bite occurs when the lower jaw shifts forward slightly and the upper and lower premolars come together evenly in the front. An even bite does allow a dog to function; however, because of the predisposition toward occlusal trauma (broken and worn teeth) due to constant friction, the even bite is not ideal.

Loss of contact between upper and lower incisors caused by short central incisors is not a result of the undershot assembly. The defect is due primarily to an insufficient amount of skeletal support underlying the central incisors. It also can be due to inadequate development of mandibular growth.

Never penalize broken teeth or those missing due to an accident. To do so places unwarranted precedence on cosmetic features and discourages the exhibition of active, working stock dogs in the show ring. It also defeats the original intent of the Australian Shepherd as a versatile breed. Denying otherwise exceptional individuals rightful consideration and placement in the show ring is to deny the fact that the purpose of the breed is first and foremost utilitarian. A mechanical injury of this nature cannot be passed on to succeeding generations.

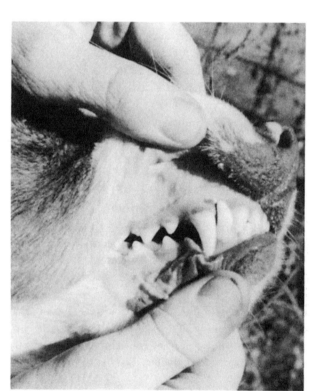

Left:
The correct scissors bite.

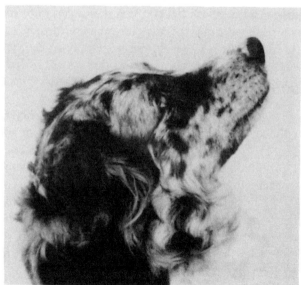

Below:
The correct scissors bite is directly responsible for the slightly tapered muzzle. An excellent example of a clean and dry head.

EYES

ASCA

Very expressive, showing attentiveness and intelligence. Clear, almond-shaped, and of moderate size, set a little obliquely, neither prominent nor sunken, with pupils dark, well defined, and perfectly positioned. Color is brown, blue, amber, or any variation or combination including flecks and marbling.

AKC

Expression: Showing attentiveness and intelligence, alert and eager. Gaze should be keen but friendly. Brown, blue, amber, or any variation or combination thereof, including flecks and marbling. Almond-shaped, not protruding or sunken.

DISCUSSION

It is often said that the eyes are a window into the soul. The Breed Standard calls for the eyes to be clear, or free from cloudiness, which can indicate impaired vision or blindness.

The almond shape of the eye of the Australian Shepherd is created by tissue surrounding the eye, rather than by the eye itself, which is round. The correct head structure dictates and allows the eye to be set obliquely, forming the almond-shaped aperture. Faults of round, bulging, and sunken, small eyes result from inadequate or incorrect skeletal features or head shapes. The relationships of the many contributing bones directly influence the shape of the orbit and the eye set, which afford proper protection to the eye. These bones include the zygomatic arch (the bones beneath the eye) formed by the joining of the zygomatic process of the temporal bone and the temporal process of the zygomatic bone, and the frontal bone (adding protection from above), which forms the forehead, inner casing, and upper portion of each orbit.

The Australian Shepherd depends upon a moderately curved zygomatic arch, which influences the slightly oblique eye set characteristic of the breed. This allows adequate protection from many objects, including briars, flying hooves, and horns, without creating a restricted visual field. The aforementioned characteristics are imperative for a dog that is working with livestock. The flatter the zygomatic arch, the more obliquely the eyes are set on the side of the head, and the greater the vulnerability of the eyes to trauma. The eyes will be more frontal if the curvature of the zygomatic arch is more exaggerated. This gives greater protection but decreases the side vision that is also important in the herding Aussie. The necessity of moderation as called for throughout the Breed Standard is readily apparent in compromising the protective properties with the visual characteristics.

Eye defects are known to occur within the breed. One clue visible to the naked eye is an offset pupil. The pupil should not be confused with the marbling (mottled) coloration of the iris, which is a trait of the merling and flecked patterns seen throughout the variety of body color. The pupil should be well defined by its positioning and darker color.

The eye color offers variety, contributing to the individuality of the breed as a whole. The eyes may be in any combination of blue, brown, and/or amber, depending on coat color. Eye color is influenced by the inherited coat color and pigmentation. Never give precedence to one eye color or combination. Remember that the wolf possesses light eyes and has very keen vision. Often, the preference of one eye color over another is generally due to familiarity with one color and lack of familiarity with another. It takes living with individuals of the various eye colors to learn how to effectively read the eyes, especially blue ones. While it is correct that the lighter-colored eyes possess less pigmentation than the darker eyes, it is entirely incorrect to assume that lighter eyes have limited visibility.

EARS

ASCA

Set on high at the side of the head, triangular and slightly rounded at the tip, of moderate size with length measured by bringing the tip of the ear around to the inside corner of the eye. The ears, at full attention, break slightly forward and over from one-quarter (¼) to one-half (½) above the base. Prick and hound-type ears are severe faults.

AKC

Ears are triangular, of moderate size and leather, set high on the head. At full attention they break forward and over, or to the side as a rose ear. Prick ears and hanging ears are severe faults.

DISCUSSION

The triangular shape, the size, and the placement of the ear as described in both Breed Standards are correct. The hound-type ear (in the ASCA Breed Standard), which was meant to describe long, pendulous ears without lift, is somewhat a misnomer. Different types of hounds sport a variety of ear types and sizes.

Long ears lacking lift interfere with keen hearing. In moist climates, drooping ears hold moisture within the canals, causing ear infections. They also are not typical of the breed and therefore should be faulted as such.

The inclusion of the term "rose ear" (in the AKC Breed Standard) is also misleading. According to the eighteenth edition of the *Complete Dog Book*, the rose ear is "a small drop ear which folds over and back so as to reveal the burr. The burr is the inside of the ear, i.e., the irregular formation visible within the cup." The naturally occurring ear of the Australian Shepherd can be small and folded over, or the upper front edges can be folded and curved outward. They should not fold over and backward (caused by the ear cartilage wrinkling inward at the rear portion), nor should they reveal the burr, as occurs naturally in breeds like the Greyhound, the Whippet, or the Italian Greyhound, where the zygomatic arch is set much more obliquely than is typical of the Australian Shepherd.

The prick ear is a different story. The prick ear is the keenest ear for hearing and is a naturally occurring characteristic in the Australian Shepherd among all foundation bloodlines, including outstanding individuals such as: Smedra's Blue Mistingo, Mansker's Freckles, and Wood's Dandy, to name a few. While this trait deviates from the ideal, it does not affect soundness, nor does it detract from the Australian Shepherd's ability to perform as a stock dog or companion.

Acceptable ear sets can vary among individuals. Diamond Spur Josey sports a typical high ear set that breaks slightly forward and over. Photo by Trish Thornwald.

NECK, TOPLINE, BODY

ASCA

The neck is firm, clean, and in proportion to the body. It is of medium length and slightly arched at the crest, settling well into the shoulders. The body is firm and muscular. The topline appears level at a natural four-square stance. The chest is deep and strong with ribs well-sprung. The loin is strong and broad when viewed from the top. The bottom line carries well back with moderate tuck-up. The croup is moderately sloping, the ideal being thirty (30) degrees from the horizontal. Tail is straight, not to exceed four (4) inches, natural bobbed or docked.

AKC

Neck is strong, of moderate length, slightly arched at the crest, fitting well into the shoulders. **Topline:** Straight and strong, level and firm from withers to hip joints. The croup is moderately sloped. Chest is not broad but is deep with the lowest point reaching the elbow. The ribs are well-sprung and long, neither barrel-chested nor slab-sided. The underline shows a moderate tuck-up. Tail is straight, and is docked or naturally bobbed, not to exceed four inches in length.

DISCUSSION

A general rule of thumb states that the length of the neck when measured from the occiput (upper, back point of the skull) to the top of the withers should approximate the length of the head when measured from the occiput to the tip of the nose.

Although described as separate entities in the Breed Standard, the head and neck work together as balancing factors. The head and neck set are marks of quality in many species. They contribute to overall character as well as to structural quality. The set of the neck is influenced by and can be used to evaluate the shoulder assembly. In order for the neck to carry back and blend well into the shoulders, the shoulder must have proper angulation (lay-back). The role played by the head and neck in maneuverability is highly influential in regulating and shifting the center of gravity. By extending the head and neck forward, the Aussie shifts his center of gravity forward. When negotiating turns, his head and neck shift to one side or the other, and the body follows. When he jumps, the head and neck lift the center of gravity and guide the body while the rear provides the power. When the dog stops, the head and neck lift up to draw the center of gravity back as opposed to propelling it forward.

A neck of moderate length and slightly arched, as called for in the Breed Standard, is most efficient for endurance and contributes to the sense of balance, symmetry, and moderation. The neck is a major influence in supporting the muscles of the front assembly. A short neck, while not lacking in strength, lacks agility and endurance and therefore does not allow maximum flexibility for the dog's body when heeling (gripping) livestock. It is dangerously ineffective in keeping the Australian Shepherd's vulnerable body away from flying hooves. The correct length of neck gives Australian Shepherd athletes (Frisbee, Agility, and Obedience competitors) the physical capabilities to perform with the greatest amount of ease.

A firm, muscular body is important to the athlete and is reflected in proper conditioning. This feature contributes to overall fitness, balance, and agility and is a prerequisite for the working Australian Shepherd. Muscles play a necessary role in holding the skeletal structure together.

(continued)

Taylor's Escalante exhibits how the neck lifts the body while working in coordination with the propelling hindquarters.

When speaking of the topline, the "backbone of the operation," an Aussie should have sufficient strength to support the organs that lie beneath. A strong, firm back is ideal. The topline that is firm should appear level and strong. Both the withers and hips should be level. A weak or sagging back tends to break down if it lacks substantial muscle. A roached back, much stronger in design, is also faulted because it deviates from the ideal and is not typical of the Australian Shepherd. Any diversion from a strong, firm back leads to undue energy expenditure.

Every aspect must complement the entire network for total efficiency and soundness. This includes the chest. The rib cage should be broad and long, gently arching outward. Ribs should be oblique to the spine and well laid back, judged by feeling the thirteenth pair of floating ribs. Moderate depth, length, and width give sufficient lung and heart room and help to combat lateral displacement in locomotion. A slab-sided body may appear long and flat, but it lacks the spring necessary for lung and heart room, while a barrel-chested body interferes with the elbow in motion and limits the depth necessary for lung and heart room. Both are faults.

Depth of body is measured vertically at the ninth rib, which is where the brisket should sweep gently upward. For the "tuck-up" or bottom line to ascend any sooner than the eighth or ninth rib is to view a restricted diaphragm, limiting lung and heart room, a fault termed "herring-gutted." The bottom line should appear level to the last long rib before tucking up. This gives the Australian Shepherd more stamina because there is adequate room for the heart and lungs to work.

The loin serves as the support to the abdominal viscera. The main muscles forming the sling that supports the abdominal organs have their origins in the loin area. Not supported by any other bones of the structure, the loin must be strong and broad. It contains thick, telegraphic muscles that surround the lumbar vertebrae and transmit the power from the hindquarter to the shock-absorbing forequarter.

*When judging Aussies, each individual must be in balance to itself.
This photo clearly illustrates the balance and symmetry described in the Breed Standard.
The length of the head (from the tip of the nose to the occiput) is the same length
as the back tip of the skull is to the withers. The length of the upper arm
approximates the same length as the shoulder blade
and the elbow is relatively the same distance from the withers to the ground.
Courtesy Mike Ryan.*

The Aussie's moderately sloping croup is most effective for the type of work that he performs. The croup is the section extending from the loin to the tail above the hind legs and includes the pelvis and associated musculature. The croup pulls the feet and legs under the body, boosts the center of gravity for fast turns during the initial part of the stride, then sends the power and thrust forward by extending the hind leg. This allows the Aussie to cover endless miles with the greatest amount of ease yet be able to turn on a dime if the situation calls for it.

FOREQUARTERS

ASCA

The shoulder blades (scapulae) are long and flat, close set at the withers, approximately two fingers width at a natural stance, and are well laid back at an angle approximating forty-five (45) degrees to the ground. The upper arm (humerus) is attached at an approximate right angle to the shoulder line with forelegs dropping straight, perpendicular to the ground. The elbow joint is equidistant from the ground to the withers. The legs are straight and powerful. Pasterns are short, thick, and strong but still flexible, showing a slight angle when viewed from the side. Feet are oval shaped, compact, with close-knit, well-arched toes. Pads are thick and resilient; nails short and strong. Dewclaws may be removed.

AKC

Shoulder blades are long, flat, fairly close-set at the withers, and well laid back. The upper arm, which should be relatively the same length as the shoulder blade, attaches at an approximate right angle to the shoulder line with forelegs dropping straight, perpendicular to the ground. Legs are straight and strong. Bone is strong; oval rather than round. Pastern is of medium length and very slightly sloped. Front dewclaws may be removed. Feet are oval, compact, with close-knit, well-arched toes. Pads are thick and resilient.

DISCUSSION

The forequarters support more than one-half of the entire body weight. They are a shock absorber during movement. They serve to oppose lateral displacement, propel (impel) turns, and control and lift the center of gravity.

The scapula (shoulder blade), often referred to as the cornerstone of the front assembly, is attached to the skeletal structure by muscle and ligament (unlike the hindquarters, which are linked by a ball-and-socket joint).

The well-laid-back shoulder is important for sufficient reach. It allows for shock absorption with the least amount of concussion under actual working conditions. It is therefore also ideal for the Best of Breed winner. While forty-five degrees is an easily estimated point of reference, most Australian Shepherds fall somewhere between thirty and thirty-eight degrees. This angle can be estimated by placing the finger of one hand on the point of the shoulder (the shoulder joint). With your second hand, guide your fingers over the cervical angle as it slopes backward. The place where it flattens is the crest of the scapula spine. By locating the ridge at the crest of the spine with one hand and the point of the shoulder with the fingers of the other hand, you can get a good estimation.

(continued)

If the humerus is of the correct length (approximately the same length of the shoulder blade) and is well angled, the front legs will set well beneath the Australian Shepherd for optimal weight bearing. The elbow is of equal distance from the ground to the withers. The attachment of the radius-ulna (forearm) should be straight and vertical when viewed from the front. Ideally, the forearm falls directly beneath the center point of the shoulder, which gives greatest support to the fore assembly.

To enable the pastern to work effectively as a shock absorber, it must be positioned directly under the center of weight bearing. Sufficient slope provides resiliency for absorbing concussion and greater lift while the Aussie is in motion. Weak or broken-down pasterns do not give adequate support to the rest of the leg. Weak pasterns predispose a dog to hyperextension of the pastern and knee at fast speeds, inducing injury. Unyielding straight pasterns with no shock-absorbing qualities jar the entire system and lead to early fatigue.

Splayed, flat, or broken-down feet are serious faults because they weaken the entire assembly and lead to early breakdown and lameness. Weak feet are more easily affected by rough terrain, rocky surfaces, briars, thorns, etc. Splayed toes expose the webbing to injury. This becomes readily apparent when the Aussie travels through rocky, brush-covered country. The tight, compact foot does not readily ball up with snow or mud as easily as the splayed foot and has better traction on icy surfaces. The feet support the entire body weight in a small cross-sectional area. Therefore, forces on them are so tremendous that compact feet are essential. The front feet are slightly larger than the back feet because they support more weight.

Dewclaws on the front legs are a matter of personal preference. Whether or not an individual has front dewclaws should have no bearing whatsoever on judging in the show ring.

The correct front. The forelegs are straight, columnar bones for the most effective support.

HINDQUARTERS

ASCA

Width of hindquarters approximately equal the width of the forequarters at the shoulders. The angulation of the pelvis and the upper thigh (femur) corresponds to the angulation of the shoulder blade and upper arm forming an approximate right angle. Stifles are clearly defined, hock joints moderately bent. The metatarsi are short, perpendicular to the ground, and parallel to each other when viewed from the rear. Feet are oval shaped and compact with close-knit, well-arched toes. Pads are thick and resilient; nails short and strong. Rear dewclaws are removed.

AKC

The width of the hindquarters is equal to the width of the forequarters at the shoulders. The angulation of the pelvis and upper thigh corresponds to the angulation of the shoulder blade and upper arm, forming an approximate right angle. Stifles are clearly defined, hock joints moderately bent. The hocks are short, perpendicular to the ground, and parallel to each other when viewed from the rear. Feet are oval-shaped, compact, with close-knit, well-arched toes. Pads are thick and resilient; nails short and strong. Rear dewclaws are removed.

DISCUSSION

This paragraph of both Breed Standards reemphasizes the concept of balance. The rear assembly must correspond to and be compatible with the front assembly for the individual to function efficiently as a whole. An imbalance occurs when the rear assembly is more than the front assembly, or if the hindquarters are angulated less than the forequarters. Therefore, the two assemblies must compensate according to the degree of imbalance (also influenced by other factors such as the length of body in comparison to the height). Lacking necessary synchronization between the support and propelling phases results in faults such as crabbing, overdriving (overreaching), pounding, paddling, pacing, etc.

While the rear assembly is not designed to support weight like the fore assembly, it is intended to energize and formulate power. The correct assembly supplies the Australian Shepherd with propelling force and drive.

The hind legs are secured to the stationary pelvis by articulated attachments (ball-and-socket joints), just as the humerus and scapula are articulated. The femur (upper leg) should be attached at ninety degrees to the pelvis in the standing position. Muscle and ligament support is important with this joint, because laxity in it predisposes the Aussie to hip dysplasia. The ninety-degree angle allows the stifle to assume a moderate bend, providing greater flexibility to the hind leg and sufficient length to both the femur (upper thigh) and the tibia-fibula (lower thigh). This gives a driving stride of sufficient speed and power without wasted energy. The correct angulation also allows the legs to gather adequately under the body. This efficient stride is necessary for maintaining endurance in the working Aussie.

(continued)

Short metatarsal bones drop directly beneath the center of weight bearing, thereby giving maximum support to the rear assembly. Moderate bend to the back, as with the moderately bent stifle, allows maximum flexibility and efficiency.

Because the feet carry the Aussie over all types of terrain, they must be as sound as the legs and body that they support. The compact foot that is close-knit with well-arched toes gives the greatest amount of strength and spring, allowing for endurance and agility.

The "width of the hindquarters approximately equal to the width of the forequarters at the shoulders. . . . The metatarsi are short, perpendicular to the ground and parallel to each other when viewed from the rear."

COAT

ASCA

Of medium texture, straight to slightly wavy, weather resistant, of moderate length with an undercoat. The quantity of undercoat varies with climate. Hair is short and smooth on the head, outside of ears, front of the forelegs, and below the hocks. Backs of the forelegs are moderately feathered; breeches are moderately full. There is a moderate mane and frill, more pronounced in dogs than bitches. Nontypical coats are severe faults.

AKC

Hair is of medium texture, straight to wavy, weather-resistant, and of medium length. The undercoat varies in quantity with variations in climate. Hair is short and smooth on the head, the ears, front of forelegs, and below the hocks. Backs of forelegs and britches are moderately feathered. There is a moderate mane and frill, more pronounced in dogs than in bitches. Nontypical coats are severe faults.

DISCUSSION

The Aussie's coat is not simply an item of great beauty, but one of utility. It should not be forgotten that the coat is a protective covering against all elements. The coat texture and its quality are as important as its length and quantity. The ideal coat is one of low maintenance, due partly to its moderate length, but equally due to the correct medium texture. When considering environmental conditions on the range such as the presence of cockleburs, sandburs, seedpods, mud, rain, snow, and heat, you cannot have a coat that requires tedious grooming. This is not to say that the coat is maintenance free, because none are. Debris seems to collect more frequently in woolly, dense, wiry, excessively curly coats or extremely fine coats and is more difficult to remove. Smooth, slick coats are uncharacteristic of the Australian Shepherd. The guard hair or outer coat provides protection against sunburn, and to a certain degree protects against insect bites and laceration by burrs and thorns while affording relatively easy removal of burrs and mud due to the proper texture. The downy undercoat insulates the Aussie against cold temperatures and will be commensurate with climatic conditions. An Australian Shepherd working for long hours under a Texas sun will not develop the same undercoat as an Australian Shepherd during a Canadian winter. The Australian Shepherd's ability to shed or grow undercoat enhances his utility in a variety of climates.

Ch. Shanahan's Phantom CDX sports a moderate coat, ideal for working in all weather.

COLOR

ASCA

All colors are strong, clear, and rich. The recognized colors are blue merle, red (liver) merle, solid black, and solid red (liver), all with or without white markings and/or tan (copper) points with no preference. The blue merle and black have black pigmentation on the nose, lips, and eye-rims; the red (liver) merle and red (liver) have liver pigmentation on the nose, lips, and eye-rims. Butterfly nose should not be faulted under one year of age. On all colors, the areas surrounding the ears and eyes are dominated by color other than white. The hairline of a white collar does not exceed the point of withers. **Disqualifications:** Other than recognized colors, white body splashes, Dudley nose.

AKC

Blue merle, black, red merle, red—all with or without white markings and/or tan (copper) points, with no order or preference. The hairline of a white collar does not exceed the point of the withers at the skin. White is acceptable on the neck (either in part or as a full collar), chest, legs, muzzle, underparts, blaze on head, and white extension from underpart up to four inches, measuring from a horizontal line at the elbow. White on the head should not predominate, and the eyes must be fully surrounded by color and pigment. Merles characteristically become darker with increasing age. **Eyes:** The blue merles and blacks have black pigmentation on eye rims. The red merles and reds have liver (brown) pigmentation on eye rims. **Nose:** Blue merles and blacks have black pigmentation on the nose (and lips); red merles and reds have liver (brown) pigmentation on the nose (and lips). On merles it is permissible to have small pink spots; however, they should not exceed 25 percent of the nose on dogs over one year of age, which is a serious fault.* **Disqualifications:** White body splashes, which means white on body between withers and tail, on sides between elbows, and back of hindquarters in all colors.

DISCUSSION

None of the accepted colors or patterns is preferred over the others as long as the color is within the guidelines of the Breed Standard and is characteristic of the breed. All colors—red, blue, and black (with or without white and/or copper trim)—receive equal billing and should be bred for and judged as such.

The black color is black. It should be jet black with no sable to the undercoat. Blue merle is a modification of the basic black body color and is sometimes referred to as "salt and pepper." It can vary in a

(continued)

---

* Note: The sections on **Eyes** and **Nose** are usually listed under the section of the **HEAD**, but for the sake of discussion they have been included with **COLOR**.

striking combination of powder blue, silver blue, steel gray, or blue black, all of which exhibit black hairs mixed with varying degrees of white or silver hair to produce the effect of blue or silver and must not be mistaken for charcoal or silver pigmentation. The red color is reddish-brown. It can be deep liver, burgundy, sorrel, mahogany, auburn, shades of rust, or chestnut in hue. The red merle is a variation of the basic red body color and is sometimes called "cinnamon and sugar" with liver skin pigmentation. The colors may be extremely contrasting to evenly blended. The patterns vary from a roan base, flecked, freckle merling (mottling) to marbling, splotches, and bold patches.

Nose leather, eye rims, and lips must correspond to the coat color, such as liver pigmentation on the reds and red merles and black pigmentation on the blacks and blue merles. Deviations from the corresponding coloration, such as black pigmentation on the red, mahogany, pumpkin, sable, and buff, are undesirable. It has been suggested that deep, rich pigmentation may help prevent sunburn, especially in reds.

Occasionally, "blue" individuals will appear with charcoal gray or navy blue pigmentation (nose, lips, and eye rims). These dogs have silver- or charcoal-colored hair instead of black, suggesting that the lethal gray gene may be present. Often these individuals demonstrate a sparser coat. While the charcoal gray or navy blue coloring is attractive and unusual, it is undesirable.

The variety in color combinations and patterns allows individuality within the breed, an important characteristic of Australian Shepherds. Each color may be with or without white and/or copper markings. White trim is an acceptable color pattern under the Australian Shepherd Breed Standard. It consists of white appearing in well-defined areas: muzzle, forehead, neck, chest, stomach, feet, and legs. It is not to be confused with other white color patterns that are genetically distinct and unacceptable under the Breed Standard. White trim can vary from small amounts on the tips of the toes to full blazes and collars, and stockings. (For a more complete discussion on white color patterns, see the coat color section of Chapter 25.) Copper varies from the deep rich color of a new penny to a creamy beige.

Pigmentation: Pigmentation on the nose leather is a concern for many Aussie owners. Pink spots on the nose, especially those that are surrounded by pigment, will usually fill in with age. Pink spots *in* the nose should not cause concern. The dudley nose (one without pigmentation) is a concern due to direct sun exposure. The sun can cause irritation to the unpigmented area; therefore, it is more susceptible to sunburn and solar dermatitis. Although the butterfly nose is faulted after one year of age, some Aussies may take two to three years for the nose to become fully pigmented. This is due to the breed's tendency for coat coloring to darken with age. Some deep-colored merles will appear almost solid in color as these individuals approach their twilight years.

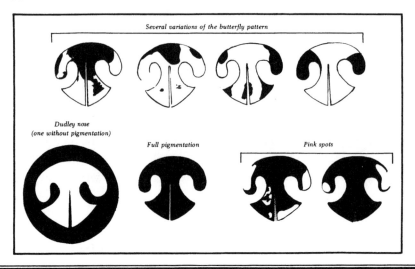

GAIT

ASCA

Smooth, free, and easy; exhibiting agility of movement with a well-balanced, ground-covering stride. Fore and hind legs move straight and parallel with the center line of the body; as speed increases, the feet, both front and rear, converge toward the center line of gravity of the dog, while the topline remains firm and level.

AKC

The Australian Shepherd has a smooth, free, and easy gait. He exhibits great agility of movement with a well-balanced, ground-covering stride. Fore and hind legs move straight and parallel with the center line of the body. As speed increases, the feet (front and rear) converge toward the center line of gravity of the dog, while the back remains firm and level. The Australian Shepherd must be agile and able to change direction or alter gait instantly.

DISCUSSION

"Gait" refers to the ideal conformation described in both Breed Standards, but in real-life action an Aussie must be able to turn on a dime and accelerate instantly in order to get ahead of livestock. He must also be able to fall behind a herd or flock and trail it for many miles. The correctly built Australian Shepherd will maintain balance and symmetry when set in motion. The individual that meets the ideals of structure should also meet the Standard's description of gait, because to move correctly, he must be built accordingly. Static conformation allows the transformation to proper kinetic conformation. Evaluation of both static and kinetic leads to a total picture of the true properties possessed by each individual Australian Shepherd.

The Australian Shepherd employs several gaits under actual working conditions but depends primarily on the trot. Therefore, gait is evaluated at a trot. The trot is a natural, two-beat, diagonal gait in which the front foot and the opposite hind foot take off simultaneously, while the hind foot strikes the ground a split second after the fore foot. Timing and coordination must be precise. It is a delicate balance. The Australian Shepherd must be able to cover ground in a minimum number of steps without sacrificing the agility necessary for sudden changes of direction. In order to exhibit ground-covering stride as well as agility, the Aussie cannot be overly angulated. In other words, agility plus ground-covering stride necessitate moderate angulation. The Breed Standard outlines the ideal gait for all physical demands on the Aussie in the variety of services that he performs for man.

Viewing the Aussie from the side reveals a smooth, effortless transition between fore and hind assemblies, or it reveals a lack of balance. Regardless of how spectacular or exaggerated the reach and drive (side gait) are, an Aussie lacking in correctness either coming or going is expending valuable energy unnecessarily, causing early fatigue. Remember: moderate, correct, and balanced are the key words.

(continued)

Single tracking, as called for in the Standard, is a natural phenomenon of gravity. The faster the trot, the more distinct the convergence as the Aussie draws his paws beneath his own center of gravity to minimize side-to-side motion, which wastes energy. This convergence formulates from the shoulder joint (point of shoulder) and from the hip joint to the feet. As the individual moves toward or away from the viewer, the legs appear to form a "V." There must be no deviation from a straight line. The joints must not bend or twist when in motion.

Agility is also dependent on convergence, which enables each Aussie to swivel (pivot) from the center line, rather than pulling himself around.

The Standard in Motion is exhibited in this excellent photo of Ch. Touchstone's Star Trekkin. The ideal, ground covering, agile gait described in the Breed Standard requires moderate angulation and perfect coordination between the front and rear assemblies.
Courtesy Cameron.

SIZE, PROPORTION, SUBSTANCE

ASCA

Preferred height at the withers for males is twenty (20) to twenty-three (23) inches; that for females is eighteen (18) to twenty-one (21) inches; however, quality is not to be sacrificed in favor of size.

AKC

Size: The preferred height for males is twenty to twenty-three inches; females, eighteen to twenty-one inches. Quality is not to be sacrificed in favor of size. **Proportion:** Measuring from the breastbone to the rear of the thigh and from the top of the withers to the ground, the Australian Shepherd is slightly longer than tall. **Substance:** Solidly built with moderate bone. Structure in the male reflects masculinity without coarseness. Bitches appear feminine without being slight of bone.

DISCUSSION

The Australian Shepherd is medium-sized in comparison to the entire canine species. Once all other qualities are brought into perspective, the importance of the Aussie's size is minimal against the appearance of the whole individual and the way in which he handles himself in action. Agility and working efficiency are based more on sound structure than on size. Exceptions to the ideal size range should be faulted only to the degree of deviation, as with any other fault.

OTHER DISQUALIFICATIONS

ASCA

Monorchidism and cryptorchidism.

DISCUSSION

Both monorchidism and cryptorchidism are fundamentally serious hereditary faults that affect the reproductive capacity of the animal.

When running at full speed (galloping), only one foot is on the ground supporting the entire body weight, especially when leaping to turn an escaping animal. WTCh. Justus Sioux performing a cow dog ballet. Photo by Cee's Pix.

Chapter 4

THE STANDARD IN MOTION

REFERRING TO THE TERM "GAIT" sets the Australian Shepherd Breed Standard in motion. Gait is the study of kinetic structure, or locomotion, as opposed to static (stationary) conformation. Gait and structure are directly related to each other. While in motion, the legs act in unison in either symmetrical or asymmetrical patterns, each of which is labeled "gait." In symmetrical gaits, including the walk and trot, the legs of either side repeat the actions of the other side, but they do so a half a stride later. In asymmetrical gaits, which include variations of the gallop, the legs from either side do not repeat the actions of the opposite side.

A stride is the complete coordinated cycle of action of all four legs, which starts with propulsion and ends with leg stabilization (support). The length of the stride is measured from the place where one paw leaves the ground to the place where the same paw again touches the ground. Each time a pad strikes the ground separately, the gait has four beats, as in walking. When diagonal legs strike simultaneously, as in the trot, the gait is two-beat, because only two beats occur for each stride.

The Australian Shepherd may have to trail stock for many miles and at any given moment be able to display great bursts of speed to outrun and turn a maverick. He often employs many forms of gait during any given day. His ability to maneuver quickly at full speed is referred to as agility. The dog that is able to cover the greater amount of steps without sacrificing agility is ideal. In other words, the moderately angulated, balanced individual is the most functional and therefore the most desirable.

The Australian Shepherd is slightly longer than tall, which gives him a moderately lower center of gravity that enhances his natural ability to duck and turn at full speed. At a natural stance, the stationary base of support formed by the paws on the ground is in the form of a rectangle (not a square).

SYMMETRICAL GAITS

Walk

At a walk, a triangular outline is formed because one pad is off the ground and the body weight is supported by the other three legs. The support role is greater for the forequarters, which are placed nearer the center of gravity, while the propulsive role is prominent in the hindquarters.

Trot

Foot timing and leg action between the forequarters and the hindquarters require absolute precision for correctness and efficiency. The trot is a symmetrical gait of medium speed in which the dog is supported by alternating diagonal pairs of limbs. The forequarter legs are off the ground only a split second longer than the legs of the hindquarter to allow the front feet to clear the ground in advance of the placement of the hind legs on the same side. When the front foot leaves the ground, the hind foot takes or "fills" its place.

When the Australian Shepherd shifts from the walk into an easy, slow trot, the gait is then called "collected." In the "extended" trot, the legs reach out to increase stride length and speed. When a period of suspension occurs between the support phases and propulsion, the gait is referred to as a "flying" or "suspended" trot.

ASYMMETRICAL GAITS

Canter (Slow Gallop)

The canter is in essence a slow gallop. It is a three-beat gait (in waltz time). Diagonal pairs of legs hit the ground simultaneously. The pattern is consistent: one hind leg, the other hind leg, and the foreleg diagonal to it simultaneously, followed by the remaining foreleg.

Gallop

As speed increases, the points of support decrease with a corresponding decrease in stability. When

The foot is flexed forward to absorb the initial shock and support the entire body weight during locomotion. The toes must be adequately arched, and the foot compact and strong to offer the maximum protection and cushion the front assembly. Photo by Trish Thornwald.

Fifteen hundred reasons why correct movement really counts.
Ch. Just Jake of Las Rocosa.

The hinge-type joint of the upper arm aids in diagonal extension of the front legs. Aussies must be light on their feet for total maneuverability.
WTCh. The Bull of Twin Oaks.
Photo by Cee's Pix.

a dog is running, his base of support is one point (foot and leg), as compared to the walk that is supported by three points (feet and legs) forming a triangular pattern on the ground. The gallop is an asymmetrical gait of fast speed. The Australian Shepherd is supported by one or more legs or is in suspension during parts of the stride. The support pattern is transferred depending upon the placement of the legs.

Analyzing Structure

It can take many years of observation to apply knowledge of gait. The interplay of strengths and weaknesses between the fore and hind assemblies is more clearly revealed in the trot than in any other gait. Leg action is more readily apparent at the symmetrical trot than in the asymmetrical, faster gaits. Sometimes a dog will appear flawless but when set in motion will have some factor that forces him to compensate considerably or "fall apart." Often this is only evident when all of the physical parts react with one another.

44 ALL ABOUT AUSSIES

Precision foot-timing is absolutely necessary for the tireless trot. Taylor's Escalante pictured along the historic Outlaw Trail, a remnant of the cattle rustling network that interlaced Utah.

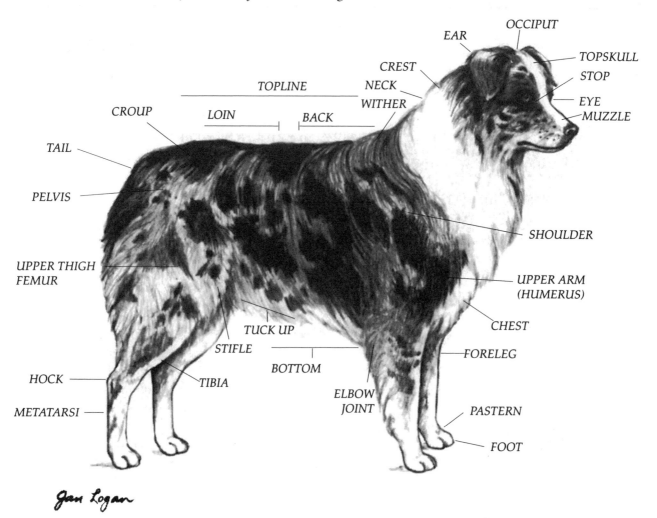

Side Movement (Reach and Drive)

When a judge views the Australian Shepherd in action from the side, he is able to study the interaction of the forequarters with the hindquarters. Foot timing is clear and easily accessible to the trained eye. The Australian Shepherd is a confident athlete. When set in motion, his gait suggests endurance. There is an effortless quality in the stride, which is deliberate without wasting energy. In this sense, the Australian Shepherd is an economist. The most effective movement does not always stand out and attract attention. However, its quality is never mistaken, because all parts harmonize without disrupting the interworking of other parts. When viewed from the side, the dog's topline should be strong and appear level between the shoulders and the loin. When the dog is trotting, there should be no bobbing, as the withers should remain level in motion. Any up-and-down movement wastes energy and indicates another structural inefficiency.

The "flying trot." Ch. Just A Sample of Sunnybrook CD. Courtesy Smith.

Skeletal structure of forearm.

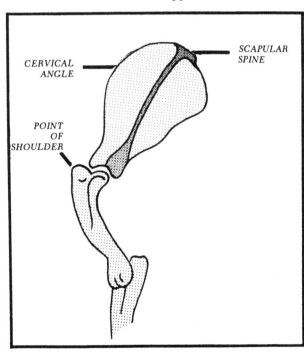

Two Track's Terpsichore of Depindet UD displays sheer agility as regulated by total balance and symmetry. Correct angulation is necessary for the thrusting power in a "kick-off," and, when coupled with balance, is also responsible for gathering the legs back under the body for maximum efficiency. Courtesy of Earnest.

Sometimes while in the working gait, the Australian Shepherd may drop his head slightly. When alert or focusing his attention on something, however, he can lift his head while in motion. The Australian Shepherd is slightly longer than he is tall. Actual body length determines foot placement, which is specifically governed by angulation. Balance and symmetry are the first and foremost requirements in a working breed such as the Australian Shepherd. This is influenced by correct static conformation but is measured by the yardstick of performance. Correct shoulder angulation that allows adequate reach but that lacks the corresponding angulation of the driving hindquarters is of little value. This kind of dog cannot "fill" his fore tracks and ends up wasting energy. On the other hand, an Aussie with well-angled hindquarters and insufficient angulated forequarters overdrives the front assembly by forcing the front feet and legs to get out of the way of the back ones, causing faults such as dwelling and crabbing.

The View Going and Coming

The Australian Shepherd is known as a "single-tracking" breed. When engaged in the trot, the dog's legs must converge toward a midpoint under his body (his center of gravity) as his movement speeds up. Strengths and weaknesses that are not readily apparent from the side view are easily seen as each dog moves away from or toward the viewer. Balance must be maintained constantly. The convergence begins from the point of the shoulder and the hip joint. The legs are strong, straight, columnar limbs. In other words, the joints of the legs should be free from any deviation or twisting actions as the legs converge toward the center line of gravity. An obvious "V" shape occurs as the leg remains steadfast within its position from either the point of the shoulder and hip joint, but the rest of the leg is drawn inward from the paws rather than from the joints of the pastern or hock, which will remain straight from the paw to their skeletal attachments at either the humerus or the pelvis.

The forequarters of the Australian Shepherd support the dog's weight. The shock caused by the weight being propelled forward by the hindquarters is absorbed by three primary features: the feet, the pasterns, and the shoulders. The feet absorb concussion somewhat like an automobile tire does. Soundness and endurance are dependent upon a combination of well-arched toes fitted snugly in a compact oval with thick pads. The toes will withstand more shock and offer more protection to the entire running gear. Flat toes that lack sufficient arch or splayed toes that fit together loosely are weak and incapable of adequately absorbing concussion. Splayed toes also expose the webbing to injury. This becomes readily apparent when the dog travels through rocky, brush-covered country. The tight, compact foot does not readily ball up with snow or mud as easily as the splayed foot, and it has better traction on icy surfaces.

The slope of the pastern acts like the shock-absorbing mechanism in an automobile. When the foot contacts the ground, the pastern flexes to accommodate the leg and then springs back to absorb the "jar" out of the gait. The absence of sufficient pastern (length and slope) results in constant concussion to the body. Weak or broken-down pasterns that are long with too much slope lack immediate spring and recovery and can cause a dog to fatigue easily and predispose the pastern and knees (carples) to hyperextension at fast speeds, causing them to be more susceptible to injury.

The slope of the shoulder (the angle between the scapula and the humerus and between the humerus and forearm) also acts like the springs in an automobile. Athletes such as skiers know the effect of the "jar" of stiff legs against a rough or hard surface. Try standing stiff-legged in the back of a moving vehicle, then bend your knees slightly. Suddenly your teeth stop being jarred. The angle of your bent legs then acts like the pastern and shoulder lay-back of the Australian

VISUALIZING THE VIEW COMING AND GOING

When converging toward the center line of gravity, the legs should remain columnar from the point of the shoulder to the paws. There should be no twisting at the pastern as the leg is drawn under.

Left: "Going." Right: "Coming." Courtesy Cornwell

Single tracking.

This dog does not display maximum reach and drive but is in total balance to itself.

Shepherd. A sloping shoulder blade and the corresponding hindquarter are conducive toward a smooth passage and transition during the various phases of kinetic balance with little lost motion.

Perhaps the main contributing factors toward tireless motion when under working conditions are the relative proportion and the angulation with the bone assembly of the running gear. The way in which the neck sets into the shoulder indicates the lay-back. The neck should always blend into the shoulders with no pronounced line of anatomical division. Long, sloping shoulders result in a moderate length neck (relative to the entire length of the top skull, the stop, and the muzzle when measured from the occiput to the tip of the nose and from the occiput to the withers), and in the appearance of a short back with a long underline that allows for a smooth, effortless gait when accompanied by corresponding hindquarters.

Left: The correct rear.

*Below, from left to right:
The correct rear in motion, bowed or open hocks, close behind, and cow hocks.*

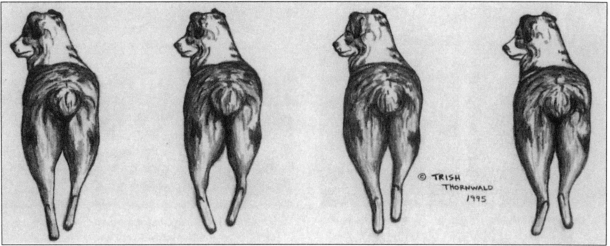

Short, upright shoulder blades produce a short neck and the appearance of a long back (not to be confused with a long body) and a choppy stride created by the limitations of the upright assembly. The blades should be broad and flat when viewed from the side. Shoulder musculature should be smooth and hard. Muscles firmly attach the shoulders to the body, allowing lateral mobility and a maximum cushioning effect.

Joints such as the elbows and hocks should be adequately broad in proportion to the bone of each dog and strong enough to allow good attachment and placement of muscles and tendons for efficient leverage. The elbows should be neither pinched nor loose. Free action of all joints is essential. The hinge-type joint of the upper arm is able to open enough to aid diagonal extension from the top of the shoulder to the tip of the extended pastern and foot. As the front pad hits the ground at the point of the dog's reach, forward propulsion is maintained. When the leg moves forward, the elbow and pastern bend to allow the leg and foot to move freely without scraping the ground. The hindquarters provide the necessary thrusting action when driving from behind. The well-angulated hindquarter permits the hind legs to extend effectively during motion.

When a judge must decide between two individuals of equal merit, but each has a fault, he must then determine which fault is the lesser. To do this, he must first understand what is correct. Then he will be able to figure out what is incorrect, what factor(s) cause the fault, and how it will affect the performance of each individual Aussie.

For example, when all else is equal, a fault such as cow hocks is more easily recognized than its counterpart fault—bowed or open hocks. Yet, it takes relatively little effort to bring the leg under the body for adequate support with cow hocks (because the support is already underneath the body) as opposed to the open hocks, which must "twist" inward and also cover a wider distance (because the leg is outside of the center line of gravity) in an attempt to converge. The effect is similar with deviations in the front legs. The individual that slightly toes out expends less energy to draw the legs underneath the line of gravity (similar to cow hocks) than an individual that slightly toes inward (pigeon toes), because the line of the leg is outside of the supporting feet. Therefore, it will take more distance to draw the legs underneath for sufficient support during movement.

Any deviation from a strong, firm topline requires the body to use additional energy to divert the power sent through the loin from the hindquarters during the transition from the hindquarters to the forequarters. When all other factors are equal, a slightly roached back would be preferable to a slightly dipped topline due to the fact that an arch is structurally stronger. It must be remembered, however, that all factors come into play when a decision is to be made.

STRIDE VERSUS SIZE

Size is not applicable when it comes to the science of soundness of gait. The factors that determine soundness, foot timing, and stride are based upon symmetry, balance, and sound structure rather than on size.

Often, an untrained eye will interpret that a larger dog is covering more ground than his smaller counterpart. This is especially apparent when comparing a larger dog that naturally stands over more ground with a smaller individual with the same angulation. Size has nothing to do with the actual length of stride when placed in proper perspective. This becomes obvious when two individuals of the same size are compared. For example, when a larger dog with straighter angulation is compared with a smaller individual that has greater angulation, the difference may not be that visible to the newcomer. But when the larger dog is compared to another dog of the same size that has a greater degree of angulation, the difference becomes more obvious.

The method of evaluating each dog in light of the Breed Standard is far superior to applying numerical increments. Each measurement should take into consideration the relationship of one part to another, and of all parts to the entire individual. This method stresses the importance of breeding well-balanced Aussies that are capable athletes.

*Ausies come in a variety of markings and different personalities.
Photo by Trish Thornwald.*

Chapter 5

FINDING THE RIGHT AUSSIE

BEFORE YOU CHOOSE AN AUSSIE, you must decide what bloodline has a consistent reputation for the traits that you most desire. The decision is yours. The variety offered within the breed is due to the fact that each breeder sets different goals for his breeding program.

It is important to buy from a trustworthy breeder. The reputable seller will lend you much assistance in making a decision. Conscientious breeders devote considerable time to studying Australian Shepherds and dogs in general. They know all of the distinguishing features of their dogs' bloodlines, including temperament and developmental patterns, both mental and physical. Conscientious breeders are aware of existing trends or problems with Aussies in general. They can inform the buyer which problems are acquired (congenital), and which are inherited (genetic). Breeders can give you particulars on their dogs' ancestral backgrounds. Over the years, breeders have gained tremendous insight about the breed and can answer many questions concerning training, grooming, and handling by giving actual demonstrations. Reputable breeders have satisfied clients because they stand behind the quality of their animals.

Pet shops or backyard breeders are not as familiar with the dog's ancestral background, nor do they understand the fine points of the breed. Registration papers are not always available due to a lapse in record keeping. They are not going to take the responsibility for or guarantee against genetic defects. They probably won't be around to answer questions or lend expertise when needed. However, conscientious breeders guarantee against genetic defects provided that the owner produces a signed veterinarian statement. If for some reason the dog doesn't work out in your situation, and if you have followed the recommendations of the breeder, the breeder is often in a position to either take back the individual, help place it, or offer an appropriate solution to the problem.

How to Find the Right Breeder

Contact the Australian Shepherd Club of America for a directory of breeders. Dog publications, veterinarians, and training clubs can also help point you in the right direction. Try to locate breeders who socialize their puppies in a home environment, and avoid any "breeder" who does not. Locate breeders who are involved with the breed. If a breeder trains and is involved in dog activities such as exhibiting, judging, stewarding, or attending seminars, this suggests that he has a well-rounded background.

Conscientious breeders feel responsible for bringing the puppies into the world and want to make sure that they will receive proper care. Breeders who care about their puppies view the sale of dogs like an adoption. The breeder must qualify the buyer. The breeder will be concerned whether the potential buyer has proper facilities, enough time, and enough money to care for the new puppy. The breeder will interview the buyer or have him fill out a questionnaire. Some of the questions may be:

- Do you have a preference for a male or female? Why?
- Do you want to get involved in the breed beyond having a companion or pet ownership?
- What areas of interest would you like to pursue with your Aussie (companion, stockdog, obedience, show, or other competitions, breeding, 4H, watchdog)?
- What future plans or goals do you have for the dog?
- Do you plan on training your Aussie?
- Have you or your family ever owned an Aussie before?
- Do you have children? (If yes, what are their ages?)
- Will they be training or handling this Aussie?
- Do you have other animals? (If so, tell us about them.)
- What type of area do you live in (rural, suburban, urban)?
- What facilities do you have now for your future Aussie (fenced yard, kennel, other)?
- How large is your yard?
- Do you work?
- How many hours will your Aussie be alone each day?
- How active are you, and do you take daily walks?
- If you are getting a stock dog, have you ever trained or worked a dog on livestock before?
- What type of stock will you be working?

These details about your needs and expectations help the breeder to determine if a suitable Aussie is available. If one is not, you will more than likely be referred to an appropriate source. It is necessary for a breeder to determine if your personality is compatible with that of the Australian Shepherd. He will further need to establish if you have the proper facilities to care for the Aussie. Apartment houses are not exactly adequate for an active herding breed.

If the breeder is reluctant to allow you to walk through the kennels, respect his wish. Due to bacterial infections and viruses that may be carried on a visitor's shoes and clothing, it may be a health risk to expose the dogs unnecessarily. However, most breeders are delighted to show you their facilities.

As a prospective buyer, you have the right to see at least the dam of the puppy and, if possible,

Ready to get out and discover the world.

the sire. This will tell you much about what you can or cannot expect. Most breeders will show you other relatives, including the grandparents and littermates.

THE RIGHT AUSSIE FOR YOU

Do not ignore your first impressions, because these are instinctive feelings that often guide your judgment. However, do not make hasty decisions or buy on an impulse. Make sure that you fully understand what Australian Shepherds are all about. Read books and magazines. Talk to different veterinarians, breeders, and trainers. Attend shows and performance events to see Aussies in action.

Theoretically, each Aussie that closely resembles the ideal described in the Breed Standard should be able to function efficiently. Realistically, an individual that is totally balanced and sound may still lack sufficient angulation, the ideal ear set, or other specific traits to be competitive in the show ring, but still will be able to function as an athletic, sound, working dog.

When you consider that Aussies live for twelve to fourteen years, it becomes important to choose a dog that has a good disposition. Environmental factors and handling affect the Aussie's attitude. Very often, breeders and buyers overemphasize show-ring winnings as a basis of selection. This method is less valuable from a breeding standpoint. It is helpful, however, when evaluating a puppy that does not yet have his own records—you must observe for consistency of desirable traits that are found in a specific bloodline that satisfy your requirements. A pedigree or registration paper does not guarantee the quality of an individual Aussie.

Male, Female, or Altered?

Males are good choices for show dogs due to the fact that they are "in coat" for more months throughout the year. Males are easier to compete with as Specials, because the frills are more pronounced than in their feminine counterpart. It must be remembered, however, that a superior individual is outstanding regardless of sex.

Both males and females can be trained and trialed in Obedience and Working with equal success. For training and trialing, the only disadvantage to owning a female is the twice-a-year heat cycle that may interrupt training and exhibition schedules, but then males in training for exhibition may also be affected by females in heat. If this creates a problem and your only interest is to get an Aussie for Obedience or Stock Trials, consider an altered male or female. However, if you plan to breed or exhibit in the Conformation ring, only whole males or females can be considered because the sole purpose of the breed ring is selecting stock to be used for the betterment of the breed.

Some males are more likely than females to roam if left unattended. If they are maintained in proper facilities, this should never become a problem.

Females are less likely to urinate on the walls, but they can squat and urinate in the middle of the floor. Cleanliness comes through proper training and management, and either sex can be clean house dogs.

Considering an Adult Aussie

Keep in mind the expectations that you have for your dog. With an adult Aussie, what you see is what you get. The Aussie has already reached physical maturity. The personality is already developed, and by close interaction and observation, you should be able to determine the quality of his disposition. This is highly important if you have children. If you have children, bring them along and introduce them, but only under close supervision. Watch for signs of aggression, avoidance, or timidity. Regarding changes in size or appearance, there will be no surprises in the adult.

Adult Aussies make excellent companions for many households, but they are particularly suitable if your lifestyle cannot accommodate the needs of a young puppy. Adults have outgrown the chewing stage that all puppies go through.

Adult Aussies become available for many reasons. Some Aussies become homeless through no fault of their own. Learn as much as possible about the individual's background. Breeders will sometimes place "retired" Aussies in special homes. Sometimes a well-trained and even possibly titled Aussie may become available. For ex-

Aussies are usually calm but can become excited when the doorbell rings. Photo by Trish Thornwald.

ample, an owner or breeder may be limited in facilities, time, or personnel and may cut back on present dogs to make room for up-and-coming individuals and trainees. A champion may even be attainable, although the breeder may want to maintain limited or unlimited breeding rights. The older stock dog may enjoy competing in the trial arena or introducing a Junior Handler to the world of competition.

The older "kennel" dog may lack confidence when taken from the security of his home. He may not exhibit as much personality as one that has had constant handling. When given special attention, however, this type of Aussie can be a very pleasurable companion. If the kennel dog possesses basic stability and the typical Aussie temperament and has had proper socialization and handling, he should be able to adjust readily to a new home and master. These dogs often flourish when given the chance to become a "special" member of the household and family.

AUSSIE PROFILE

Heritage:	Herder/guardian
Function:	Stockdog
Size:	19 to 23 inches, 25 to 65 pounds
Lifespan:	12 to 14 years
Personality:	Intuitive, affectionate, loyal, enthusiastic, high-spirited, protective, boundary-oriented
Intelligence:	High
Trainability:	High, eager to please
Activity Level:	High energy, requires daily exercise and play
Excitability:	Varied
Coat Type:	Double-coat (downy undercoat with coarser guard hairs)
Shedding:	Seasonal
Grooming:	Moderate; requires weekly brushing
Children and Other Pets:	Good with children and other pets; may try to herd them. Some may show aggression with other dogs
Strangers and Acquaintances:	Aloof toward strangers; may relate to drop-in neighbors (children and adults) as intruders
Ideal Home Situation:	Rural or suburban with large fenced yard
Ideal Owner:	Active or with patience and time to invest in regular training, exercise, and play to burn off excess energy

Aussies are a high-spirited, high-energy breed. The company of another dog may invite a good romp, but if not, it is up to the owner to provide an adequate avenue for sufficient exercise and play. Courtesy Anne Furnish.

Aussies will gently watch over their charges, but will fiercely protect them if necessary. Aussies are territorial, and with the breed's history as guardians, don't be surprised if they won't let strangers (even acquaintances) come and go without their owner's approval first.

Aussies that do not have an opportunity to work can learn tricks to keep them occupied.

Aussies are not machines that can be forced into obedience without damaging the desire. Aussies want to please and do best when taught with reward, be it getting to herd livestock, retrieving a ball, or other favorite activity.

Allow the dog to make the initial moves to make up to you. Do not force yourself upon him.

The conscientious breeder and kennel manager will make every attempt to socialize each of his Aussies by allotting special time for each individual. Regular grooming and handling are necessary for the dogs' health and welfare. Short trips in the car on errand days add variety and expose kennel dogs to unfamiliar situations, strangers, and children. Time in the house is beneficial in developing confidence and personality. Breeders often rotate their dogs from the yard to the house so that each dog has exposure and experience in different situations. Many Aussies maintained in a kennel situation have had former Obedience, Show, and Working careers and therefore are a marvelous introduction to the breed and to the dog world as a whole. Some of the best-behaved Aussies are those individuals raised in the kennel, providing they have had proper socialization and training.

The Family Companion

Personality is the most important consideration for the family companion. An experienced breeder generally knows what type of home each puppy is ideally suited to and can assist you in choosing the one that best matches your personality and activity level.

The disposition and activity level of the mother and the father (if he is on the prmises) will give an indication of the potential temperament of the litter. With the breeder's cooperation, you can perform the basic personality tests described in Chapter 28 (The Nursery). Each puppy should be handled gently in all of the tests. The puppies will not be as alert if they have recently eaten or have just woken up from a nap.

Skittish puppies that cower, are nervous, or that are highly submissive are poor choices for impatient people or families with small children who may force attention on him. This type of puppy will not adapt readily and will require special

Aussies are not suited to an independent lifestyle. Aussies rely on human companionship. They often follow their owners from one room to another just to be with them.

handling to develop confidence. This type of puppy frightens easily and may snap at a child when severely stressed.

Bold puppies that are highly dominant, that fiercely resist restraint, that jump and nip, and that growl or bark are also not good candidates for children or inexperienced owners. This pup will not readily accept children as pack leaders and can be provoked to bite if challenged. Similarly, overly independent puppies (especially when combined with highly dominant or submissive characteristics) are poor risks as pets, because they are not likely to socialize well, they do not enjoy affection and attention, and they may dislike social interaction.

Households with another dog should probably avoid the bossiest puppies that initiate puppy fights and lead in the puppy games. The "middle of the road" puppies that join in on puppy play and hold their own will generally fit in best and get along with another family dog.

The Obedience Companion Prospect

No two Aussies are alike, and no two will respond exactly the same to each person. The puppy that chooses to be with you will more likely be responsive and willing to perform with you. You must determine what temperament is best suited to you, because a dog with a compatible personality will make the most enjoyable companion for you. Do the parents and grandparents respond with a "what can I do to please you" attitude? The type of Aussie that will bounce back from timely corrections followed by praise is the best choice for training. Obedience companions must be structurally sound so that they can jump to height specifications in the Obedience ring and compete in other Aussie activities such as Agility.

Selecting the Stock Dog

In addition to temperament, other traits must be evaluated when selecting a stock dog. Gathering instincts, fetching/driving, heading/heeling (high or low), wide running/close running, silence/bark, grip/lack of, hard-mouthed/soft-mouthed, degrees of eye, degrees of force, and tail pulling must all be considered.

Training can alter and inhibit approximately 50 percent of the natural Working instincts. It is better to choose a stock dog with lots of "want to" than to try to encourage one lacking the appropriate instincts and drive to work.

If you are considering an older Aussie that has never been exposed to herding livestock yet that comes from Working ancestry, do not be discouraged if interest is not immediately aroused on the first introduction to livestock. Aussies are quick to respond to their natural herding instincts and may start to take interest after a couple of sessions.

Most breeders will guarantee that Working prospects, especially puppies, will have herding instincts. It is up to you, however, to provide a suitable environment, proper training, and handling to bring out these instincts. Herding prospects should be free from debilitating inherited defects that affect soundness and ability to function as a Working dog. There is no guarantee against faults that are acquired by injury or mismanagement.

Selecting the Conformation Prospect

The Conformation prospect should be a good representative of the breed according to the Standard and should be guaranteed to be free from disqualifying faults. It is impossible to guarantee that the individual will win when entered in competition. Winning is the combination of many variables, including each judge's interpretation of the Standard, condition of the Aussie, management (care and nutrition), handling, and competition.

Breeding Prospects

Breeding-quality Aussies must be sound in temperament and conformation. Breeding quality predisposes that the Aussie can be bred and is fertile, provided he does not contract diseases such as brucellosis after leaving the breeder's premises. The individual should be free from hereditary defects that could affect breeding soundness.

Once the Aussie is used for breeding by the buyer, it is assumed by the breeder that the buyer has given his approval. If the Aussie is good enough to breed, he will probably not be replaced.

GET IT IN WRITING

Guarantees and Adjustments

Breeders often place time limits on certain guarantees, such as up to twenty-four hours or thirty days after purchase. The reason for time limits is because exposure to health hazards, such as disease, parasites, injury, emotional trauma, abuse, and improper management, are all out of the breeder's control.

It is generally understood that the buyer will have the dog examined by his veterinarian. This is done to establish a record of health and to detect any possible or potential problems within the necessary time requirements established by the seller at the time of sale.

Any defects deemed necessary for replacement or adjustment commonly require appropriate documentation—a veterinarian's statement, Orthopedic Foundation for Animals (OFA) evaluation, eye certification (from a certified ophthalmologist), or an Obedience certificate from an approved training center—at the time of adjustment or replacement. The breeder has the right to require the necessary documentation at the buyer's expense (unless otherwise specified) to substantiate the claim. This is especially applicable in the case of hereditary defects that are not apparent until later but that affect suitability for the purpose purchased.

If an Aussie is replaced by the breeder, the breeder may require that the buyer pay shipping expenses for the Aussie's return. Depending upon the breeder, he will usually pay shipping charges for the replacement. If a replacement or adjustment is necessary, the breeder often will offer you a choice of a replacement individual or a total or partial refund. Some breeders will allow the purchase price or part of it to be applied to another Aussie. Sometimes Aussies are sold as show or breeding quality with the agreement that if the individual does not develop as anticipated, the neuter or spay fee will be refunded. Some breeders will refund or apply the purchase price toward a more suitable dog upon proof of alteration.

Aussies sold as pet quality may or may not have registration papers, or papers will be furnished when proof of alteration is supplied in the form of a veterinarian's statement. For many reasons, breeders may sell an individual for a pet price but reserve the option (usually at the request of the buyer) to reevaluate the quality of an individual. This evaluation generally takes place when the Aussie is between six and eighteen months of age to conclude whether or not he is of breeding or show quality. If the breeder finds that the Aussie is of this quality, he will issue registration papers with the difference between pet-quality price and a show/breeding-quality price satisfied. If the breeder finds that the Aussie is not of show or breeding quality, then registration papers will be given when there is proof of alteration.

Money, Contracts, and Registration Papers

All transactions must be well defined, and the cost and method of payment should be clearly understood by both parties before closing the sale. Most breeders require a deposit. Methods of payment vary with the breeder. Cash or money orders with purchase price paid in full are the most widely acceptable methods of payment. Most breeders will accept time installments (to be paid in advance, or a percentage of the total price to be paid in advance and the remainder to be paid in a manner specified and agreed upon by both parties). Some breeders will accept checks but will keep the paperwork until the check clears. In some cases, they will keep the dog until the check clears. Some breeders will accept credit cards, although this is not a common method of payment.

Dogs sold with breeding rights, or with partial payment to be made in stud rights on a male or puppies back on a female, are said to be sold with "breeder terms." Paperwork is generally held by the breeder until all terms are met as agreed upon. With co-ownerships in which two parties own the individual and each handles specific responsibilities and expenses, it must be fully spelled out who is to do what. In these cases, registration papers may be maintained in both the breeder's name and the buyer's name. When all obligations are met, the breeder generally will transfer sole ownership to the buyer.

Australian Shepherds can be registered with the Australian Shepherd Club of America (ASCA), the American Kennel Club (AKC), the Canadian Kennel Club (CKC), the United Kennel Club (UKC), and/or the National Stock Dog Registry (NSD). To participate in club shows and events, Conformation shows, Obedience, Agility, Tracking, or Herding/Stock-dog trials, each Australian Shepherd must be registered with that association. Many Aussies are eligible for more than one registry.

Registration papers or applications should accompany each individual. If they do not, proof of registration of both the sire and dam (with the same association) should be provided. For the individual to be registered, the breeder must first submit a breeder's certificate to the registry and then be issued a litter number. If the breeder has received this paperwork from the registry, he should then supply that litter number on the bill of sale along with a brief description of the individual, including sex, date of birth, color (including eye color), registered names and numbers of both the sire and the dam, and the name of the breeder (the owner or lessee of the dam).

It should be clearly understood or specified in the contract (if applicable) that registration papers will be provided with the individual or transferred or forwarded upon receipt from the registering association after they have been processed. Registration papers will be supplied upon fulfillment of "terms" either agreed upon as usually specified in contracts, or they will be signed over when proof of alteration is received in the form of a signed veterinary statement in the case of neutering and spaying.

Pedigree and Health Records

The breeder should supply a three-, four-, or five-generation pedigree, in addition to a record of inoculations, including dates of worming.

Taking the perfect puppy home.

Chapter 6

YOUR NEW AUSSIE

THERE ARE MANY RESPONSIBILITIES that you must assume when you get a new puppy. Puppies are irresistible, but as they grow into adulthood, they will require daily care (food, water, shelter) and training. You must have appropriate facilities to accommodate your Aussie. Medical care must be provided. You must assume full responsibility for all of your dog's actions.

Try to make the ride home a pleasant one. It is beneficial if the puppy has had previous experience. Many breeders give their puppies short rides in an automobile to precondition them prior to going to their new homes.

THE HOMECOMING

Allow your new puppy time to freely explore his yard and house. He will be anxious to become acquainted with the new territory and people.

The first night away from home and the security of his dam and littermates will be a difficult adjustment. Provide a dry, clean, comfortable place for him to sleep that will lend a sense of security. Prepare for the puppy by obtaining ahead of time a crate, bedding (washable), safe puppy toys (rubber ball, chewable toys, a squeaky toy), a collar and leash, puppy food, bottled water, dog biscuits, nonchewable and nonbreakable food and water dishes, a brush, nail clippers, styptic powder, tearless baby shampoo, cleanup equipment, carpet stain and odor remover, a baby gate, a first-aid kit, and a copy of *All About Aussies*.

Don't buy or make toys that are small enough to swallow or that can become lodged in the puppy's throat. An old sock with a ball or knots tied in the end is also an amusing toy.

Puppy-Proof Your Home

Just like toddlers, puppies are curious and explore the world by putting everything in their mouths. Carpet, drapes, and furniture legs can be sprayed lightly with extra-dry (unscented) antiperspirant or commercial dog repellents to discourage chewing. Put house plants up and out of the puppy's reach. Tape electrical cords to baseboards, or hide them under rugs and behind furniture. Don't leave cigarette butts in ashtrays—they can cause nicotine poisoning. Many objects, if swallowed, cause intestinal blockages and require surgical removal. Keep tiny objects such as pills, small toys, jacks, marbles, pins, needles, pencils, and anything that can splinter, such as chicken bones, glass, or wood, out of your puppy's reach. Put everything away in closets, on cupboard shelves, or in drawers. Put up the children's toys and clear away the books and magazines. Put the fishing-tackle box out. Empty all trash cans, and don't leave the toilet paper dangling. Keep the toilet lid down (especially when it contains sanitizing chemicals). Put the kitty-litter box where your puppy cannot reach it. Don't leave shoes and socks lying around. Puppies enjoy chewing on your new shoes just as devotedly as they enjoy the worn-out ones. Household cleaners of every kind are hazardous for puppies and must be stored away carefully.

In the garage, antifreeze/coolant (ethylene glycol) is highly attractive *and deadly*. Clean up antifreeze spills with soap and water. Even if they are stored in tightly capped containers, poisonous substances can be dangerous if the puppy chews on the container. Carefully store away all weed killers, insect and rodent poisons, and fertilizers.

Remove any poisonous plants or other substances (snail bait, etc.) from the yard. Yard edging can severely cut up the pads and toes of your puppy's feet.

Give your dog safe toys.

When you first bring the new puppy home, you need to provide a secure place of his own. Touchstone's Brassy Executive of Las Rocosa in her own special little bed with her favorite toy. Courtesy Carol Madsen.

CRATES

A dog crate is a safe place for your puppy when you are not able to keep an eye on him and protect him from harm. A crate should be used like a crib or playpen for a baby. The crate can protect a puppy from many dangers like chewing on an electric cord or eating a poisonous substance.

A dog crate is your Aussie's private den or cave. Your puppy needs a special place where he can have his own space and feel secure. When you have a house full of company, when there is danger that someone may let the puppy outside, or when your puppy needs a break from constant handling or inconsiderate children, or is underfoot, the crate is the safest place to put him.

The crate provides a safe place for your puppy to ride. It serves much in the same capacity as a child's safety seat. In the event of an accident, a puppy confined to a crate that is secured in the vehicle will have more protection from being thrown through the window. The crate is your Aussie's home away from home. Refer to the chapter on traveling with your Aussie.

Crates should be long enough to accommodate the Aussie when he is stretched out. It should be tall enough to allow him to stand comfortably with his head held in a natural posture. Crates are excellent training tools when used correctly and are a real help when you initiate house training.

THE FIRST NIGHT AWAY FROM MOTHER

The first night away from home and the security of his dam and littermates will be a difficult adjustment for your puppy. He will feel lonely and restless. The first night, and possibly for several nights until he becomes adjusted, he may cry or whine. Place his crate or bed next to your own bed or that of another family member. During the night, you can reach down and comfort him with reassuring strokes until he settles down and falls asleep. You can also play the radio softly or let him listen to the ticking of a clock, which might be calming to him. Under no circumstances should you punish your puppy.

Always take your puppy outside to relieve himself just before retiring for the night. If after the first few nights the puppy continues to whine, tap on the crate and tell the puppy, "That's enough."

CRATE TRAINING

Introducing your Aussie to a crate should be a pleasant experience. Prop the door open and allow the puppy to check it out. Place a few doggie treats or a dog bone inside at the back of the crate. To begin crate training, place the puppy's food inside. While he is eating, close the door. When he is finished, let him out unceremoniously. Confine your Aussie to the crate for short periods, such as for a drive around the block. If he starts whining or barking, do not let him out. Otherwise, the puppy will learn that you will let him out every time he complains. Your Aussie will be most eager to enter the crate if he knows that it is a temporary situation and that he will be getting out again—soon.

Crates are excellent to use for house training as well as to establish a schedule and introduce a place for feeding and sleeping. An Aussie that needs special socialization can gain exposure to normal activities surrounding him when he is placed in a crate. Your Aussie gains the added benefit of being handled as he is placed in and out of the crate.

In warm months, take special care to place the crate in a cool, shaded area with adequate ventilation. Water must be available at all times. If necessary, a small water bucket or "lick-it" type of watering device can be used.

If your Aussie must be crated for several hours at a time while you are away at work, make sure that he receives adequate exercise when you get home. It is also important that you give him

*The best way to house train a puppy is to anticipate his needs. Puppies can be distracted easily, so give them ample time to take care of business.
Photo by Trish Thornwald.*

ample opportunity to exercise and to take care of business prior to placing him in the crate before you go away. Otherwise he could develop bladder problems.

HOUSE TRAINING

If you feed and exercise your puppy on a regular schedule, house training will be no problem, providing you promptly take him outside every two hours. Puppies do not have any more physical control than a baby does. By the time your puppy nears five months of age, he should be able to hold himself for a few hours at a time. Whenever your Aussie is having a problem making messes in the house, it probably can be traced to neglect or to an inconsistent schedule. For example, on weekends, family members are home to let the puppy out the door. When everybody is away at work or school, however, nobody is home to open the door, yet they expect the puppy to control himself throughout the week. If you arrive home and there is a mess in the house, don't make a big deal out of it. Do not punish your Aussie for events beyond his control. Dog doors are ideal in this situation. If you suspect a physical problem (parasites or other ailment), take your puppy to the vet.

You must first understand your puppy's natural inclinations and apply them in training. In the wild, young pups are taught at an early age to go far from their den or nest to defecate. If the pup is confined to his crate, he has no other choice than to soil his bed unless you let him out when he needs to go.

To be successful, you must take your puppy out just as soon as he wakes up from a nap, and within fifteen minutes after eating or drinking, and after exciting play. Take him outside the very first thing in the morning and the last thing before going to bed. This will establish a pattern and good habits for him. Whenever you have been away, take him outside immediately. Use the same door each time you take him out to eliminate. Your puppy will soon go to that door to let you know when he needs to go out. If you take him to the same spot each time, he will soon go there on his own. You can use any word or command—"outside," "yabba dabba do"—to indicate that it is time to take care of business. Don't rush him, and don't leave him unattended. Always praise him once he has completed his business. This is invaluable when you are traveling to unfamiliar places.

Pick of the litter. Courtesy LeDine Denzin.

If you see your puppy sniffing the ground, turning in circles, or beginning to squat, take him outdoors, because he is about to eliminate. When you take your puppy outdoors, allow him sufficient time to complete his business. Stand there quietly with him until he urinates or defecates. Praise him. Do not bring him back inside until he finishes (even if the World Series is on television). The puppy may be anxious to get back indoors, especially during foul weather. Even during these times, you must allow him ample opportunity.

Your Aussie's nose is so keen that he can smell one part urine in thirty to sixty million parts of water. If he smells urine (as he should when he eliminates in a familiar place), he will be inclined to urinate in that spot. A mixture of vinegar and water or odor neutralizers will eliminate the urine odor. The scent of ammonia is confusing to puppies, so avoid using it when cleaning up urine. After applying the vinegar to neutralize the urine, use soap and water to clean the spot thoroughly.

Whenever you are unable to keep an eye on your puppy, confine him to a specific area that you can easily clean up in the event of an accident. Child/baby gates are helpful as a divider between two rooms. If an accident does occur, *do not* punish your puppy or rub his nose in the mess (especially if you didn't see the act take place). Scolding or spanking only increases the problem and makes your puppy more nervous. Simply take your puppy outside. If you see the accident take place or about to take place, give an "ah-ah" correction and calmly take the puppy outdoors. Use common sense. Your consistency will bring about positive results and will help your puppy become secure and confident. If you become anxious, your puppy will begin reacting out of fear. This, in turn, will bring more negative results.

SOCIALIZATION AND TRAINING

In order to develop into a well-adjusted adult, a puppy must be conditioned to handle the challenges of everyday living. At certain times in a puppy's life, he will be ultrasensitive toward new experiences. When your puppy reacts adversely to a new experience (veterinary examination, meeting new people, riding in a car), it is important for you to be the leader and to respond in a positive manner. This will be reassuring to your puppy and will convey that everything is under control. When your puppy is frightened by a certain stimulus (thunder, firecrackers, vacuum cleaners), don't spend a lot of time cuddling and petting him. Unknowingly, you are actually rewarding him and are thus encouraging fearful behavior.

Early conditioning or socialization involves subjecting the puppy to mild stress in everyday

First encounter with a goose.

living (meeting new people, seeing new places). When introducing your puppy to strangers, you can give the strangers food treats to offer the puppy. Allow only friendly people to interact with your puppy. Do not allow strangers to play roughly or to restrain the puppy, because this can foster inappropriate behavior (fear or aggression). When these experiences are positive, they build confidence in the puppy.

Enroll your puppy in a puppy kindergarten class for socialization and gentle play training. Puppies should have the opportunity to play with other puppies. Many important skills are learned through play with other puppies. The class should also involve interaction with many friendly people. While the inherited temperamental traits form the basic personality, it is the interaction of those genetic traits with environment and handling in the early part of life that greatly influence the dog's behavior and personality for a lifetime. Socialization is the most important aspect of raising a puppy during his first six months.

Play

Play is highly important in your puppy's development. Encourage him to retrieve a ball or toy. Toss or roll the toy, and lavishly praise your puppy for going after it. Encourage him to bring it back.

Do not let the kids roughhouse with the puppy unless you are trying to encourage more aggressive behavior.

Dominance and Leadership

Whenever you walk away from your puppy and he follows, praise him. Always praise your puppy for seeking your attention. In order to establish yourself as the pack leader, gently roll your puppy over and hold him down until he relaxes, or pick him up and hold him until he settles. Do this several times a day. Praise your puppy and release him.

Take your puppy on outings to the park. An older dog helps give the puppy confidence in strange surroundings. Photo by Trish Thornwald.

LEASH TRAINING

Leash training is important because many training lessons will utilize a lead and collar. Proper leash training also establishes the foundation for teaching your puppy to come when called. The first lessons on lead should begin with a nylon web or leather collar. Training collars (choke, pinch, or electronic) are far too severe on puppies and should not be used until much later, if at all. The collar must fit snugly enough so that it won't slip off if the puppy tries to pull back against it, but not so tight that it is uncomfortable for the puppy. Once the collar is on the neck, you should be able to slip one or two fingers underneath it.

The first lessons should occur in the familiar surroundings of home. Early handling can set an impression in the puppy's mind to last a lifetime. A negative experience also can leave a lifetime impression. Place the lead and collar on your puppy and let him drag it around the house or in a secure fenced yard or empty tennis court—but only while you are present to keep an eye on him.

After a lesson or two of letting the puppy drag the leash, you can practice walking your puppy by carrying the lead. Clap your hands and call your puppy to you. When he arrives, give him praise and a reward (food or a toy). The reward must be in the form of whatever motivates your puppy. Walk a short distance in the opposite direction. Now call your puppy's name. If he responds immediately, give lots of praise and a reward. If he is slow to respond, snap the leash and run away from him. Your puppy should chase you. When he reaches you, praise him, give him a treat, and pet him. Whenever you pop the leash, you must immediately release the pressure and put slack into the line (just like snapping your finger).

Too often, inexperienced owners forget to release the pressure by keeping continual tension on the leash. The puppy will be less likely to fight the leash if it has slack in it. If the puppy learns to walk on a lead without tension, he will be more reliable in responding to commands when he is off the lead. Don't focus your attention back at the puppy—set your sights ahead. Call your puppy's name and walk from one side of the

Many important skills can be learned through play. Photo courtesy of Talena Smith.

Aussies often use their feet to hold a ball or toy during play.

yard to the other. Don't make a big fuss over the puppy, but talk happily as you walk. Pretty soon he will be trailing right along.

If your puppy balks or panics and jumps around and fights the leash, *do not* scold or tug on him. Keep hold of the lead, but release the tension. Now, call the puppy to you, and clap your hands to encourage him to come. You can also offer a little food treat. Remember to praise him and talk happily. Every time the puppy balks or resists, give a gentle but quick jerk and release (making sure that there is slack in the leash after the jerk) and keep moving forward. It won't take long. A little food might be an appropriate treat to encourage your puppy to follow along.

Work on the leash will be beneficial in teaching your puppy to come when called. When on lead, your puppy cannot get into the habit of running in the other direction when you call his name. Always praise him for coming. *Under no circumstances should you ever call your puppy to you for any type of discipline.*

FINDING THE RIGHT PUPPY CLASS

Not all dog trainers are knowledgeable about Aussies or canine behavior. Carefully screen the instructor. No matter how great a trainer is at working with dogs, he also must be able to communicate his knowledge to people. Puppy training must teach good manners without inhibiting your Aussie's spirit. Positive experiences are imperative in fostering sound temperaments and confidence. The breeder of your puppy, a kennel club, your veterinarian, or a groomer may be able to recommend a good kindergarten puppy class. Many recreation associations and community colleges offer dog-training classes. Check the bulletin boards at pet-supply outlets or supermarkets, and peruse the newspaper and yellow pages for class listings.

Whenever possible, visit the class prior to enrolling. It is important that the class be small enough to allow a certain amount of personal attention. Does the instructor relate well to the dogs? Do you approve of the training methods? If the Obedience training methods are too disciplinary for you or your Aussie, try other options, such as a Conformation class. These types of classes are good opportunities for social exposure; they offer food rewards and rarely discipline.

Among the numerous books and videos on raising and training puppies, try the following: *How to Raise a Puppy You Can Live With* by Clarice Rutherford and David Neil, *Owner's Guide to Better Behavior in Dogs* by William E. Campbell, and *The Art of Raising a Puppy* by the Monks of New Skete.

Preventative Care

Between six to eight weeks of age, your puppy should receive a well-puppy exam and begin a preventative health program. Health care includes vaccinations, parasite control, proper nutrition, and dental care.

Choosing a veterinarian is no different than trying to locate a pediatrician for your child. Above all, you will require a vet whom you can trust completely. You need to feel comfortable talking with your vet. He should be willing to answer questions and explain any procedures performed on your Aussie. The fees should be discussed prior to treatment. It is beneficial if the vet is familiar with Aussies or is willing to do homework to learn more about them. Competence, compassion, and friendliness are all important characteristics in a vet and staff.

Your Aussie's breeeder may be able to refer you to a vet in your area who has experience in treating Aussies. Other breeders, handlers, trainers and training centers may be able to make recommendations. Veterinarians are also listed in the yellow pages of your telephone book.

Visit the veterinary practice. Cleanliness of the facility should be apparent. You should feel comfortable with the staff's willingness to assist. Check out the hours offered at the clinic. Are emergency services available when the clinic is closed? What services are offered at the clinic? Is grooming or boarding available? Are specialists (ophthalmologist, dermatologist) or a veterinary hospital available for referral?

Vets who are members of local, state, and national veterinary medical associations are usually very interested in continuing education. This is important due to rapidly advancing scientific techniques.

Coccidiosis

New owners need to be aware of the symptoms of coccidiosis. The symptoms may go unnoticed (mild diarrhea) and eventually disappear, while severe cases of coccidiosis cause highly virulent infections that are rapidly fatal.

The incubation period from initial exposure to coccidia is about 13 days. Coccidiosis is spread from feces or from carrier hosts (including flies and cockroaches that mechanically carry the parasites).

Illness is often manifested during the stressful period of adjusting to a new home, sickness, or when the immune system is suppressed from an infestation of other parasites (worms), bacteria, or viruses. It is more common in puppies or young dogs, as healthy adults usually develop natural immunity. Coccidiosis is treatable. See Health Care.

The New Adult Aussie

If you purchase an older dog, give him time to settle in. Wait until you have had him about a month before you begin formal training. By that time he will be accustomed to his new home and will have regained his confidence. Even an Aussie that has had Obedience or other training needs to attend a class with his new owners so that you and your Aussie can become a team.

Although the adult Aussie may be housebroken, it is beneficial to establish a new schedule by taking him outside at regular intervals.

Keeper of flock, home, and heart . . . We have a responsibility to him, too.

Chapter 7

RESPONSIBILITIES OF OWNING AN AUSSIE

WITH EVER INCREASING ANTI-DOG attitudes and anti-dog legislation, dog owners must go out of their way to protect their Aussies and the right to own animals. Actions of dog owners will affect how dog ownership is perceived by society in the future.

URBAN AND SUBURBAN AUSSIES

Aussies are adaptable and in many cases can live harmoniously in the city, providing they receive the right kind of daily exercise and care. Due to restricted space, urban living requires careful planning and a commitment. In the streets, dogs face danger around every corner. They can be hit by a car or be dognapped, or they can lick antifreeze on the pavement. Unless you have a fenced yard for your Aussie, you will have to schedule regular outdoor outings, first thing in the morning, at noon (perhaps during a lunch break), when you arrive home from work, and prior to retiring for the evening.

Although life in the country may be less restricting than in the city, Aussies should not be allowed to roam at will. Unsupervised dogs are at risk of getting killed by vehicles, poisoned by pesticides, killed by coyotes, shot by a neighboring farmer or rancher, or stolen for resale to laboratories. Not only is the unsupervised dog in danger, but he also can develop bad habits. Whenever you can't be with your dog, he should be safely contained in a fenced yard, kennel run, house, or barn.

Be A Good Neighbor

In order to be a good neighbor, you have to live cooperatively with others by observing the laws. Keep all vaccinations up to date, and be sure that your Aussie is free of parasites.

Don't allow your Aussie to run at large. When he does so, he may intimidate small children; chase bicycles, the neighbor's cat, or livestock; soil the neighbor's yard; or dump over the garbage. These antics will not make you a popular neighbor. And remember the safety factor—your Aussie simply is not safe when he is running at large.

Without exception, clean up after your Aussie. Don't allow your Aussie to defecate in areas where children play. When strolling through the neighborhood, you can carry a disposable scooper. Most dog-supply catalogs and pet stores carry such items, or you can make your own. They are discreet and convenient to use.

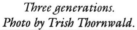

*Three generations.
Photo by Trish Thornwald.*

An Aussie against the silhouette of a rough-coated Pyrenean sheepdog in Europe. Courtesy Claude De Salis.

Barking, howling, and whining are natural behaviors, but at three o'clock in the morning, these sounds can be a real problem if they wake up your neighbors. Barking and howling often occur when you are away from home, because your Aussie is bored and lonely and will bark at anything that passes by. Barkers can be curbed through behavior modification and proper management. Aussies are natural guardians. When someone knocks at your door, allow your Aussie to bark a couple of times. Praise him with "good dog," then curb the action with a vocal command, "that's enough."

To avoid a visit from an animal-control officer, it may be beneficial to bring the outdoor barker indoors at night and when you must go away. If you need to confine your dog to a certain area in the house, you can use a child's folding gate. A crate is ideal for Aussies that are not house trained. Music playing softly on a radio or a program on television may help comfort your Aussie as well as mask neighborhood noises.

Teach Good Manners

An Aussie with good manners (acquired through training and handling) is appreciated by everyone who encounters him. Most people do not appreciate being jumped on, humped on, or slobbered on. Nor do other dog owners appreciate a strange dog rushing up to or challenging their dog.

Basic obedience is necessary and desirable for Aussies in all communities. The AKC offers an excellent program to promote training and care necessary to properly integrate Aussies into society. The Canine Good Citizen (CGC) Program rewards responsible dog ownership. A Canine Good Citizen is an Aussie that makes his owner happy, while not making anybody else unhappy. The CGC program is not limited to AKC purebreds but also allows unregistered and mixed-breed Aussies to gain certification.

The CGC Program involves a noncompetitive, ten-part, pass-or-fail test that evaluates the Aussie's behavior in practical situations at home, in public, and in the presence of other dogs. Aussies must demonstrate sociability, be able to walk on a loose leash, and respond to basic Obedience commands (sit, down, and stay). Owners are allowed to talk to their Aussies throughout the tests as they would in everyday, normal situations. In order to participate in a CGC test, your Aussie must also be groomed and have a current rabies shot.

For more information, contact the American Kennel Club:

THE WORKING OWNER

Rarely can you be with your dog twenty-four hours a day. Although some places of employment will allow your dog to accompany you to work (if he is trained and well behaved), not all employers are receptive to the idea.

Aussies are social animals and thrive on the companionship of their owners. Periods of isolation may cause separation anxiety, which can result in destructive behavior such as barking, howling, chewing, and messes on the floor. Punishment for negative behavior that you don't actually witness only increases anxiety upon anticipation of your return home. Emotional departures and returns also increase anxiety.

You can minimize the effects of separation, loneliness, and boredom by leaving squeaky toys, chew toys, and bones to occupy your dog while you are away. A playmate—another Aussie perhaps—can provide companionship in your absence. Perhaps you can hire a friend or young adult in the neighborhood to spend some time each day after school walking and playing with your Aussie.

When you make a big production out of leaving or returning home, you are actually contributing to the problem. Some Aussies become chronic escape artists. Escapees are vulnerable to many dangers. They dig holes around the yard, chew an escape route through the fence, or jump the fence in search of companionship or to pursue tormentors. Unneutered males escape in search of a female in heat. Fear of thunder in stormy weather can also provoke an Aussie to escape.

You can confine a jumper by either raising the height of your fence or by adding extension slants that tilt inward. A strand of electric wire strategically placed only inches from the bottom of the fence, or an invisible transmitter and collar receiver, may discourage your dog from getting close enough to dig. Metal bars driven deep into the ground or a sunken fence may discourage escape attempts. A kennel run with a wire top and cement floor is always a good investment.

You must protect your Aussie from becoming the target of cruel and bored children who get a kick out of taunting dogs, or inflicting pain and fear. When you are away, your dog should never be left in a place that is accessible to passersby. Aussies are vulnerable to being abused and dognapped when they are left unattended in a yard or on a chain.

IDENTIFY YOUR DOG

The use of collars for temporary identification is ineffective in the case of stolen, stray, and often lost individuals. The role of positive identification afforded through tattooing is limitless. It gives protection to valuable breeding stock, champions, working Aussies, and faithful companions. Positive identification is often necessary during litigation regarding stolen Aussies, as well as for other transactions including artificial insemination, registration, and sale transfers. With each individual that is sold, a transfer slip should accompany each Aussie to the new owner. Nose and paw prints, freeze-branding, microchips, and tattooing are all methods of permanent identification. While microchips can't fade or become distorted, they are not a viable form of identification due to potential migration of the chips after implantation. At this time, tattooing is the only reliable, absolute proof of ownership accepted in a court of law.

By law, a tattoo is considered in the same classification as a brand. Branded animals are subject to federal laws that are enforced by the Federal Bureau of Investigation (FBI). The abdomen and inside right thigh are the safest areas to tattoo and cannot be easily mutilated through amputation. Positive identification consists of tattooing an owner's social security number or registration number on this area. For a minimal one-time fee or lifetime rate, this number can be registered permanently with the National Dog Registry (NDR) or with I.D. PET. Once the initial fee is paid, there is generally a tattooing fee of a few dollars for each additional Aussie. Tattoo clinics are often available in conjunction with local shows and matches and through your veterinarian. Once registered with the NDR or I.D. PET, a missing or stolen Aussie can be readily identified. Both organizations also aid in pet recovery.

Tattooing is a quick (it usually involves no more than a few minutes), painless procedure. A vibrator unit is used to permanently apply the numbers, then tattoo pigment (ink or paste) is applied for easy identification. Numbers on the thigh should be made readily visible by clipping the hair. Tattoos on the abdomen are often more visible than anywhere else.

To obtain further information and registration forms, write or call the National Dog Registry or I.D. PET (see appendices).

If Your Aussie Is Lost or Missing

Every year, Aussies are stolen out of vehicles, kennels, and yards. Immediate action is essential

Urban dogs with proper ID tags. Photo by Trish Thornwald.

It is evident by his appearance that this Aussie is well loved and cared for. Photo by Wayne Rogers.

if you are going to recover your dog. Visit all of the animal shelters in your area. A phone call is not always adequate. Shelter volunteers are often not knowledgeable about dog breeds or familiar with terminology regarding color or markings and may not recognize your Aussie as such. Contact local veterinarians, animal-control offices, and law-enforcement agencies.

Make up flyers and posters. Color copy machines can reproduce a good, clear photo. Include pertinent information such as size, color, and identifying marks or tattoos. Distribute flyers throughout the neighborhood by leaving them in doorways and mailboxes. Post flyers with local boarding kennels, schools, supermarkets, and stores and on telephone poles near intersections. Ask the mail carrier, paper carriers, meter readers, neighbors, and their children to keep a lookout. Advertise in newspapers and on the radio. Get in touch with local Aussie breeders and Aussie rescue programs that may encounter your dog. Be persistent.

Visit animal shelters daily to look for yourself. Most hold stray dogs for only a few days. Persistence is imperative, because it may take a couple of months to locate your lost dog.

Do not list your dog's name, because this makes it easier for a thief to become acquainted with your Aussie. *Do* give a couple of phone numbers to contact in the event your Aussie is spotted. If you are offering a reward, don't list the amount. Be aware of scam artists requiring money to be sent before the return of your dog. Call the police if the party seems suspicious.

CONTROLLING REPRODUCTION

Reproductive control of unaltered females involves constantly supervising the bitch throughout the twenty-three-day estrous cycle twice a year. You must take full responsibility for providing a secure enclosure that is inaccessible to other dogs. If you do not have a secure area, you will have to keep your female with you and take her out to exercise on lead, never leaving her unattended even for one minute. You might want to place your female in a reliable boarding kennel during this time to eliminate the chance of an unwanted litter and also to discourage stray male dogs from creating a nuisance. Unless you intend to breed your Aussie or exhibit in the Conformation ring, you should consider spaying your female or neutering your male to reduce the number of unwanted, homeless animals born through accidental matings.

Spaying

The surgical removal of the female's uterus and ovaries (ovariohysterectomy) can be performed as early as six months of age, when the female is between heat cycles or litters of puppies. It is not necessary for the female to experience estrus or have a litter prior to being spayed. Spaying eliminates heat cycles and the chance of developing a uterine in-

A black tri affair. Raising puppies takes a lot of time and a commitment. Photo by Trish Thornwald.

fection or ovarian and uterine cancer, and it reduces the incidence of mammary tumors.

Although there is the possibility that one out of a thousand females will end up dribbling urine after being spayed, the condition can be controlled by periodic doses of medication. Talk to your vet about the risks.

Neutering (Castration)

The surgical removal of testicles (orchidectomy) should be done after your Aussie reaches puberty, at approximately six to eight months of age, when the male begins to lift his leg. Neutering reduces the incidence of testicular infections, cancer, and prostate problems. It may also reduce roaming, aggressive behavior, and fighting.

AUSSIES AND THE LAW

Everywhere you go, there are laws that affect you and your Aussie. Many municipalities have laws to govern the dog owner's responsibilities. There are leash laws, noise laws, dog licenses, zoning laws, cleanup laws (poop and scoop), nuisance laws, cruelty laws, liability for property damage, vicious dogs, and so forth.

You need to be familiar with local and state laws (which can vary from jurisdiction to jurisdiction). Laws can change from time to time and are subject to the interpretation of circumstances by a judge, existing laws, and court precedents throughout the country. In some states, a "BEWARE OF DOG" sign might protect the owner from liability for injuries sustained from his Aussie in cases of unlawful entry. In other states, such a sign could be interpreted that the owner admittedly had prior knowledge that his dog bites or could bite, even in cases of trespassing (even if the trespasser is a burglar).

Licensing

In most cities, Aussies are required to be licensed and registered for regulation and control purposes. Under the law, an unlicensed dog may be handled differently than a licensed one. If a li-

Typical Aussie grin. This is NOT an aggressive gesture.

censed Aussie is found running at large, he may not be destroyed by authorities without adequate notice unless he is found attacking a person or livestock. Before an Aussie is licensed, you must provide a certificate of vaccination for rabies by a certified veterinarian. Although your dog is licensed, it does not protect you from liability for your dog's actions.

Some areas impose restrictions regarding the number of dogs allowed in a household, including visiting dogs. Puppies may be exempt in the case of a litter or up until a certain age. Owners housing more than the allowed number may be penalized with fines. In some cases, owners may be able to obtain a special permit to house a kennel.

Vaccinations

Rabies is the one disease that has specific regulations to preserve and protect public health. In certain conditions, unrestrained Aussies may be seized and destroyed if you cannot provide a valid certificate of inoculation.

Leash Laws

An Aussie is considered to be running at large or trespassing when he is beyond the control of his owner and is acting on his own initiative. In some areas, restraint does not necessarily have to be physical but may depend upon the training and actions of the individual Aussie when he is off his owner's property.

Casa Buena Kameo CDX, OTD (Ch. Fairoaks Stormy Streaker ex Lingle's Foxie) shows natural retrieving instincts at eight weeks of age. Courtesy Middleton.

If your Aussie is running at large, you may be liable if an accident or injury results therefrom (dog bites, traffic accident). In the event of an escapee, you may still be liable but may not be deemed negligent, providing you took proper precautions to secure your dog and take immediate action to recover him.

Waste Removal

Many municipalities have pooper-scooper laws that require owners to clean up after their dog on sidewalks and city streets. Summons are issued to offenders for noncompliance.

Bateham's Out of Mist. Courtesy Talena Smith.

Trespassers

A trespasser is anyone who is not an invitee. If an innocent or unintentional trespasser gets injured by a dog on the dog owner's premises, the owner may be liable. Only if a trespasser enters another's premises with the intention of committing a crime, or contributes to the negligence, is he prevented from recovering damages for injury in most cases.

When an Aussie trespasses on another person's property and as a result is killed or injured, the owner may have legal rights for compensation providing the dog wasn't worrying livestock or endangering a person or property. Each case will depend upon individual circumstances and upon the court of law deciding the case.

Zoning Laws

Zoning ordinances commonly restrict or limit the use or intended use of property. In the event of new zoning regulations, an established, licensed kennel may be granted a nonconforming status or may be issued a variance.

You should contact the state veterinarian at the Department of Agriculture for rules and regulations governing kennels and licensing requirements. A licensed kennel is generally subjected to periodic inspections for the health and welfare of the animals. Your veterinarian should be able to direct you to the correct person in your state.

Tenant Restrictions

Some communities restrict dog ownership by limiting the numbers allowed per residence. Some housing authorities within a community don't permit dogs at all. Special permits may be obtainable in cases such as seeing-eye dogs and hearing dogs for the hearing impaired.

Nuisance Laws

Whether or not an Aussie is considered a nuisance depends on the disposition of the Aussie and the manner in which he is kept. Any dog that is not properly restrained and that aggravates or annoys persons traveling on a public street or road is considered a nuisance. An Aussie chasing or worrying a neighbor's livestock, digging holes in the neighbor's yard, chasing cars, or scattering garbage is also considered a nuisance. If a barking or howling Aussie or whining puppies interfere with neighboring premises, causing annoyance and interrupting sleep, this can be grounds for a nuisance action. Offensive odors emanating from an unkempt kennel situation could be deemed a nuisance. If there are other dogs in the neighborhood that make noise and emit odors, you may be able to defeat an injunction against yourself.

Dogs As Property: Your Rights and Responsibilities

Dogs are recognized as personal property, and you as the owner have legally enforceable rights. Legal action can result in injury, theft, or death, and you are entitled to compensation. Pedigree, purchase price, value, and future income from the Aussie in either puppies or stud services may all be considered in a settlement.

Neglect

Negligence enters into the picture when you are careless and you neglect to instill reasonable care and to take proper precautions in preventing any person (provided he is engaged in lawful and common activities) or property from sustaining harm.

Liability

Generally, you as the dog's owner are liable for property damages and personal injury caused by your dog. These damages may include medical expenses and compensation for loss of earnings due to the injury, which can be enormous.

Insurance

Homeowner's or renter's insurance usually covers injuries sustained when your dog bites or injures someone. The cost of the insurance is based on the probability of a bite or injury occurring and potential damages resulting in the form of a settlement. Read the policy carefully. Most plans limit coverage to the first incident. After that, you may be on your own. Protection-trained dogs are not covered and may be considered grounds for cancellation of coverage altogether. Word to the wise: don't advertise the fact or post "GUARD DOG" or "BEWARE OF DOG" signs. The behavior of a properly trained and handled dog is more predictable and controllable and is a much better risk for insurance companies, but most insurance companies are not properly educated regarding this matter.

Cruelty

Any act that causes pain and suffering to an Aussie is, upon conviction, punishable by law. Confinement of a dog to a motor vehicle on hot days, abandonment, theft, hit-and-run, and neglect (passive cruelty) for not providing proper care (shelter, food, or water) and attention are also considered cruelty whether the Aussie belongs to that person or to another.

Burial

Home burial is restricted in many areas. Check with your municipal government. Most rural and suburban areas permit home burial, but whenever in doubt, check your local laws.

See the appendices for further information and addresses where you can obtain help with legal questions.

Partners in crime. Aussies often fill the gap and function as a human substitute when parents are away at work and there are no siblings to play with.

Chapter 8

KIDS AND AUSSIES

AUSSIES CAN TEACH CHILDREN about love and respect, life and death. Children can learn responsibility and commitment from their pet. An Aussie will give unconditional love and companionship that can build confidence in a child. Children and Aussies have boundless energy and make excellent partners for discovering the world together.

Aussies are natural protectors of children. The two innately go together, but with guidance. Establish a few rules in the beginning. Puppies and children need time away from each other. Children must be taught to respect a puppy's need for rest. Young children have no comprehension of the damage and serious injury that can occur if they drop, hit, pounce on, jump on, or step on a puppy. Young children should not be allowed to pick up puppies because children sometimes get tired of holding the puppy and may thrown him down. Above all, children should be taught to tend to the needs of their pet. An Aussie is a sensitive, feeling creature; he needs water when he's thirsty, food when he is hungry, and shelter from the weather. Children must also learn never to hit or abuse their Aussie, which should help teach kindness. Parents must be willing to oversee the care, welfare, and training of the dog until such time as the child is able to assume full responsibility.

While caring for an Aussie can teach responsibility, breeding a litter so that the kids can learn about the birds and the bees is irresponsible. There are too many abused and unwanted pets in the world.

Aussies can be excellent with children. They have been known to pull their sleighs and assist them when learning to walk, and entertain them for hours by fetching a ball. Little Ty Taylor and his most trusted friend, Poco.

THE AUSSIE AND YOUR NEWBORN BABY

If you own one or more Aussies and are an expectant parent, part of your parental planning should include (if you haven't already) an Obedience course for your dog. Obedience training will help you and your Aussie to adjust to all of the changes that are about to take place in your family. Sometimes this can be a stressful time for an Aussie that has never been around a baby.

There is no reason to give up your Aussie when you add a baby to the family. When you first bring the baby home, allow several days before officially introducing your Aussie to the baby. At first, your dog will be excited with the smell and sounds of a new baby. No matter how trustworthy or kind your dog is, *do not under any circumstances leave your Aussie unattended with the baby.*

After a week or so, your husband or wife should sit down on the sofa or a chair with the baby. You can bring your Aussie into the room on a leash. If he approaches calmly, you can let him sniff at the baby's blankets, but *do not* allow him to stick his face in the baby's face or to jump up on the baby. He might unintentionally scratch

Never leave babies — human or animal — unattended.

him. Quietly pet your Aussie and tell him that he is a good dog. If the baby cries and your dog gets overexcited, take the Aussie away. Do not rush or force the acquaintance period. Parents should oversee all interactions with babies. Aussies that have not been mistreated or overly dominant will usually adjust with little difficulty to a new baby.

At first, toddlers may be somewhat cautious around larger Aussies (unless raised with them). If toddlers have not been frightened or made fearful by the actions of adults or other children, they will be eager to interact with the dogs, especially smaller Aussies. Emily Wilke with her faithful companion, Las Rocosa Wizard of Aus CDX. Curtesy Paul Wilke.

INFANTS TO PRESCHOOLERS

By the time the baby is able to sit up, crawl, and toddle around, your Aussie should have accepted the new pack member. As with newborns, children of this age should never be left unattended with a dog. Toddlers will often grab the dog's coat when learning to walk. Most Aussies are generally tolerant of this unless they are ultra touch-sensitive or overly dominant. Always supervise playtime, because even a kind and loving Aussie can get excited and unintentionally knock a baby down or scratch him.

Adults must oversee interactions between children and puppies. They can be taught to live and play together harmoniously. Establish a few rules in the beginning and adopt safety precautions. Young children should be allowed to hold puppies only while sitting on the ground or on the floor, and they should be taught how to hold a puppy properly. They must also be taught never to pounce on the dog.

Preschoolers are sometimes excessively rough with dogs because they equate them with toys. Babies and small children can unintentionally abuse and hurt the dog by stepping on his feet, pulling his ears, yanking on his hair, poking his eyes, and sitting on him.

Young children must be taught not to touch or poke the eyes, or to pull the ears and hair. Dogs must be protected from sharp or foreign objects being poked into their eyes or ears. Young children have been known to place rubber bands around the dog's limbs. Without parental intervention, the dog may try to avoid the situation, or he may simply growl and snap at the

Gentle guardian. Courtesy Paul Wilke.

Chance Chipman and his buddy. Photo by Cee's Pix.

child. But he also may be provoked to bite and injure the child through no fault of his own.

You must show your children how to pat the dog with calming strokes, and you must protect young children from sharp teeth and toenails. Young puppies have no conception that their nails can scratch or that their teeth can injure delicate skin.

Never allow your children to bother the dog when he is eating. Aussies and children need time away from each other. A certain room, yard, or crate can provide such a place. Do not let young children carry food around the house or yard where an Aussie can snatch it away. In the process, the dog can inadvertently scrape or pinch tiny fingers. It is also dangerous and negligent to allow children to crawl or walk among more than one dog because the dogs could get into a fight.

AUSSIES AND THE KINDERGARTEN-AGE CHILD

A four- to five-year-old child is nearing the age where he can participate in more activities with the Aussie. He can begin to help care for the dog by brushing him and filling the water bowl and food dish. He can tag along when the Aussie is

Patrick Straube knows that his friend Red will keep a secret better than anyone else. Courtesy Friedhelm Kolb.

Aussies can share moments of active roughhousing . . .

taken for his daily walks. Children don't know that all Aussies are not as friendly as their own Aussie. They must be taught *never* to approach strange dogs without asking for permission first. They must also be taught not to disturb a sleeping dog, or one that is eating.

Children in this age group still need supervision when playing with the Aussie. Parents should exercise good judgment when including the dog in activities involving other children. Puppies are easily excitable. They like to play tug-of-war. In the presence of children running, squealing, yelling, crying, and waving arms, the Aussie can become excited, leading him to play too roughly or even nip. The needle-sharp teeth can be piercing and can easily penetrate skin and clothing. Sometimes the teeth get caught up on

. . . or quiet times of reflection.
Vince Renna and Wolf.

a sleeve or pant leg when the puppy jumps up to grab or catch a ball. He can accidentally pinch or bite in the confusion of a keep-away game. Toenails can scratch, too. Toenails must be kept trimmed, and puppies must be taught not to jump up. This task will be impossible, however, if you allow your children to overexcite the puppy.

When your child has young friends visiting, it is wise to pay close attention to the manner of play. Rough play between children might alarm the Aussie and cause him to protect "his" child from harm. Never allow the strange children to put their faces in the face of your Aussie, to grab him, or to wrap their arms around his neck. With visiting children, it is always wise to give your Aussie refuge in a place away from the activity.

You cannot scold the puppy for behavior encouraged through improper handling. It is not the puppy's fault for jumping up and scratching, or for grabbing children in play, unless he has been taught otherwise. This type of play can get rough and out of hand. When your Aussie is in a crate, yard, or pen, children should not be allowed to put their faces against the fence or their fingers through the wire, nor should they be allowed to tease him in any way.

At this age, young children may not understand death. The loss of a pet might best be explained by telling the child that Fido had to go to doggie heaven. Children can write a note or draw a picture and send it to doggie heaven in a helium balloon to help keep the Aussie's memory alive in their minds.

SCHOOL-AGE CHILDREN AND DOGS

At approximately seven years of age, children demonstrate an active interest in taking care of their Aussie. Between six and ten years of age, a child cannot and should not be expected to take full responsibility for the care and welfare of the dog. Simple tasks like brushing and bathing the Aussie can further develop the friendship and

The unconditional love and friendship a child experiences from an Aussie helps develop self-assurance. Katy Lynn Taylor and Beatrice.

bond. The love between a child and his Aussie is unconditional. An Aussie is a wonderful companion, especially for children whose parents work and who return home to an empty house each day after school. Now is the time, if the child shows an interest, to get him involved in training and showing his Aussie.

Children comprehend death much better between five and eleven years of age. They will be inquisitive about the loss of their Aussie. Be honest with your answers, but do not burden the child with gruesome details. If the pet had to be euthanized, don't tell the child that the dog had to be "put to sleep." You don't want the child to

Aussies are natural hams and love to perform. Just Jake as "Sandy" in Little Orphan Annie.

feel guilty or assume responsibility for the death. Memories of Fido may best be remembered in a special book compiled of favorite photographs, drawings, and stories of events and other activities involving Fido.

AUSSIES FOR PRE-ADOLESCENTS AND ADOLESCENTS

The ages of eleven to sixteen are probably the most uncertain years for young adults. The companionship of an Aussie can lend security and company during this time of great emotional stress and transition. A pet offers a noncritical ear. A child in this age group is capable, if he shows an interest, in taking responsibility for full care of the Aussie. The parent, however, should always govern the pet's care.

A child in this age group with an active interest in working with a dog may benefit greatly from getting involved with one of the local dog clubs: Obedience, Agility, or 4-H.

At this age, youth who have owned an Aussie since early childhood may have to deal with the death or illness of their beloved companion. When dealing with the death of a pet, be frank with children of this age group. Planting a tree or favorite perennial may help memorialize Fido.

In the quiet solitude at the end of a day.

Chapter 9

NO PLACE LIKE HOME

YOU MUST PUPPY PROOF YOUR Aussie's environment for your puppy's safety. Ponds and swimming-pool areas should be properly fenced to prevent accidental drowning. The safest way to protect your Aussie is to provide a fenced area where he can play and exercise. If you can't fence in an area outside, let your dog out only when you can supervise him. Trolley systems, tie-out stakes, and cables can provide unrestricted movement and safety but should be used only with your dog wearing a wide leather or nylon collar. Never use thin or choke collars.

Make potable water available to your dog at all times. There are many types of pet-watering systems (automatic, heated, insulated) to provide a constant supply.

Your Aussie is vulnerable to attack from both humans and animals when he is tied up, so do not leave him unattended. Exercise caution when tying up your dog next to a fence. He may jump or climb the fence and strangle if he gets hung up.

Hidden or invisible fence systems are an excellent option. A thin wire loop transmits a radio signal to a receiver that your Aussie wears on his collar. Whenever your dog approaches the boundaries that you set, the receiver produces an audible warning beep. If the dog disregards the warning, he will feel a harmless but effective mild correction. While the boundary is effective for keeping your dog in, it will not keep predators (human or animal) out.

YARDS AND RUNS

Every Aussie needs a yard or run in which to exercise safely. Running at large, unsupervised, is not only dangerous, but it is irresponsible. At the other extreme, you see Aussies chained up to any type of contraption, and this is equally thoughtless and certainly not recommended.

If you have only one or two Aussies, a securely fenced yard is probably sufficient. Even with only one or two Aussies, it is wise to have a secure run, especially for females in estrus or when you are unable to be with your Aussies to supervise.

All indoor/outdoor facilities should have connecting outdoor runs to ensure adequate exercise, fresh air, and natural light. The more confined your Aussie is, the more exercise he will need to maintain his mental health and muscle tone. The Australian Shepherd is an active herding breed. It goes without saying that each individual needs sufficient room to exercise regularly.

Any and all runs should be securely fenced with dog-proof wire and equipped with good latches and hooks. For your dog to be safe, you must be certain that the entire area is free from broken glass, sharp objects, and edges such as rusty metal, torn and broken wire, and holes. The area should be at least six feet high. Aussies have been known to climb or jump over or dig out from under a secure fence. If you are in doubt, install an overhang or top. Six feet of height will maintain most Aussies.

Make a platform available, especially to allow mothers to get away from their babies on occasion and when they are weaning. A jungle gym, crate, or large wooden box are wonderful for Aussies of all ages. Rubber tires also make excellent objects to stand on and jump across. Rubber balls, plastic milk jugs, old tennis shoes, rubber thongs, and slippers make good chew toys to carry around.

Youngsters in their play yard.

Play and exercise areas should also have a shady spot to lend protection from the sun in warm weather. Kennel covers made of monofilament fabric, nursery netting, or any other fabric that is mildew- and rot-resistant are excellent sources of ventilated shade. Canvas tarps also work well, but only if they are ventilated. Kennel covers should withstand the elements and protect dogs living in indoor/outdoor kennels.

Ideally, runs should be six feet wide by thirty feet long. The longer they are, the better. The thought behind the length is that it gives each Aussie the opportunity to run without running in circles. A solid stockade-type fence between six and eight feet in height, made of wood, cinder blocks or similar materials, as well as trees, shrubs, and vines around the perimeter of the kennel, will help muffle sound and may form a screen to help block airborne disease. Soothing music played constantly from a radio will also have a calming effect on your Aussie to further eliminate disturbance.

During summer months, carefully locate your dog's house so that it has the benefit of maximum shade. A spot that is shady during the morning can become sunny and unbearably hot in the afternoon. In winter months, make sure that the entrance is protected from cold winds, driving rains, and lack of sun. Don't put the dog house next to the fence, because it will be too easy for your dog to use the roof for an easy escape.

Caught napping.

Aussies that live primarily outdoors need a water supply that won't freeze and shelter from the elements. Windchill can cause temperatures to drop severely. You need to provide a solid, watertight dog house that is elevated off of the ground and filled with clean, dry bedding (carpet, towels, blankets, shredded newspaper). A wet dog can chill and become sick. The dog house should have either a door or be designed in such a way as to prevent wind or precipitation from infiltrating the dog's safe haven. It should be neither too large nor too small for the Aussie, thus allowing him to feel comfortable while still retaining warmth from the dog's body within the walls.

When weather conditions become extreme, keep your Aussie indoors. If your dog becomes wet after a romp in the rain or snow, dry him off thoroughly indoors before you allow him to go outside again. Make sure to get your dog out of the wind, because he is prone to frostbite.

Sanitation

Sanitation is a constant concern. There should be no accumulation of debris or excreta. Replace soiled gravel and sand frequently, and be sure that you have adequate disposal for such wastes. A good pair of Dooling sticks or set of poop scoops for sanitary waste removal will aid in quick cleanup. Several varieties of mini septic tanks (systems that use live organisms and enzymes to dissolve excreta) also are available. The liquefied material from the septic tank leaches into the ground through a miniature leaching field to make disposal sanitary and manageable.

To prevent contamination, all food must be stored in a sanitary manner. Rodent and insect-proof containers are a good investment. You must be able to provide a safe food supply for your animals. If you experience any problem with insects or rodents, seek professional help (often county extension agents are available).

DOG HOUSES AND KENNELS

While cleanliness is imperative, fancy operations with expensive, made-to-order houses, chain-link fencing, cement runs, and stainless-steel pans are impressive. Just remember that a showplace does not guarantee the health or welfare of its occupants. The most important aspect of any kennel is that the Aussies are cared for and managed with common sense.

Certain features of a dog house for the outside or a dog bed for indoors are necessary for your Aussie's comfort and safety. Outdoor dog houses, regardless of architectural design, should be constructed and insulated with weather-resistant components to prevent leaks and drafts for ultimate protection from the elements. Synthetic materials (structural foam, polymers, and fiberglass) are beneficial because they are fully waterproof and rot proof and are washable for easy cleaning. Traditional materials (exterior plywood, bricks) also offer good protection from the elements when used properly. The inside should be tightly sealed for proper cleaning and sanitation to prevent parasite or germ infestation.

A piece of canvas or carpet or a mud flap hung over the entrance will block drafts, rain, sleet, or snow and will hold in warm air. Elevate the house several inches off of the ground on bricks, concrete or cinder blocks, or wooden blocks to keep the floor dry and free from rot. Dampness

Creative Playthings like this miniature obstacle help develop confidence in young Aussies.

from snow and rain amplifies the cold. Maximize protection by lining the floor of the dog house with a thick, insulating layer of dry, thermal bedding (or rugs, blankets, shredded newspaper, wood shavings, hay, or straw) that can be laundered easily or replaced frequently.

Crates and dog beds offer a comfortable place to sleep indoors with protection from drafts and cold floors. Dog mattresses with removable, washable covers are ideal.

Plans for your kennel do not need to be expensive or complex. With a little imagination, you may be able to convert existing buildings into an adequate setup. You must also consider local zoning regulations. Consult your state, city, and county departments for specific requirements. Some research facilities or other breeders may provide blueprints or share their ideas with you.

Suitable and necessary features of your Aussie's shelter should include smooth, impervious walls to avoid breeding areas for germs and parasites and to facilitate effective cleansing and disinfecting. Situate the housing so that the drainage is good, sloping away from the shelter. Do not locate your kennel near stagnant water or swamps.

There is a well-founded belief that the best layout is for the long axis to lie in a north-south direction, which means an easterly exposure. A northern exposure is cold and, because of a lack of direct sunlight, is frequently damp, although it does offer the advantage of coolness during the hot months. A southern exposure is hot and more likely to subject your Aussie to pesky insects. An eastern exposure at least compromises many of the disadvantages of either northern or southern exposures. Ideally, the layout should offer relief from the sun in the warm months and allow maximum exposure to the sun during the coldest months. An overhang of corrugated tin or fiberglass can provide shade along with trees, shrubs, and nontoxic vines.

A kennel should be a sound, waterproof structure in good repair. A good, reasonably high foundation and double walls or walls of porous material (with impervious inner surfaces) afford the best insulation. Although they are more difficult to clean, floors with broom-finished cement give Aussies better footing. The coldness of cement floors may be largely prevented by insulating them with a thick layer of cinders or with hollow tile or brick under the concrete. Or, you may place loose, properly fitted wooden platforms on top of the cement floor. Floors should also have drains to carry away liquid waste. This does not necessarily involve an extensive system, because all you really need are shallow gutters directed toward a common channel. Floors should be sloped slightly to provide proper drainage. All wooden or concrete surfaces should be sealed with a coat of epoxy (or similar substance such as lacquer) to further protect against parasitic infestations and disease.

Proper ventilation in your kennel is essential. Screened, louvered windows and sunroofs (with or without a screen) can all provide fresh air and natural light. You also must have a decent source of natural sunlight either directly or through light-pervious material other than ordinary glass (ordinary glass does not allow ultraviolet rays to filter through). Sunlight is a source of germ control (sunlight filtered through ordinary glass is not destructive to germs) and plays a vital role in enabling your Aussie to absorb nutrients such as calcium from food.

You should have an adequate service room for cleaning equipment, washing water bowls, etc. You may also want a grooming area with a sink for bathing.

When you have more than one Aussie, you must be able to provide an adequate place that isolates sick individuals from the others until veterinary care is available.

Groomed and ready to show. Photo courtesy Heidi Gorchals.

―――― Chapter 10 ――――

KEEPING UP APPEARANCES

GROOMING IS A COMPLEX BEHAVIOR displayed by domestic dogs and their ancient ancestors. In general, grooming equates to hygiene. Aussies practice grooming by licking, rubbing, rolling, scooting, scratching, and shaking debris from their coats. Aussies care for their eyes, nose, and nostrils by rubbing their faces with their paws and forelegs.

In the wild, wolves can be observed rubbing against bushes and brush to remove dead hair—in essence, some form of brushing. They may roll on their back, twisting their body from side to side to improve stimulation. They clean and moisturize their coat and skin by licking.

During illness, wolves and Aussies alike lack the desire and capability to care for themselves. Because the cells of the skin and coat are subject to rapid turnover, disease states are soon reflected in them. Also, lack of general attention can cause deterioration of the coat and body. Grooming keeps the skin functioning naturally and lessens the chance for the skin to become diseased. It also improves the dog's overall condition and muscle tone.

The Australian Shepherd Coat

Length, strength, density, texture, and condition of the hair coat depend on the genetic makeup, nutrition, environment, proper care, and health of your Aussie. A straight coat will appear to grow faster and will look slightly longer than a wavy coat because the shortest distance between two points is a straight line. The typical Aussie coat varies between being straight and slightly wavy.

The hair root determines coat texture and shape because it lies in the follicle—a tubelike depression or pocket encasing the hair root. Straight hair grows from a straight hair root and is round in cross-section. Wavy hair is oval in cross-section and is grown from a slightly curved hair root.

Each strand of hair has three distinct layers, none of which contains blood vessels or nerves. The first layer, the cuticle, surrounds and protects the underlying two layers. The cortex, in the middle, gives the coat elasticity and strength and contains the pigment that designates coat color. The center core, called the medulla, resembles marrow in a bone. The papilla, lying beneath the hair root, supplies blood and nerves that contribute to the growth and regeneration of the hair.

Coat activity is divided into three distinct stages: (1) anagen, an active growing stage; (2) telogen, a resting stage; and (3) catagen, the transition between the first two stages. It is during the latter stage that shedding takes place; new hair pushes out the old hair as it surfaces.

Results achieved through proper care are determined by the limits of genetic makeup. The quality of inherited coat texture can be enhanced through a maximum state of health but can never be changed.

The Aussie's coat is a mirror reflection of his body. Coat condition accurately reflects his state of health. A dry, lackluster coat may indicate that some factor is out of balance. It may be the result of an internal illness, an infestation of parasites, or an inadequate diet. A glossy coat with a lively resilience begins inside. The coat is nourished only after all of the vital organs and body have been fed.

Shedding

Shedding is a natural process that is governed by the length of daylight more than by temperature changes. It usually takes place during early summer or late spring. The long hours of sunlight activate the systems of outdoor Aussies into shedding their heavy winter coats. Modern Aussies living under artificial conditions, such as house dogs or indoor kennel dogs, become confused with the shedding cycles. Unnatural light lends no lengthening and shortening of days to indicate natural cycles; consequently, these Aussies shed lightly all year. If the home is overheated, there may be excessive shedding as well as dry skin during the winter. Exercise will stimulate blood circulation and tone up the skin to encourage the growth of new coat.

Even if the coat is heavily matted, do *not* shave it. Shaving the coat leaves the individual (especially the light-colored or merled dog) vulnerable to painful sunburn and scarring. When the Aussie is shedding, it is important to brush the coat out *first*, making sure to lift out all of the dead undercoat to prevent additional matting. A slicker brush may be helpful in removing undercoat. Saturate any burrs or mats with olive or mineral oil, which will make them easier to work out of the coat.

Grooming Table Training

Grooming establishes a healthy rapport between you and your Aussie when it is done in a kind manner. Harsh handling only builds a resentment toward this necessary chore. Grooming can have a calming effect that can build a strong foundation for future handling. If a puppy is managed and socialized properly from his earlier stages, he should be a pleasure to teach.

Set a grooming routine. Begin his first few grooming periods while you both sit together on the floor. Teach him to accept and enjoy brushing while standing up and lying down. Keep each session short to hold your puppy's interest.

An active youngster will easily learn to submit to this type of restraint while his mind is flexible and his body is small. You will want to eventually graduate to the grooming table, which allows you to work easily without stooping or bending. Yet, any dog crate, bench, or flat surface will serve the purpose if it is sturdy and of adequate size and height. Place a rubber mat, thick rug, or towel on it to give your Aussie secure footing. A grooming noose may be helpful by giving the Aussie additional security and aiding in restraint.

Combine short sessions on the table with a soothing voice and gentle hands. Your Aussie may be frightened or unsure at first, but kind, patient handling will give him confidence. Initially, do not be concerned if he does not lie or stand perfectly still. Perfection comes with practice. Make each session a pleasurable experience. A few minutes every day will familiarize him with handling.

Always lift a youngster on and off the table. If a young Aussie is allowed to jump off of the table, he may get injured. As he gets older, he can be taught to jump up. Never leave him unattended or tied on the table without supervision, or he may jump off and strangle himself. Keep one hand on him to prevent him from leaping off. This will also reassure him.

ROUTINE GROOMING CARE

Eyes

The eyes can be bathed with a soothing eyewash made by dissolving one-half teaspoon of salt in a cup (eight ounces) of tepid, distilled water. Stir well before using. Saturate gauze pads in the mild saline solution and gently cleanse the eyelids. Wipe the inside corner of each eye, out toward the outside corner of the eye. Afterward, apply a drop of olive oil in each eye.

If a persistent discharge or inflammation of eye tissue is present, consult your veterinarian. Runny, weepy eyes can be a sign of serious illness.

Ears

Examine ears frequently. Check ears for wax, ear mites, and any other irritations. Healthy ears smell clean and are pale pink. Clean the inside ear leather and ear opening only, and do not probe or push beyond what you can see. A small amount of wax is normal. Wipe away any visible dirt with a gauze pad and olive oil. Place a few drops of lukewarm olive oil in the ear canal with an eye dropper. Then massage the base of the ear. You also can use a commercially prepared formula. Some veterinarians recommend cleansing the ear with a solution of one part alcohol to one part vinegar. In the event of bacterial and yeast infections, the solution should have a low pH (slightly acidic) to discourage their growth. Ear powders are not recommended because they can get caked against the eardrum and on the lining of the canal.

Consult your veterinarian whenever:

- your dog's ears are red and inflamed,
- there are odorous secretions or excessive wax,
- your dog carries one ear lower than normal, or
- your dog is scratching or rubbing his ears.

You will need a proper diagnosis in the event antibiotic, anti-inflammatory, or antifungal drugs are indicated.

Ear infections are serious. Inflammation or infections of the external ear canal (otitis externa), if untreated, can lead to inflammation of the middle ear (otitis media). If the infection progresses to the inner ear (otitis interna), your dog may experience permanent damage to his hearing or balance. From the inner ear, the infection can enter the brain and be fatal.

Nose

Apply olive oil with a gauze pad or cloth to cleanse and condition the nose leather.

Teeth

If your Aussie has healthy teeth and gums, his breath should not be offensive. Bad breath is often caused by different grades of periodontal disease. Red, irritated gums and yellow-brown deposits of tartar are signs of trouble. The problem begins when plaque, harboring bacteria and tartar, builds up on the teeth. As a result, the gums become irritated and inflamed. If left unchecked, tartar deposits actually erode the gums and cause the teeth to loosen. Worse yet, periodontal disease leads to heart, liver, and kidney infections. In advanced cases, drooling, blood in the saliva (noticeable on chew toys or the dog bowl), reluctance to eat, and foul breath are noticeable. In these cases, it may be advantageous to have your dog's teeth cleaned professionally with ultrasound. Because cleaning releases bacteria into the bloodstream, antibiotics are generally indicated. Your vet will probably recommend a regular oral hygiene program.

Light cases of tartar can be removed with a charcoal pencil, a fine emery board, or a tooth scaler. Teeth should be scaled from the gums to the tip of the tooth, or you can use a finger toothbrush, a soft, child-sized toothbrush, a pet toothbrush, or gauze wrapped around a finger to gently massage your Aussie's teeth and gums. To acquaint your dog with good oral hygiene, gently massage his gums and teeth a few seconds at a time, brushing from the gum line to the tip of the tooth with a circular motion. *Do not* use human toothpaste because it can upset your dog's stomach. Use special canine toothpastes (formulated with flavor enhancers for easier acceptance) and oral rinses containing chlorhexidine, or make your own by mixing one teaspoon of salt with three teaspoons of baking soda.

With your dog's mouth closed, you can lift up his outer lips and gently rub his teeth and gums using small circular strokes. It is usually much

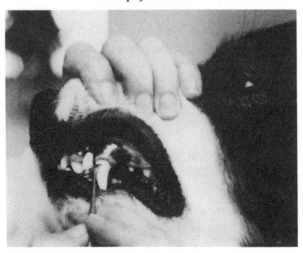

Teeth should be scaled from the gums to the tip of the tooth.

The back molars often accumulate agreater amount of tartar. Scale teeth from the gums to the tip of the tooth.

TOOTH BISCUITS

2 cups of flour (preferably whole grain)
1 cup of cornmeal
1/2 cup brewer's yeast
1/4 cup pumpkin or sunflower seeds
1/4 cup parsley flakes
1/4 cup powdered milk
1 tablespoon garlic
1 cup meat (chicken or beef) broth
1 egg beaten and thinned with milk (glaze)

Combine dry ingredients in large bowl. Stir in meat broth. If the mixture is too stiff, add more meat broth. Roll dough on a floured surface or waxed paper. Roll out to approximately a 1/4-inch thickness. Cut into different shapes with a knife or dog-bone-shaped cookie cutter. Place shapes on greased cookie sheet, then brush with egg glaze. Bake for 45 minutes at 300 degrees. When golden brown, turn off the oven and allow biscuits to dry in oven for approximately 8 hours.

---

easier to start practicing oral hygiene during puppyhood, but it is never too late to begin. Go slowly by handling your dog's mouth a few minutes every day. Be patient, and remember to stroke your dog and reassure him with gentle praise in order to establish a pleasant routine. After a few days, you can open his mouth by inserting your thumb and finger directly behind the canine teeth and pulling his head up and back. This will encourage your dog to open his mouth. It helps if both you and your dog are relaxed. This can be a therapeutic time for both of you if you approach it with a positive attitude. If your dog totally opposes the idea, even after several weeks, you may need to restrain him by wrapping him in a large bath towel with only his head sticking out.

Rawhide bones and raw beef bones are nature's toothbrush. Given to your dog once a week, they will keep your dog's gums tight and his teeth free of tartar. While dry dog food and dog biscuits will not prevent tartar buildup, they will help reduce the amount of buildup when compared to a diet consisting exclusively of soft and semi-soft foods.

Toenails

Begin the practice of pedicuring when your dog is very young. You must nip small bits in the beginning to build your Aussie's confidence in allowing you to work with his feet. Too few Aussies have occupations in which their nails are worn down naturally. Most Aussies must have their nails maintained by artificial means.

Nails can be trimmed with one of several varieties of nail trimmers or grinders. A nail file, emery board, or jeweler's file may be used to smooth the rough edges of the nail. Nails left untrimmed and allowed to grow long put undue stress on the paw by forcing the weight on the back of the pads. This condition tends to spread and break down the foot. Regular attention to the nails will help maintain the proper length. The quick will recede with regular and frequent trimming. Correctly trimmed nails should not touch the ground, allowing the individual to stand squarely and compactly on the pads. Nails left long can get torn off or snagged and can also scratch furniture and skin.

It is easier to differentiate the quick from the nail when the nails are white, as opposed to liver or black. The quick appears to be a pink vein and travels approximately three-fourths of the way through the nail. In actuality, the quick is living tissue that gives rise to the nails.

Begin by trimming off the hook of the nail. Then take off the remaining dead nail in smaller bits. If you accidentally nick the quick and draw

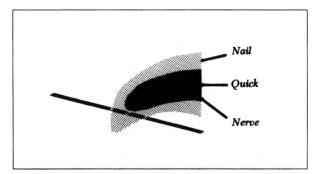

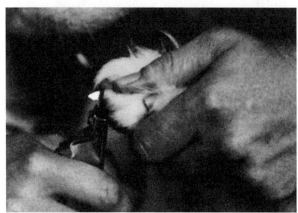

Using guillotene nail clippers.

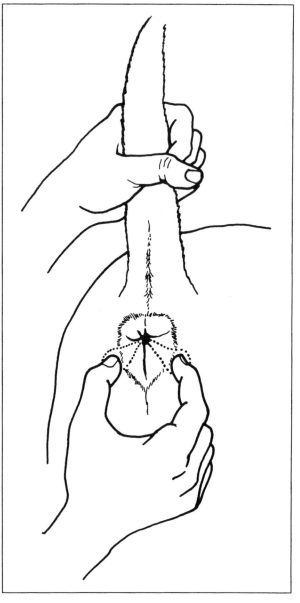

Expressing the anal glands.

blood, dab an alum powder, styptic powder, or styptic pencil on it. Ice may also be used, but you should follow up by applying iodine or a similar antiseptic. Your Aussie may be nervous and may not want you to continue, yet you should do so as if nothing happened. Continue with patience and a little more caution. Do a few nails at a time, and break up the procedure with intervals of brushing until all nails are completed. If your Aussie has front dewclaws located on the inner legs above the paws, trim them. Untrimmed dewclaws will curl inward and pierce into the foreleg, causing considerable pain, possible infection, and perhaps abscess.

Anus

Active, healthy Aussies rarely have any problem with anal glands. The anal glands, located at either side of the anus (at approximately four and eight o'clock), are emptied naturally with bowel movements. They can become expressed when the Aussie is frightened. When the glands become full and uncomfortable, the Aussie may scoot along the floor or may lick or chew at the perineum to express them.

Check the anal area for cleanliness. If the area is soiled, brush away any dry matter. Shampoo the area, rinse it thoroughly, and dry it.

BRUSHING

Brushing distributes natural oils throughout the coat, thus improving the elasticity of the hair and giving the coat body and strength. Brushing your Aussie's coat cleans it and brings out shine and natural luster. It also dislodges loose hair and whisks away surface dirt, debris, and the daily accumulation of dust and lint.

Effective brushing begins with using the correct brushes. The best choice for general purposes is a quality pin brush (one with large, blunt pins set on a rubber cushion base). Incorrect brushing or poor grooming tools can cause considerable damage to the coat and skin. Brushing by dragging an implement across the coat can break, split, and uproot the hair. Bristles shaped at a sharp angle will scratch the skin, cause irritation, and make your Aussie reluctant to be brushed.

Daily brushing is far superior to any other routine, but a thorough brushing several times a week will maintain most Aussies in good condition. The chore of getting a neglected coat back into shape can be quite an ordeal if a regular schedule is ignored.

The proper way to brush is from the ends of the coat, clear down to the skin (back out to the ends). This stimulates circulation, aids in removing dead cells, and distributes natural oils. As you brush outward from the skin, brush with the direction of growth, or "grain." After you have brushed the coat in this fashion, brush the hair *against* the grain to promote better circulation from blood to skin. Now work the coat back in the direction of regular growth.

Some groomers prefer starting at the head and working back to the hindquarter. Others prefer to work from the feet up. Choose whatever process works best for you and your Aussie.

Natural shine is encouraged by using a natural bristle brush. Natural bristles have imbrications that are remarkably similar to canine hair, unlike smooth plastic, nylon, or wire bristles. This leads to absorption and greater distribution of natural oils.

The Aussie's double coat is a medium-textured, moderate-length outercoat, and a shorter downy, water-resistant undercoat. Photo by Cee's Pix.

Inherited coat texture will dictate the appropriate texture of the brush—softer bristles for finer hair, stronger bristles for a coarser coat. For the average Aussie, you will need to choose a medium-textured bristle brush for medium coarseness.

Brushing is the ideal time to look for parasites and skin problems (hot spots, eczema, sores, tumors) that may require medical attention.

BATHING

How frequently you bathe your Aussie depends on his coat texture and on the climate and environment in which you live. If you brush him regularly, baths can be held down to twice a year (in the spring and fall). However, whenever there is a doggie odor, or when your dog's skin and hair are dry and dull, your dog may benefit from a bath. Bathe your Aussie whenever necessary. If he is in good health, any odor should be eliminated with a bath. If it is not, consult your vet, because the cause may be medical.

Before bathing, brush the coat thoroughly. Pay special attention to the fine hair behind the ears and the long hair on the legs and hindquarters, referred to as "feathers." Remove any mats before bathing. With the help of a wide-tooth comb, gently work mats out with your fingers. A drop of oil may help. Do not rip out any mats from your dog's ears, because the ears are extremely sensitive and your Aussie will not respond favorably. If there are large mats that do not work out with this method, make several lengthwise cuts through the mats, then work them out gently. If possible, try to avoid cutting off the entire mat (it will look "chopped"). *Do* place a comb next to the skin under the mat to protect the skin from an accidental nick.

If it is necessary to cut the mat, place your blunt-nose scissors just under the mat and over the comb, then slowly snip the mat. Never point the scissors toward the body, the head, or the eyes.

For secure footing in the tub, you may want to place a rubber mat in the bottom. Fill the tub with lukewarm water, making sure that the water is comfortable to touch.

A cotton ball placed in the ears will keep water from entering them, and a drop of olive oil, mineral oil, or eye ointment will protect the eyes. Saturate your dog with warm water, but avoid getting water in his ear canals. Dilute a small amount of shampoo by half with water (ratio of 1:1) in a plastic container or applicator bottle. Then work it through the coat with your fingers, massaging your dog's entire body with shampoo from head to tail. Never pour shampoo directly on the coat. Use a sponge or terry cloth to cleanse the face and genital areas. Rinse the entire coat thoroughly with warm water. A sprayer attachment will make this much easier. Soap residue will not only leave a dulling film, but it can also irritate the skin. Shampoo and rinse again.

Many shampoos contain harsh detergents that damage the coat by indiscriminately stripping it of natural oils and penetrating far into the hair shaft and skin. The ideal shampoo is pH balanced to leave the hair resilient and shiny. In order to keep your Aussie's coat in its healthiest, strongest state, use an alkaline-balanced shampoo similar to Johnson's No More Tears Baby Shampoo. On a scale from 0 to 14, anything between 0 and 7 is acidic, and between 7 and 14 is alkaline. The Aussie's skin is nearly neutral, with a slightly alkaline pH of 7.5. Human hair has more acid and is therefore nonalkaline with a pH of 5.5. Many excellent dog shampoos are available from top manufacturers. You can find all-purpose, conditioning, herbal, medicated, hypoallergenic, flea and tick, tearless and color-enhancing shampoos—all for your Aussie.

Many groomers use a few drops of bluing in the water to bring out the sparkle in white trim. *Do not* use bleach or other chemicals. Never scrub the coat or use detergents in an attempt to highlight the white trim. Scrubbing may cause skin irritation and may actually damage white hair. Shampoo the white areas with a sponge or a gentle bath brush, using only a mild shampoo. The face may be washed with a washcloth or sponge and clean water. Be sure to rinse all shampoo thoroughly from the skin and coat with lukewarm water.

EMOLLIENT CONDITIONER

1 cup safflower oil, sunflower oil, olive oil, or almond oil
¼ cup dried rosemary leaves
¼ cup chamomile flowers (for light coats) or
¼ cup sage (for dark coats)

Place oil and herbs in a double boiler and heat for at least 30 minutes or until there is a pronounced aroma. Store in a glass container. Depending on the size of your dog and the quantity of his coat, mix 1 to 3 tablespoons in a gallon of warm water to use in his bath water or as an after-bath rinse. Too much oil will make the coat greasy. Instead of using herbs, you can use herbal oils. Blend 4 parts of any of the above oils with 1 part of lavender or thyme in a bottle and add it to the bath water.

A dry coat and skin will benefit from a good conditioner and a quality intensive-conditioning treatment. Alpha-Keri can be added to your dog's bath water with excellent results. Be sure to use conditioners correctly, because when they are used improperly or are not rinsed out thoroughly, they can weaken the hair by coating the hair shaft with an oil residue, thus clogging the hair follicle and attracting oils and dust. Emollients (vegetable and animal oils) are best applied after a bath, providing an oil barrier to retain moisture in the skin. Emollients protect and soften the skin. There are many emollient conditioners formulated for your dog's coat, or you can make your own.

In certain cases, an oil-free humectant may be the most beneficial for your Aussie's skin and coat. Humectants often contain glycerins, propylene glycol, lactic acids, urea, and carboxylic acids. Humectants act as a rehydrant by pulling moisture to the skin from the dog's own body fluids. They can be used daily to alleviate dry skin. If your dog experiences skin and hair-coat problems, consult your veterinarian for the best treatment.

Throughout the entire bath, until the time your Aussie is completely dry, protect him from any drafts. An Aussie can suffer upper-respiratory problems if he gets chilled while wet.

If possible, allow your Aussie to shake off excess water. Towel dry him gently. A leather chamois works well on the coat, and a blow dryer will be helpful. Start drying at a higher setting, then switch to a lower one when the coat is still somewhat damp. Always hold the dryer at least six inches away from the coat, and keep the dryer in motion. Not only is excessive heat damaging to the coat, but you can burn your Aussie's skin. Use a warm, not hot, setting, then switch to a cool setting to finish.

You can use the blow dryer to get the appearance of more volume by brushing the coat against the growth pattern. For a smoother appearance, brush the coat with the grain. After bathing, be sure to remove the cotton from your Aussie's ears.

Dry Cleaning

Dry cleaning should be used whenever there is a possibility of your Aussie becoming chilled. Aging Aussies, young puppies, ill or recovering Aussies, and bitches nearing the last stage of pregnancy should be guarded against becoming entirely wet. Dry cleaning can also be used when your Aussie needs a simple freshening up.

You can wash off the feet and legs in either a bucket or tub. Take a damp cloth and work it over the entire coat, paying special attention to the dingy areas. Do not use a wet or sopping cloth, and dry your dog thoroughly.

Several commercial dry shampoos are available expressly for this purpose. Fuller's earth, baby powder (talcum), or cornstarch can be sprinkled throughout the coat. Be sure that you avoid the eyes. The coat must be completely dry before you sprinkle the dry cleaner into the coat. For better penetration, you can brush the coat against the grain of growth, then rub the dry cleaner into it. Allow the dry cleaner to remain in the coat long enough to absorb odors. Then brush out all remains. If any dry cleaner is left in the coat, it will dry it out and absorb essential natural oils. Use a leather chamois or a natural bristle brush to brighten the darker colors and distribute these natural oils back through the entire hair coat. Let your Aussie shake afterward to loosen any cleaner.

Desert Sky Diablo expresses the Aussie's eager "What can I do to please you?" attitude. Photo courtesy Barbara Sims.

Chapter 11

NUTRITION

NUTRITION IS THE SINGLE GREATEST factor responsible for enabling each Aussie to realize his full inherited potential. Your Aussie's system is a complex myriad of functions. To operate smoothly, the system requires energy that comes from proteins, fats, and carbohydrates. Before these nutrients can be utilized by the system to provide energy, they must undergo a chemical change called metabolism. Metabolism consists of two basic activities:

- Anabolism—the building process in which the absorbed nutrients and complex chemical compounds that have been stored in the system are used in the formation or repair of the cells that form body tissue.
- Catabolism—a process in which the decomposition of nutrients under the influence of hormones, enzymes, and the nervous impulses are oxidized for the production of heat and work.

In order for metabolism to be most effective, it must be governed by enzymes that require vitamins and minerals for performance of regularity tasks. The lack of one vitamin or mineral can totally upset various biochemical processes.

There are six basic elements to nutrition: water, protein, carbohydrates, fats, vitamins, and minerals.

Basic Nutrients

Water

Next to oxygen, water is the most crucial substance for all plant and animal life. The need for water in the canine individual is regulated by thirst, and the amount required by each dog depends on gestation, lactation, growth, stress, environment, activity, age, and temperament.

Water aids in temperature control. It acts as the medium in which blood carries nutrition to the cells and removes waste products from the system. The need for water is often overlooked and neglected. An abundant supply of fresh, clean drinking water should be available to your dog at all times.

Protein

Protein is essential for the repair and maintenance of all body tissue, hormones, enzymes, and antibodies. It is needed for the development of strong muscles, ligaments, organs, bones, teeth, and coat.

Proteins are complex organic compounds made up chiefly of amino acids. The amino acids may therefore be called "building blocks" from which proteins are made. The quality of protein is determined by its profile and balance of essential amino acids and by the availability of digestible material within food substances. A shortage of one single amino acid will limit the utilization of all others and will therefore reduce and limit tissue repair and growth and break down the body's resistance to infection. Any shortage will also contribute to a lack of stamina and loss of condition.

Carbohydrates

Carbohydrates are made by plants in the process of photosynthesis. They are energy foods often called the "protein-sparing" nutrients, and they consist mainly of sugars, starches, and cellulose.

Unlike proteins, unused carbohydrates are stored in the body as converted fat and as glycogen in the muscles and liver. Starches and sugars provide the most readily available sources of energy. In the absence of carbohydrates, the Aussie's system is able to employ fat and protein

"Cooling off."
MacSpadden Photo.

Initially, the pup depends on his other for a balanced diet. Later, the owner will be responsible for good nutrition.

in terms of energy. Although fat and protein can supply these needs, they are less expendable. Protein provided primarily as an energy source can cause severe stress on the liver.

Cellulose forms fiber and governs the resorption of water. This, in turn, aids the body in the proper formation and elimination of wastes.

Certain sugars and starches, such as the large amounts of lactose found in cow's milk, are often difficult for the Aussie's system to digest and absorb—many times causing diarrhea. Uncooked starches, such as those found in cereal grains and various other food products, must be properly cooked and processed before they can contribute any nutritional value and avoid causing diarrhea.

Fats

Fats are the most concentrated source of energy. When the glycogen stores are used up, fat comes into play. The fuel value is about twice as great per ounce as the fuel of carbohydrates. Fat increases the palatability of the diet. It helps maintain and alleviate dry coats and scaly skin and conveys fat-soluble vitamins to the system. Rancid fats, however, destroy valuable fat-soluble vitamins and must be guarded against.

Vitamins

Vitamins yield no energy, yet they play an integral role in maintaining anabolic and catabolic functions. Certain vitamins are dependent on one another. One cannot be substituted or replaced by another. Vitamins fall into two categories—water-soluble and fat-soluble. Water-soluble vitamins include B-complex and C, which must be replenished on a regular basis. Fat-soluble vitamins include A, D, E, and K. These vitamins are absorbed and stored within the system.

Minerals

Minerals are not sources of energy. They regulate the system's dynamic balance. An intricate relationship between minerals and other dietary constituents can be affected by a change in only one. Minerals must be supplied in adequate amounts and in proper ratios in order to maintain the dynamic balance.

Diet

Your dog's diet must be complete and balanced. To be complete, it must contain all the necessary ingredients vital to his nutritional needs. A diet is balanced only if all vital nutrients are in proportion with energy (calories) to provide needed fuel that will enable utilization of proteins in the body-building processes.

Metabolism is crucially dependent on certain quantities of individual nutrients. The lack of a single ingredient can halt or diminish the metabolic chain of events, while an overdose of an ingredient or nutrient can mask or interfere with the properties of the nutrients that are so necessary to complete vital chemical interrelations.

Homemade Diets

A homemade diet, including the finest cuts of meat and fresh vegetables combined with necessary vitamins and minerals, may or may not be totally balanced. If the homemade diet is formulated by a nutritionist, it can be excellent.

Commercial Diets

Commercial diets are by far the most practical and are usually less expensive. These diets are available in dry, semimoist, and canned varieties. The major dog-food manufacturers maintain research facilities to control, maintain, and regulate proper rations of nutrients including vitamins and minerals. There is a constant effort to utilize the latest knowledge of nutrients and canine nutrient requirements to improve existing products.

Dry

The dry foods can be broken into three types: kibble, meal, and expanded.

Kibble—Kibble and biscuit varieties are a baked dough prepared from soybean flour, wheat flour mixed with meat meals, milk products, yeast, vitamins, and minerals. The heat process in baking cooks starch granules, which make carbohydrates in these biscuit-type foods readily available to your Aussie's system.

Meal—Meal consists of dry ingredients either as a blend of granular powders or as flakes mixed together to form a ration.

Expanded—Expanded nuggets and pellets are homogenized foods that are made by blending ingredients such as cereal grains, meat meals, vegetable products, fish meals, fat, and milk products along with vitamins and minerals. The blend is then cooked and formed into pellets or expanded into nuggets of varying shapes and sizes. The stability of the mixture is improved through cooking, which makes nutrients more readily available to your Aussie. Prior to packaging, fat is sprayed onto the food.

Of the available commercial diets, dry foods are the least expensive per pound of dry content. Dry diets are easily sorted and can be free fed (see the section on Methods of Feeding later in this chapter). They provide good exercise for teeth and gums and help prevent accumulation of tartar on the teeth.

Generally speaking, meat products contain a higher quality protein than cereal products. Therefore, dry foods *may* contain a lower quality protein. However, protein quality depends on the ingredients used by the manufacturer, not on the form of diet.

Because manufacturers are limited in their choice of ingredients that can be used successfully in the dry-food process, essential fatty acids may or may not be present. The lack of fat also limits the caloric density of food. A dry, dull hair coat with scaly skin can be one of the first signs of a fatty acid–deficient diet. One or two teaspoons of a vegetable oil may be added per cup of dry diet. Vegetable oil contains more essential fatty acids than pork, poultry, beef, or butterfat.

The working dog burns lots of energy. Snacks given during the day will help him to work at peak efficiency.

Vegetable oils are usually a better choice than wheat germ oils high in vitamin D, or the commercial oil supplements with vitamins and minerals. The addition of these nutrients to an otherwise balanced diet may cause an imbalance that in turn may create an overall deficient diet through vitamin overdose.

The addition of at least one teaspoon of vegetable oil per cup of dry food (four teaspoons per pound of food) and no more than two teaspoons per cup (eight teaspoons per pound) of dry food will also increase the energy content.

Without supplementation, most dry dog food contains approximately 1,350 to 1,700 calories per pound of food, or 300 to 350 calories per cup. The digestible energy ranges from 65 to 75 percent. Dry foods contain approximately 8 to 12 percent water and 88 to 92 percent food solids.

Semimoist

Semimoist foods have a fairly long shelf life and require no refrigeration. Semimoist foods cost about the same as canned diets when purchased in individual, premeasured packages. Semimoist diets purchased in ten- or twenty-five-pound bags will slightly lower the cost per feeding.

This form of diet provides the highest digestible energy due to the sugars used to preserve the food. An advantage to a semimoist diet is that a greater variety of ingredients, such as fresh and frozen meats, can be used. Semimoist diets contain about 1,350 calories per pound, or 500 calories per each six-ounce package. They contain about 30 percent water and 70 percent food solids.

Canned

All types of ingredients may be utilized in the manufacture of canned rations. These diets generally contain more fat per pound of dry matter than any other form of diet and therefore yield more energy per pound. Complete and balanced canned rations can meet the needs of lactating bitches whose higher caloric demands require an easily available energy source. A disadvantage to the canned and semimoist diets is that they are more expensive.

Canned Meat—Some of the more expensive canned products are compositions of meat by-products either alone or supplemented with vitamins and minerals. While the palatability is extremely high and the protein quality good, your Aussie is forced to use protein as his main energy source, which puts undue stress on the system. These products can be used to increase palatability to a dry diet when added at 10 to 25 percent.

How To Find the Right Diet

You can judge the quality of any diet by the vim and vigor of your Aussie. You should be able to run your hand alongside his ribs and feel them, but not the concave between his ribs. The coat should have a healthy glow.

The only avenue to an accurate evaluation of any diet is through results obtained in feeding trials. To evaluate particular diets, feed a maintenance level for six days. During this time, standardize your Aussie's daily activities, and determine maintenance amounts accordingly. You must also consider your Aussie's stage of life.

Avoid diets that cause diarrhea after the first two days. On the third, fourth, fifth, and sixth days, weigh the total amount of diet fed. Collect the excreted feces and place them in a plastic bag. Clearly label the package, stating the contents. Weigh the stools, and divide the weight of the stool by the weight of food fed to produce a percentage. The diet is an acceptable ration if the stool weight is less than 25 percent of the weight of the canned food that was fed, 70 percent of the semimoist diet, or 90 percent of a dry diet.

If water is normally added to the dry diet, then mix one part dry food with three parts water *by weight*. The stool should weigh no more than 25 percent of the dry food intake. The quality of diet is directly reflected by what is able to be digested and absorbed by your Aussie. Poor-quality rations contain ingredients that your Aussie's body cannot utilize; therefore, a larger volume of undigested, unabsorbed material passes into the feces as waste material.

You can perform an easy test by feeding an adult Aussie according to the instructions on the package daily for three weeks. Maintain and organize daily activities as evenly as possible. Take a beginning weight and an ending weight. Weigh your Aussie at the same time before feeding. Avoid all diets that are unable to maintain a normal weight evidenced by the fact that your Aussie loses weight.

You also can compare your litter's growth to a standard growth curve. When you wean your litter of puppies, free-feed them and then make comparisons, keeping in mind that there will be slight differences between breeds of similar developmental patterns and even between individual bloodlines within the Australian Shepherd breed. However, any food that fails to support a constant growth rate during the first nine months should not be considered adequate.

Supplementation

Supplementing a professional-quality, complete, balanced ration is not recommended in most cases. To do so may upset the balance and therefore create an inadequate, nutritionally deficient diet. On a dry-matter basis, an acceptable diet should consist of at least 25 percent protein, 10 percent fat, and at least 1,400 calories, but more acceptably 1,600 to 1,800 calories per pound of dry matter. The addition of selected ingredients may be necessary if you are feeding a grocery-store-variety diet as compared to a professional mix. Fat is the most expensive ingredient, and a quality diet can be determined by the percentage of fat included.

It is possible to supplement 10 to 25 percent (no more than 25 percent, however) without affecting the overall balance of a good dry diet. The best choice for increasing palatability and available energy is to add two teaspoons of a cold-pressed vegetable oil per cup of dry food (eight teaspoons of oil per pound of dry food).

Butter, margarine, animal fats (meat fats), lard, and tallow are saturated fats, as compared to unsaturated fats such as vegetable and fish oils. Margarine is a solidified vegetable oil that is generally fortified with vitamin A and is therefore nutritionally similar to butter. Margarine is recommended over butter due to its higher unsaturated fatty-acid content. Coconut and palm oils, used in some nondairy products, are high in saturated fats, even though they are vegetable oils.

Vegetable and meat broths and even water drained from cooked pasta or rice are ideal for increasing the palatability of a good dry diet.

During periods of physical or mental stress, your Aussie will require larger caloric intake without added bulk. Hot climates decrease the desire to eat, yet increase the energy needed for cooling, whereas cold climates increase the calories expended for warmth or heat.

It is preferable to give your Aussie a top-quality professional feed and thus eliminate unnecessary supplementation. It is always best to consult your veterinarian before supplementing your Aussie's diet, especially with vitamins and minerals. The fat-soluble vitamins are quite easy to overdose, causing nutritional imbalances. Generally, more nutritional deficiencies are due to unnecessary supplementation with improper quantities. Never supplement more than 25 percent of any diet.

Vegetables and Vegetable Juices

Vegetables are composed mainly of carbohydrates and water but contain very little protein. Vegetables and vegetable juices are an excellent source of vitamins and minerals. Juices are digested easily, and vegetables provide necessary bulk to a diet. Vegetables are usually available in fresh, frozen, canned, and dried varieties. Fresh vegetables must be rinsed thoroughly to remove chemical residues and dirt. Quick-frozen vegetables are comparable in nutrient content to fresh vegetables. Drying, on the other hand, tends to decrease nutritional value. Whenever possible, vegetable skins should be left on because of the nutrients found in the skins.

Light green vegetables provide many carbohydrates, vitamins, and minerals, but the richest source of nutrients is found in the greener varieties. Vitamin A is contained in both yellow and dark green vegetables. Potatoes are a good source of vitamin A, vitamin C, and some of the B vitamins, as well as protein.

Meats

Liver is especially nutritious. The supplementation of liver at least once or twice a week will provide protein, fat, carbohydrates, minerals, and vitamins. Liver also helps to combat iron-deficiency anemia due to its high iron and B_{12} content. Liver is also available in tablet or powdered form called "desiccated" liver.

Meat should always be well cooked to avoid the transmission of parasites. This is especially important in the case of pork and wild game. Lamb, beef, and pork are also good sources of the B-complex vitamins and certain minerals, including phosphorus and iron. Organ meats, including the liver, tongue, kidneys, heart, brains, and sweetbreads (glands of lambs or calves), are generally richer in vitamins and minerals than the muscle meats. The leaner the meat, the more protein is available per pound.

Poultry

Poultry also contains B-complex vitamins as well as iron and phosphorus. It is a good source of protein. White poultry meat contains less connective tissue and fat than the dark meat and therefore is easier to digest. However, the dark poultry meat is richest in vitamins B_1 (thiamin) and B_2 (riboflavin). Poultry must be cooked thoroughly to prevent food poisoning.

Fish

Fish is an excellent source of high-quality protein. Fish is rich in polyunsaturated fatty acids

Solid food can be introduced by making a gruel of a high-quality dog food with meat broth and boiled rice. Photo by Cee's Pix.

and minerals, including iodine and potassium. Fish is available in fresh, frozen, canned, dried, salted (not recommended), and smoked varieties. Due to possible bacterial infections, fresh fish should be carefully stored, wrapped, and cooked. Fish, as with the varieties of meat, should be well cooked to prevent the transmission of parasites. In either case, bones must be removed completely. Canned fish are nutritionally balanced and are highly palatable to most Aussies. Freshwater fish provide minerals, including phosphorus and iron. Saltwater and shellfish lend rich iodine sources. The unsaturated-fat levels fluctuate with the season and the species. Salmon, halibut, mackerel, and other fatty-type fish provide good sources of the fat-soluble vitamins A and D.

Dairy Products

Dairy products boast the best protein-calorie ratio without disturbing the calcium-phosphorus ratio of the diet. Supplementing with dairy products such as cottage cheese is the most naturally balanced diet, although cheeses, yogurt, and milk can be used. Many dairy products also come in powdered and canned varieties. Dairy products are excellent sources of complete protein, and they provide one of the safest supplements in regard to the calcium-phosphorus ratio. Milk must be pasteurized in order to kill bacteria. Homogenized milk is more easily digested than unhomogenized milk due to the blending of fats within the milk itself.

Milk contains between 3 to 4 percent fat, but when the fat is removed, the milk is classified as "skim." Two-percent milk contains 2 percent fat. Milk is often fortified with the fat-soluble vitamins A and D. Skim milk and nonfat dry or powdered milk must be fortified in order to contain these fat-soluble vitamins. Skim milk and nonfat dry milk are still rich in protein and calcium. When one-half of the water content is removed from whole milk, the milk is classified as "evaporated." When the water is removed and sugar is added, it is classified as "condensed milk."

Although yogurt is made from milk that is fermented, it contains a greater percentage of A, D, and B-complex vitamins than milk and is high in protein. Yogurt has been reported to improve the intestinal flora and is especially beneficial in restoring intestinal flora after the use of antibiotics. Yogurt is easily digested and has been reported to aid in yeast infections in the bitch.

Buttermilk is the by-product of churning butter, but it is generally cultured. Cultured buttermilk results when specific bacteria are added to skim or churned buttermilk. Buttermilk is an excellent source of the bacteria that aid in digestion in the intestinal tract. Powdered buttermilk is also an economical supplement and is easier to store than fresh buttermilk. Butter itself contains a high percentage of saturated fat as well as the fat-soluble vitamins A and D.

Once milk solids are separated from the water, a variety of cheeses are produced. Regardless of flavor and texture, cheeses contain protein, fat, calcium, and phosphorus.

Milk has been known to cause diarrhea in Aussies, especially if given in too large of a quantity, and should either be decreased, varied, or eliminated from the diet if the condition persists after the third day of supplementation. Goat's milk is an excellent substitution because it is highly digestible. Dairy-vegetable blends also can be used.

Eggs

Eggs are an ideal source of protein because they contain all of the essential amino acids and iron. Eggs must be cooked. If fed raw, they will "tie up" biotin, a necessary B-vitamin in the Aussie's body system. The egg yolk also provides lecithin, which helps to break up fats and aids in digestion.

Lecithin

Lecithin is available in granule, capsule, and liquid forms. Although it is high in phosphorus, lecithin unites with iron, calcium, and iodine to aid in the digestion and absorption of fats. Lecithin has been reported to help increase immunity against viral infections. There are no toxic levels for lecithin.

Molasses

Regular molasses is rich in iron, calcium, phosphorus, and other minerals and vitamins. One tablespoon of regular molasses can also be dissolved in one cup of warm liquid (water, vegetable broth, or milk) and added over a dry diet to increase palatability.

Brewer's Yeast

Brewer's yeast can be obtained in powdered, tablet, and flake forms. Brewer's yeast helps to increase the nutritional value of foods. It is a natural source of protein, B-vitamins, and minerals, including phosphorus. Brewer's yeast has more phosphorus than calcium. In order to balance the calcium/phosphorus ratio of the supplement, it is necessary to add a form of calcium in order *not* to upset the calcium/phosphorus ratio of the diet. Supplement four tablespoons of dry powdered milk or the equivalent of eight ounces of skim milk for every tablespoon of brewer's yeast. Brewer's yeast is nonleavening and cannot be substituted by regular yeast. Brewer's yeast provides possible protection against the vitamin-D toxicity that can occur through incorrect supplementation. It has been reported to increase the Aussie's resistance to flea infestations.

Wheat Germ and Wheat-Germ Oil

Wheat germ is an excellent source of protein, vitamin E, B-complex vitamins, and minerals, including iron. Wheat germ also contains calcium and phosphorus. As with brewer's yeast, wheat germ must be supplemented with either four tablespoons of dry milk powder or the equivalent of eight ounces of skim milk to every tablespoon of wheat germ. Wheat germ must be properly stored and refrigerated. The wheat-germ oil extracted from wheat germ is one of the richest sources of vitamin E, a fat-soluble vitamin.

Bone Meal

Bone meal is one of the safest and most natural calcium and phosphorus supplements available. A tablespoon per day will aid in bone, teeth, and tissue development. Bone meal is especially beneficial to individuals on a limited milk intake. It is difficult for your Aussie to overdose on bone meal. A source of vitamin D, such as in egg yolks, milk, and fish-liver oils, is necessary to regulate the absorption of calcium and phosphorus and to distribute the minerals to the bones and teeth.

Kelp

A natural source of iodine, kelp has been reported to produce a calming effect. It also helps to induce a richer skin pigmentation in nose and eye leather. Kelp is rich in vitamins D and E, B-complex vitamins, and vitamin K, as well as calcium and magnesium. As with all seaweed, kelp is rich in all minerals.

Garlic

Garlic, an essential medicinal food for centuries, inhibits viral multiplication. Its antibiotic action is actually equivalent to 1 percent penicillin. Because of its natural antibacterial properties, garlic is highly beneficial to sprinkle on your Aussie's diet. Garlic greatly enhances palatability.

Apple-Cider Vinegar

When given with dairy products, apple-cider vinegar has been reported to decrease the chance of digestive, urinary, and reproductive-tract problems.

Pedialyte

Pedialyte and other electrolytes can be beneficial for hard-working individuals or those under stress.

METHODS OF FEEDING

Portion Feeding

Portion feeding requires feeding a premeasured amount of food on a regular schedule. The amounts fed can be controlled or adjusted according to individual requirements—for weight loss, weight gain, or weight maintenance. Portion feeding may help regulate the metabolic changes for inactive, spayed, neutered, or elderly individuals that still retain large appetites as you adjust the amount of food to meet actual physical requirements. With this method, your Aussie should be fed at regular intervals to maintain a steady appetite, proper digestion, and regular elimination. Be sure that fresh, clean drinking water is available at all times.

Free Feeding

Commonly known as self-feeding, free feeding has many advantages. By consuming small amounts of food on a frequent basis, the level of nutrients in the bloodstream remains more constant. Free feeding has a quieting effect on dogs, because there is no before-feeding excitement. Food is always available to nibble on, which helps prevent boredom and discourages the investigation and eating of stools. If more than one Aussie is present, free feeding assures meeker or more submissive Aussies of getting sufficient quantities of food.

There are containers designed for free feeding. Individual pails or dishes can be chosen to hold one or several day's ration of a dry or semimoist diet. Semimoist diets must be replenished more frequently. Because moist or canned foods spoil easily, they should never be fed by this method.

Convert your Aussie from portioned feedings to self-feeding gradually over a period of several days. Feed the regular ration, then place the free-feeding container out. Eventually discontinue the scheduled rations. An ample supply of fresh drinking water should be available at all times.

QUANTITIES TO FEED

Feeding instructions offer a guideline. The actual amounts required are determined by individual needs and environmental conditions. Individuals with the same weight, genetic background, general environment, and activity can have as much as 100 percent variation in daily food intake. One individual may actually require twice as much food as a similar individual. The amount fed and the type of diet will vary during different stages of the dog's life cycle and also according to the dog's use for breeding or performance.

Maintenance

Maintenance diets are for Aussies that have reached physical maturity and are engaged in normal activity. This type of diet should provide adequate quantities of nutrients to support a mature Aussie with a steady, consistent body weight and help promote general health.

Reproduction

Gestation and lactation greatly alter nutritional needs due to additional stress on the female. The Aussie female's body depends on previously stored nutrients obtained from a highly digestible, balanced ration. Females deprived of an adequate diet will not have sufficient levels of energy, amino acids, vitamins, or minerals, resulting in low conception rates, abnormal fetuses, and a reduction in milk production. From the fourth week of gestation until parturition and weaning, the female Aussie will require a higher caloric density.

Nursing is the most taxing element in a female's life. Not only must she meet her own energy and maintenance needs, but those of her rapidly growing litter as well. A high-quality diet is imperative. Your Aussie female will require three and one-half times more food than during her maintenance stage. Many diets based on requirements for growth may not have sufficient nutrient density to meet the needs of a bitch nursing a large litter.

If a top-quality, well-balanced ration formulated for lactation is fed, no supplementation is necessary. A complete, all-meat supplementation between 15 and 25 percent (not to exceed 25 percent) of the overall diet can be given. The addition of vegetable oil is acceptable in increasing caloric density but should add up to no more than eight teaspoons per pound of the total diet.

The nursing bitch will also require more water in order to produce sufficient quantities of milk.

Free Feeding the Lactating Bitch

Free feeding helps supply and distribute the nutrient levels required by the bitch. The bitch's caloric needs will increase until the litter is weaned. A top-quality diet designed to meet the nutritional needs of a lactating bitch is the most economical and by far the wisest choice. If necessary, a ration containing a larger amount of calories per pound of dry matter can be supplemented with vegetable oil or bacon grease to boost the energy level. There is no substitute for quality ingredients presented in a form available to the canine system.

Reproductive Problems Related to Nutrition

Diarrhea caused by excessive food consumption can occur during lactation. Because a low-calorie diet is incapable of providing sufficient energy, the bitch if forced to consume larger amounts of food in an attempt to meet essential nutrient and energy needs. It is a progressive problem, because the diarrhea makes the nutrients even less available to the bitch.

When a bitch is deprived of an adequate diet, she may suffer from dehydration and lack of muscle tone (atrophy). A loss of body weight will be evident after whelping and especially after weaning. Other symptoms related to dietary deficiencies are agalactia (fading puppy syndrome), a condition where the mammary glands fail to produce milk; acidic milk (bacterial mastitis changes the nearly neutral 7.1 pH of the bitch's milk to a more alkaline pH); anemia; and toxic milk, caused by decomposing tissue and fluids from the placenta.

Growth

A growing Aussie requires twice as much energy as an Aussie in another stage of life. Youngsters use their accelerated energy levels in enabling their systems to utilize essential nutrients for the building of the skeleton, muscles, and vital organs. The system also begins to establish and build a resistance to disease during this time. Feed a diet designed specifically for growth during this active stage.

Working and Performance

You get back what you invest. A hard-working Aussie may require two to four times the energy level of an Aussie during a maintenance period. Temperature also plays a role. In cold environments, an Aussie requires energy for work and for maintaining adequate body heat. For an Aussie that is in a demanding, high-energy athletic performance, it may be necessary to feed a light meal two to three hours before performing or working and then give the remainder of the meal after he has cooled off several hours later. Depending on the environmental temperature, an Aussie worked for a long session or during a heavy period may show signs of ataxia or fatigue. He may suffer from hypoglycemia, and in such instances, convulsions are not uncommon. A snack and water, if fed at least once or twice during the day and periodically during a heavy day, will help sustain your Aussie until he can consume the bulk of his meal.

Periodic drinks of water throughout the day will boost energy levels approximately 75 percent in a working Australian Shepherd. Water is essential for hard-working Aussies in all stages of life.

Semimoist diets are an excellent "pickup" during times of stress because of their high levels of digestible energy. Dry diets are advantageous for energetic, active, and hard-working Aussies due to the greater number of calories available per pound of dry matter. Professional diets have been designed to meet the needs of active Aussies. These dry-type diets contain increased amounts of nutrients in addition to boosted levels of energy. Unlike many products designed for the average pet, these concentrated products do not contain bulky fillers. These diets allow your Aussie to consume higher energy levels in smaller quantities due to their denser contents.

Aging Aussies

The metabolic rate in the older Aussie is reduced. An older Aussie requires an easily digestible diet due to internal changes in the intestinal tract, the liver, and the pancreas. Extreme levels of protein are hard on the liver and kidneys of older dogs. Unsaturated fats help maintain the skin and hair coat in a healthy condition, but diets rich in excessive fat are not easily digested by aging Aussies.

Worn-down or missing teeth make it difficult for an older Aussie to consume a diet of hard biscuits and bones. Many good-quality diets are available in dry, semimoist, and canned varieties

This magnificent champion mirrors the keen and eager expression that displays intelligence as described in the Breed Standard.

Left: An outstanding rich, deep chestnut red merle with light, cream copper trim. Courtesy Duncan.

Ch. Colorado Sizzlin Sioux (Higgins Fast Buck of Berrycreek ex Colorado Sharade) displays a beautiful coat, ideal for work or show. Courtesy Linda Wilson.

Puppies become richer in color as they mature. Often the flecked red merles will look like a blend of cinnamon and sugar which can become a blend of silver and sorrel/liver, similar to that of a red roan. Pictured are three eight-week-old littermates. Left: blue merle. Middle: red merle with predominately liver coloring. Right: red merle with freckled merling.

Above: One eye of each color is commonly found in merles. This lends individuality to the breed. Upon retiring, Ch. Stonehenge Justin Case of Las Rocosa CD had forty breed wins. MacSpadden Photo.

Right: Due to the breed's tendency for the merle colors to become deeper with age, pink spots on the nose leather that are surrounded by pigmentation will usually fill in over time. The marbled eyes are also characteristic of the merle color patterns.

Above: The burgundy hue of this deep red coat accents the balance and symmetry of ASCA Hall of Fame sire, Ch. Chulo of Fairoaks. Courtesy Sandy Cornwell. Left: A beautiful example of the rich reddish-brown color of chestnut.

Ch. Gefion's Out Of The Fire CD. Courtesy RaDeena L. Burgess.

From left to right: Ch. Casa Buena Calico Cowgirl (Ch. Chulo Rojo of Fairoaks ex Ch. Cascade Blue Bonnie), a red merle; Ch. Casa Buena Mariquita (Ch. Silvertone Amazing Blue Light ex Ch. Cascade Blue Bonnie), a silver blue merle; Ch. Silvertone Amazing Blue Light (Ch. Las Rocosa Ricky Taylor ex Allee's Silver Foxie), a steel blue merle; Casa Buena Cayenne (Manchado Red River ex Ch. Casa Buena Mariquita), a deep liver red-tri; Ch. Fairoaks Stormy Streaker (Ch. Cornwell's Cody ex Fairoaks Sweet Gypsy Rose), a jet black bi. Courtesy Weaver.

Ch. Southern Cross Crimson King CD, OTD-SD (Ch. Some Like It Hot of Adelaide ex Wildfire of Windermere CD, STD-DS) in an eye-catching shot at the 1994 National Specialty. Photo by Cee's Pix.

Ch. Briarbrook's Can Can Girl. Courtesy Linda Wilson.

Ch. Copper Canyon Caligari CD.

Lovely Aussie puppies.
Photo by Cee's Pix.

Above: Bringing home the ribbons. Left to right: Kalypsos Marshmallow of Ken-Lin CDX, Las Rocosa Kahlua Koa of Van-B CDX, Mi Keoke Ki Mist of Snow CDX. Photo by Kohler.

Left: Las RocosaCherokee Chilie. Photo by Max Schroeder.

These four-week-old Aussie puppies are in a critical developmental stage, and they need to remain in the security of the litter. By the fourth week of age, the head is beginning to take shape. Courtesy Vicky Whipp.

According to legend, the blue-eyed dogs, were held in reverence and came to be known among Native American Indians as sacred ghost-eyed spirit dogs.

Oakridge Classic Impression. Photo by Bobbie W. Myrick.

Right: Photo by Trish Thornwald.

Although Aussies are biddable (able to be trained and willing to take direction), they are not robots that can be taught to obey without thinking. When you command your Aussie to come home, but you fail to see an injured ewe or newborn lamb hidden in a ravine, your Aussie's instincts will direct him to bring the stray home or stay behind to protect it from danger. Photo by Dan Moos.

WTCh. Windsong's Falcon RTD-SC altering these steers' travel plans. Photo by Cee's Pix.

An Aussie in action. Photo by Cee's Pix.

that are easily consumed by the older Aussie and that also meet his physical needs. Liquids such as water and meat or vegetable broth can be added to moisten dry foods and make them easier to eat.

Due to individual differences in the aging process, it is best to consult your veterinarian. Your vet can help you determine the specific needs of your Aussie in this stage of life. Through proper management, you can prolong an enjoyable life!

The Importance of Good Nutrition

There is no substitute for a good diet. Choosing a top-quality diet over a bargain or generic brand has sound economic reasoning behind it. The initial investment may be a few more dollars, but when you consider that it takes a smaller quantity of a superior product to satisfy the need of your Aussie, it only makes good sense to choose the better diet.

Even if your Aussie is allowed to eat as much as he can of an inferior product, including supplementation with the finest quality ingredients, there is no guarantee that he will receive adequate levels of balanced nutrition. Inferior products often contain poor-quality ingredients that cannot be digested, absorbed, and utilized by the Aussie's system.

Nutrition is the single greatest factor that enables your Aussie to reach his maximum inherited potential. It is the very factor that boosts performance levels, whether on the range or in the whelping box. Diseases such as skeletal disorders and allergies can in many cases be avoided or prevented with a proper diet. Essential nutrients are responsible for all bodily functions. They aid in building the body's defense against disease and help develop resistance to infectious agents. Never underestimate the power of good nutrition for your Aussie.

Las Rocosa Dally of Copper Canyon was the inspiration behind the Super Sid and Dally comic strip.

Chapter 12

HEALTH CARE

VACCINATIONS AND INFECTIOUS DISEASES

Vaccinations are a preventative measure but will not cure disease. Bacterial diseases can be treated with antibiotics, but in viral diseases, no specific treatment or drug will kill the virus once the infection begins. Therefore, preventing disease through vaccination is imperative. Immunizations stimulate the Aussie's immune system to produce disease-fighting antibodies against infectious diseases. Even Aussies that have minimal contact with other dogs should be vaccinated.

Colostrum from the dam's milk during the first twenty-four hours of a puppy's life provides the puppy with temporary, or passive, immunity. The maternal antibodies are received from vaccinations given prior to breeding. Maternal antibodies have limited effectiveness and gradually decrease during the first few months of the puppy's life (five to twelve weeks of age) once the puppy is weaned. Because maternal antibodies can interfere with the vaccine, a series of doses is the best way to ensure a blanket coverage.

The American Veterinary Medical Association recommends that Aussies receive their first vaccination at the age of six to eight weeks, followed by revaccination, or booster shots, four weeks later—at ten to twelve weeks—and then at fourteen to sixteen weeks. Booster shots should be given annually thereafter. Rabies vaccinations should be given at twelve weeks, sixty-four weeks, and then annually.

Viral and Bacterial Diseases

Distemper

Distemper is a highly contagious viral disease that spreads through the air. Distemper is the most common infectious disease of dogs and occurs throughout the world. Distemper attacks the Aussie's respiratory, digestive, and nervous systems. It is a primary cause of illness and death in unvaccinated Aussies, especially puppies, which are particularly susceptible after weaning. An Aussie with distemper may develop diarrhea, fever, respiratory disease, seizures, muscular twitches, and watery discharge from the eyes and nose.

Hepatitis

Hepatitis is also known as canine adenovirus (CAV-1 or CAV-2). Most adult Aussies that develop infectious canine hepatitis recover, but the disease is most severe and often fatal in puppies. Hepatitis is spread primarily through infected urine, stools, or saliva. Typically, hepatitis affects the liver and tonsils, but it also attacks organs throughout the body. It is characterized by vomiting, diarrhea, abdominal pain, poor muscular coordination, convulsions, and changes in the appearance of the eyes.

Leptospirosis

Leptospirosis is a bacterial disease that causes hemorrhaging in the digestive system, the kidneys, and the liver. Symptoms include bloody vomiting and diarrhea, listlessness, jaundice, ulcers in the mouth, loss of appetite, lethargy, fever, and extreme weight loss. Leptospirosis is painful and life-threatening. Aussies of any age can be affected. An Aussie infected with leptospirosis can spread the bacteria for many months even after he has recovered. Other dogs and even humans can pick up the bacteria from the infected Aussie's urine through skin contact or by ingesting contaminated food.

Viral Diarrhea

Parvovirus and coronavirus are highly contagious gastrointestinal viruses characterized by odorous diarrhea and possibly vomiting. The initial symptoms are depression and a lack of appetite. Sometimes Aussies can be infected with both viruses at once, leading to extremely serious bloody diarrhea, elevated temperature, and vomiting. Healthy adult Aussies generally survive viral diarrhea, but the loss of fluids in puppies and old Aussies can lead to rapid dehydration, depression, and shock, followed by death within hours. In very young puppies, parvovirus can affect the heart, with no outward signs, and be fatal in a matter of hours. Viral diarrhea is transmitted through the infected Aussie's nasal secretions or stools.

Respiratory Disease

Kennel cough, or canine cough (tracheobronchitis), characterized by a dry, hacking cough, is a highly contagious, stubborn respiratory infection. Kennel cough can have serious complications if multiple infections set in. It isn't usually fatal unless pneumonia develops. In severe infections, heavy discharges from the nose and mouth occur along with depression, lack of energy, loss of appetite, and poor appearance.

The disease is passed through the air and spreads rapidly among dogs that live together in close quarters. Aussies at dog shows, boarding kennels, grooming shops, and veterinary clinics

Table 12-1
SUGGESTED IMMUNIZATION SCHEDULE

Age	Interval	Type of Vaccine
6 to 6½ weeks	first shots	Distemper Measles vaccine (effective regardless of maternal antibodies present in puppy's system). Killed Parvovirus vaccine (given separately or in combination).
10 to 12 weeks	4 weeks	DA2PL+CPV+CV (Distemper, Hepatitis [Adenovirus Type II], Parainfluenza, Leptospirosis, Canine Parvovirus, Corona Virus (These are given in various combinations or all in one. Follow recommendation of your veterinarian.) Bordatella. Lyme disease when available in your state.
14 to 16 weeks	4 weeks	Booster shot of all above DA2PL+CPV+CV, bordatella, lyme disease. First Rabies shot.
1 year	8 months	Booster all vaccines.
Annually as adult	1 year	Booster Distemper, Hepatitis, Lepto, Parainfluenza, Parvo and Corona Virus, Bordatella vaccines.
1 year	1 to 3 years	Rabies booster (Varies according to state and local laws. Vaccine is good for 3 years after initial booster at 1 year).

are at a higher risk. Vaccine comes in two forms—injectable and intranasal. Three commonly involved viruses and bacteria are canine parainfluenza virus, canine adenovirus type 2 (CAV-2), and Bordetella bronchiseptica bacteria.

Rabies

The rabies virus can infect all warm-blooded animals, including humans. Rabies is a deadly viral disease that affects the brain. Rabies develops slowly over ten days to several months as the virus attacks nerve tissue. Once the infected dog develops signs of rabies, death always occurs.

Rabies takes one of two forms—furious rabies or "dumb" rabies. Signs of the disease include stages of excitability (furious rabies), and paralysis (dumb rabies). In furious rabies, the animal becomes unnaturally aggressive because it becomes ultrasensitive to noise and may bite any moving object. In dumb rabies, the lower jaw drops, excessive drooling occurs, and the animal avoids contact.

Rabies is spread by the bites and saliva of infected animals. An unvaccinated Aussie involved in a fight with a wild animal should be a suspect for rabies. There is no cure for rabies, and when it is diagnosed, infected animals must be humanely euthanized.

LYME DISEASE

Lyme disease, a bacterial infection caused by a spirochete identified as borrelia burgdorfei, may not show up for months after initial exposure to an infected tick. The appearance of arthritic symptoms characterized by stiffness, lameness, and pain in the joints is characteristic.

The Lyme vaccine (borrelia burgdorfei bacterin) is used to provide protection from the disease but is also indicated in treating Aussies already infected with Lyme disease.

AUTOIMMUNE PROBLEMS

Viral disease and recent vaccinations with single or combination modified live virus vaccines, especially those containing distemper, adenovirus 1 or 2, and parvovirus, are being recognized as increasing contributors to immune blood disease, organ dysfunction, and bone-marrow failure.

The increased frequency of autoimmunity involving more than one gland may also be related to viruses appearing over the past decade along with other environmental influences such as nutritional factors, chemicals, toxins, and drugs. Drugs associated with aggravating immune and blood disorders include more recent heartworm preventives, certain anticonvulsants, and trimethoprim-sulfa antibiotics.

Four main causative factors of autoimmune disease are stress, infections (especially viral infections), genetic predisposition, and hormonal influences. Immunosuppressant viruses (parvoviruses and retroviruses) have been implicated in hematologic disease (immune-mediated blood disease), autoimmune organ failure (kidney and liver), and endocrine disorders, especially of the thyroid gland (thyroiditis), the adrenal gland (Addison's disease), and the pancreas (diabetes).

It is impossible to cover the entire extent of diseases that may affect Aussies, because it would necessitate a veterinary manual. More importantly, you need to be able to recognize the signs of illness.

SIGNS OF ILLNESS

Early treatment usually reduces the seriousness of disease and hastens recovery. Early detection and accurate diagnosis are important. Call your veterinarian if your Aussie exhibits any of the following signs:

- Blood in the stool, urine, or any other body part. Black stools indicate blood or a problem in the digestive tract. Medium-colored blood indicates a colon disorder, and bright red blood in the stool indicates damage or disease in the rectum.
- Convulsions (dazed appearance; violent shaking of head or legs)
- Vomiting or diarrhea persisting more than twenty-four hours. Once the stomach is emptied, repeated vomiting of yellow bile indicates possible intestinal parasites, an infection, or liver or kidney disease. Bloody discoloration (dark red, brown, or black) commonly occurs when there is an internal injury, inflammation of the stomach lining, or an ulcer.
- Pain (exhibiting pain when touched or lifted; limping)
- Lethargy (lack of normal energy or reduced tolerance for exercise)
- Weight loss (dramatic changes in body weight)
- Changes in urination (increased or frequent urination; strained and accidental urination). An Aussie naturally drinks more water in hot weather or after exercise. But if your Aussie exhibits increased thirst and urination when he is cool and calm, it could indicate urinary-tract infection, diabetes, kidney or liver failure, or endocrine abnormality. Straining to urinate can indicate injury, a urinary-tract blockage, bladder stones, or prostate or vaginal infections. Accidental urination (incontinence) may indicate injury or infection of the urinary tract or a hormonal imbalance in spayed females.
- Unquenchable thirst
- Persistent coughing (dry, scaly nose; nasal discharge)
- Eye abnormalities (squinting, discharge, redness, film over the eye)

- Lumps beneath the skin (bleeding or rapid growth)
- Scratching (frequent scratching or biting at any body area; pawing at face or ears; shaking or tilting of the head)
- Changes in eating habits (eating more or less or refusing food). The appetite usually increases with more activity. When your Aussie exhibits constant hunger, with or without weight gain, it may be a sign of hyperthyroidism or diabetes. If your Aussie refuses to eat one meal, there is no reason to become alarmed. If he stops eating for more than forty-eight hours and exhibits other signs of illness, he may have a viral infection, gastrointestinal upset, or a fever.
- Labored breathing during rest. Heavy, quick panting after exertion is normal, but not once your Aussie has cooled down and is resting.
- Constipation. A sudden change in diet or stress can cause constipation. If the condition persists for more than forty-eight hours and is accompanied by apparent discomfort, stomach rumbling and bloating, or depression, it could indicate a blocked digestive tract.

Treating Stomach Upsets and Diarrhea

Whenever treating stomach upsets and frequent, loose, watery stools from changes in food or water, stress, parasites, etc., withhold food for twelve hours. Give Pepto Bismol or other antidiarrheal every four to six hours for twelve hours.

Following the period of twelve hours with no food, feed three to four small meals per day of a bland diet consisting of one part boiled hamburger, chicken, or cottage cheese to four parts of boiled rice. Rice aids in forming firm stools and supplies the necessary B-vitamins.

By the third or fourth day, blend a small amount of the regular food with the bland diet. Gradually increase the regular diet and decrease the bland diet so that the dog is on regular food by the sixth or seventh day.

Electrolytes are necessary to treat rapid dehydration. In addition to fluid therapy, antibiotics are often indicated to treat viral diarrhea such as parvo and corona. Due to the seriousness of rapid dehydration, it is urgent to contact your veterinarian.

Common Antibiotics

The following antibiotics are most commonly prescribed for dogs by veterinarians. Always follow the directions of your veterinarian when administering antibiotics.

- Amoxicillin—Broad spectrum, respiratory. Give five milligrams per pound every twelve hours.
- Ampicillin—Broad spectrum for wounds, uterus, skin, mouth, genitourinary tract, respiratory tract. Give ten milligrams per pound every six hours.
- Erythromycin Tablets—Penicillin substitute. Give five milligrams per pound every eight hours orally.
- Tetracycline—Broad spectrum, Lyme disease, brucellosis, leptospirosis, kennel cough, skin problems. Give ten milligrams per pound every eight hours.

Protozoal Intestinal Infections

Two common protozoal infections that affect Aussies are coccidiosis and giardiasis, both of which affect the intestinal tract.

Coccidia

Coccidiosis is widespread throughout the United States and is particularly prevalent throughout the South. Coccidia often affects young Aussies. Older Aussies typically display no signs of the disease. Younger Aussies and puppies may experience diarrhea, weight loss, diminished appetite, dehydration, vomiting, anorexia, fever, depression, and even death.

These parasites invade the cells of the small intestine, where they multiply rapidly and destroy tissue. The organisms eventually give rise to resistant, egglike forms (oocysts) which are eliminated in the feces. Under favorable conditions (humidity and warm temperatures), the oocysts become infective in a few dogs and are transmitted to susceptible hosts in contaminated feed and water. The parasites destroy the intestinal wall, leading to poor absorption of nutrients. The stools are fluid, containing mucus and blood.

While coccidiosis has often been associated with unsanitary conditions, an outbreak of the disease can occur even with a good sanitation program. Coccidiosis is induced by physiological stress, such as shipping, weaning, dietary changes, cool and damp weather, overcrowding, and fatigue.

To control the spread of coccidiosis, it is important to maintain strict sanitary conditions, proper nutrition, and the use of coccidiostatic drugs. Therapy is aimed at controlling diarrhea with intestinal sulfonamides or antibiotics and correcting fluid and electrolyte imbalances.

Giardia

Giardia is also called backpackers' disease, because it is commonly acquired by drinking infected water in high mountain lakes and streams and in irrigation ditches. This intestinal organism is commonly passed in the feces of beavers. Giardia infects dogs, deer, and even humans.

Giardia causes inflammation of the bowels. It is less severe in mature Aussies than it is in puppies. Adult Aussies often show no clinical signs, but younger Aussies may have persistent soft, light-colored stools, dysentery, and diarrhea. In heavy infections, the bowel movements are bloody and mucoid and generally have an offensive odor. Weight loss is a common side effect.

Giardia infections are difficult to diagnose and are equally difficult to get rid of. The organisms are tiny and can be easily missed in a fecal examination. The giardia organism is shed in the feces of infected Aussies for a while. It then disappears, but reappears again at a later time. It is usually necessary to repeat the test several times before giardia is diagnosed. Once your dog is infected, he may develop symptoms again when he is under stress.

Treatment is given to control secondary infections. Aussies infected with giardia have been reported to respond to metronidazole, available under the trade name of Flagyl.

WORMS (INTERNAL PARASITES)

Chances are that sometime during your Aussie's life, you will have to deal with parasites of one type or another. In spite of ever-improving medicines, sanitation, and management practices, the unique biology of parasites allows them to thrive under adverse conditions. Dogs can be born with them or can easily acquire them.

Hormonal activity during pregnancy can activate ascarid and hookworm larvae that are encysted in the mother's tissues and that migrate to the unborn whelps. Furthermore, emotional and physical stress, such as that involved in shipping, trauma, surgery, injury, illness, and in the administration of certain medications like cortisone, can reactivate dormant larvae in the tissues and vital organs. This situation can become fatal if left untreated.

Internal parasites cause damage in a variety of ways. They can interfere with digestion, allow bacterial complications, lead to heart disease, damage the tissues and vital organs, and be fatal if left unattended.

COMMON DRUGS

In the event you cannot reach your veterinarian immediately, the following list of over-the-counter medications can be safely used in dogs.

- Acetaminophen (Tylenol)—not recommended.
- Aspirin, buffered—for pain relief and as an anti-inflammatory. Give one five-grain tablet per thirty pounds every six hours (five milligrams per pound every twelve hours). One "baby" tablet per fifteen pounds; one-fourth tablet if under fifteen pounds every six to eight hours.
- Benadryl—for allergies and itching. Give up to two milligrams per pound every eight hours.
- Charcoal—for diarrhea and flatulence. Give one tablespoon in four ounces of water per thirty pounds (two to six tablets three or four times daily).
- Cheracol-D—for coughing. Give one teaspoon per thirty pounds every four hours. Up to thirty pounds, administer child's dose.
- Di Gel Liquid—antacid and antigas. Give four tablespoons every eight hours.
- Dramamine—for travel sickness. Give twenty-five to fifty milligrams one hour before traveling.
- Epinephrine—for reactions following insect stings and medical allergies ($1/10$ to $1/2$ ml subcutaneously).
- Hydrogen peroxide—antiseptic and emetic for inducing vomiting. Give one tablespoon per thirty pounds every five to ten minutes until vomiting occurs.
- Imodium A-D for diarrhea. Give two teaspoons after the first loose bowel movement and one teaspoon thereafter, but no more than four teaspoons per day. (See page 133.)
- Kaopectate—for diarrhea and vomiting. Soothes stomach and intestines. Dosage is the same as for humans.
- Milk of Magnesia—antacid, anti-toxin, and laxative. Give one-half to two tablespoons per day.
- Mineral oil—to eliminate constipation and absorb solvents and petroleum products. Give one-half to two tablespoons per day.
- Pepto Bismol—for stomach gas, diarrhea, or vomiting. Give one to two teaspoons per five pounds every four to six hours.
- Sodium bicarbonate (baking soda)—neutralizes acid. Give one teaspoon in eight ounces of water.
- Syrup of Ipecac—an emetic to induce vomiting. Give one teaspoon per ten pounds of body weight.
- Vinegar—neutralizes alkalines. Give one teaspoon in eight ounces of water.
- Vitamin B—an appetite stimulant. Give one-half to one milliliter subcutaneously every twenty-four hours.
- Ivermectin—see page 133.

Anthelmintics (Dewormers)

Canine anthelmintics (dewormers) differ drastically in their effectiveness in expelling worms from the body. Some anthelmintics are parasite specific, while others have a broad spectrum of activity. As with any treatment, always consult with your veterinarian first. Effective results depend on an accurate diagnosis for the problem. The best all-around anthelmintic for Australian Shepherds is fenbendazole. Panacure is a trade name for fenbendazole. It is a broad-spectrum medication with a wide margin of safety. Fenbendazole can be used during pregnancy and is safe in heartworm-positive dogs and in puppies older than four weeks of age. This drug is 100 percent effective against whipworms, 99 percent effective against ascarids, 98 percent effective against hookworms (98 to 99 percent effective against migrating ascarids and hookworms), and 100 percent effective against the taenia species of tapeworms. It must be used for three consecutive days, then repeated in three weeks.

Pyrantel pamoate is one of the safest wormers on the market. It is an excellent choice for puppies and is safe for use in pregnant bitches and nursing puppies. It is 95 percent effective against both ascarids and hookworms.

In addition, adequate exercise, proper nutrition, and nutritional supplements (ground up pumpkin seeds, black walnuts, and garlic) are beneficial. Once a week, feed your dog raw beef bones instead of his regular diet. The fast helps cleanse his system, while the bones help slough off the worms by mechanically removing them from your dog's system.

Heartworms

Heartworms are potentially the most dangerous parasites known to modern dogs. Mosquitoes transmit the disease by biting an infected dog and then depositing the heartworm larvae in a healthy dog, where the larvae pass through the dog's tissues and later into the bloodstream. When they reach the heart, they mature into long (six to fourteen inches), slender worms four to six months later.

Signs of Heartworm

Although some infected dogs may show no outward signs, most will exhibit weight loss, fatigue after even light exercise, poor appetite, and a chronic cough. Most of these symptoms do not appear until the damage is extensive and the disease is well advanced. A blood sample can be drawn by your veterinarian to detect the presence of microfilariae in the bloodstream. If your dog is diagnosed positive for heartworms, an intensive course of action must follow.

Treatment

Heartworm treatment is risky and should not be attempted at home due to the life-threatening complications that can occur. X-rays can be taken to reveal the severity of damage. Depending on your dog's overall health, he may require further testing to determine if his present state of health (liver and kidney functions) can tolerate the treatment. Preliminary treatment may be necessary to stabilize and support your dog to increase his chance for survival.

Once all the necessary preliminary treatments have been done, the vet will inject a drug to destroy all of the adult heartworms. The patient must be given a week or two of cage rest. Exercise can cause fatal blood clots to form in the lungs.

In the second phase of the treatment, your vet will follow up with another injection and will administer oral medication to eliminate any remaining larvae, followed by four to eight weeks of restricted exercise.

Prevention

Preventive heartworm medication must *never* be given to dogs that are already infected with adult heartworms. A simple blood test can detect the presence of microfilariae in the bloodstream. If your dog is diagnosed with the disease, he must be treated as described above prior to being placed on preventive medication.

Warning! It is important that you carefully consider which heartworm preventive will be the most beneficial for your dog. Although Ivermectin is a highly popular and effective medication, be sure to exercise great caution when using it. Even with the small amounts contained in the preventive available under the trade name Heartguard, Australian Shepherds are highly sensitive and at risk of adverse reactions. Ivermectin can affect the central nervous system, producing warning signs such as depression, excitability, tremors, drooling, and even coma and death in some cases. Manufacturers warn that individuals should be observed for unusual signs such as vomiting, staggering gait, dilated pupils, and depression for at least eight hours following each treatment. Ivermectin accumulates in the nervous system and toxicity can occur in a matter of months. Seizures are a classic symptom of Ivermectin toxicity.

Diethylcarbamazine citrate has long been a standard heartworm preventive available under the trade names of Filaribits, Caricide, Nemacide, and Decacide. Diethylcarbamazine must be given daily. When used correctly, it is also 100 percent effective against ascarids. Side effects reported are occasional vomiting and diarrhea.

Milbemycin oxime is the most recent addition to the list of heartworm preventives. It is available under the trade name of Interceptor and is popular because it is given on a monthly basis rather than every day. It also helps to control hookworms and removes and controls adult ascarids and whipworms.

Hookworms (Ancylostoma)

Hookworms are only about one-half inch long and about as thick as an ordinary straight pin. They are bloodsuckers that attach themselves to the intestines and cause anemia. Hookworms have a number of "hooks," or cutting teeth, that attach to the lining of the small intestine. They damage the lining, then migrate to new areas, leaving the abandoned sites bleeding long after the worms have moved. Because of their small size, they are not easily detected in your dog's feces.

Hookworm eggs pass in the fecal material and hatch into larvae. Ingested larvae can pass through the lungs, the windpipe, and the throat. A dog can become infected by licking his contaminated feet, by coming into contact with larvae on a ball, or by consuming contaminated food or water. Larvae can penetrate the skin. Furthermore, larvae can become dormant and develop weeks later into adults in the intestine. Pregnancy can stimulate encysted larvae, causing them to migrate to the mammary glands and be passed to nursing puppies. Hookworm larvae also can infect developing fetuses in their mother's uterus and mature into blood-sucking adults once the puppies are born.

Signs of Hookworms

Common signs of hookworms in young puppies and in debilitated and malnourished individuals include life-threatening anemia manifested by extremely pale mucous membranes (gums and eyelids), diarrhea with black, tarry stools, feces streaked with blood and mucus, pneumonia, depression, and weight loss. Hookworm infestation can prove fatal.

Treatment

Hookworms are diagnosed by the detection of eggs on a stool sample. Blood transfusions may be necessary in severely anemic dogs before they can be wormed. Pyrantel pamoate or fenbendazole are excellent and safe choices for Australian Shepherds. Consult your vet for dosages. Puppies should be treated two to three weeks after birth and again at two- to three-week intervals until they are three months of age. The mother of the puppies should be treated at the same time. Fenbendazole can be given to bitches from the fortieth day of pregnancy until the fourteenth day after whelping to reduce transmission of hookworms to the litter.

Prevention

Hookworms are contracted through contact with infected feces, which means that sanitary measures are vitally important. Daily removal of all feces is highly recommended. Concrete runs should be washed biweekly during warm weather. Sodium borate (Boraxo) applied on dirt or sand kennel runs is the most effective decontaminator. When you are walking in public places, keep your dog from coming into contact with other dogs' feces, and clean up after your own dog.

Hookworm infections are more difficult to control in temperate zones. Larvae on hard surfaces or bare dirt runs in kennels may be destroyed with a saturating solution such as sodium borate. Larvae in the soil in outdoor runs are destroyed by freezing temperatures. How frequently you treat the soil depends on the type of soil and the degree of infestation. Applications should be repeated more frequently during spring and summer months in colder parts of the country and on a year-round basis in warmer climates.

Roundworms (Ascaridoid nematodes)

Ascarids are the most common and injurious worms in puppies, and they cause many complications, including pneumonia. A puppy can be born with roundworms even under the most sanitary conditions. The worms are white and yellowish and are two to eight inches in length. They resemble spaghetti and tend to coil in a spiral when they are alive.

When the eggs are swallowed, they hatch into larvae and can take several routes. They can enter the bloodstream and encyst in connective tissue. Encysted larvae, which become active in a pregnant female, can infect the puppies through the mother's uterus and develop into adults in the puppies' bowels. Puppies can also become infected by their mother's milk or by walking in their mother's feces.

Once in the bloodstream, roundworms also can circulate to the lungs via the liver and heart. From the lungs, they are coughed up and swallowed. Numerous eggs of ascarids are passed in the feces of dogs and become infective within a few days under favorable conditions. The eggs are then swallowed by a dog that eats an infected rodent, rabbit, or even an earthworm, all of which act as transfer hosts.

Signs of Roundworms

Puppies with roundworm infections are thin and potbellied. The hair coat will be dry, dull, and rough looking. Diarrhea, mucus-stained feces, coughing (when larvae are migrating through the lungs), and lethargy are common symptoms. In heavy infestations, puppies may cry from intestinal discomfort. Ascarids are easily detected by locating eggs in a stool sample and by examining expectorated segments passed in the feces or vomitus of puppies.

Treatment

To reduce transmission to the litter, fenbendazole can be given to a bitch from the fortieth day of pregnancy to the fourteenth day after whelping. Puppies should be treated three weeks after birth and again at two- to three-week intervals with either pyrantel pamoate or fenbendazole. The dam of the litter should be treated at the same time.

Prevention

Because ascarid eggs are resistant to cold temperatures and common disinfectants, and because they adhere to hair, skin, paws, and other surfaces, good hygiene and strict sanitation are important to minimize contact with contaminated surfaces. Feces should be picked up daily.

Tapeworms (Cestodes)

Tapeworms are ribbonlike, flat, and several feet long. They are composed of numerous segments, each of which contains hundreds of eggs that break away from the rest of the worm. The head, or scolex, of the tapeworm fastens to the wall of the gut with rows of large and small hooks. While not life-threatening, tapeworms are definitely a problem.

There are many varieties of tapeworms, but only three seem to pose a problem for Aussies: *Dipylidium caninum* (in which fleas and lice act as intermediate hosts), *Taenia pisiformis* (in which rabbits act as the intermediate hosts), and *Echinococus granulosus* (in which domestic livestock are the intermediate hosts). Infections occur when your dog accidentally ingests a flea, when he nips at his skin, or when he scavenges or eats the viscera or offal of wild game or domestic stock.

Signs of Tapeworms

The segments are shaped like cucumber seeds and resemble grains of rice when dried. They cling to the hair under the tail, around the anus, or in your dog's stool. Unless a segment ruptures, no eggs will appear in the fecal sample. Weight loss, irregular appetite, colic, rough hair coat, lethargy, and irritability are typical symptoms, with seizures occurring in severe infections.

Treatment

It is difficult to get rid of tapeworms because you must be able to successfully purge the scolex. If you don't, the tapeworm will regrow a new body. Currently, praziquantel, available under the trade name of Droncit, is the most effective drug against larvae and adult tapeworms (not the eggs). It should not be used in puppies less than four weeks of age.

Control of fleas and lice is essential to avoid reinfection. If you live on a farm, be sure that you properly dispose of any carcasses, and do not allow your dog to scavenge.

Whipworms (Trichuriasis)

The whipworms found in dogs are white or gray, and they appear in the cecum or colon, where they attach to the lining and suck blood. When they are mature, whipworms are two to three inches long and no thicker than a needle. Dogs ingest the eggs when they lick their feet and hair. The worms hatch in the small intestine, and young worms reach maturity in the cecum about three months later.

Signs of Whipworms

Typical signs and symptoms of whipworm infestation are chronic diarrhea or alternate periods of runny stools and constipation, anemia, abdominal pain, weight loss, and mucus and blood in the stools. The heavier the infection, the more pronounced the symptoms. Mild infections produce no obvious symptoms in healthy individuals.

Treatment

It is difficult to get a positive diagnosis for whipworm infections, because the worms are very small and the adult females produce a relatively small number of eggs that are shed intermittently. It may be necessary to do at least four fecal exams over a four-day period to get a positive diagnosis.

Once infected with whipworms, a dog can easily contaminate the soil in his kennel run or fenced yard, where the worms remain in the ground for a long time. Dry conditions, good drainage, sunlight, and aeration of pens and exercise areas will help destroy whipworm eggs. The thick, impervious shell of the egg of this parasite does not permit easy destruction by chemical agents but is subject to drying and temperature extremes. Furthermore, prompt and frequent disposal of feces will minimize contamination.

EXTERNAL PARASITES

Fleas

Fleas are only about one-eighth inch long, but they have such powerful legs that they can jump 150 times the length of their own bodies. They are black or brown wingless bloodsuckers. They are responsible for spreading tapeworms to dogs and can cause severe allergic reactions. One bite can cause itching for days. In heavy infestations, they can cause anemia.

If you want to eradicate fleas from your Aussie, you must also get them out of your house, your dog's house, and all the areas that your dog frequents, even the automobile if your dog goes for rides. When fleas lay eggs on your dog, some can also fall around his environment.

Fleas pass through four different stages: the egg, the larva, the pupa (cocoon), and the adult. After the eggs are laid, they hatch several days later into wormlike larvae. Larvae are not parasites; rather, they live on organic matter called "flea dirt," which actually is dried blood that is passed in the feces of the adult fleas. Several weeks later, the larvae are full grown and spin tiny cocoons in which they transform from larvae into pupae. The pupae change to adult fleas about a week later. They thrive in warm, humid climates.

Treatment

For any treatment to be effective against fleas, you must treat your dog and his environment at the same time. There is a wide and varied selection of flea products. Wash your dog's bedding, dust and mop the floors, and vacuum all carpets to pick up eggs, larvae, and pupae. Dispose of bags, because flea eggs can hatch in them. Treat your dog's bed, the carpet, outdoor yards, and kennels with a safe product. Diatomaceous earth and powdered African chrysanthemums can be mixed together for a safe, natural flea powder. Sodium borate (Twenty Mule Team Borax or Boraxo) can be applied to the ground. Due to the toxic nature of many commercial and natural products, follow the directions carefully.

For heavy infestations, a dip will provide the most effective protection after the application has dried. Dips can be absorbed through the skin and are toxic, and you must use them with caution. The same goes for powders and flea collars if they are ingested or get wet. Fabric (cotton) collars can be renewed with a few drops of essential oils, cedarwood, citronella, eucalyptus, pennyroyal, orange, sassafras, or lavender for added protection. Flea shampoos will kill the fleas and rid the body of flea dirt.

Pyrethrins (derivatives of African chrysanthemums) are mild and among the safest choices. Many times, manufacturers will combine synthetic pyrethrins with natural ones, or they will combine pyrethrins with insect growth regulators that break the fleas' life cycles by preventing eggs and larvae from further development.

Not all products are safe for use in puppies or bred bitches. In these cases, you can use a tearless baby shampoo followed by a rinse made by steeping a sliced lemon or lime in a quart of hot water for ten to twelve hours. This solution can also be sponged on the individuals between baths. Brush and comb your dog with a flea comb daily. Aromatic cedar bed pillows act as natural insect repellents while providing a natural fresh scent.

Avon's Skin-So-Soft bath oil is a safe and popular insect repellent. It can be sprayed on the coat directly or mixed with water as an after-bath rinse. Use oil in moderation, because too much can make the coat greasy. One-half ounce to two ounces mixed in a gallon of water, or a few drops of insect-repelling herbal oils—eucalyptus, citronella, mint, pennyroyal, orange, or lavender—can be added to the bath water.

Lice

Lice are tiny, wingless, pale-colored insects that lay eggs (nits) that look like grains of sand. The nits adhere to the hair shaft. Lice fall into two categories—sucking lice and biting lice. Lice are not common in healthy, well-groomed individuals. Lice usually appear on weakened, unkempt individuals. Transmission occurs by contact between dogs. In large numbers, lice can cause death associated with anemia (more common in young and debilitated

dogs). Heavy infestations can lower the dog's resistance and make him susceptible to other diseases. They also can lead the way to secondary bacterial infections and/or fly infestations due to the small wounds that they create. Lice can also cause a severe allergic reaction. A rough, dry coat with or without mats can indicate lice. Scratching and biting are also signs of lice.

Treatment

Anemic dogs may require a blood transfusion, vitamin/mineral supplements with iron (ferrous sulfate), and a better diet. Affected individuals should be bathed in a medicated shampoo. All grooming tools should be disinfected, and infected bedding should be removed and disinfected or destroyed. Pyrethrins that control fleas also control lice. Two treatments given two weeks apart should effectively get rid of lice.

Mange Mites

Mange mites are microscopic parasites in the spider family. Two types of mites cause mange—sarcoptic and demodectic. Sarcoptic mange, or scabies, is highly contagious. Intense itching occurs when the females burrow under the skin of the ears, face, and legs to lay their eggs. Once the eggs hatch, the larvae grow to nymphs by molting, and they live under the scaly skin on the surface. Veterinary attention is necessary to correctly diagnose the presence of mange mites through microscopic examination of skin scrapings. Mange mites are considered a secondary bacterial infection and must be treated accordingly to prevent them from spreading.

Demodectic or red mites feed primarily on the cells in hair follicles and can be found on normal Aussies, especially puppies. They may first be noticed by hairlessness around the eyes

Three is a charm.

and reddened, scaly skin on the face and forelegs. Mange generally occurs in young Aussies and when the immune system is weakened and unable to function properly. A good diet, good grooming, and clean living quarters increase your Aussie's resistance to mange.

Ear mites cause an Aussie to scratch and paw at his ears, carry his head to one side, and rub his head on the ground. A foul-smelling, dark ear wax and a black grainy debris (dried blood) resembling coffee grounds can indicate ear mites.

Ear mites do not burrow under the skin. They live deep in the ear canal near the eardrum and feed through the delicate skin. Ear mites are highly contagious and can be contracted from cats and other affected dogs. Ear drops containing pyrethrins are necessary to kill mites followed by application of an antibiotic ear ointment such as Panalog.

Ticks

Ticks are small, blood-sucking parasites. They are flat and oval-shaped and are members of the spider family. After burrowing its head into your Aussie's skin, the female engorges with blood and expands many times its original size. Both sexes go through four stages (egg, larva or seek tick, nymph, and adult).

Your Aussie is most likely to pick up ticks in wooded areas, overgrown fields, and sandy beaches. Ticks are most active during the warm months (year-round in the southern states).

Ticks are dangerous because they can secrete a paralysis-causing toxin and can spread serious illnesses such as Lyme disease, Rocky Mountain spotted fever, Texas fever, tularemia, babesiosis, and canine ehrlichiosis. Large tick infestations can cause severe anemia and even death.

Ticks are commonly embedded between the toes, in the ears, and around the neck but can also be found elsewhere on the body. Prompt removal reduces the chance of infection. Care should be taken when removing ticks, because they can spread infectious organisms that cause spotted fever. A few seconds prior to removing the tick, use a cotton swab to apply a tick-killing insecticide or clear fingernail polish to kill the tick. Grasp the tick with tweezers or gloved fingers as close to the skin as possible. Use steady traction and pull firmly upward. Once the tick is removed, apply an antiseptic such as hydrogen peroxide to the wound.

A periodic sponging with an insecticide solution (dip) may be necessary to control ticks. Effectiveness of commercial products is highly variable. Use caution when applying insecticides because they can be harmful to your Aussie. Pyrethrins provide a wide margin of safety due to their lower toxicity. Carbaryl, such as found in Sevin dust, is quickly eliminated once it is absorbed and therefore has a relatively low level of toxicity. Carbaryl can be sprinkled on your Aussie's coat as well as throughout the premises (sleeping quarters, inside kennels, outbuildings, and garage) for effective tick control in the cracks and crevices.

The lawn and weeds should be mowed and discarded, and trees and shrubs should be treated once in the spring and again in the summer.

Ivermectin and Other Drug Related Toxicity to Aussies

A number of Australian Shepherds have been found to be susceptible to neurologic toxicity induced by pharmaceuticals including ivermectin (worming), loperamide (Immodium), digoxin, ondansetron, many chemotherapeutic drugs including vincristine, vinblastine, and duxorubicin, and other drugs. Neurologic signs include hyper salivation, ataxia, blindness, coma, respiratory compromise, and death.

According to Washington State University, a veterinarian at WSU, discovered the cause of the neurotoxicity was due to a deletion mutation in the MDR1 gene. This gene encodes P-glycoprotein (large transmembrane protein), part of the blood-brain barrier that is an essential to transport medications out of the brain and back into the bloodstream where they can be metabolized safely.

There is a simple test developed by WSU to screen the presence of the mutant gene. The benefit of having your Aussie tested is that it will help to determine the appropriate pharmaceuticals needed for medical treatment.

The owner can obtain a test kit from the Veterinary Clinical Pharmacology Laboratory at WSU. The process is no different than as in brushing cells from inside the dog's cheek for a DNA test and then mailing to the laboratory. To find out more about the test you can contact the Veterinary Clinical Pharmacology Laboratory at WSU (See Appendix for information).

Exploring the world.

Chapter 13

EMERGENCY FIRST AID

ONE OF THE MOST DIFFICULT CHALLENGES facing you as an Aussie owner is being able to recognize a medical emergency. Urgent situations that require immediate attention include:

- Convulsions
- Loss of consciousness
- Sudden paralysis
- Collapse
- Accidental poisoning
- Traumatic injury
- Foreign objects (if inhaled or swallowed)
- Inability to urinate
- Repeated or continuous vomiting and/or diarrhea (lasting for more than twenty-four hours)
- Shock (rapid pulse and breathing, lowered body temperature, or lack of normal response)

Accidents often occur at unexpected times far from a place where you can get immediate help. You must be able to stay calm and act quickly and effectively in order to save your Aussie's life or to prevent further complications of an injury until you are able to get your dog to

135

the vet. Familiarize yourself with the following first-aid information *before* an injury occurs. Remember that these procedures *do not* take the place of professional veterinary care. The following guidelines are organized as a quick reference guide to help you deal with an emergency just prior to going to or while en route to the vet. In some cases, home treatment should *not* be attempted. A lack of knowledge can do more harm than good!

If you are traveling and you do not know where to get veterinary assistance, make phone calls rather than driving around trying to find someone to treat your Aussie.

FIRST-AID PROCEDURES

When an accident occurs, treat the injuries in their order of severity. The principles of first aid are:

1. Check for regular breathing and then check the pulse rate.
2. Maintain open air passages and respiration.
3. Maintain cardiac function.
4. Control bleeding.
5. Prevent or treat for shock.
6. Restrain your dog if necessary to prevent further injury or to keep yourself from being bitten.

Applying an Emergency Muzzle

Even the most trustworthy Aussie can become frightened or panic-stricken when he is injured and in pain. You may need to restrain him from biting while you are trying to help him. If necessary, apply a regular muzzle or use approximately two feet of gauze bandage or nylon stocking. Make a double half-hitch by wrapping the bandage twice around your dog's muzzle and securing it with a knot under his chin. Tie the ends together behind his ears at the back of his head to keep the bandage from slipping off. The muzzle should fit securely but not so tight as to interfere with circulation or breathing. Be alert for signs of vomiting. If your dog vomits, remove the muzzle immediately to prevent choking or suffocation. Do not leave your dog unattended when he is wearing a muzzle. Remove the bandage as soon as possible, because dogs perspire through their tongues.

Artificial Respiration

If your Aussie has stopped breathing, you will need to administer artificial respiration. Place your dog gently on his side. Quickly check inside his mouth to be sure that no object is blocking the air passage. Pull the tongue forward, and extend the head and neck forward to establish an open air passage to the lungs.

The most effective method of artificial respiration is by mouth to nose. Place your mouth over both of your Aussie's nostrils. Cup your hands over the entire muzzle, forming an airtight seal, and begin to blow air into the lungs. Observe your dog's chest and stomach to ensure that his *lungs* are being inflated and *not the stomach*. Give one deep breath every five seconds. Continue this procedure until your dog begins to breathe strongly on his own.

Vital Signs: The normal respiration rate for the average Aussie is approximately eighteen to twenty-two breaths per minute but can vary from twelve to thirty per minute.

Heart Massage

If your Aussie has no pulse, you will need to massage his heart. Place your Aussie down on his right side on a firm surface. Put the palm of one hand on his lower chest, right behind his left front elbow where the tip of the elbow rests at the bottom of the chest cavity. Place the other hand, with the palm facing up, on the same spot beneath your Aussie's body. Firmly press both hands together, then pause. Repeat this action

Emergency First Aid

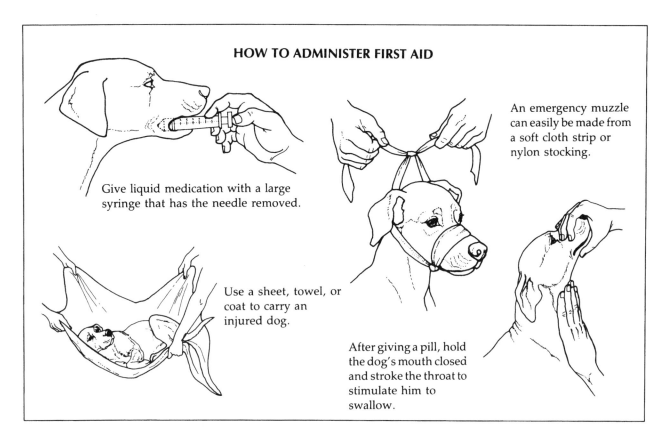

HOW TO ADMINISTER FIRST AID

Give liquid medication with a large syringe that has the needle removed.

Use a sheet, towel, or coat to carry an injured dog.

An emergency muzzle can easily be made from a soft cloth strip or nylon stocking.

After giving a pill, hold the dog's mouth closed and stroke the throat to stimulate him to swallow.

approximately sixty times per minute. When treating puppies or small Aussies, adjust the force of resuscitation to the size of the Aussie. Pushing too forcefully can break ribs and puncture the lungs and heart, and may even damage the liver.

Vital Signs: Normal heart rates for Aussies range between 70 to 100 beats per minute in adults and 90 to 140 beats per minute in smaller and younger Aussies. To check the pulse, place your fingertips on the inside of your dog's upper hind leg, one-half to three-fourths of the way up (where the femoral artery is located). Count the beats for fifteen seconds, then multiply this number by four.

Cardiopulmonary Resuscitation (CPR)

CPR combines artificial respiration and heart massage. Massage the heart five times with one compression per second (at the rate of sixty per minute), then give one deep breath.

Compress the chest for a half second, then relax for a half second. Compress again. As you compress and relax, count 1-1000, 2-1000, 3-1000, 4-1000, 5-1000. After you have done five compressions, take your hands off the chest and place your mouth over your dog's nostrils (as described under Artificial Respiration), and give a deep breath. Now resume giving five more chest compressions. After every fifth compression, give a deep breath.

Shock

Any injury, especially one in which your dog loses a lot of blood, can throw your Aussie into shock. Stop the bleeding first, then treat the shock. One sign of shock is slow capillary refill. To check for refill time, press your thumb firmly against the gum area above your dog's tooth until the gum becomes white. If the gum takes more than a second to return to a pink color, there is serious trouble. Other signs of shock include shallow breathing, pale or white mucous membranes, dilated pupils, dull-looking eyes, glassy-looking eyes, rapid and weak pulse, rapid and irregular breathing, and a cold, clammy feeling.

Keep your Aussie warm and get him to the vet immediately. This is an urgent, life-threatening situation. *Don't waste time.* Intravenous fluids and drugs may mean the difference between life and death.

During transport, maintain, but do not raise, your dog's body temperature. If the weather is cold or damp, place blankets or extra clothing over and under your dog. Provide shade if the weather is hot. A light, gentle massage of the limbs may be helpful. *Do not* give your Aussie food or liquids. If he is thirsty, offer him ice cubes to lick. Control bleeding, and ensure adequate breathing. Keep your dog quiet.

Carrying an Injured Aussie

If you need to transport an injured Aussie, use a solid, flat surface, such as an ironing board or door, or any strong cloth, such as a blanket, rain slicker, shirt, coat, or pup tent, as a stretcher. If you use cloth, tie knots in each corner and insert a strong branch or pole in the knots or through the sleeves of a shirt, jacket, or slicker to form a sling. A small Aussie with minor injuries can be carried by supporting his stomach, chest, and hindquarters in the crook of one arm. The other arm can support his head and neck. A larger Aussie with minor injuries can be carried by wrapping one arm around his front legs and the other around his hind legs.

Abdominal Injury

If your dog sustains blunt trauma to the abdominal region, internal hemorrhage is possible. In a rare occurrence, a dog may sustain a tremendous force or penetrating injury to the abdominal area, rupturing the abdominal wall and spilling the intestines. *Do not* attempt to wash off or replace the organs in the abdominal cavity, because they will become contaminated. *Do* prevent your dog from licking or chewing at the organs. Wrap the organs in plastic wrap or a thermal space blanket to retain moisture. Then place towels and blankets over this dressing to keep the organs warm. Treat for shock. Your Aussie may also vomit blood. If this happens, lie him on his side, with his head slightly lowered, so that the blood will not be sucked back into the lungs, especially if the dog is unconscious. Get immediate professional assistance.

Allergic Reaction

Aussies can be allergic to insect bites, foods, and medications. If breathing becomes labored, he needs prompt veterinary care. If the throat swells shut and breathing stops, you need to perform CPR. Get to the vet immediately.

Animal Bites

Puncture wounds naturally occur from animal bites. Because all animals harbor bacteria in their mouths, contamination and subsequent infection may result. Wash the bite wound with antibacterial soap, then consult with your veterinarian. Only he will be able to determine whether systemic antibiotics are indicated.

Bleeding

Bleeding from superficial wounds caused by minor injuries is stopped by the natural clotting of blood upon contact with air. If this does not stop the bleeding, apply direct pressure over the bleeding point with your finger or thumb. Be sure that your hands are clean, or place a piece of clean—preferably sterile—material over the wound before applying pressure. If the injury is to a limb, elevate the injured leg while applying direct pressure. Pressure can also be applied above the artery that serves the injured limb. For example, to control hemorrhage of a lower-hind-leg injury, apply pressure to the femoral artery on the inside of your Aussie's thigh. Continue the pressure until the bleeding has stopped.

Profuse arterial bleeding is dangerous, because blood in an artery is under direct pressure from the heart. If the artery is severed or torn, the blood will be bright red and will flow out irregularly in spurts, timed with the heartbeat. To stop bleeding from an artery, apply pressure between the heart and the wound.

If the wound is gaping or jagged, place gauze over it and hold the gauze in place with adhesive tape until you can get your dog to the veterinarian. Never place cotton directly on the wound, because it leaves fibers that are difficult to remove.

Internal Bleeding

Even if there is no apparent injury after an accident, your Aussie may be hemorrhaging internally. If he is weak or prostrate, if mucous membranes (gums, tissues surrounding the eyes) are pale, or if you notice distention of the abdomen, he may have been injured internally. Internal bleeding induces shock. Wounds of the chest or abdomen may cut or tear large veins, causing severe internal hemorrhage. This situation requires immediate professional attention. If there is bleeding from the nose, mouth, or ears with no apparent damage to those areas, it may indicate a head injury. Treat the condition by keeping your dog as quiet and immobile as possible. Carry him on an improvised stretcher, and get to the veterinarian immediately. Treat your dog for shock (see pages 137–138).

Brain Injury

A brain concussion can occur as the result of any trauma to the head. Other types of brain injury may appear similar. Signs of possible brain injury are shallow respiration, feeble pulse, dilated or pinpoint pupils, or pupils of uneven size. If he is conscious, your Aussie may carry his head cocked to one side, or he may become uncoordinated. The dog may demonstrate partial or total unconsciousness. Blood appearing from the ears or nose may indicate brain hemorrhage. Vomiting may occur. Be careful to observe that vomitus does not get sucked back into the lungs, especially if your dog is unconscious. As with any type of severe injury, treat your dog for shock (see pages 137–138). Do not give any stimulants. Keep your dog quiet to avoid further trauma. Seek professional assistance as soon as possible, because swelling of the brain can lead to additional damage.

Broken Teeth

Tooth dislocations and fractures in a working breed like the Aussie are not uncommon. Injuries range from teeth being jarred loose, chipped, or broken to being totally uprooted. Teeth can be driven into the nasal cavity, lip, cheek, or tongue. Hemorrhage is usually present, and the movement of the tongue will slow clotting.

If the wound is minor and hemorrhage is at a minimum, apply an ice pack to control bleeding. Bleeding from a single cavity can also be controlled by applying direct pressure to the wound. Your veterinarian may have to suture large lacerations and use a form of immobilization such as pinning and wiring to heal fractures of the teeth and the jaw assembly. In certain cases, a dislocated tooth with a root can be replaced in its cavity and remain functional with proper dentistry. If the tooth is not too dirty, rinse it with cold water. Preserve all gum fibers still clinging to the tooth. If the tooth is excessively soiled, rinse it with eight ounces (one cup) of ice water mixed with two tablespoons (one-fourth ounce) of salt. In both cases, seek veterinary care immediately.

Bruises

Bruises accompany many types of injuries. Apply a cold pack to prevent swelling of a new injury. Use a warm compress to improve circulation on an already swollen injury.

Burns

Get veterinary attention immediately. Burns can be extremely serious and may require the administration of antibiotics. Burns are extremely painful and are prone to infection, and they can lead to shock. Flood the burned area with cold water. *Do not* apply ointments, greases, or powders.

Thermal Burns

If your Aussie is scalded by hot liquids or hot objects, and if the burn is minor, immerse your dog in cold water or saturate the area with liberal amounts of water. Apply clean, cold, wet towels and get to the vet. *Do not* add salt to the water.

If the burn is severe and covers a large area, *do not* immerse it in cold water as you would a minor burn. Cover the burned area with a clean, moist cloth to keep out air. If burns are extensive, keep your Aussie quiet and warm, and maintain open breathing passages. Coax your Aussie to drink water. If he refuses, administer water with one-half teaspoon salt and one-half teaspoon baking soda. Treat your dog for shock (see pages 137–138). Take your dog to the vet immediately.

Chemical Burns

If the burn is from a chemical substance, flood the entire area liberally with cold water. Read the manufacturer's label to determine what type of chemical was involved. Call the veterinarian without delay.

Electrical Burns

Disconnect the power source if possible, or pull the victim away from the source using wood or dry cloth. *Do not* use your bare hands or metal objects. Electrical burns may require CPR. All electrical burns must be evaluated by your veterinarian, because they can be worse than they appear.

Turpentine, Kerosene, and Gasoline Burns

Use mineral oil *instead* of water to absorb petroleum liquids. Apply it liberally and rub it in thoroughly. Then wash your Aussie with a mild soap or baby shampoo.

Choking

When your Aussie is choking, he may begin to paw violently at the side of his face and make retching motions. His tongue and lips may turn bluish, then he may collapse. Pull your Aussie's lower jaw open and tilt his head upward. If a foreign object is visible, remove it with a blunt instrument, taking care not to push the object farther down his throat.

If you are unsuccessful, wrap your arms around your Aussie's body just behind his ribs (holding him from behind). Wrap one hand around the other to make a double fist. Squeeze sharply, pressing upward until the object is ejected from the windpipe. Use quick, sharp blows up and forward to push the solar plexus until the object is expelled.

When dealing with puppies, modify the procedure. Place your hands around him (with your thumbs on his back) instead of your arms.

Constipation

Constipation is a condition of the bowels in which defecation is difficult and irregular. It is characterized by recurrent attempts to defecate and is sometimes accompanied by a whimper of sharp pain. Sometimes the feces will be blood-streaked or hard and dry.

Aussies confined for long periods of time without proper exercise and debilitated individuals are prone to constipation. A poor diet can result in constipation. The condition can also be caused by an obstruction, a hernia, a tumor of the colon, a swollen prostate gland, parasites, abscesses, or a foreign object. Consult your veterinarian.

Treat mild cases by applying warm soapy water to the external area and anus in case dry feces have formed an external block. A teaspoon of vegetable oil on your Aussie's feed may help soften the feces. You may also want to reevaluate your Aussie's exercise program. If your Aussie is constipated after two days or is showing other symptoms, do not hesitate to call your veterinarian.

Cuts and Wounds

There are several types of wounds—lacerations, punctures, incisions, abrasions, and bruises. Lacerations are common and may occur upon the impact of a kick, a vehicle collision, a dog fight, or a snag from a piece of wire or a branch. An irregularly shaped wound is caused by a ripping effect. Puncture wounds may result from a dog fight or porcupine quills and occur when a sharp object penetrates deeply into the tissue. An incision is caused when a sharp object such as glass makes a clean, slicing cut. Abrasions are made upon contact with a surface that scrapes the skin and tissue. Bruises can accompany many types of injuries but most commonly occur upon impact with an object not sharp enough to penetrate the skin.

Cuts and wounds should be covered with a clean—preferably sterile—dressing to prevent further contamination. Have your Aussie examined by your veterinarian. If the wound is jagged or gaping, place a strip of adhesive tape over the dressing until treatment can be administered. A cold compress will help to control swelling and pain. A hot compress improves circulation of an already swollen wound. If necessary, control hemorrhage.

For minor, superficial wounds, remove any foreign object such as glass or slivers. Cleanse the area with soap and water and apply 3 percent hydrogen peroxide or a mild antiseptic germicide such as Betadine (povidone iodine).

In the case of puncture wounds, pour 3 percent hydrogen peroxide into the wound. Wash the surrounding area with germicidal soap or a mild antiseptic. In order to heal properly, puncture wounds must heal from the inside out. Shave or trim hair surrounding the wound. Do not allow the skin to heal quickly over the top. Wash the wound several times a day, then apply peroxide and insert an antibiotic ointment. As with any healing wound, observe closely for signs of infection, such as redness, swelling, or the feeling of heat over the involved area. In case of deep puncture wounds, consult your veterinarian.

Diarrhea

Diarrhea is an intestinal disorder in which the bowel movement is fluid and frequent. As with vomiting and seizures, it is not a disease itself but a symptom of another disorder. It can occur from allergies, infectious diseases, metabolic disease, parasites, foreign bodies, an unclean feeding utensil, overfeeding, or a change in diet. Lactose found in milk is a common cause of loose or watery stools. Check your Aussie's stools regularly for indications of a possible problem.

Normal feces vary in color depending on the individual and his diet. Normal color usually ranges from light brown to dark or ruddy brown. Black feces may result from a diet high in meat content, while grayish-white stools may indicate the presence of large amounts of bone. Nursing puppies or Aussies on a diet high in milk or cereal grain will exhibit a light brown or tan stool. Any blood, mucus, foreign substances, or abnormal color and consistency should be brought to the attention of your veterinarian.

Dislocations

Dislocations, fractures, and sprains can be caused by any strong impact. A dislocation is a displacement of a bone that is entering into a joint.

Joints in the shoulder, hip, jaw, knee, toes, and pasterns are all susceptible to dislocation. The affected limb is, in essence, out of joint and will be held in an abnormal position. Reluctance to bear weight and swelling will occur.

Apply a cold compress to relieve pain and minimize swelling. Do not try to readjust the dislocation, because you may further damage the tissue and nerves surrounding the bone. Keep your Aussie as quiet and immobile as possible to prevent further injury. Take the patient to your vet to reposition the joint. Prolonged delay may add complications and make it impossible to reset the joint by manipulation.

Electrical Shock

Electrical shock can be transmitted by electrical cords, power lines, and lightning. Death usually results from respiratory failure or cardiac arrest.

If your Aussie is in contact with an electrical current, *do not* touch him. If he has urinated, be cautious not to step in any moisture when you touch him. Try to turn off the current by unplugging the cord from the outlet, or by switching off the circuit breaker. If you are unsuccessful, get assistance. *Do not* put your own life in jeopardy.

Once your Aussie can be approached safely, begin supportive measures if his heart or breathing has stopped. Treat him for burns and shock if necessary. Get veterinary assistance immediately.

Eye Injury

The correct eye placement in Aussies allows protection from traumatic blows (such as flying hooves) as well as from scratches and lacerations. Sometimes, however, the eye may become injured. Injuries that result in varied pupil sizes between the right and left eye, pupils that are unresponsive to light, and graying of the cornea are all emergency signals that require immediate veterinarian attention.

A severe blow can cause the eye to become dislocated from the socket. This is a true emergency and requires immediate professional care. *Do not* attempt any cleansing or manipulation of the eye, because you could damage it further.

Any foreign bodies in the eye that cannot be washed away by irrigating the eye with a gentle stream of lukewarm water poured from a glass two to three inches from the inner corner of the eye should be treated only by a veterinarian. If a superficial foreign body is removed by irrigation, continue to observe the eye for irritation or pain, which indicates that professional attention is required. *Do not* attempt any manipulation of an eye that has a penetrating foreign body.

Fish Hooks

Fish hooks can become caught in the mouth or feet. Cut the barb off of the end of the hook with a pair of wire-cutting pliers or similar tool so that the remaining end can be pulled through. If possible, cut off the eye of the hook so that you will not have to pull the barbed end back through. Clean the wound and apply an antiseptic. Observe for signs of infection.

Foreign Body

Objects can become lodged behind back teeth, wedged across the roof of the mouth and between the teeth and cheeks, and sometimes driven into soft tissue. This usually causes your Aussie to panic. He may paw frantically at his muzzle or shake his head, choke, or cough. Sometimes he cannot close his jaw. You may notice unusual salivation, difficulty in swallowing, lack of appetite, weight loss, and depression. The symptoms vary depending on the location of the object.

Examine your Aussie's tongue both on top and underneath. Examine the gums, the teeth, and the hard palate. If your dog is extremely agitated, seek professional help to avoid being bitten. To examine the throat, place a handkerchief over your Aussie's tongue for a better grip. Pull the tongue out to view the throat. Sometimes thread becomes looped and imbedded around the tongue. Your Aussie may show signs of retching, gulping, salivation, and decreased or no appetite. In cases of imbedded thread, there is a linear reddening that can be seen on and underneath the tongue.

If you find that the object is not imbedded too deeply, you may remove it with a pair of tweezers or dental forceps. If the object is in close proximity to the throat, do not attempt to remove it yourself. Also, if the object is deep or is not easily dislodged, have it removed by your vet.

Food gulped down without your dog chewing it first can result in vomiting or retching of a mucous substance. If you can see the object, you may be able to grasp it and remove it with forceps. If you cannot remove it easily, leave the job to a trained specialist. You may cause complications and force the object farther down your dog's throat. Some foreign objects must be located by radiography.

Foreign Objects in the Intestines

When a foreign body is present in the intestines, your dog will attempt to vomit, he will experience abdominal pain and sensitivity to touch in the abdominal area, and he will show signs of excessive salivation, constipation, retching, and possibly diarrhea.

Never attempt to induce your Aussie to vomit if you suspect that he has a foreign body in his intestines. This is a job for your vet. If the object is rough or sharp, you may cause considerable damage, lacerations, and even perforation, which can cause death.

Foreign Objects in the Rectum

Foreign objects in the rectum can cause symptoms similar to those of constipation. If you suspect a rectal foreign body, contact your veterinarian.

Fractures

Although Aussies are sturdy working dogs, a blow or other abnormal force on the skeletal structure can fracture bones and cause considerable damage.

A fracture is a broken bone indicated by an inability to bear weight on or use a leg or jaw. Another symptom is swelling or abnormal alignment of the injured structure. An Aussie with a broken bone must be moved carefully so as not to risk further damage.

Do not try to set the fracture. In a compound fracture where the bone protrudes through the skin, a sterile dressing is required to prevent further contamination. Keep the broken limb immobilized. The use of a temporary splint will help prevent the sharp edges of the bone from cutting a blood vessel or puncturing a vital organ. However, if excessive manipulation is required to apply the splint, it is best not to attempt it. Tie the limb gently and loosely with bandages or cloth to a pillow, board, or similar item. Some fractures, such as of the skull and shoulder assembly, cannot be splinted. Keep your dog as immobile as possible during transport. Treat for shock if necessary (see pages 137–138).

Frostbite

Frostbite is a rare occurrence in Aussies that are healthy and well nourished. However, dogs exposed to long periods of extreme cold may suffer from frostbite. Frostbite generally occurs on the ears, scrotum, nipples, and feet. Signs of frostbite include reddened or flushed tissue, which then becomes white or grayish. If frostbite occurs, bring your dog into a warm area and allow him to thaw out gradually. If shelter is unavailable, gently warm or massage areas with your hands. Never rub or massage a frozen area such as the ears, because you can induce gangrene and easily bruise, tear, and irritate frozen tissue. Instead, soak affected areas in lukewarm water. Vinegar (approximately two ounces per cup of water) may also be added to the lukewarm water to help thaw the tissue. Gently dry the affected tissue.

Cover your Aussie with a blanket, sweater, or coat to help him maintain body heat, and get him to a warm shelter as soon as possible. With severe cases of frostbite, as seen in physically injured Aussies, get to a vet immediately. Antibiotics, among other therapies, are necessary to avoid complications such as gangrene.

Gunshot Wounds

Gunshot wounds are traumatic emergencies. Check your dog's heart and respiratory functions, and treat him for hemorrhage and shock (see pages 137–138). Get to a vet without delay.

Heat Stress

Overweight Aussies, puppies, and geriatric Aussies are more vulnerable to heat stress than Aussies in good condition and excellent health. The specific heat-related health risks for Aussies are heatstroke, heat cramps, and heat exhaustion.

Heatstroke
Heatstroke is the most frequent type of heat stress. It is most commonly due to exposure to high temperatures where the atmosphere is windless (inadequate ventilation) and humid.

Initially, heatstroke is characterized by panting, bright red mucous membranes, an increased heart rate, and an elevated body temperature. This is followed by a stuporous state and pale mucosa due to the onset of shock. The body is hot to the touch, and your Aussie may exhibit a watery diarrhea. Final stages of heatstroke are coma and respiratory arrest. The onset of heatstroke is rapid. Your Aussie can withstand fevers of 105°F and above for only a few minutes before permanent damage to the brain and central nervous system occurs.

If your Aussie has collapsed and is hyperventilating, get him to a cool, shaded place and immerse him in cool water immediately. Otherwise, cool him off by applying cold water to his body in any way possible in order to avoid death. Heatstroke *is* life-threatening. *Do not* use ice water, because the shock may result in death. Ice packs, however, may be applied to the head and neck. If your Aussie is conscious and is not suffering extreme symptoms, allow him to lick ice cubes. Recovery depends on prompt treatment. Get veterinary help as soon as possible. Make every attempt to prevent heatstroke by keeping your Aussie in a shaded, well-ventilated area with constant access to fresh, cool water during warm weather.

Heat Cramps
Heat cramps are the early warning signs preceding heat exhaustion. They are painful and are caused chiefly by the loss of salt from the system and by extreme exertion in hot weather. Heat cramps do not commonly occur in dogs but can affect Aussies working in intense heat. Get your dog to a shaded area. Give him small drinks of cool (not cold) water with one teaspoon of salt added per eight ounces of water. Gently massage sore muscles to help relieve spasms. Give your dog several days of rest before you allow him to work again.

Heat Exhaustion
Heat exhaustion can occur when your Aussie has been exposed to intense heat and heavy exercise, when he has been worked hard without adequate water, or when there is a lack of salt in his system. Symptoms are fatigue, muscular weakness, and circulatory collapse. The pulse is fast and feeble, and the temperature is normal or slightly elevated. This is an emergency situation that requires immediate action. Get your dog to a cool environment. Replace fluid loss with cool (not cold) water, adding one teaspoon of salt per eight ounces of water. Immerse your dog in cold water or apply it to his body. Get veterinary assistance immediately.

Quiet class. Photo courtesy Paul Wilke.

Hypothermia

Hypothermia is a severe lowering of the body temperature that occurs when an Aussie gets wet and is exposed to cold weather and wind. Hypothermia is seldom seen in a healthy Aussie that can seek shelter. It is more commonly seen in old or unconscious Aussies that are injured or diseased and then exposed to cold.

Hypothermia is characterized by violent shivering, drowsiness, slow or absent pulse, dilated pupils, and shallow, infrequent respiration. As the temperature drops below 90° F, shivering will be absent, and the body will become stiff due to increased muscle tone. Bring your dog into a warm place and allow him to warm up slowly to a normal temperature. Cover him with blankets to aid in heat retention. A light massage of the limbs may be helpful. Administer CPR if necessary, and treat for shock (see pages 137–138). Get veterinary assistance as soon as possible.

Insect Bites and Stings

Insect stings are usually minor, but an allergic reaction can occur. For simple bites and stings, you may apply ice to the area to relieve pain and swelling. Benadryl (diphenhydramine hydrochloride) can be administered for minor irritations. Severe reactions can vary from pain, local swelling, burning, and itching to excruciating pain, muscular cramps, fever, nausea, abdominal pain, convulsions, severe swelling, blisters, shallow respiration, and unconsciousness. Respiratory difficulty is one of the main signs of an allergic reaction.

At the first sign of a reaction, get your Aussie to a vet immediately. If breathing stops, administer artificial respiration. Avoid unnecessary movement, and keep your Aussie quiet.

Lung Injury

Any blow to the chest or inhalation of certain chemicals can cause lung damage. A fractured rib may puncture the lung. There may or may not be external, visible hemorrhaging. Bleeding is likely to occur in the chest cavity. Labored breathing (you can sometimes hear the air rushing in and out) or irregular breathing are accompanied by pain in the chest and coughing of foamlike, brilliant, crimson blood.

If a foreign body is present, *do not* pull it out. Place a wet cloth around the object. Protect the area to prevent the object from being driven deeper into the wound. If the lung injury is an open wound, cover the opening with a damp cloth and secure it in place. Get immediate veterinary assistance.

If your Aussie is unconscious, keep his head extended and hold his mouth open to maintain an air passage.

Near-Drowning

Aussies are instinctive swimmers. However, even the strongest swimmers can become exhausted and drown. If your Aussie has sustained an injury, he may be incapable of swimming well enough to keep from drowning. If your Aussie can be rescued safely and is conscious, cover him with a blanket or coat to prevent chilling, and dry him thoroughly. If he is willing to drink, a warm liquid may be helpful. Watch for signs of shock. It is advisable to have your dog examined by a veterinarian.

If your Aussie is unconscious, administer artificial respiration. If vomiting occurs, do not allow vomitus to be sucked back into your dog's lungs. Treat for shock (see pages 137–138), and get your dog to the vet immediately.

Nose Injury

A blow or trauma to the nose can cause pain, bleeding, and swelling. Apply an ice pack or cold compress to the nose. This should curb swelling and stop the bleeding. Watch for signs of difficulty in breathing. Consult your vet if bleeding continues or breathing difficulty becomes apparent.

Paralysis

Paralysis might indicate an injury to the spinal cord. No pain reflex will be evident when your Aussie is pinched in the area between the toes. Place him on a stretcher and cover him. Take him to a vet as soon as possible.

Poisoning

Due to the serious nature of poisoning, timing is crucial. A poisoned Aussie must be treated immediately and correctly. Certain poisons require very specific treatment. Poisons can enter the system through ingestion, inhalation, injection, or absorption. Always suspect poisoning if your Aussie has an abrupt onset of unexplained symptoms.

SIGNS OF POISONING

- Odor of poison on your dog's breath
- Traces of suspicious or toxic substances or plant parts nearby
- Dilated or pinpoint pupils
- Bleeding mouth, nose, or genitals
- Salivation
- Watering eyes
- Weak or difficult breathing (gasping for air)
- Respiratory spasms
- Gurgling sound in the lungs
- Severe abdominal pain (sensitive to touch)
- Weak pulse
- Abnormal heart rhythms
- Twitching, staggering, incoordination, unusual excitability, or shaking
- Depression
- Rear-end paralysis
- Paddling of legs
- Muscular spasms
- Unconsciousness

Treatment for Poisoning

If you see your Aussie eating or drinking a toxic substance, or if you suspect poisoning or see an empty or opened container nearby, check the label on the container for a recommended antidote. If none is listed, call your veterinarian immediately. In the event your veterinarian is not readily available, call a local poison-control center or the National Animal Control Center, which maintains a poison-control hotline.

Do not wait for symptoms to develop. With the instructions of your veterinarian or poison-control center, take the container with the substance or a sample of vomitus (if present) to your

---

Poison Control Hotline
1-800-548-2423 ($30.00/case, credit cards only; follow-up calls, no extra charge) or 1-900-680-0000 ($20.00 for five minutes, plus $2.95 for each additional minute; $20.00 minimum; no follow-ups)

EMERGENCY FIRST AID

> ## TOXIC SUBSTANCES
>
> - ANTIFREEZE (ethylene-glycol)
> - ALCOHOLIC BEVERAGES,
> - COLOGNES/PERFUMES (containing ethanol)
> - CHOCOLATE (theobromine, a bitter, caffeine-related alkaloid, contained in chocolate)
> - COAL TAR (disinfectants, clay pigeons, tar paper)
> - DEICERS
> - FERTILIZERS
> - FUNGICIDES
> - GARBAGE
> - HERBICIDES (weed killers, etc.)
> - INSECTICIDES (snail bait, etc.)
> - LEAD (surfaces painted with lead-based paint, batteries, plumbing materials, solder putty, fishing weights)
> - MEDICATIONS (drugs of all kinds)
> - MOTHBALLS
> - POLISHES
> - PLANTS (plants such as mistletoe are highly toxic)
> - RODENTICIDES (rat poisons, etc.)
> - SALTS (fire salts)
> - WOOD PRESERVATIVES, among hundreds of other products that contain toxic substances such as arsenic, cyanide, strychnine, mercury, copper, and fluoride.

> ## ACIDS, ALKALIS, AND PETROLEUMS
>
> **ACIDS:**
> Battery acids, bleach, toilet-bowl cleaners, solvents
>
> **ALKALIS:**
> Lye, ammonia, drain cleaners, potash, washing powders, paint removers
>
> **PETROLEUMS:**
> Gasoline, kerosene, coal oil, turpentine, lighter fluids, benzene, furniture polish, cleaning agents
>
> ### SYMPTOMS
>
> **Acids and Alkalis:**
> - Burning sensations in the mouth, throat, and stomach • Obvious abdominal pain (sensitive to touch) • Cramps • Disorientation • Bloody diarrhea • Possible vomiting • Difficulty in breathing
>
> **Petroleum Toxicity:**
> - Irritated coughing due to chemical pneumonia if inhaled or aspirated
>
> **Treatment:**
> - *Do not induce vomiting.* Vomiting can further damage the esophagus and the lungs.
> - Administer activated charcoal (a protectant and adsorbent)—20 to 120 mg/kg body weight, mixed with water to coat the gastrointestinal tract and prevent irritation or erosion.
> - Or give your dog liberal amounts of mineral oil, milk of magnesia, milk, cream or water, bread soaked in milk (cream or water), egg whites, or vegetable oil to coat the esophagus and bowels, dilute toxins, and reduce absorption into the system.
> - Contact your vet immediately.
> - Be prepared to treat for shock or administer artificial respiration.

vet for easy identification. Always keep syrup of ipecac (an emetic) or 3 percent hydrogen peroxide on hand to induce vomiting. This will remove some of the toxins from your dog's system. You can also give your dog activated charcoal to bind or neutralize certain poisons.

Do not induce vomiting if your Aussie is unconscious; if several hours have passed since ingestion; if he shows signs of nervous disorder, tremors, or convulsions; if he cannot swallow or has ingested tranquilizers; or if he has ingested caustic chemicals (acids, alkalis, and petroleums).

If your Aussie exhibits nervous symptoms, he may already be in a serious, life-threatening condition. *Without delay*, get to the nearest vet. Treat your dog for shock (see pages 137–138) by keeping him quiet and warm. Unnecessary handling or stimulation (bright lights, touching, loud noises) can trigger convulsions.

ABSORBED AND INHALED POISONS AND POISON IN THE EYE

ABSORBED POISON

Dermal contact with corrosives, insecticides, agricultural, lawn and garden products, and poisonous plants can injure the skin and become absorbed into the body's tissues. Flush the affected area liberally with water for ten minutes, then gently cleanse the area with a mild soap or baby shampoo and rinse thoroughly. Watch for shock.

POISON IN THE EYE

Flood the eye(s) with lukewarm (not hot) water poured from a large glass two or three inches from the inner corner of the eye. Repeat for fifteen minutes. Do not force the eyelid open.

INHALED POISON (CARBON MONOXIDE, SMOKE, FUMES FROM SPRAY CHEMICALS)

Get your Aussie out in fresh air. If he is breathing, use ammonia inhalants. If he is not breathing, start artificial respiration. Use ammonia inhalants as soon as breathing starts.

Porcupine Quills

Armed with a bristling coat of approximately 30,000 quills, the porcupine can drive his well-aimed tail at his enemy, leaving the barbed spears in the victim. Quills are extremely painful. They can vary in length from one to four inches. Each quill is needle sharp with fine barbs that flare in opposition. Each movement can work the quills in deeper. Quills should be worked out gently, not yanked, because this is an extremely painful procedure for your Aussie. If there are more than a few quills, take him to your vet. Your Aussie will be put under anesthesia to remove the quills, thus minimizing tissue damage. The vet will have to use a pair of pliers or forceps and slowly twist out each quill. Quills in the chest area and behind and under the shoulder may work their way through the skin into the vital organs.

If you remove the quills yourself, apply an antiseptic over the wounds once the quills are gone. Check your dog's mouth and throat carefully. Cactus thorns may be removed in a similar fashion. Treat your dog for puncture wounds.

Seizures

Mild seizures may go unnoticed. Your Aussie will appear to be in a hypnotic trance, staring into space, but he will probably recover in a matter of minutes. A more severe seizure will include the above signs, in addition to panting, drooling, and slight muscular tremors.

A grand mal seizure occurs if your dog is thrashing on the ground, drooling, and making running motions. His body will stiffen and he will lose control of his bladder. The only action that you can take at this point is to protect your dog by removing objects that can injure him. If he is near a stairway or by a fireplace or some other dangerous area, gently grab the ruff on the back of his neck and drag him to a better spot. If necessary, restrain him by placing a blanket over him and holding down the blanket (not your

Aussie) to keep him from beating himself. Be careful not to get your hands near his mouth, because you can easily lose a finger.

When he first comes out of the seizure, he will be disoriented and confused. Once he has recovered and is more aware of his surroundings, you can offer him a drink of water or ice cubes to lick. If the seizure lasted more than five minutes or your dog goes into another seizure, take him to your veterinarian immediately.

Skunks

Skunks have a pair of perineal glands from which a pungent, offensive-smelling secretion is sprayed when the animal is startled. If your Aussie encounters a skunk, wash the eyes liberally with cool, clear water. Bathe him in tomato juice or a feminine douche followed by a bath with baby shampoo.

Snakebite

A snakebite is a true emergency. Snakebites are not uncommon and can be fatal in working stock dogs. Most types of poisonous snakebites in North America occur from rattlesnakes, copperheads, water moccasins, and coral snakes.

Speed is essential. Kill the snake whenever possible and take it to your vet for positive identification. This is important for proper treatment. Keep your stricken Aussie as quiet as possible, and restrain or immobilize him if necessary. Pick him up and carry him to a vehicle (or across your saddle), then confine him to a travel crate or force him to lie quietly as you travel to your vet's office. The more excited your dog becomes and the more he moves, the faster the venom moves through the bloodstream. If your dog stops breathing and there is no pulse, perform CPR. While getting your dog to the vet, do not administer sedatives or tranquilizers or any products containing aspirin, because aspirin dilates the blood vessels and causes the venom to circulate faster.

The size of the snake and the location of the bite will affect your dog's prospects of recovery. Bites to the thorax or abdomen generally have a higher death rate than bites to the head or legs. Administration of antivenin is the only direct and specific treatment for neutralizing snake venom. Symptoms of snakebite include swelling, pain, muscular weakness, impaired vision, breathing difficulties, drooling, vomiting, bleeding, shock, paralysis, and convulsions.

The use of constricting bands or incision and suction is *not* recommended unless medical help is more than an hour away. If you plan to be in a remote area where poisonous snakes are prevalent and veterinary assistance is not within close reach, contact your vet to learn the specifics of emergency snakebite procedure. Learn how to recognize symptoms that require use of a constricting band and how to perform this procedure effectively. Your vet can give you several vials of antivenin with specific instructions for storage and use if this is legal in your area. Carry the antivenin with you in your vehicle, your saddlebags, or your backpack. In an emergency, human hospitals may be a quick means of obtaining antivenin.

Sprains

Sprains and other injuries to ligaments and muscles are often difficult to distinguish from fractures. The injury occurs when there is torque on a joint that elongates the ligament. The affected area is swollen and tender. Keep your Aussie quiet and, if necessary, apply a temporary splint (see Fractures). If you are unsure of the kind and extent of the injury, treat it as a fracture.

Throat Injury

A blow to the throat can damage and injure the larynx and is manifested by labored breathing, pain, and swelling. Severe injury and swelling can

Due to life-threatening complications that can occur in puppies with persistent vomiting and watery, bloody diarrhea, immediate veterinary attention is necessary. Photo by Cee's Pix.

even lead to suffocation. If the larynx is penetrated, you will hear air leaking out, with blood seeping from the wound.

Apply a cold pack to the wound. Do not cleanse the area with liquid, because you want to avoid getting moisture in the air passage and possibly the lungs. Take your Aussie to the vet immediately.

Toad Poisoning

Exposure to some species of toads causes your Aussie to be poisoned. Signs of toad poisoning are excessive salivation, incoordination, convulsions, vomiting, and urination. Defecation occurs within ten to twenty minutes after an encounter.

Douche or sponge your dog's mouth out with plenty of water using a garden hose, basting syringe, or sponge. Administer activated charcoal.

Traumatic Physical Injuries

A vehicle accident is the most common way in which your dog can receive a traumatic injury. An automobile collision can cause considerable physical damage—bruises, abrasions, broken bones, abdominal injury, and skeletal damage. An Aussie that has been hit by a car or that has broken bones must be moved carefully. Sometimes there are no visible lacerations or fractures, but there may be internal injuries, a ruptured organ, and slow bleeding. Control hemorrhage. Administer CPR if necessary, and treat for shock. Without delay, get professional veterinary assistance.

Vomiting

Persistent vomiting often indicates a more serious disorder. It can be caused by poisoning, infectious diseases, or foreign bodies and can lead to life-threatening dehydration. Treat your dog for fluid loss. Administer electrolytes, such as Pedialyte, to replace lost electrolytes. If vomiting is persistent, recurrent, or accompanied by other symptoms, or if vomitus contains blood or abnormal material, consult your veterinarian immediately.

Occasionally your Aussie will suffer from a simple upset stomach. He may vomit when he eats grass, when he gets extremely excited or nervous, or when he gulps down food or water quickly. This type of vomiting is not alarming and should be followed by normal behavior. If you know your dog and his normal behavior and attitudes, you can easily determine if he is ill or depressed.

Lois George with her friends. Photo by Thom Carter.

The aging Aussie who knows his job can perform with great efficiency in his older years.

Chapter 14

THE AGING AUSSIE

BECAUSE OF THE "WILLING" AUSSIE attitude, aging is hardly apparent. The older Aussie is still an excellent companion. He has adapted to your routine and lifestyle so well over the years that he has become an important member of the family. The aging Aussie plays a vital role in any home. He will be nonetheless eager to please. He will guard the flock, home, and heart with as much courage and devotion as he displayed in his younger years. He may be your self-appointed public-relations chairman.

The older, experienced Aussie may play an active part in teaching young, inexperienced Aussies the "ropes," but he will maintain dignity and sometimes a degree of aloofness toward the youngster's antics. The older Aussie will often surprise you and join in on the fun and games with the vitality of puppyhood.

You will have to make it a point not to take your old friend for granted and put him on a shelf. There will be special times ahead for both of you. Keep in mind your Aussie's physical and mental well-being. Do not allow or ask him to engage in activities that are beyond his physical capabilities. Simple jobs around the farm or ranch, a little swimming, or a game of ball or Frisbee, if not exerting, are excellent. A peaceful walk will give you and your Aussie pleasure and will provide exercise that is not too taxing in the older years. Your old Aussie may not understand having to share your time and attention with the youngsters. He will be indignant to think of another taking his place while he is left at home to "hold down the fort." He will nevertheless anxiously await his turn.

Grooming and handling are enjoyed immensely by the Aussie. The well-kept individual is testimony to the health and longevity represented in your breeding stock. For the breeder, there is no greater honor than to be able to "show off" the veterans of the breed, especially those grand foundation sires and dams.

MANAGEMENT

Caring for the geriatric Aussie should not only prolong life, it also should prolong an *enjoyable* life right up to the end. With a little thought and effort, you can help your best friend adjust accordingly. In turn, you are rewarded with unconditional love and devotion. Australian Shepherds live to an average age of fourteen years.

The Aging Process

Aussies age just as people do. The hair around the muzzle and whiskers will become gray. The aging process also affects the nervous system, which indirectly affects all of the senses. Irritability and disorientation are also attributed to aging.

Audio-visual senses are diminished with age. Nuclear sclerosis, the cloudy, bluish-white appearance of the eyes, is common with aging but does not affect eyesight. A hazy, whitish growth—cataracts—can lead to blindness. When your Aussie's eyesight is failing, avoid needlessly rearranging the furniture. Hearing loss also occurs and is evidenced when your dog doesn't respond to familiar commands or to his name.

Muscle tone atrophies in old age. The bones are more subject to fracture due to their brittle nature. Hip, shoulder, and leg action can become

Hall of Fame sire, Las Rocosa Sydney (Taylor's Whiskey ex Ch. Las Rocosa Leslie CSD) possessed longevity that he transmitted to his offspring. At sixteen years of age, Sydney was active, athletic, and healthy. Sydney inspired the character "Super Sid," the ever-popular comic strip based on his adventures as an almost human.

slowed by different types of arthritis. Stiffness and limping are often indicative of other problems as well, including injury and neurological disorders. Internal organs are more susceptible to disease and infection with age. Respiratory and cardiovascular functions also begin to lessen, and the endocrine system becomes deficient. Mammary-gland nodules, uterine infections, and tumors on the testicles are frequently seen in unspayed and unneutered individuals. Tumors may or may not cause damage. Depending on their location and size, they may eventually disrupt the capacity of specific organ functions. Incontinence (uncontrolled urination) may be due to a hor-

The Aging Aussie

Harper's Old Smokey (1957–1972), Tucson's Joe ex Tucson's Sis. Foundation sire of the breed.

monal imbalance, to diabetes (if water intake increases), or to bladder or kidney trouble associated with old age. Tissue repair and recovery from disease, illness, and surgery are slower. Dehydration can more commonly occur from reduced water intake. Bad breath and difficulty with eating can be caused from gum disease.

You will notice, too, that your old Aussie requires more sleep. When his metabolism slows down, his body produces fewer of the hormones that help maintain normal body temperature. Obesity occurs frequently in old dogs. Reduced levels of dehydroepiandrosterone, a natural hormone produced by the adrenal glands and ovaries, may be responsible for obesity in senior dogs. Reduced activity levels and increased food intake can contribute to weight problems. A little weight gain is not unusual for aging dogs, but excess weight can drastically reduce your Aussie's life expectancy. Heart and lung disease, gastrointestinal disturbances, and bone, joint, and muscle problems become worse in overweight Aussies. Medical procedures are also more dangerous in obese dogs where anesthesia is indicated.

Regular checkups by your veterinarian should diagnose existing problems in the earliest stages before they become more difficult to treat. Warning signs include frequent urination, increased water consumption, sudden weight loss or weight gain, change in bowel habits, behavioral changes, coughing, shortness of breath, foul breath, and stiff joints or lameness.

Weight is best determined by the condition of the individual and is evidenced by the tuckup behind the rib cage. Pads of fat on the hips, a bulging midriff, and a sagging abdomen may suggest that your Aussie is carrying extra weight. You can flatten your hand and gently guide it along his rib cage. There should be a thin layer of fat tissue overlying the ribs.

Special Diets

Your Aussie's diet needs to be balanced to meet his changing metabolic needs. Caloric requirements of older Aussies need to be determined on an individual basis. Smaller rations of a higher quality diet will alleviate additional stress on urinary functions. Weight loss and harsh, dry coats in certain individuals can result from the inability of the intestinal tract to absorb and utilize nutrients efficiently. Overfeeding can hasten internal organ degeneration. Prescription diets are often indicated for individuals with heart and kidney trouble, obesity, or other problems diagnosed by your veterinarian.

Too much protein will burden the system and can cause kidney failure. Some fats are necessary for absorption of certain vitamins. Fats also increase palatability but can be difficult for older Aussies to digest. Additional fiber will help regulate bowel movements and alleviate constipation. Supplementation of the water-soluble vitamins is necessary to replace what is frequently lost in the urine. Kidney stones and other kidney problems require greater water intake, and a higher level of sodium may be required to stimulate thirst. Dehydration can more commonly occur due to reduced water intake. On the other hand, inappropriate amounts of sodium may be detrimental for individuals with heart problems. A complete health assessment by your veterinarian will help determine the best diet for your Aussie. (See the chapter on nutrition, Keeping Up Appearances.)

Grooming

Daily brushing is important. (See the chapter on grooming.) Grooming provides an excellent opportunity to check for tumors, cuts, or any other abnormality. Cysts or benign tumors, or cancer, may be evidenced by large lumps under or on the surface of the skin. Keep the coat in good condition to improve circulation and skin tone and, to a slight degree, help maintain subcutaneous muscle tone. Skin and hair problems are attributed to less active hair follicles and decreased elasticity of the skin. The hair thins out and natural oils are reduced. Due to the activity of the sebaceous glands, fatty secretions sometimes develop little cysts on the skin. These are harmless.

Old Aussies are susceptible to respiratory infections. Extra precautions must be taken to keep the old Aussie warm and protected from drafts to avoid chilling when bathing.

Oral hygiene is part of daily grooming. If the teeth contain slimy tartar, extensive plaque, gingivitis, or varying degrees of periodontal disease, paint the teeth and gums with 2 percent tincture of iodine on a cotton stick. Do not use so much that it can be swallowed. Evidence of oral ulcers may also result from insufficient food consumption.

Housing

Old Aussies are sensitive to extremes in temperature. A senior citizen should be maintained where he may be cooler in the summer and warmer in the winter. His sleeping quarters should be clean, dry, and warm in the winter. He must be kept from lying in drafty places or on the cold, damp ground. In the summer months, his quarters must be cool and airy. He must be kept from lying in the hot sun or in a hot vehicle. Lack of proper ventilation or water can lead to heatstroke.

Exercise

Moderate exercise in the form of daily walks will benefit senior dogs immensely. If old Aussies sit around or sleep away their later years, they are more likely to lose flexibility in the joints, gain unnecessary weight, and become depressed. Don't overexert an old Aussie that is out of condition. Pay special attention to signs of tiring or breathing distress. Slow down or stop and let the old dog rest if the activity is too strenuous. Obese, unconditioned, and old dogs fatigue more quickly.

Never exercise your older Aussie during weather extremes. Whenever possible, don't walk him during the heat of the day, and shorten his walks in severe winter weather.

Working the Aging Aussie

As long as your Aussie has the desire to work and is physically capable, he can work right up to the end. Because of his will to please, an Aussie will do anything asked of him. Don't push your old Aussie beyond his capabilities. Situations such as deep sand can be taxing, and an Aussie may easily overexert himself. Remember that he may not have the stamina that he once had. Back off when your Aussie is getting tired, and learn to recognize those signals. The older Aussie may not be able to get in and away from flying hooves and horns with youthful ease. The aging, experienced Aussie is often aware of his own limitations and will calculate carefully before he moves in to grip. Because old bones do not heal as well as young ones, avoid sending your dog into tight, vulnerable places, and do not let him become fatigued.

The old stock dog will still be a valuable hand on the operation. Younger Aussies can carry out the strenuous tasks, while the older Aussie is there to oversee a job and even bark out a few commands. Simple jobs will make him feel like a useful hand. The dedicated Aussie has learned his job well and is a pleasure to handle. He also can help your promising youngsters get a solid start in their careers. The older Aussie's smooth style is calming to inexperienced young stock dogs. The presence of the older Aussie will give the youngster confidence but will not "wind him up" as will the presence of a fiery young Aussie.

How long you can work an Aussie depends largely on what he is conditioned to do. In any event, do not work him as hard as before. Muscular soreness can affect the older working Aussie and usually comes from exertion. When you see that your Aussie is stiff after working, a warm massage or even warm packs will tend to ease soreness. One or two tablets of buffered aspirin may also be effective in relieving muscular discomfort. Consult your veterinarian for an exact dosage.

TRAVELING

Travel should pose no problem for a healthy senior Aussie that is accustomed to traveling. Older Aussies may appreciate more frequent stops to take care of business and loosen up stiff joints. Emotional and physical stress should be minimized wherever possible. Take his own water supply from home, and feed him his regular diet.

SAYING GOOD-BYE

There may come a time when your Aussie is not able to enjoy life. As an old dog, he may suffer with pain and discomfort. As your Aussie's best friend, you owe him the blessing that only you can grant. While in the comfort and security of your arms, you can let him go painlessly in seconds without further suffering.

GRIEF

Grieving over the death or illness of your Aussie is natural. To some, Aussies are old companions and friends. To others, their Aussie is a vital member of the family. The sense of loss can be overwhelming and may trigger deep depression in some. In general, society does not understand that the feelings toward companion animals can be so special. Even friends may not lend adequate support or understanding in this time of need.

Most experts agree that emotions go through several stages. You have feelings of denial, and you don't want to believe that your pet is seriously ill or gone. If your dog is ill, you may try to bargain with mother nature for more time. You promise to take better care of your Aussie if he is spared. When you lose your Aussie, anger and frustration can cause you to lash out unfairly against others. The next stage of grief encompasses sadness, guilt, and anger. Recognizing these stages can help you cope with grief. Finally, the passing grief resolves itself as time leads to memories of the good times. A friend who is buried in his owner's heart never really dies. More times than not, a new Aussie is a great healer, as long as you accept the new Aussie as an individual. There will never be another Aussie like the one you lost. The new Aussie will offer love and devotion if he is given a chance.

If the burden of grief is too overwhelming, seek counseling. Several universities of veterinary medicine have specially trained individuals available to counsel pet owners. Your vet or a veterinary college may be able to recommend a counselor. Support groups are also available around the country to aid the grieving pet owner.

Places to go and things to do.

Chapter 15

TRAVELING WITH YOUR AUSSIE

TRAVELING WITH AN AUSSIE IS MUCH like traveling with a small child. He gets thirsty and restless and needs to make pit stops to relieve himself and stretch his legs. If your Aussie is adaptable, he won't care where you go or what you do as long as he can spend time with you. Travel disrupts the regular routine and creates new surroundings, unfamiliar situations, and a constantly changing schedule.

TRAVEL TRAINING

The stress of travel is something that your Aussie can be successfully prepared to handle. It is always ideal to accustom your Aussie to travel while he's young and adaptable, but Aussies at any age can be conditioned to travel if you give plenty of training prior to the trip. Start out by taking a short trip around the block, or drive down the road. Each time, add a little more distance, perhaps when running an errand. Always make the trip a positive experience. Put a favorite toy or treat in the crate. Driving to a local park to take your Aussie for a short walk or to play will give him something to look forward to.

Obedience training is important if you are going to be traveling. Not only does it make an Aussie easier to travel with, but it may also decide whether or not you are welcomed back.

TRAVEL CARRIERS

A travel crate is a must for any type of travel. A crate is no different than a child's safety seat. It gives your Aussie a safe place to ride when in transit on a plane or in your car, and when you make rest stops and stay at motels. When you must leave your Aussie in a strange place, such as a motel room, a crate is a secure, familiar place for him. Aussies that are crate-trained are not as likely to whine or bark when left alone, and hotel personnel are more likely to accept a dog that will be crated.

When you are moving to a new home, a crate will help make the transition much easier. Because Aussies, like all dogs, are den animals, your dog will enjoy the security of a private place that is all his own. Whenever possible, introduce your Aussie to the crate prior to adding the stress of a trip or new environment. Crate training is covered in Chapter 6.

OTHER ESSENTIAL ITEMS FOR TRAVEL

Take your Aussie's leash and collar with identification tags, because at roadside areas, parking lots, and gas stations, there is always a danger from traffic. It is simply safer not to take chances in strange areas. The leash will prevent your Aussie from jumping up to greet strangers.

You will need a current rabies certificate, health papers, and a copy of your dog's medical records in the event of an emergency. Any written prescriptions or other medications that your dog is taking, along with good identification (color, distinguishing marks, height, and weight) and a photograph will be imperative in case your dog becomes lost or stolen.

A trip is not the time to change your dog's diet. A sudden change in food and water can cause intestinal problems. Use bottled watter or take water from home, and introduce new water gradually. You also can dilute the original water supply by adding new water to it gradually. On foreign or back-country trips, use a portable water system (the type that backpackers carry) to purify the water. Don't forget to bring a dish and water bucket.

Also include wet wipes or paper towels, a favorite toy, grooming aids, a first-aid kit, sunscreen, insect repellent, bedding for his crate, and a portable scooper and small plastic bags to aid in clean-up. Plastic bags can be turned inside out over your hand to quickly pick up dog waste.

HEALTH REQUIREMENTS

Before you leave town, make an appointment to visit your veterinarian. This is an excellent time to update all of your Aussie's inoculations and to ask about putting him on a heartworm preventative if he is not already on one. Airlines require a health certificate obtained from a licensed veterinarian within a few days of the flight. Check with your airline for details. Some states require a health certificate. Hawaii and many foreign countries quarantine dogs upon entry.

ACCOMMODATIONS

Hotels and Motels

Call ahead to be sure that your Aussie will be welcome. Not all motels and hotels accommodate guests with dogs. Some hotels accept dogs in the room, and others provide kennel facilities. It is important to make reservations in advance. Auto clubs list approved lodging that accepts dogs. Most major motel/hotel chains offer toll-free numbers so that you can check on the policies of individual members. Some require a deposit for damage or extra cleaning. If you are unable to locate accommodations that allow dogs, inquire about local boarding facilities.

Observe hotel policies and other rules of travel etiquette. Whenever you leave your Aussie alone in the room, confine him to a travel crate. When you return, you will find the room in the same condition in which you left it, and you won't have to risk your Aussie nipping or escaping in case the maid comes in to clean. Even well-trained Aussies can panic in strange surroundings and may resort to howling or destructive behavior. When you leave your dog alone in the room, display the DO NOT DISTURB sign on the door. Play the television quietly for him. Put food and water in his crate dishes. Without exception, clean up after your Aussie. Pick up dog hair, and always carry along plastic bags and a scooper to pick up dog droppings. This will help welcome you and other dog owners back.

Campgrounds

Not all public parks or campgrounds allow dogs even with current health documents. Recreational-vehicle directories list campgrounds and pet policies. Campgrounds have rules and regulations for dogs and owners. Abiding by the rules makes you and your Aussie welcome back. Leash laws are strictly enforced to protect the wildlife, your Aussie, and other campers. Never leave your Aussie tied outside your tent or camper, especially at night when wild animals like skunks, porcupines, or bears can attack him.

TRAVEL BY VEHICLE

The safest place for your Aussie to ride is in a travel kennel, where he won't be jumping around the vehicle or in your lap, or lunging at toll collectors and pedestrians. Never put your dog in the trunk of the car. If your vehicle is too small to allow your Aussie to ride in a crate, train him to ride quietly in a comfortable space of his own in the vehicle. A seat-belt safety harness designed for pets can be beneficial. A dog leaping around the vehicle can cause a serious accident. Never allow your dog to hang his head out of the window of a vehicle in motion. He can end up with insects and other flying objects in his eyes and sucked down his windpipe. A collapsible wire crate is an excellent investment.

Never allow your Aussie to ride unrestrained in the back of a pickup truck, no matter how well trained he is. Not only is this unlawful in many states, but it is also extremely dangerous. Hundreds of Aussies have been thrown out of trucks going down a road and have been seriously injured or killed.

If you must leave your dog alone in a parked vehicle, take precautions. During warm weather, don't park in the direct sun. Remember—the sun moves, and even a cool, shady spot can become a dangerous place at a later time. Outdoor temperatures as low as 70°F (22°C) can approach well over 100°F (37.8°C) on the inside of your car in a matter of minutes. If your dog is riding in his crate, it will be easier to leave the windows open wide enough for necessary ventilation. A dog left alone in a vehicle is an open invitation to dognappers, however. If you must keep your dog in the car, be sure to leave a supply of cool drinking water, and leave the windows open as wide as possible for proper ventilation but not so wide as to allow your dog to escape. Ventilation grills available in pet-supply outlets are designed to allow air flow without leaving an escape hole.

Unless your dog is acclimated to extremely cold weather, he could be in danger of frostbite, hypothermia, and other cold-related injuries. Proper bedding in his air kennel will add comfort and warmth.

Whenever traveling, always stop to exercise and water your dog. If you maintain a strict schedule for feeding your Aussie at home, he may enjoy the security and act more settled if he is fed at approximately the same times on your trip.

Many auto clubs offer directories and vacation guides for trips by automobile. Some give good information on whether or not dogs are accepted.

> ### CHECKLIST FOR TRAVELING
>
> - Crate
> - Water from home
> - Food and bowl
> - Toys
> - Collar with I.D. tag
> - Leash
> - Medications
> - Health certificate if required or record of immunizations
> - Dog's bedding
> - Prescriptions, if any are needed
> - Copy of dog's medical records
> - Plastic bags for cleanup
> - Paper towels
> - Insect repellent

TRAVEL BY AIR

Traveling by air is the quickest way to get from one point to another, but it does involve preplanning. For the very old, young, or unhealthy, air travel involves a risk.

The United States Department of Agriculture (USDA) and the International Air Transport Association (IATA) regulate the transportation of animals. These regulations are safety precautions to minimize potential dangers.

Prior to traveling, confer with your veterinarian or the state veterinarian's office for requirements and quarantine restrictions for all destinations. Check with the embassy or consulate of any foreign country included in travel plans a month prior to departure.

Airline Reservations

Try to avoid peak travel periods, holidays, and weekends, when delays and stopovers are longer. Whenever possible, schedule nonstop flights. Plan the trip with as few layovers and transfers as possible. Book international flights at least three days prior to traveling and domestic flights at least forty-eight hours before departure.

Not all airline carriers accept animals. Most airlines limit the number of animals accepted on each flight. Service dogs (seeing-eye, hearing, wheelchair, search-and-rescue, and law-enforcement) are usually allowed in the cabin without a carrier. Most airlines will allow the dog to be shipped as baggage or cargo, depending on whether the dog is traveling with or without a companion. When you are traveling on more than one airline, verify transfers between airlines so that you know where and when you can pick up your dog.

Foreign Flights

Always check with the local consulate of any foreign country that you are planning to visit. There may be specific health requirements that need to be met prior to entry. Beware! Third-World countries such as Mexico may require additional paperwork and fees before allowing you to leave the country without prior notification. Pet-import regulations differ drastically. Some countries have quarantine periods up to one year. Quarantine facilities often do not meet the highest standards of quality, nor do they offer the best care. A dog boarded in quarantine is boarded at the owner's expense.

Check-In

Arrive at the airport well in advance of the flight's departure. Allow your dog ample time to exercise, relieve himself, and get a drink prior to traveling.

Requirements and Restrictions

Aussies must be at least eight weeks of age and have a current (dated within ten days) health certificate signed by a licensed veterinarian. Dogs older than three months of age must have a rabies certificate. Puppies less than eight weeks of age and weaned for less than five days are susceptible to dehydration.

In order to protect dogs from extreme temperatures, the airlines have established a guideline. Dogs can be shipped when temperatures range between 45°F (6°C) and 85°F (30°C). When temperatures are forecast to be below 45°F, but no lower than 10°F (–12°C), a licensed veterinarian must confirm that the animal is accustomed to lower temperatures by issuing a certificate of acclimation.

Whenever possible, book midday flights during the winter months when temperatures are likely to be warmer. During warmer months, travel in the early morning or late evening to avoid higher temperatures. Verify that temperatures are within acceptable ranges with cargo or reservation offices.

Airline Kennels

USDA rules are very specific. No more than one adult or two puppies (less than twenty pounds or less than six months of age) can be contained in a single carrier. The travel kennel must be large enough for the dog to stand up, turn around, and lie down in a natural posture. Travel carriers small enough to fit under the seat—approximately eight inches high, twelve to sixteen inches wide, and seventeen to twenty-one inches long—are often not big enough even for puppies.

The crate must be sturdy and must provide cross ventilation. No part of the dog's body can protrude through any openings in the crate. Therefore, wire crates are not suitable. Metal crates can get very cold or hot. High-strength, copolymer plastic crates with welded steel doors and side ventilation grills are ideal. There should be a rim projecting on the outside of the crate to keep air from being blocked by adjacent cargo.

The door latch must fasten securely but cannot be locked. In the event of an emergency, your pet must be accessible. Crates with wheels are not recommended unless they have a locking device or can be removed or secured to prevent rolling in transit.

The crate should be leakproof and should contain an absorbent bedding material like shredded black-and-white newspaper, a crate pad, or a cushion for added comfort.

Labeling

Federal regulations require that kennels must be marked clearly in at least one-inch-high letters with "Live Animal! This Side Up!" indicated with arrows. The kennel must be marked with the shipper's name, address, and telephone number. Tape a sign indicating the final destination to the top of the kennel.

Feeding and watering instructions must be displayed on the top of the kennel. There should be two dishes, one for water and one for food, on the inside of the door.

The dog must have been watered and fed within four hours of travel. Freeze a small block of ice for the water dish, because it melts without sloshing all over the crate. If the puppy is less than sixteen weeks of age, a small bag of dry food must be attached firmly on the outside of the crate.

Identification

Even if your Aussie is tattooed, waterproof identification tags with your current phone number and address and your dog's destination can be attached to a simple buckle collar. An emergency contact number (possibly your veterinarian's) should be available in the event someone is not at your home to receive a call. Do not put your Aussie's name on the collar. This makes it easy for a dognapper to become familiar with your Aussie.

Preparation

Tranquilizers are not advised due to unpredictable effects at high altitudes. However, if you do give your dog any medication, note the type and the dosage on the crate in case your dog has an adverse reaction.

Motion sickness can be alleviated by giving your dog twenty-five to fifty milligrams of Dramamine an hour before traveling, not to exceed fifty milligrams every eight hours.

Never ship your dog with a leash in the carrier or attached to him, because he could slip through a ventilation hole or become tangled in the leash during the flight and choke. Take a leash and collar along for walking your Aussie prior to departure and upon arrival or extended layover, but never ship your dog while he is wearing a muzzle or choke collar.

TRAVEL BY SHIP

Some ships have special kennel areas. Pets are rarely allowed in the cabins. Check with the travel line first. If dogs are allowed on board ship, you may not be allowed to take them on shore due to quarantine restrictions.

TRAVEL BY BUS OR TRAIN

Some railways may allow dogs to travel in a carrier in the baggage compartment, but baggage compartments are not air-conditioned or heated, and you must be careful of extreme weather. In the United States, service dogs are the only dogs allowed to travel on interstate bus lines. Some local buses will allow dogs. Always inquire first.

LOST DOGS

In the sad event that your Aussie becomes lost while traveling or moving, you must take immediate action. The quicker the loss is reported, the better your chance of recovering him. A lost dog may become confused and leery of strangers. If you are unable to find him after several hours, contact the animal-control and veterinarian offices. Personally visit the humane society and walk through all possible areas where a dog would be held (receiving, holding, quarantine, isolation), calling your dog's name as you go. Give them a written description and photograph. Post signs at intersections and in store fronts, on bulletin boards in local grocery stores, and at laundromats. Ask children and local delivery people if they have seen your dog. Advertise in the local papers and on the radio.

As long as you don't give up, there is a chance for you to be reunited with your dog. If you cannot stay behind, make arrangements for the motel/hotel clerk, the humane society, and the animal-control officers to contact you when your Aussie is found.

WHEN YOUR DOG CAN'T GO

Boarding

For times when you cannot take your Aussie with you, you may have to consider boarding. Even if your dog goes on vacation with you, certain plans may exclude your dog. If your dog will be left unattended for extremely long periods (hours on end), boarding for a day may be the most practical answer.

Check out the facilities yourself. Just because the reception area looks inviting doesn't mean that your dog will receive proper care. Take a tour of the facilities and evaluate the conditions in which your dog will be kept. If the staff refuses to show you the living quarters, don't leave your dog. The kennel should look and smell clean. Stools should be picked up at least twice a day. Indoor runs must be in good repair and have adequate ventilation. Outdoor runs should

Lois George with buddies "Jimmie" and "Red."

be secure and should provide necessary protection from the elements. Do the dogs have plenty of fresh water? Are the water bowls clean?

In other words, is your dog going to receive the kind of care for which you are paying? All too often, behind closed doors, devices like electronic bark collars are used without the owner's permission or knowledge. Unless authorized by the owner when dogs are double booked, your dog should *not* have to share a run with another strange dog. This can be extremely stressful, especially if the combination is not compatible. An old dog may suffer from being bullied, roughed up, or just aggravated by an overplayful kennel mate.

Boarding in a strange place can break your Aussie's heart. The deprivation of usual affection and attention can be extremely stressful. If this is your only option, try to instruct his caregivers to walk and feed him at regular times, and to give him some specialized attention that might bolster his spirits and give him confidence. Ask your vet and other dog owners for recommendations, especially if they know of a kennel that offers more personalized service.

Always leave complete pet-care instructions, your itinerary, and numbers to contact in the event of an emergency. Emergency care should be readily available.

Dog-Sitting Services

Aussies that are not used to traveling may be more comfortable left at home in the care of a responsible friend, relative, or neighbor. In the event such a person is not available, you may want to consider a professional dog-sitting service to care for your dog at home. Be sure that the business is bonded. When your Aussie is in his usual surroundings, he will be more secure and comfortable during the stressful separation from you.

Chapter 16

PRACTICAL TRAINING FOR YOUR AUSSIE

REWARDS AND CORRECTIONS

NO MATTER WHAT YOUR GOAL OR MOTIVATION—to compete in Obedience or Agility trials, to train a working stock dog, or to have a family companion—some form of training is necessary for every Aussie. Obedience can be incorporated into everyday life.

It has been proven time and again that positive motivation is the most effective training technique, because any behavior that is rewarded will be repeated. When you are teaching a new behavior, give your Aussie positive reinforcement immediately after he performs a desired behavior. Rewards should be something that the puppy will actively work to attain, such as food, verbal praise, play, and petting. Food is a highly motivating reinforcer and is the reward most often used by animal behaviorists and trainers. When you use food as the reward, gradually phase it out, rewarding your dog only occasionally as the behavior is learned.

An effective correction should interrupt behavior in progress. In some cases, a sharp noise is all that is necessary to alter poor behavior. Verbal corrections can be quite effective with most Aussies when given in the correct tones. Verbal corrections can be combined with other types of corrections for greater impact.

When your Aussie is behaving inappropriately—barking undesirably, digging, or chewing on forbidden items—toss a large plastic bottle filled with a handful of pebbles to the side or behind him. The bottle should not touch him, but only startle him. He will associate the correction with the undesirable act, not with you.

One effective correction is worth ten thousand ineffective ones. An ineffective correction is no better than nagging. Nagging produces little or no results except resentment. Nagging also desensitizes your Aussie.

Timing is the key to effective correction. A poorly timed correction produces confusion and dampens your Aussie's spirit. For example, upon arriving home you punish your Aussie for a grievous act (defecating in the house or chewing up an item) that occurred several hours earlier. Your Aussie associates the punishment with greeting you at the door. If this happens on more than one occasion, your Aussie will cower when you arrive home. You think that your dog is cowering to admit his guilt. In this scenario, you are damaging your relationship with your dog and are no closer to solving the problem.

Harsh corrections do more harm than good. They are abusive, they produce fear and unreliability, and they destroy your Aussie's sound temperament.

Lastly, *practice* and *repetition* are necessary in all phases of training.

TRAINING TOOLS

You will need a collar—preferably a buckle collar—and a leather or nylon lead that is at least six feet in length.

TEACHING THE COMMANDS

Come

To come when called is the very first command that every Aussie should learn. To teach your Aussie to come to you, each and every time you call him, regardless of distractions, there are three points you must remember. First, when teaching the come command, never call your Aussie unless you can follow through and enforce the command. Second, never call your Aussie to scold or punish him. Even if he did a grievous act, don't call him to you to correct him. *Go to him*. Third, when you call your Aussie, give him a reason for wanting to come. Make the practice session exciting and fun. Invite your Aussie in a friendly, enthusiastic voice. When he arrives, praise him lavishly. Reinforce the positive response with food or play.

To teach the come command, place a long lead on your Aussie's collar. Walk him on a slack, loose line. Call out your Aussie's name (in a happy voice) to get his attention, followed by the command, "Come!" Run away from him. If he is slow to respond or tries to take a detour, pop the line (remember to release the pressure) and repeat the command, "Fido, Come!" Continue to move away quickly from your dog, encouraging him to chase you. When he catches up to you, praise him lavishly. By making a game out of the lesson, you will keep your Aussie's interest high.

Practice calling your Aussie on many different occasions and in many different situations. To test how reliably he will respond when he is off lead, take him to a secure, fenced area. If he ever chooses to ignore you when he is off lead, calmly place the lead and collar back on and reinforce your commands.

Stay

The second most important command is to stay. The stay teaches your Aussie to remain in one place. Many trainers use a stationary posture, such as when the dog is sitting or lying down, to teach the dog to stay in one position.

The stay can be taught effectively and easily on a long line or lead. Loop the lead over a stationary object such as a fence post or around a tree trunk. In a calm but firm voice, tell your Aussie to stay. It is not important whether he is standing or sitting. Walk away several steps. As you walk away, he will surely want to follow. If he tries to follow, give him a verbal correction, "Ah, ah" or "No." At the same time, give a leash correction by popping and then releasing the line to reinforce the stay. Follow this by repeating the stay command.

Begin by leaving your Aussie for thirty seconds at a time, then gradually increase and vary the distance and time. At first, return to release your Aussie from the stay. When you return to his side, release him by telling him, "Okay, that will do," or "That is enough," or whatever command you wish to use each and every time. Give him abundant praise. Eventually, you can also practice releasing him at a distance by calling him to you. When he is released from the stay, always remember the praise.

Practice leaving your Aussie in a variety of places with different distractions. To test how reliably he will stay while off the lead, practice in a secure area.

Sit

A morsel of food can lead or lure your Aussie into the sitting position. With the food concealed in your right hand, hold it at your Aussie's nose. Speak your Aussie's name, followed by the command, "Sit." Move your hand, concealing the treat, up and back over his head toward his rear end. As he raises his head to follow the treat over the top of his head, tuck his hind legs under his body by placing your other hand just above his hocks. There is no opportunity for your Aussie to resist. It is very similar to sweeping a human's legs out from underneath him by bumping him behind the knees. Once your Aussie is sitting, open your closed fist to reveal the reward.

You also can teach the sit while your dog is at your side. Place your right hand on his collar. Place your left hand with your thumb on one side and your fingers on the other side of his loin. Speak your Aussie's name, followed by the command, "Sit." With your right hand, pull your Aussie's collar toward his back. At the same time (in one continuous action), your left hand can place gentle pressure on his loin to get him into a sitting position. Once he sits, reward him without delay. Always give your Aussie an incentive to work.

Down

A treat can be used to lead your Aussie into a down position. With the treat concealed in your right hand and held at your dog's nose, speak his name followed by the down command. Lower your hand to the ground. As he follows the treat with his nose and extends his head forward, place pressure over his withers (down and forward) with your left hand to guide him into a down position. As soon as he is lying down, open your hand to reward the food.

The down command also can be taught by taking hold of the lead with your right hand next to your dog's collar. Place your left hand over his withers. Speak your Aussie's name, followed by the down command. In one continuous motion, push down and forward with both hands. The lead guides the Aussie while the hand over the withers puts him into the down position. Without delay, reward your Aussie for lying down.

Stand

By applying the above training techniques, you can teach the stand by leading your Aussie out of a sitting or down position with food or a toy. With the food concealed in your right hand, speak your Aussie's name, followed by the stand command. Use the food to lure him forward and upward. Use your left hand to gently tickle under his body to discourage him from sitting back down. Give plenty of praise and the reward.

Teaching the Sit.

Teaching the Down.

Or, take the lead in your right hand and pull forward on his collar. As you pull forward on the collar, use your left hand to tickle under his belly to encourage him to stand. Grooming is a perfect and enjoyable time to practice the stand.

Correcting Problem Behaviors

When problems occur, it is not because your Aussie is a bad dog in need of punishment, it's because he's a good dog with inappropriate behavior. The cause of behavioral problems in Aussies can be physical. Whenever your dog's behavior changes suddenly, have him examined by your veterinarian to rule out physical causes. Some problems occur as a result of training and handling errors. Consult a certified canine behaviorist before little problems become big ones.

Aggression

Canine aggression is a behavior exhibited when a dog postures himself (gets big) as a warning or challenge, when the hair on top of the neck or back stands up (dorsal piloerection), or when the dog growls, barks, nips, snaps, or snarls as a warning to cause the offender to retreat. Being able to recognize different types of aggression and the situations that trigger aggressive behavior is imperative in resolving problem behavior. Dr. John Paul Scott addresses the subject in his book *Aggression*.

Types of Aggression

Trained aggression may occur upon the presentation of the conditioned stimulus if the Aussie has been intentionally or unintentionally trained to respond to that stimulus. A protection Aussie may be trained to bite and hold a suspect if the suspect runs.

Pain-elicited aggression may be directed at any person, animal, or object a split second after the Aussie experiences pain for whatever reason. Aggression caused by pain generally occurs when someone tries to handle an injured Aussie. Pain-elicited aggression also occurs when you severely punish your Aussie. According to Dr. Scott, "since pain itself is a stimulus to fight," physical punishment is a less desirable method of control.

Teaching the Stand.

Aussies can demonstrate aggression from fear. A fear-aggressive Aussie reacts out of self-defense when he is cornered, threatened, or punished, especially if he cannot escape the situation. It can surface while a dog is being handled harshly or when he doesn't understand what his owner wants of him. The Aussie responds by growling, barking, snapping, or biting at the fear-inducing stimulus. Dr. Ian Dunbar, author of *How To Teach A New Dog Old Tricks*, warns that "A fearful dog in the hands of an owner that physically dominates and punishes the dog, gives the dog ample reason to physically protect itself. Physical abuse intimidates and irritates the dog, which understandably becomes more fearful or aggressive toward humans. The family dog needs control and education, not physical trauma."

Maternal aggression occurs when humans or other animals approach the puppies or whelping nest. Females will growl, bark, or bite. False pregnancy can also elicit maternal aggression.

Quick-moving objects that run away when the Aussie approaches (such as bicycle riders, joggers, and automobiles) can trigger predatory aggression. Predatory aggression is the innate tendency to chase or hunt.

Several types of aggression surface between one and three years of age. Aggression between males and females can occur but typically occurs between dogs of the same sex. Aggression between males or between females trying to assert their dominance by establishing a pecking order or fighting over territory is common.

Redirected aggression is aimed at an animal, person, or object other than the stimulus. The Aussie is aggressive toward someone or something other than whom he intended. When a person steps in to prevent or break up a fight, the Aussie might redirect the aggression and attack the person interfering or another dog nearby.

Dominant aggression is directed toward the Aussie's family members and stems from an innate tendency to gain control over every member of his family or pack. The dominant-aggressive Aussie commonly resists being groomed, rolled over, or even petted. If he is disturbed while sleeping or eating, he may become aggressive. This individual often guards his food, his objects, or certain areas. Sometimes (unknowingly), a family member may challenge the Aussie and get bitten. A bite on the face is not uncommon when an owner or other person hugs the dog around the neck if that Aussie has not accepted that person's dominance over him.

Conversely, territorial aggression may occur when a strange person or animal that the Aussie has not accepted as a friend comes near the Aussie's family members or crosses his territory, which might include more than the owner's property.

Unlike dominant aggression, which occurs more commonly with unneutered males, possessive aggression can occur in both neutered and unneutered Aussies. A possessive Aussie that is eating or playing with toys or other objects highly valued by the dog will growl, bark, or snap at approaching humans or animals. Dominant, overprotective, and possessive traits usually develop by three years of age.

Owners can affect the behavior of their Aussies and often contribute to their problems by rewarding them for unwanted behavior. For example, when the Aussie barks or growls at visitors, the owner usually tells the Aussie, "It's okay, Fido." In the Aussie's mind, he is being told that he is doing a good job by protecting and showing aggression. An owner can also give his Aussie the wrong message by making whining sounds that make the Aussie feel that his owner is distressed.

In some families, one member may be the strict disciplinarian and may become overdemanding and physical with the dog. There may come a time when the Aussie reaches his limit and can't take any more pressure, and he may redirect his frustration toward a different member of the family.

In some situations where the Aussie sleeps on the bed with the owner, he gets the idea that the owner is a subordinate member of the pack rather than the leader. Roughhousing, tug-of-war, letting the puppy bite the owner's hands and arms, and being kept on a chain can heighten aggressive tendencies. Other factors, such as organic brain disorder, diet, and health problems, can also contribute to aggressive behavior. When aggression is a problem, you must know how your *Aussie* interprets what he is trying to communicate.

With aggression problems, you must be able to anticipate and avoid situations that provoke problem behavior. You must be able to redirect your Aussie's attention to an acceptable alternative when problems occur, and this can best be accomplished through obedience training. If you have difficulty pinpointing the problem or finding a solution, seek professional advice before the situation gets out of hand.

To avoid aggression problems, keep your Aussie in a dog/child-proof area. Never allow strangers (children, delivery people, meter readers, etc.) access to your Aussie unless you are present to supervise interactions. Do not leave infants or toddlers alone with a dog. Children can unknowingly provoke a dog to bite by pulling the dog's hair and hurting him or playing inappropriately.

When problems occur, consult a canine behaviorist before beginning therapy. In an article titled "Disarming Aggression," Ian Dunbar, Ph.D., a veterinarian and animal behaviorist, recommends two booklets, *Fearfulness* and *Preventing Aggression*, for anti-aggressiveness exercises. The books are available from the Center of Applied Animal Behavior (see Appendix).

Fear of Thunderstorms (Storm Phobia) and Firecrackers

Fear of thunder is common in Aussies, as it is in all breeds of dogs. However, your Aussie can be desensitized to lessen the fear. A cassette tape with a recorded thunderstorm can be played just below the threshold (the level at which your Aussie would become upset). Play the tape at a low level, and build up the level on a daily basis over a period of weeks. When you introduce the sound of thunder during play, you can preoccupy your Aussie with a favorite toy or activity and gradually increase the fear-producing stimulus.

Avoid encouraging fearful behavior by petting and coddling your Aussie. Immediately after conditioning, feed your dog. This way, he will associate the sounds of the thunderstorm with being fed.

Fear of firecrackers is as common as fear of thunder. With firecrackers, it is beneficial to have an assistant. A training pistol that fires blanks can be substituted for firecrackers. However, because firecrackers and pistols have no volume control, the assistant must discharge the stimulus from a distance far enough away so as not to startle your Aussie. If your dog becomes inhibited while engaged in a favorite activity or play, the assistant is too close and should move even farther away to a distance at which your Aussie displays no sensitivity. With each session, over many weeks, the assistant gradually moves closer until your Aussie is not bothered or affected. Avoid this type of conditioning during critical developmental stages. If the stress of loud or startling noises triggers aggressive behavior, contain him in a crate in a quiet room or other secure area until he calms down. If necessary, contact a professional trainer for assistance.

Jumping Up

Never invite your Aussie to jump up on you to receive praise, and never pet him when he does jump up. Your Aussie cannot tell the difference between your old clothes and your Sunday best. The worst problem with jumping up is that company will usually violate your training by letting your dog climb in their lap or by inviting him to jump up.

Each and every time your Aussie does jump up, draw your knee up into his chest with a vocal correction and command, "Ah, ah," "Off," or "No, off." If that is ineffective, put on his collar and leash and give him a collar correction backward and down when you draw your knee up into his chest. Then give him lots of praise. After several times, he may hesitantly approach you. Pet him and give him lots of attention when he is sitting or standing in front of you. Whenever company arrives, put on his collar. Whenever he attempts to jump up on strangers, give him a hefty collar correction backward and down, accompanied with vocal disapproval. When he responds, praise him lavishly.

Obedience will further develop the bond between you and your Aussie, which will help you gain reliable control over him. Enroll in an Obedience class. The contact with other people and dogs will be ideal. It's an opportunity to socialize as well as teach your dog under the professional guidance of an experienced trainer or handler. It is most beneficial for you to learn to train and handle your own Aussie rather than have someone else do the training.

Destructive Chewing

Most destructive chewing behavior is caused by separation anxiety. Aussies usually chew on objects because they are bored and lonely or are teething.

Don't correct your Aussie unless you catch him in the act. His memory is short, and he probably won't relate the punishment to the damage. If you catch him in the act of chewing a forbidden object, scold him with a sharp "Ah ah" or "No," then divert his attention by removing the forbidden object or taking him away from the scene of the crime and giving him an appropriate chew toy. Show him affection, and praise him for chewing on the right item. It may be helpful to paint the furniture legs with an unpleasant-tasting substance such as Bitter Apple or an extra-dry unscented antiperspirant for the times when you are unable to supervise.

Daily exercise and play are necessary to burn off pent-up energy and alleviate boredom.

Barking or Howling

An Aussie will bark to protect his property and to relieve boredom and anxiety, and he will bark or howl to object to being confined and to indicate physical needs for food and water or to relieve himself. Make sure that your dog has adequate food and water. When was the last time you let him out to do his business?

Once you've seen to his basic needs, there may be other reasons for barking. Separation training is necessary to condition your Aussie to your absence. Short sessions with unemotional and uneventful returns, combined with regular exercise and play and Obedience training, will produce satisfying results.

Territorial barking can be minimized by not putting your Aussie in a situation where he is likely to protest (such as behind a fence or window) when people and animals passing by are perceived as intruders.

A water pistol filled with a mild vinegar solution (eight ounces water with two ounces vinegar) can be beneficial to interrupt indiscriminant barking. When your Aussie is barking inappropriately you can squirt the solution at his mouth, while at the same time telling him, "That's enough." The solution is unpleasant tasting, but harmless.

Peter Bloeme, Director of the Friskies Canine Frisbee Championships, and his Aussie "Magic." Magic and Peter perform at major sporting events around the country and overseas. Courtesy Friskies PetCare Company.

Chapter 17

FUN ACTIVITIES FOR YOU AND YOUR AUSSIE

AUSSIES ARE ACTIVE, FUN-LOVING DOGS. They love being with you and doing things together with you. The Australian Shepherd is the perfect breed for the family or person who enjoys lively outdoor activities and competitive events. Competitive events include Conformation shows, Obedience trials, Herding/Stock-dog trials, Frisbee contests, and Agility trials for adult and Junior Handlers. Noncompetitive tests include Tracking and the Canine Good Citizen (CGC) program.

CANINE GOOD CITIZEN TEST

A Canine Good Citizen (CGC) makes his owner happy without making anyone else unhappy. The CGC program promotes the training and care necessary to properly integrate dogs into society. It rewards responsible dog ownership. The program is not limited to AKC purebred Aussies, but also allows unregistered and mixed-breed dogs to gain certification.

The Canine Good Citizen program involves a noncompetitive, ten-part (pass or fail) test that evaluates the Aussie's behavior in practical situations at home, in public, and in the presence of unfamiliar people and other dogs. The exercises test the Aussie's reaction to distractions and supervised isolation. Aussies must demonstrate sociability, accept a friendly stranger, sit for petting, walk on a loose leash, walk through a crowd, and respond to basic obedience commands (sit, down, and stay). CGC Aussies must also be groomed and have current rabies shots.

Local dog-training clubs and dog trainers offer the test. After successfully completing the test, your Aussie is awarded a certificate stating that he is a Canine Good Citizen. For more information, contact the AKC.

FRISBEE[1]

Perhaps you have been fortunate enough to see one of the Come 'N Get It Canine Frisbee Championships cosponsored by participating park and recreation departments, the Carnation Company, and the Wham-O Manufacturing Company. These contests are held throughout the country at the community level, at regional finals, and at a climaxing world finals championship.

There is no entry fee, and all materials are provided for competitors without charge. At community finals, each Aussie gets to perform individually in a basic throw-and-catch competition, a freestyle segment, or both. At regional finals, the freestyle is performed exclusively for a ninety-second duration. Both regional champions and runners-up receive an all-expense-paid trip to the world finals, which includes food and lodging for you and your Aussie.

Even if you are not interested in Frisbee as a competitive sport, this game is a lot of fun and is good exercise for both you and your Aussie. The following text is based largely on Alex Stein's widely emulated training regimen for three-time World Champion Ashley Whippet, plus valuable input from Eldon McIntire, owner and trainer of the famous Hyper Hank, world-class Frisbee disk star, and Peter Bloeme, owner and trainer of the 1984 World Champion, Whirlin' Wizard.

Before you start training, check with your veterinarian to make sure that there are no physical problems that would affect your dog's ability to leap for the disc. Always conduct training sessions in a safe area on a grassy site. Running on asphalt or concrete is harmful to the pads of your Aussie's feet. Work in a safe area away from the street so as to avoid passing cars or bicycles that can injure your pet.

Don't be impatient to see positive results. Let your Aussie warm up slowly like any good athlete before a workout. Stop if your Aussie becomes overtired or bored with the game. Don't forget that this can be a strenuous activity. Keep workouts short at first. To keep your Aussie at peak enthusiasm, do not repeat the exercises more than two or three times a day. Especially during hot weather, take it easy. A wet towel on your Aussie's back helps cool him down.

Take clean, fresh water with you to refresh your Aussie if he gets thirsty. Only give your Aussie small quantities of water for the first half hour after the training session. Wait until he stops panting heavily before you give him the water. (See Emergency First Aid for heat-stress problems.) It is a good idea to feed your Aussie after a training session, allowing a half hour before feeding.

Ashley's Proven Five-Point Training Program

Familiarization With Disc
The first thing to do is establish in your Aussie's mind that the disc is a friendly object, like you would with a ball. As a puppy, Ashley was fed his water and dog food out of a Frisbee disc. Then when his owner, Alex Stein, slid the empty disc across the floor, Ashley pursued it to make sure that it was there for his next meal. Before you attempt any effort at play with your Aussie and the disc, make sure that your Aussie knows that the disc is his or her "sports toy."

Basic On-the-Ground Training
While the goal should be getting your Aussie to leap skyward in pursuit of the disc, first things

---

[1] By Irv Lander.

The dynamic duo, Bert Eliason and Las Rocosa Jessica Jazz, qualified for the World Finals by winning the Northwest Regional Competition three years in a row. Photo by Chris Pietsch.

first. You want to begin training the way Ashley did on the way to becoming a three-time World Champion.

Start your Aussie off with tug-of-war play. Let your Aussie get a good grip on the disc. After about fifteen or twenty seconds, release your own grip so that your Aussie can feel triumphant about taking his disc away from you. Do not let your Aussie chew on the disc. Repeat this tug-of-war play often, but stop before your Aussie wants to stop.

Focusing on the Disc

A good way to teach your Aussie to focus on the disc is by playing keep away five to ten yards apart with a friend, while your Aussie watches. When he shows interest in joining in the play, float the throws and let him intercept it frequently. After awhile, your Aussie will become your full-time catching partner—but don't expect him to throw it back to you.

Introducing Motion

Roll the disc on its edge in plain sight of your Aussie so that he has eye contact and can chase and catch up with the disc. This is sheer fun for your Aussie and helps in the familiarization process and the desire to retrieve the disc in motion. Even if your Aussie doesn't grab the disc while it's rolling, praise him and keep trying until he scoops it up consistently. Make your roller throws short at first, and gradually lengthen them as your Aussie becomes more proficient.

Bringing the Disc Back

This can be difficult at first, but be patient, because it is so much more gratifying if your Aussie acquires this habit. You can help by going to meet him when he catches up with the disc, taking the disc from his mouth, and praising him. Then, go back to where you started and repeat the exercise. If your Aussie is trained to come on command, this exercise will be that much easier. Just make sure that your Aussie brings the retrieved disc along. Jeff Gabel, owner and trainer of two-time World Champion "Casey," taught his great dog to bring back the disc by tying a long rope to his collar and pulling it gently but firmly toward him until Casey got the message to consistently fetch the disc back on his own. Each time Casey did this correctly, Jeff praised his dog. Repetition and praise helped a great deal in forming Casey's good habits.

Midair Catches

This is the ultimate joy and exhilaration for both Aussie and trainer in disc play. The key is patience, patience, patience. Ashley was taught to leap up and take the disc out of Alex's hand, starting slowly, with progressively higher levels. Then, and only then, did his trainer throw the disc a short distance away so that Ashley could pursue it and soar skyward to catch it before it hit the ground. Praise profusely for successful efforts.

Three-time World qualifier Paul Gebauer of Anchorage, Alaska, found his Aussie "Jaeger" in a newspaper ad. He trained him to catch a Frisbee disc and the rest is history. Courtesy Friskies PetCare Company.

Never scold your Aussie for failure to catch the disc. Always make sure that your Aussie has eye contact with you and with the disc before you release it. Some people forget that the dog must have eye contact with the disc, and they throw the disc too far at first. Success breeds success. It is very important to remember that disc sport is a team effort, and each member of the team has to know his role.

Establishing a Routine

Once your Aussie has learned to catch the disc and can make midair catches, you may wish to establish a routine for both exercise and possible competition. This involves the use of more than one disc thrown sequentially, trick catches, and stunts, such as leaping over the thrower's back to snatch the disc in flight. Your best bet for learning some of these advanced maneuvers and incorporating them into a routine for your Aussie is to attend some of the Come 'N Get It contests. Even if you do not compete, this will give you an opportunity to observe how other teams go about it.

Frisbee Throwing Tips[2]

Since most experts agree that improving your throwing skills will greatly enhance your Aussie's catching proficiency, his enthusiasm, and his enjoyment of disc play, these throwing tips can be most helpful, particularly for beginners or the inexperienced.

Proper Grip

The proper grip is as important in disc sport as it is in golf, for instance. In the basic grip, preferred by most players and owners of disc-catching Aussies, one places the thumb on top and the forefinger along the rim, while the other fingers are curled on the underside of the disc. The disc is held in this grip firmly but not tightly. Through constant practice, the basic grip should become second nature to you, and you won't consciously have to think about it when throwing the disc.

As you progress in your skill level, the power grip is recommended. Make a fist with your palm up, open your thumb to the "hitchhiking" position, loosen your fingers just enough to slip the disk between your palm and fingertips, and place your thumb down on top—just like you would hold a fan. This may feel awkward at first. Now bring your other hand up and hold the far side of the disc temporarily. With your gripping hand, move your bottom fingers slightly toward your thumb (while trying to maintain as much contact as possible with the inside/underneath rim) until

[2] By Peter Bloeme.

they feel relatively comfortable. Once mastered, this grip is good for accuracy and best for distance, and it helps you cope with heavier wind conditions.

The Backhand Throw

This is the most versatile and easy-to-learn method of throwing the disc. Once mastered, it is good for accuracy and distance.

The Stance: Stand sideways with your right foot forward. Your feet should be shoulder width apart, with your knees slightly bent and parallel to each other. Your leading shoulder should point toward the target. The throwing motion should be left to right, smooth and even, with a good wrist snap upon release. Your arm should be bent slightly, your wrist cocked backward, and the disc held horizontal to the ground. Do not rotate your wrist side to side, only front and back. Follow through with your right hand pointing at your target (reverse if you are left handed). Keep your eyes forward. Start the throwing motion with two-thirds of your weight on your back foot. As you bring your arm and wrist forward, shift most of your weight to your front foot. Don't lift your back foot off the ground, as it will cause you to lunge forward. Always keep some weight on each foot. If your throw veers to the left of the target, you've released the disc too soon. If it veers to the right, you've released the disc too late. If the disc wobbles, check your grip, speed up your delivery, and concentrate on keeping the disc level from beginning to end. Increase your throwing distance only as your skill increases.

Overall

The most important rule to remember when starting out, or as you progress, is to keep the disc's flight as flat as possible. The disc will react differently if it is released with the nose (front) pointed up or down, or if it is angled to either side. Always try to throw across the wind instead of upwind or downwind. When practicing with your Aussie, work at short range—ten- to fifteen-yard throws that are between the waist and shoulder in height. You want to be able to make smooth, level, and accurate throws. Increasing the distance of your throws before mastering the basic fundamentals is not recommended.

TRACKING

Tracking with Australian Shepherds is one of the most exciting and enjoyable experiences imaginable. As with Obedience and stock work, it is a team effort, except that in Tracking, the Aussie knows far more than the handler.

In Tracking, your Aussie learns to follow the scent of something or someone often unknown to him. He must be trained to work under all weather conditions and in all kinds of terrain. When your Aussie has been trained, you depend solely on his ability to discern the correct track. You therefore need to be able to "read" your dog to determine when he is "on."

Any Aussie of any age can be encouraged to track. The Australian Shepherd is superior when it comes to tracking. His inborn abilities enable him to excel in practical situations as well as competitively. Tracking is unique in that no Obedience is required or employed. Tracking is totally an incentive/reward association for the Aussie.

Tracking tests are designed to accredit an Aussie's ability to work under a variety of scenting conditions. First, however, the dog must be certified by a licensed Tracking judge to determine whether or not the dog is qualified to compete. Tracking judges must be thoroughly familiar with the various conditions that may exist when a dog is required to work a scent trail. The actual Tracking test is somewhat more difficult than the preliminary certification. Once an Aussie has passed an accredited Tracking test, the letters "TD" follow his name. If the Aussie already has a UD (Utility Dog title), the letter "T" is added, "UDT."

UCD Rowdy's High Caliber Scraps WH, BH, SCHH, CDX "on the track" with handler/owner Sue Mikes. Courtesy Sue Mikes.

Once an Aussie has earned a TD, he can work toward the Tracking Dog Excellent, in which the degree of difficulty is increased. In the first test for the TD, the track is between 440 and 500 yards on a trail that is between one-half hour to two hours old. It also involves turns (changes of direction). The Tracking Dog Excellent test is laid out between 800 and 1,000 yards on a trail that follows a scent that is between three and five hours old, with newer, distracting tracks somewhere in between. A dog that passes this test may use "TDX" behind his name. The UDT title becomes "UDTX."

Beginning Tracking Training[3]

Aussies can be started on Tracking at a very young age—six to seven weeks if possible. Beginning with the puppy on a nonrestrictive harness, one person hides behind a tree or any other barrier that conceals him, about twenty-five feet away. The puppy should see him leave. The person calls to the pup but stays hidden. Most pups will "air scent" at first, but with practice, that little nose soon scoots right along the ground. When the person is "located," a *big* fuss should be made over the puppy!

Start early to use certain words such as "find it" or "track it," and as the pup progresses, start pulling back just a bit so that he has to drive into the harness. He should get used to pulling strongly.

An older Aussie can be started without the benefit of puppy training. Use a toy or other favorite object. The track layer dangles the object enticingly above the Aussie's head, while the handler holds on tightly to the lead. The Aussie should be wearing a nonrestrictive harness. The track layer walks off in a straight line away from the Aussie, about twenty-five feet. Calling the Aussie's name to attract his attention, he drops the article about eighteen inches away from his body and to the side so that the Aussie sees it fall. He then moves away from the article. The handler points to the ground to get the Aussie's attention and draw it to the spot where the article has been dropped. Again, make a big fuss—throw the article in the air to get the dog excited. Not too much encouragement is needed to put Aussies on a Tracking high! Lay two to five tracks a day, always in a fresh and unused area. If the Aussie gets tired or bored, *quit*. This is a fun sport, and there is no way anyone can *force* that nose to quiver along the ground unless the dog enjoys what he is doing. Training for Tracking is entirely motivational and positive.

[3] By Rose Spicuzza.

Over the course of two to three weeks, make the tracks longer, add a corner or two, then "age" the tracks gradually up to an hour or so before running them. Do this until the Aussie is tracking over 600 to 800 yards in length on an hour-old track with four or five corners. Now you are ready to try for your "T."

AGILITY

Agility tests an Aussie's control, desire, and athletic ability at three levels of difficulty. There are basically two different styles of Agility—the International style (originating in Britain) and the National Club for Dog Agility (NCDA) or Kramer style. The International style emphasizes speed. The Kramer style does not place as much emphasis on speed, and the obstacles are slightly smaller (not as high or as long) than the obstacles used on International courses. Kramer also includes several obstacles not included in International competition, such as the sway bridge, the slide, and the crawl tunnel.

The ASCA Agility program is based on the North American Dog Agility Council (NADAC) rules and regulations, which are patterned after the International style of Agility competitions. The UKC adopted the NCDA rules and regulations. AKC Agility events combine elements from both the International and Kramer styles of Agility.

Aussies fall into two categories for jump heights: Aussies up to twenty-one inches (and over sixteen inches) jump twenty-four-inch-high hurdles (the most competitive division), while any Aussie over twenty-one inches competes in the thirty-inch division.

Beginning Agility Training[4]

Agility training first and foremost should be fun for the dog and the handler. There is no place in Agility training for heavy-handed training methods. Peter Lewis, one of the pioneer Agility trainers from England, emphasizes in his video *Training the Agility Dog* that Agility can be taught completely using play. Before Agility training begins, it is important that the dog be under some reasonable level of control. At a minimum, the dog should be able to walk at heel, sit, down, wait, and recall, and it is better if the dog performs these commands off lead. It is not important that the dog perform these exercises with the precision expected in Obedience competition, but good (and fast) compliance is important. Since you are going to use play as the strong motivator, an interest in retrieving toys is also useful, and the use of treats can be effectively utilized. An Aussie that gets excited about retrieving a tennis ball is good Agility dog material. It is important that the Aussie return the toy to you, because you don't want to spend all of your time trying to get it back.

Weave Poles

I have often stated that if I had the choice of only one obstacle to train with, it would be a set of weave poles. Notice I use the singular, since I believe that the weave poles should be perceived as a single obstacle rather than a series of single poles. Most dogs at the national championships can negotiate a set of ten poles in a time of two to four seconds, some even much faster than is possible to command the dog on individual poles.

There are a number of ways to put together a set of cheap practice weave poles. One of the easiest ways is to buy ten-foot sections of three-fourths-inch PVC pipe and cut each section into three poles, each forty inches long. You will need a total of ten to twelve poles. These poles can then be slipped over electric fence posts stuck in the ground about twenty inches apart to form a line of weave poles.

There are a number of methods that can be used to start the dog on the weave poles. I strongly recommend the "wire and channel" method that Peter Lewis describes in detail in his

[4] By Kent I. Mahan.

Mahan's Red Bandit CDX, AD. Courtesy Ken Mahan.

video. In this method, the weave poles are offset for the beginning dog as much as eighteen or twenty-four inches, with the poles on either side of the "channel" being about forty inches apart. Each side of the channel created by this offset is connected by wires, as shown in the diagram below. Note that as the Aussie enters the wired

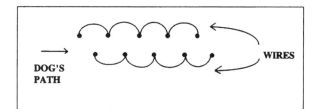

channel, the first pole is to his left and the second pole is to his right. This trains the Aussie for proper entry by International rules that are followed by the North American Dog Agility Council (NADAC), the United States Dog Agility Association (USDAA), the Canadian Dog Agility Council (CDAC), and other international bodies that state that the dog must enter between the first and second poles from the right to left. In the diagram, ten poles are used. You could begin with six or eight, but use an even number so that correct entry will be made from either end of the channel during your practice sessions.

Begin training by walking the Aussie down the channel, on lead, giving him a command you plan to use for the weave poles, such as "poles" or "weave." Do this many times over a period of days or weeks, because it is very important that the Aussie become comfortable with the constriction imposed by the wires. After a period of time, the Aussie can then be placed in a sit or down between the first pole (on his left) and the second pole (on his right).

The handler will then back off to the end of the poles and call the dog through the channel. After this is done many times, the handler can send the Aussie, tossing a toy as the Aussie exits the channel to generate enthusiasm and condition the Aussie to look ahead when he gets to the end of the channel. The handler can also run with the dog on the right and left sides of the channel and work on the dog entering the poles at various angles.

When the Aussie can do all items well over a period of weeks, it is time to narrow the channel from, say, eighteen inches to twelve inches and begin the sequence of training just described all over again over an additional period of weeks. This cycle continues until eventually the channel is narrowed to the point where the Aussie actually begins to weave and ultimately the poles are in a straight line.

Once the Aussie is negotiating the poles in a straight line, begin removing wires from the middle of the channel, and repeat the cycle of training until the wires can be removed completely. If at some point the dog starts missing poles or jumping out of the channel, widen the channel again a little and repeat the cycle. It appears to be those last two or three inches of offset that take the dogs the longest to overcome. Usually the channel is three to six inches wide at a point where the dog first starts to weave, and at this point you may have to narrow the offset no more than one-half inch at a time.

It has been my observation that the weave poles are usually the last obstacles mastered by most Agility dogs and are usually the obstacles that keep the dogs out of competition the longest. Because of this, and because of the fact that there is little chance of injury with the weave-pole training method just described, I decided to train an Aussie pup on the weave poles starting at about four months of age. By about six and one-half months of age, he had graduated to a regular game using a variety of toys and treats for motivation and producing a near-weave-pole "frenzy" during the training sessions. Teaching the weave poles requires patience and a willingness to work with the dog at least three to four times a week, if not every day. And remember, if the Aussie makes a mistake, don't give him a negative like "No!" Just withhold praise or give him a mild reprimand like "Ahh" and make him do it over until he gets it right. When he does it right, heap all the enthusiastic praise on your Aussie that you can muster.

Tunnels

Tunnels are perhaps the easiest obstacles to teach. Generally, after one or two times through the open tunnel, the dogs just love it and become tunnel happy. Begin by shortening the open tunnel to about five feet and have the handler go to the opposite end while the dog is held

Having fun with Obedience.

by a second individual. The handler then calls the Aussie through the tunnel using a command that the Aussie is familiar with, such as "come" and a command that you plan to use for the tunnel, such as "tunnel" or "through." If the dog is a large adult Aussie, he may want to look around or over the tunnel rather than through the tunnel at the handler. In this case, the helper may want to push the head of the dog down so that he can see the handler through the tunnel. If the Aussie still resists, then a gentle shove and/or pull on the lead will help get him through. Generally, once or twice through in this manner and you can't keep the Aussie out of the tunnel.

Once the Aussie is going through on his own, gradually lengthen the tunnel and then put a bend into it so that the Aussie can't see the handler. Then walk or run with the Aussie as you send him through, tossing a toy to retrieve as the dog emerges through the tunnel. Remember to give your command for the tunnel each time and lots of praise when the Aussie goes through.

The procedure for the collapsed tunnel is the same, except that the handler must pick up the chute and look at the Aussie through it, then call the Aussie through with the chute held up. After two or three times, the handler calls the Aussie through again, and as the Aussie passes into the chute, the handler lowers it so that it just rubs the Aussie's back as he passes through. The chute is lowered a little each time until the Aussie is pushing through on his own. Remember to give lavish praise and/or a toy reward as the Aussie exits from the tunnel. Once the Aussie is pushing through on his own, run with him and send him through the tunnel. It usually only takes one session to teach the tunnels unless the Aussie is extremely timid.

Contact Obstacles

There are three types of contact obstacles that are normally used in all Agility competitions—the A-frame, the dog walk, and the see-saw. In training the contacts, you must first select a command for each of these obstacles. Some people choose a single command for all three obstacles; however, I prefer a separate command for each—"Walk" or "Walk it" for the dog walk, "Teeter" for the see-saw, and "Scramble" for the A-frame. What you use is not important, but it *is* important that you stick with what you use. Keep the command short and simple so that the Aussie will eventually understand and respond immediately.

The key to training the contacts is for the dog to have confidence in scaling the obstacle and for him to hit the contact zones. Normally, training is started on lead, in order to control the Aussie so that he hits the contact zones from the very beginning of his training. Contact training for Aussies usually begins with the A-frame lowered to a training height of about four feet. This gives the larger dogs a wide base on which to work and gain confidence. Simply walk the Aussie over the A-frame on lead, giving the command that you have chosen and lots of encouragement and praise. Be sure that the Aussie hits the contact zones on both the up and down ramps. Once the Aussie is going over the lowered A-frame well, gradually increase the height.

Puppies may be started on the dog walk. It is important that the puppy *does not fall*. Use a spotter on the opposite side of the walk so that someone is situated on both sides to catch the puppy if he falls or jumps off. If possible, begin on a dog walk with low sawhorses for safety and control. Walk the Aussie over on a lead, giving the command that you have chosen, and make sure that the Aussie hits the contact zones on both ends. If you look at the dog walk or A-frame from the Aussie's level, it appears to be a ramp to nowhere, and in many cases this makes the dog hesitant. In this case, lift the Aussie onto the bridge section next to one of the down ramps, and walk him down the ramp. Repeatedly move the Aussie further back down the ramp until he is going the full length of the bridge section next to one of the down ramps. Then walk the Aussie down the ramp. Next, try the up ramp and across and down. This is difficult if you have a large, heavy-boned Aussie, in which case you may want to detach the ramp from the dog walk

Fun Activities For You and Your Aussie

To teach your dog to slide, you must first teach him by your side, with the first lessons in your lap. This way you will be security for him, and you can prevent him from jumping. Never allow your dog to jump from a slide. The slide should have a "slow" surface so that your dog can maintain his balance, and the grade should be moderate to prevent injury.

and place it on the pause table at eighteen or twenty-four inches and have the Aussie walk down. Don't forget the command for the obstacle and praise for the dog.

Once the dog walk is mastered, teach the see-saw. By this time, the Aussie can scale the ramp and must be taught to hesitate just beyond the pivot point to give the see-saw time to deflect. Give the Aussie the command for the see-saw, and walk him up the ramp on lead. Just when the teeter begins to deflect, make the dog wait and catch the ramp as it comes down. Gently lower it to the ground so that it does not slam down as the dog comes down the ramp. Make sure that the dog hits the contact zones at each end and does not leave the see-saw until the ramp contacts the ground. Repeat catching the ramp until the Aussie shows confidence, then let the ramp come down harder a little at a time. Don't forget to praise the dog!

Hurdles

The key to teaching hurdles is to start with the hurdle low and to not move the jump height too fast. With puppies, start low and stay low until they have a chance to mature physically.

The easiest way to teach the hurdles is to get a long lead, put the dog in a sit-stay, and step over the hurdle, calling the Aussie across with an appropriate command such as "Over" or "Up." Once the Aussie is jumping the hurdle, try running with him on lead over the hurdle, again keeping the jump height low. Once the Aussie is going over on lead, try the exercise off lead.

The hurdles are the simplest and best obstacles to use in introducing the Aussie to a series of obstacles. Start by putting the dog over a single hurdle and throwing a toy in front of him as he comes over the bar. This conditions the dog to look ahead. Then try two hurdles in sequence, throwing the toy after the second. Finally, go to three hurdles, throwing the toy after the third. Remember—you only want the Aussie doing obstacles on command. Therefore, once you get the dog sequencing three jumps, try calling him away from the second or third to make sure that he is under your control. This is where your recall training comes into play. You may have to go back on lead if the Aussie is not responding.

Tire

The tire is rated by Peter Lewis as the second most difficult obstacle next to the weave poles, because many dogs want to go under or around the tire. Select a command like "Tire" and lower the tire nearly to the ground so that the dog cannot go underneath. Put the dog in a sit and pass the lead through the tire. Call the dog through as in the case of the hurdle. Once the Aussie can be called through reliably, try running with him as you send him through the tire. Do not raise the tire until you can send the Aussie through with both you and the dog on the run. Raise the tire only a few inches at a time.

Pause Table

Under International rules, a dog is required to mount the pause table and do a five-second down. You should not teach the down on the pause table. Rather, teach the down like it is normally taught in Obedience before you make the dog down on the table. You can then teach the dog to mount the table using an appropriate command such as "Table." Some people like to teach an automatic down on the table in which the table command means to mount the table and do an instant down.

In discussing beginning training, the commands that have been emphasized are commands for the obstacles such as "Over," "Tunnel," "Teeter," "Weave," etc. In addition to obstacle commands, directional commands must be used to maintain control on the Agility course. Most people use hand signals along with voice commands such as "Come" or "Come in," "Go out," "Right," "Left," "Turn," etc., to maintain directional control while running the Agility course.

Course Handling

Sharon Nelson has spent hundreds of hours watching video tapes of Agility dogs in competition in search of reasons why mistakes are made on the course. In the vast majority of cases, she finds that course errors, particularly refusals and off-course errors, are the result of improper positioning of the handler.

Many handlers overly rely on voice commands to direct the dog through the Agility course. Sharon finds that body language, including positioning and hand signals, is the most important factor in directing the Aussie through the Agility course. Most often, the handler will want to either send the Aussie away to an obstacle or call the dog in or toward the handler to position for the next obstacle. Usually it is more natural for the dog to come toward the handler, rather than to move away from the handler. The handler's body becomes, in effect, a magnet for the dog. It is a good strategy to position yourself so that you can bring the dog toward you to prepare for the next obstacle. It is important to position yourself early for the next obstacle as well as to give an appropriate voice command and/or hand signal for the next obstacle.

As soon as the dog commits to an obstacle, you should be getting into position for the next. For example, if the dog must take a hurdle and make a sharp left turn for the next obstacle on the course, the handler should position himself on the Aussie's left, facing the next obstacle as soon as the Aussie is in the air over the hurdle. Simultaneously, the handler should be giving the commands for the dog to turn toward him.

Usually I run into the biggest problem if the Aussie gets too far in front of me where he cannot see the direction that I am turning. There are situations where you must send the Aussie away. It is important, therefore, to teach the Aussie to "Get out" or "Go out." The context of this command is that the distance between the handler and the Aussie is going to increase, which means that the Aussie moves away from the handler or the handler moves away from the Aussie.

A good exercise for teaching the go out command is to set up four or five hurdles so that they are facing the same direction but are offset by a few feet in such a way that if the handler starts the first hurdle and runs a straight line, the hurdles will progressively get farther away from the handler, as will the dog as he runs the hurdles. Give the Aussie a get out command before each hurdle after he has completed the first. If the

Illustration by Trish Thornwald.

Aussie seems unsure, step toward him and swing your arm toward him with each command.

Eventually, the Aussie should be able to do all of the hurdles even though you are running a straight line and the Aussie is angling away from you. I find that the get out command is particularly useful in obstacle discrimination. One of the frequent challenges on today's course is the tunnel placed next to and under the ramp of the dog walk or A-frame. In the example below, the handler should be on the Aussie's left side to be in proper position as the Aussie exits the tunnel. When the Aussie completes the hurdle, a get out command and tunnel command while the handler steps toward the dog should send the Aussie far enough out to push him into the tunnel and avoid the ramp of the dog walk. On the other hand, if the handler moves away from the Aussie and gives a come or here command along with the walk command, this should pull the Aussie away from the tunnel and up to the ramp of the dog walk.

In summary, let me reiterate that there are two types of commands—commands for control and directions, and commands for individual obstacles. Do not rely on commands for individual obstacles exclusively. Work on those direction and control commands, and remember to not be too hard on the Aussie if he makes a mistake. The mistake was probably yours.

OTHER ACTIVITIES

There are a multitude of other, noncompetitive activities in which you and your Aussie can participate. If you enjoy hiking, teach your dog to carry a backpack and take him with you in approved areas. If you want to donate your time and your Aussie's love to a good social cause, enroll in a program for Therapy Dog training. You'll be rewarded richly in the personal satisfaction that you get from seeing a handicapped or elderly person respond to your dog. More active owners may enjoy participating in search-and-rescue teams. Young people can enroll in 4-H or Junior Handling programs and competitions. The possibilities are almost endless. Don't just "own" an Aussie—get out and enjoy working and playing with him.

Aussies are a close-working, authoritative breed. Heavy (sticky) sheep and large range flocks require a closer working distance between themselves and the dog in order to make them move.
Ch. Las Rocosa Little Wolf STD CD.

Chapter 18

BORN TO WORK

HERDING INSTINCTS

The instinct to herd is innate in Aussies whose ancestors were cultivated for their working abilities. Herding is the primary instinct necessary in developing an effective stock dog. Herding is the natural inclination of an Aussie to keep livestock bunched in a group. When one head of livestock breaks away from the group, it is the *heading instinct* that compels the Aussie to run to the front or head of a runaway and block it from escaping. Without supervision and training, some Aussies may demonstrate tendencies to head, then rehead the escapee, preventing it from returning to the herd or flock. A *driving dog*, whose natural inclination is to stay behind the livestock, working the flanks to keep the bunch grouped, won't naturally race to the head of escaping stock. The *heeling instinct* gives the dog the ability to nip or *grip* the heels (or front legs) of a maverick and convince it to return to the rest of the group.

Just because the dog has heeling instinct, do not assume that he has a lot of force or power. Sometimes an Aussie bites out of lack of confidence. Force or power is evident in an Aussie that takes a deliberate approach to handling livestock. Biting or gripping is important in handling obstinate livestock, but it is not effective unless it is backed by confidence. Power can be developed in an Aussie through proper handling. Never put your Aussie into any situation that he is not mentally or physically ready to handle.

By the same token, *barking* may or may not be a sign of a lack of confidence. Young or inexperienced Aussies may bark when they are in a challenging situation. With some Aussies, a well-placed bark or growl is the most effective and natural tendency when forcing difficult, heavy stock or in turning a bunch of runaway cattle.

Eye is another inherited trait, recognized by the puppy's gaze or fixed stare. Eye is a form of concentration that develops steadiness in the Aussie. Too much eye, however, causes the Aussie to be sticky, with so much hesitation in his approach that it lacks power.

The ideal Aussie has a good balance of the above instincts combined with *trainability*, which encompasses the "want-to-please" attitude.

Frequently, young puppies from working lines will attempt to herd animals and even their littermates. It is important to choose a herding Aussie by considering what kind of stock the dog will be working. Some Aussies bred for handling cattle may be too rough to adapt easily to herding sheep. Conversely, many sheep dogs may not have the grit or power necessary to handle cattle or hogs. Some Aussies, however, are versatile and can work more than one class of stock effectively. Remember to select a puppy from good working stock whose ancestors were top-notch performers in herding, not ancestors that were pets or show dogs.

Evaluating a Litter

A puppy that is being selected for use in herding work must be evaluated on his own merits as well as on those of his ancestors. Perhaps the best indicators of the kind of Aussie he will grow into are the traits of his parents and grandparents. Evaluation can be achieved by examining pedigrees for working-quality bloodlines. In addition, look carefully at the puppy. A number of traits can be observed that will help predict the puppy's stock-dog potential.

When a puppy is about seven weeks old, you can begin to assess the strengths and weaknesses of a litter. One of the first tests evaluates the social attractiveness that the pup has for people. The test involves observing how eagerly and readily the pup follows a person who is walking away from him. The pup's enthusiasm to follow predicts his future willingness and desire to please his trainer.

One of the best predictors of success is the young Aussie's desire to retrieve an object. If the pup readily and repeatedly chases the object and brings it back or chases it and carries it off, he has good drive or desire and has a high probability of success.

The last test assesses the dominance of the pup. For herding, it is important to have a "middle-of-the-road" dog—one that is neither too submissive nor too dominant. To evaluate dominance, the pup is rolled over on his back and held in this position for approximately thirty seconds. The ideal puppy struggles to get up but does not become frantic or overly aggressive.

In all of these tests, the pups should be evaluated in an environment new to the litter. It is important to see the puppy under the mild stress of a new place, because this will give a clearer indication of the puppy's character and confidence level.

Standing "Eye." Loida's Just Plain Charlie OTD-sc ATD-d demonstrating the intense eye characteristic of his working style. Courtesy Loida.

Puppies should be allowed to be around livestock as youngsters but never should be left unattended, even as puppies, with ducks. Introduce them to ducks at a young age, but never rush them or try to push them too young. They will tell you by their actions when they are ready to start working.

Puppies from the age of five weeks may be observed around ducks. No two puppies will react the same way toward the flock each day. Their interest or curiosity may be exhibited by their watching, following, or chasing the ducks. Some puppies will even take hold of the duck's tail feathers, which can be an indicator of the heeling instinct. Other puppies will move to the head of the ducks. Some puppies use varying degrees of eye, which you can recognize when the puppy drops his head ever so slightly and stares at the ducks. It is apparent even at this early age that the working instinct is present. However, you cannot accurately determine the working style completely until the Aussie is older—perhaps a year or so—although this will vary.

A summary of some of the research on dogs indicates the following: First, the puppy needs to stay with his litter until the seventh week. If he is removed too soon, he will not form appropriate attachments to people. For the best man-dog relationship, the time between the seventh and twelfth weeks is the best time to bring a puppy into a home. However, this time can be somewhat delayed if appropriate individual socialization is given regularly to the pup. Second, a

Aussies are versatile and are able to work all types of stock, including turkeys. Photo by Jeff Swain.

puppy needs much specialized attention to establish his self-importance. Finally, character traits are inherited and can be effectively evaluated in a puppy at an early age.

Introduction To Livestock

Once the correct puppy has been selected, there are several ways to create or spark his interest in herding. You can use ducks to create a focal point. If the puppy is wandering around, sniffing the ground, and acting generally disinterested, you can call his name or whistle to attract his attention. When he looks up, you can direct his attention by moving and making a hissing or clicking sound toward the flock. This kind of early exposure to the flock can be repeated every two or three days or even weekly until the puppy shows some interest and learns that the ducks will react to his movements. You should always be present to make sure that the puppy does not get too rough with or exhaust the ducks and that the flock doesn't spook the puppy. If the puppy gets too rough with the ducks, never punish or scold him. Simply take him away. To scold him in these early stages may totally inhibit or squelch his herding instincts.

Some Aussies will not "turn on" until later, perhaps between nine and eighteen months, even after repeated exposure to the stock for several months. Another effective tool for encouraging the young Aussie is to use an experienced Aussie in the pen. This can give the pup confidence as well as trigger his own instincts.

Some youngsters are extremely fragile in their confidence. They can quickly become inhibited or lose interest. If this happens, it is possible to get the young Aussie's attention and redirect it to the flock once again. When the pup shows interest, praise him and end the training session on this positive note. As a rule, concentration and intensity do not come in the early sessions. Young Aussies are often inconsistent.

Conversely, young Aussies with a strong desire to herd tend to get very enthusiastic around stock. Their instincts tell them that they should do something, but they are not always sure what or how. Do not assume that because these Aussies are so eager to work, they are mentally mature enough to accept corrections. Training with stock at too young of an age can actually be detrimental to the pup. Untimely corrections or a traumatic experience during these early stages can inhibit and destroy the herding instinct and make the young Aussie less inclined to use his own initiative. The Aussie should always associate working with a positive, rewarding experience. There is no exact mold into which each Aussie will fit—especially when you add the human element, which will either make or break the Aussie.

Play Training

There are times when an Aussie is not yet ready for formal training or when stock is not available. Nonetheless, games can be introduced that are very beneficial in teaching the young Aussie his basic commands.

Begin by using a toy or ball attached to a pole or rod with a string. Toss the toy and drop it to the ground. As you lure the puppy with the toy, you can make sounds to stimulate interest. It is much like a game of cat and mouse. Let the Aussie catch the toy to give him a continued incentive to play. To get the toy back, go to the Aussie and say, "That'll do," then ask him to "give" and gently take the toy from his mouth. Follow this with much praise. This basis will set the groundwork for most of the basic commands that he will need to know.

Walk On

This command tells the Aussie to go to the stock from any direction. In order to teach this command, you can turn it into a game. Lower the ball or toy to entice the Aussie to go after it. Tell the dog to "Walk on." Occasionally, you can pull

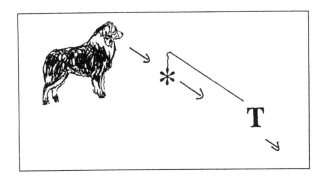

the object toward yourself as you walk backward. Other times, move the object from left to right and from right to left. The Aussie should follow this object.

Steady ("Take Time")

This command may also be learned in a game format. Hold an object in front of the Aussie above his head. Lower the object, and if the dog rushes to get it, raise it out of his reach. While raising the object, say the word "Steady." As he concentrates on the object, lower it gradually as the dog walks toward it in a steady, deliberate manner. It is noticeable here if the young Aussie has eye.

Skit a Hold

There are times when you need to let the Aussie know that it is permissible to use stronger force on the stock. This is necessary when the stock decides that it is not going to be moved without more pressure. The Aussie can also learn this important skill by way of a game. The game involves saying, "Skit a hold" ("Get a hold") to the Aussie and allowing him to grab the toy. Once he grabs the toy, he can shake it and play a game of

Using the ball to develop "eye" and teach the steady command.

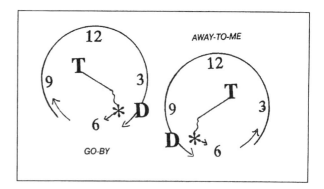

The trainer can teach the Aussie to grip with the skit a hold *(or* get a hold*) command by letting the dog grab the toy after giving him the command.*

Using the away to me command (counterclockwise). Goats can be used instead of sheep.

tug-of-war. Ultimately, this game teaches the Aussie to move in and use whatever force is necessary to move the livestock.

Away To Me/Go By

The side or directional commands for the Aussie to move around the stock to the right or left are "Go by" for clockwise movement and "Away to me" for counterclockwise movement. "Go by" can be taught by pulling a toy clockwise with an Aussie in pursuit. To change direction, flip the toy to the other side of the Aussie, and use a cane to block the Aussie from continuing in the first direction. While doing this, the Aussie hears "Away to me." The cane or pole is only to be used as a gate to stop the Aussie by tapping it on the ground. It is *never* used to hit the Aussie.

Back Out

This command alerts the Aussie that he is too close and must back away. To teach this command, tap the cane on the ground while stepping toward the Aussie. At first, the young Aussie is only asked to back up a few steps. Once he does this, reward him for responding to the command. A way to do this is to throw a ball for him or to play tug-of-war while giving him lots of praise.

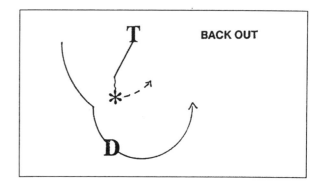

Over time, he will learn to back away to a greater distance. The reward is very important to keep his spirits high. If he cowers or sulks at any time during his play-training, the teaching has been too harsh and should be made more enjoyable.

Look Back

The last command that the Aussie can learn through play is "Look back." This alerts the Aussie that he must leave one group of stock and turn back and look for the next one. While the Aussie's attention is focused on the object on the pole, toss a different ball or toy behind him. Raise the object on the pole and tell the Aussie to "Look back." Direct the Aussie's attention back to the object lying on the ground, then repeat the command, "Look back." When the Aussie retrieves the object, reward him.

Any of these exercises can be utilized to let an extremely exuberant Aussie run off extra energy prior to an actual training session with stock. Don't overdo it during the heat, and remember to give him a drink of water when he needs it. Any Aussie can enjoy these games at almost any time or place. These games also help *you* learn the commands. It avoids confusion later when you add the third element—the livestock. Train-

Mini Acre Peppermint Patti (Claussen's Ramrod of Mini Acre ex Claussen's Tina of Mini Acre) demonstrating the type of eye characteristic to Australian Shepherds. Courtesy Warren.

ing an Aussie creates an eminently satisfying relationship between you and your Aussie. The Aussie senses that he is well loved, and he exhibits confidence and loyalty. You experience the rich reward of watching your Aussie perform successfully, and you gain a devoted companion.

Before the Aussie's formal stock-dog education begins, he must be self-confident in any environment and have a strong bond with you. The Aussie will not give his full attention to learning if either of these two elements is missing. Extensive socialization with friendly people in different places is critical. Introducing a variety of loud noises (the clanging of pots and pans, music) and different surfaces in a secure, friendly environment will help prepare him to deal with the unexpected situations that can occur on the job.

In order to cultivate your Aussie's trust while exposing him to new situations, always make sure that he can't get hurt in unfamiliar surroundings. Keep your young Aussie with you as much as possible. This creates a good relationship between you and your dog. The Aussie will recognize you as the leader of his pack and his companion. With this kind of conditioning, new places soon lose their frightening dimension to the young Aussie and become interesting places to explore.

Teaching Basic Commands

Come Here

The first and most important command that any Aussie should learn is to "Come here" when called. This is imperative if you need to call the Aussie off the stock. You may need to use this command if the stock are out of control or if you need to reposition your Aussie.

Teaching your Aussie to come is relatively easy. When he is only a puppy, he should have learned the rewards of coming to your voice by receiving plenty of attention and a tidbit of food with praise

Sakonnet Royal. Courtesy Linda Gray.

and petting. He needs to know above all else that the command, "Come here," is rewarding. Either food or abundant praise or play must await him when he responds by coming. Always make it worth your Aussie's time to respond and come.

Never punish your Aussie for coming. Even if he has committed a grievous act and then comes to you, do not punish him. If the dog makes an error, give vocal disapproval by telling him "No." If necessary, go to the Aussie to correct him.

In teaching the Aussie to come, it is important that you have a way to reinforce the command "Come here." This means that when the Aussie is older, he will need to learn to work on leash (wearing a collar and a long line) when practicing the command at first. Otherwise, there is no effective way to correct the Aussie and bring him to you if he decides to disregard the command. The collar must fit loosely enough to allow adequate air intake, but must not be so large that it can slip off over the Aussie's head. When the collar is on his neck, you should be able to slip a couple of fingers under it easily.

Initially, the Aussie drags the long line. When you first pick up the leash, the puppy may balk at the end of the lead or may jump around wildly when he realizes that he is "on lead." When and if he panics, *do not jerk or pull on him*. When he realizes that he is fighting against himself, he will probably let up. When he does, immediately put slack in the leash to release the pressure and reward the Aussie. In addition, give the young Aussie praise by petting him and telling him that he is a good dog.

Working Indian Runners. Ch. Beauwood's Out Rustlin Bear CDX STD-d (George's Red Rustler ex Beauwood's Caligari Bear).

Once the Aussie is used to having the leash attached to his collar, you can pick it up, call the dog's name in an enthusiastic, inviting voice, and give the command, "Come here." Pop the leash, switch directions, and begin running backward away from the Aussie. He will dart to his escaping trainer. As soon as he reaches you, reinforce him with abundant praise, a tidbit of food, and/or play with a ball or toy. The motivator (food, toy, or praise) can be varied according to the temperament and drive of the Aussie, but it must be present during the initial stages of training. After the Aussie clearly understands the command and eagerly bolts to you upon hearing the command, then the reinforcement can be intermittent so that the Aussie never knows when to expect it. Verbal praise is important in motivating the Aussie and is vital in communicating to the Aussie that he is on the right track. Word of caution—never leave the collar or leash on your Aussie unless he is under supervision.

Lie Down

The second most important command is "Lie down." The down is used to stop the Aussie and take pressure off the stock, to drop the Aussie in a stationary position, thus allowing you to reposition him, and for many other uses. It is like having brakes on a vehicle.

Probably one of the easiest ways to teach an Aussie to lie down is to hold a piece of food in your right hand next to the ground. When the Aussie takes an interest in the morsel and reaches down to pick it up, place your left hand over the Aussie's withers and press down in a forward motion. When the Aussie is lying down, give him the food as well as lots of praise. As long as the Aussie goes down, even if for only a short time, it is okay.

If the Aussie is not motivated by the food, use the lead and collar to get the same result. Ask the Aussie to lie down. With the leash in your right hand, place your left hand over the Aussie's withers and apply firm pressure in a forward and downward motion while pulling the leash in a forward and downward motion.

Stay There

Once the Aussie has learned the lie down command, you can teach him to stay put with the stay there command. "Stay there" can be taught once the Aussie has been told to lie down. If he gets up or moves, put him back in the same place and repeat the command, "Stay there." Once the Aussie does stay, leave him for only a few seconds. Then, in an enthusiastic voice, release the Aussie by telling him, "That'll do." Gradually, the Aussie can be left for longer periods of time. You also can build up the distance at which you leave your dog.

To further reinforce the stay there command, hook the end of the leash to a stationary object (looped over a fence post or around a tree trunk, door knob, etc.) and tell the Aussie, "Stay there," then walk away. If the Aussie tries to follow, repeat the command "Stay there" as the Aussie reaches the end of the lead.

Firm, but patient and kind handling will produce more rewarding results than a rough, abusive approach to training. Aussies are very anxious to please the master who he loves and trusts, not the one who he fears. However, to respond correctly, he must fully understand the com-

Using a long line to reinforce the stay there command.

A natural leader going to the head to stop the herd dead in their tracks. Berkshire's Beau Diddely CDX (Berkshire's Spot of Bar Lazy K ex Stoll's Misty). Courtesy Pardridge.

mands. Otherwise he will become frustrated and perplexed. If he does not understand what you expect of him, it is usually because he hasn't been properly taught.

It is important that you use correct intonation when giving commands. When you call the Aussie to "Come here," the command should sound inviting. Commands like "Lie down" and "Stay there" should settle the Aussie, because they are given in distinct and firm (matter-of-fact), but not scolding or threatening tones.

The split decision. Courtesy Donham.

Left: In perfect balance to keep the flock under control, preventing any ducks from splitting off and keeping them moving in the desired direction. Courtesy Donham.

A good example of how the working distance affects different kinds of animals. WTCh. Las Rocosa Pecosa Rojo R.D. (Ch. Just Lake of Las Rocosa ATD, CD, ex Las Rocosa L'oreal) is in good balance to the sheep (not too far, not too close). The lambs are responding to the pressure, while the ewes are just beginning to take notice.
Photo by Dan Moos.

Chapter 19

TRAINING THE STOCK DOG

THE TRAINING ENCLOSURE

Because the basic commands may be completely ignored when the trainee first goes to stock, a controlled environment (such as a round pen or an oval-shaped pen) will keep the situation from getting out of hand. The stock will be less stressed if they have not been chased all over a big field or arena. In this smaller area, you can be on top of most situations that may occur. Once the building blocks are laid here, the Aussie can then graduate into a larger area—but not before! Fortunately, all training will transfer from one class of livestock to another.

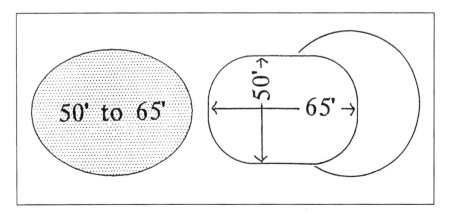

SELECTING LIVESTOCK FOR TRAINING

In order to effectively train your Aussie, you must be able to "read" the livestock, just as you must skillfully "read" your Aussie. This comes from understanding the nature and habits of the stock. Some stock are gregarious, meaning they possess bunching or grouping instincts. For example, Dorset sheep, which tend to bunch together (often noticed with range flocks), are excellent to use for teaching your Aussie to herd. Another example of gregarious stock is Indian Runner ducks, which are like a school of fish in their habits. Muscovy ducks, on the other hand, tend to string out and gravitate in various directions and require more work by the dog to keep them together. This is also true for some types of cattle and sheep. Gregarious stock are ideal for teaching young or inexperienced Aussies to herd, because they are not as likely to split into multiple directions unless they are scattered by the Aussie.

Generally speaking, all livestock flow to the point of least resistance. Some stock are "heavy" or "sticky" and do not move readily without more direct pressure being applied at a closer working distance (perhaps six feet away). This is in contrast to "lighter" or "flighter" stock, which are more responsive to the Aussie's movements farther away (perhaps a hundred feet, for example). Too much pressure on such stock by an Aussie right on their heels may cause them to explode in quick flight, running to escape the pressure. The flight/fight zone is an invisible barrier. Yet when it is penetrated, an individual or group of stock will either move away or become defensive.

When the stock—whether they be cattle, sheep, ducks, or goats—have been gathered by you or by your Aussie, there are several methods of moving them from one point to another. One method is to have you and your Aussie push from behind the herd to get it to its destination. A second method is for you to lead the way, with the stock in the middle and your Aussie bringing up the rear. A third method is especially effective when gathering wild cattle that are likely to break away from the herd. Here the Aussie works at the head of the herd to keep the cattle contained while you push the herd from behind (generally on horseback).

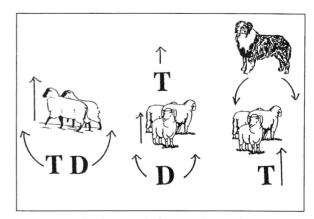

The three methods of moving stock.

For the average person getting started, it would be best to use five to ten head (definitely no less than three head) of gentle stock that won't unnecessarily challenge your Aussie. It depends entirely upon your situation, the availability of stock, and the nature of your dog. Some Aussies show an interest in sheep or goats when they won't even look at ducks. Others may be intimidated by sheep but are motivated by ducks or cattle. When cattle are not available, goats are the next best choice to use for Aussies that have a strong cattle-working background.

Indian Runners move like a school of fish, with the slightest movement or change of direction. MacSpadden Photo.

First Lessons On Stock

When your Aussie is around nine or ten months of age and shows an interest in wanting to work, it is your job to direct and guide him in order to channel this raw instinct. You must step in to lend a helping hand when needed, the same way a parent guides a toddler learning to walk.

When the young Aussie first gets around the livestock, he may forget all he has been taught. He might want to chase the stock, bark, run straight through the middle and scatter them, bite them, keep them in a tight group against the fence, or demonstrate little or no interest. If the Aussie shows little or no interest, you may move the flock around yourself. You can use a sharp whistle to attract the Aussie's attention. Direct the Aussie toward the stock with a hissing sound to stimulate the Aussie and say, "Watch 'em." Hopefully, the Aussie will take notice and make some move at the flock. Even if he makes a wrong or wild move or nips at the sheep or ducks, do not discourage him. He must be motivated to take an interest in them. These sessions should be short—no more than five to ten minutes every couple of days—until the young Aussie develops a sustained desire to move the stock. When he develops a "want-to" work attitude, it is time to begin training.

When you enter the round pen, put your dog on a slip cord. Ideally, the stock should be standing quietly in the middle away from the fence, but this is not always the case. If the flock is crowding the fence, move them while keeping your Aussie at your side next to the fence.

When the flock moves away from the pressure of you and your Aussie, a gap or space will be created along the fence. When a space opens, release your Aussie and step toward the middle of the pen. As the Aussie slips through the gap, the flock should veer away from his pressure and move toward the middle of the pen. You should keep walking backward, because it allows the flock to walk forward without your getting in the way. Otherwise, the flock will turn back against the fence or the dog. In this method, the Aussie is pulling or fetching the flock and is bringing them to you. In essence, the Aussie is driving in that he is behind the stock but the focal point is you. The driving Aussie will probably be content to keep the sheep or ducks moving forward, but the heading Aussie will be anxious and will try to race ahead to check the flock's forward movement. If he races to the head of the stock, use a lightweight cane or pole to block him from continuing forward. Tap it on the ground to encourage the young Aussie to move back to the rear of the flock.

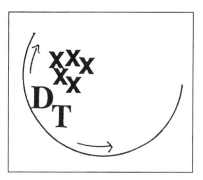

The flock moves away from the dog and trainer.

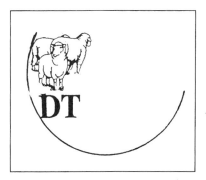

Moving the flock away from the fence.

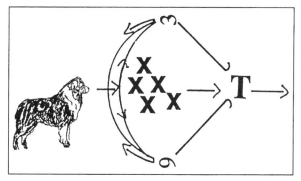

The trainer encourages the dog to keep the flock together while taking them toward the trainer, who continually walks backward.

Sometimes an eager, young Aussie chooses to ignore the cane, and instead of going back behind the flock, he cuts in between you and the flock. You should then step to the opposite side of the group in order to keep the flock between you and the Aussie. If things get chaotic or out of control, the Aussie can be dropped with the lie down command. Allow the Aussie to drag a light cord attached to a leather collar (not a choke collar) so that you can control him in these situations.

Let your Aussie and the flock of sheep or ducks settle for several minutes, then begin the exercise again. When your Aussie reaches what is referred to as the twelve o'clock position, fall back approximately to the six o'clock position and start walking backward again. Whenever your Aussie nears the three o'clock or nine o'clock position, send him to the rear by tapping the ground with the cane to create a barrier. When the Aussie gets to the other side of the pen, swap ends with him and continue in the opposite direction back across the pen. Initially, the biggest problem will be keeping the flock together.

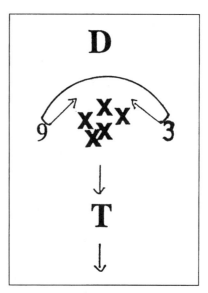

Fetching (pulling).

If the Aussie gets too close, cuts in, and tries to split the sheep or ducks, tap the cane on the ground and tell your Aussie, "Back out." If he grips one of the flock, make an audible growling sound, "Ah, ah," and tell him "Back out." When he releases on command and backs away, give him praise.

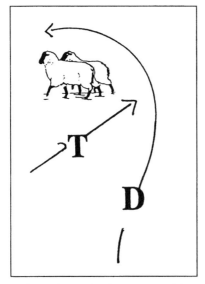

The trainer is in the correct position to cast the dog to the opposite side of the flock.

When the trainer and dog get to the end of the pen, the trainer moves to twelve o'clock and encourages the dog to pick up the six o'clock position.

Dog is too close and must back out.

Occasionally, a sensitive Aussie may become distracted or inhibited and may lose concentration and interest. When this happens, call his name, or use a sharp whistle to attract his attention, and redirect him back to the flock with a hissing sound and the words, "Watch 'em" as you move the flock. You will need to give this type of Aussie a freer rein to encourage him and to build up his confidence.

If aggressive biting is a constant problem, you can put a muzzle on your Aussie until he settles down. This allows you to teach without the constant worry about injury to the sheep or ducks. It is important, however, that your Aussie practice wearing the muzzle prior to working the stock. Otherwise, the young Aussie may become inhibited, focusing all of his attention on the muzzle. Also, be sure that the muzzle doesn't restrict the Aussie's ability to open his mouth to pant, putting him in danger of overheating.

If the Aussie is reluctant to bring or fetch the stock, modify your position from twelve o'clock off to one side or the other, and encourage your dog to follow the flock. You must always be flexible in your teaching in order to get the best results from your Aussie.

If the flock is moving at a pace that you cannot maintain, drop your Aussie with the lie down command. You also can change directions. If at any time the stock chooses not to move away from the Aussie and keeps facing or challenging him, encourage your Aussie and allow him to grip. This is a controlled situation in which you give your Aussie permission by telling him to "Skit ahold." As soon as the Aussie has done so, he is told, "Good dog, that'll do."

If your Aussie lacks the confidence to assert himself, step in to give him confidence by turning the aggressor's head away from the Aussie. You must also keep the welfare of the livestock in mind. You must make sure that your dog is not stressing the stock. Heavy panting with mouths open (or ducks with their bills open) is a strong signal that the stock has been overworked. They must be given ample time to catch their breath before continuing to train.

It is not uncommon for stock that have never been worked by the Aussie to become panicked. There are a few ways to prevent the stock from running into and bouncing off of the fences. You can use an experienced Aussie to condition the stock or work the new group with several head of "dog-broke" stock. If this is not possible, calmly move the stock around the enclosure several

"Lifting" takes place the moment the Aussie makes contact with the livestock. Ideally, the stock should melt calmly away from the Aussie.

times with the inexperienced Aussie on leash. By doing this, the stock will become acquainted with the boundaries of the enclosure and more comfortable with the presence of the Aussie. Whenever you obtain new stock, be sure to condition them to being handled by Aussies several days in a controlled situation prior to turning them out to pasture. The stock become much easier to handle later on.

Once the Aussie realizes that his place is on the opposite side of the flock while keeping them grouped together, he is ready to graduate into a

One of several different methods to move livestock. Ty Taylor leads the way home while his Aussie, Poco, brings up the rear.

When teaching the Aussie to drive, it is the handler's position that changes, not the Aussie's.

larger working area. Drop him with a "Lie down," and stand slightly ahead of him and between the flock so that you can guide him around to the far side of the sheep while discouraging him from cutting in or running straight at the flock.

Casting dog to opposite side.

Dog cuts in and trainer is out of position to prevent dog from cutting in.

The Aussie should veer out away from you. When he reaches the far side of the flock at approximately twelve o'clock, fall back to six o'clock and start walking backward, as practiced in the round pen.

Some trainers believe that the Aussie is in balance when he is directly opposite his handler. An Aussie in balance moves the stock by being in the right place at the right time to discourage escape attempts and applies the appropriate pressure to move his flock. You do not need to worry about teaching your Aussie directional commands until he has learned how to control and take the flock wherever you walk around the pasture.

Wherever possible, encourage the young Aussie to think on his own. A good example of this is when one head of stock breaks away from the group, and the heading Aussie's instincts prompt him to stop the runaway and put it back with the others. Interfering with the dog's natural inclination discourages his natural herding instincts, because it doesn't allow him to think for himself. The result is a mechanical Aussie. You will have control of your Aussie once the Aussie has control of the livestock. You will also have a better Aussie. To help him gain experience, take many walks around a pasture or field while your Aussie brings the flock. Stop every now and then to allow the flock to graze and the Aussie to settle.

DIRECTIONAL COMMANDS

The directional commands are introduced during this next phase of training. Flanking is a circling movement that the Aussie uses to skirt around livestock. The flanking commands are "Away to me" (think of it as "going back in time") for counterclockwise movement around the stock, and "Go by" (think of it "as time goes by") for clockwise movement around the stock. Drop your Aussie and stand slightly ahead of him between him and the flock. Send him in a clockwise direction with "Go by." You should also walk around the flock in the same direction, but stay next to the stock in a smaller circle to keep your dog from getting too close. If necessary, you can stop your Aussie with the lie down command. Always be in a position to make sure that your Aussie goes in the desired direction on command. Send your Aussie clockwise again by telling him, "Go by." After doing this two or three times, let the Aussie bring the stock back to you.

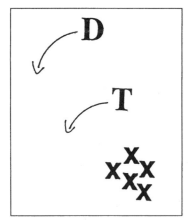

Flanking the dog counterclockwise.

If the young Aussie is excitable and rushes into the stock prior to fetching them to you, stop him and wait a few seconds. Then allow your Aussie to lift or pick up the stock by telling him, "Steady." The stock should move quietly away from the Aussie. When you practice this, you are helping your dog understand how to pick up or "lift" the stock in a controlled, deliberate manner.

Now send your Aussie in from the other direction. Make sure that he stays far enough from the stock so that he does not put unnecessary

Flanking the dog clockwise.

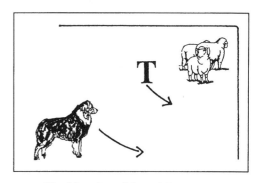

Flanking dog with stock in a corner.

Gripping or heeling is necessary for bossing livestock.

pressure on them, but not so far that he loses contact with them. Continue with this a few more times before letting the Aussie bring the flock to you. Aussies with a calm approach do not need to be stopped prior to lifting the flock.

If the flock is not cooperative, use a corner of the field to keep them contained while introducing flanking commands.

As the training progresses, you will be able to increase the distance you are able to send the Aussie to gather the flock. If at any time your Aussie cuts in, stop and redirect him. Next time, send him a shorter distance to the flock. This is a very gradual process. It is important not to send the Aussie too far or too wide too soon. This way, you build the length of the outrun a few feet at a time.

As you cast the Aussie from your side to the far side of the livestock, you are laying the foundation for the outrun. This is necessary to get the Aussie from your side to the opposite side of the stock without disrupting the stock or sending them bolting in the wrong direction.

The same training principles can be applied to cattle, because all training transfers from one class of stock to another. Generally speaking, cattle are not upset as easily as ducks or sheep. Using cattle for training allows a greater margin of error if the dog is young and enthusiastic. If the Aussie has been bred to herd cattle, he will probably be forceful and exhibit strong tendencies for gripping. This type of Aussie is ideal to teach using calves (or goats) as a starting point.

When you introduce an inexperienced Aussie to cattle, it is preferable to work in a space where the cattle can move freely away from the dog. In a small, confined area, there is a greater risk of injury or challenges from the cattle to the Aussie.

When the Aussie is sent through a space or gap to move the cattle off the fence, it is important for him to have sufficient space to get through. If he gets kicked against the fence, he may get hurt and lose his confidence. There are three important safety issues to keep in mind when working cattle. Always be sure that the cattle are in motion before you let an inexperienced Aussie make contact with them. Cattle have binocular myopic vision. They have a broad visual field to the side and to the rear. As a result, they are in a position to kick with better accuracy when they are standing still.

The dog should not wear any kind of collar because it can get entangled on a horn or hoof. If this happens, your Aussie could be severely injured. If your Aussie gets kicked, do not say anything to him for a second or two, because you do not want him to associate the kick with you. Look to be sure that your dog isn't limping or wasn't kicked in the head. Blinking or rubbing his eye with a paw would indicate a problem. Veterinary care is necessary if the pupils (the black centers of the eye) are of two different sizes or if the cornea becomes hazy or gray. Other post-traumatic signs are: blood or clear fluid draining from the ears or nose, poor coordination (unsteady walking), convulsions, fatigue, excessive sleepiness, intolerance to noise, slow thinking, or vomiting more than twice. Fortunately, these types of incidents are not frequent.

It is helpful to work as many types of stock as possible in many different situations. This keeps

No nonsense! Las Rocosa Cornflower isn't about to take "No" for an answer by the forceful way she is stalking this obstinate steer.

your Aussie keen and makes him versatile. It is also important to keep the sessions short and enjoyable. Repetition is essential to enable the Aussie to master his lessons. If at any time your Aussie seems confused, tired, or reluctant, give him a break for several days or even a few weeks. This should be a time of exercise and play, but not training or work. When he has finished his break, he will be fresh with renewed interest and excitement in training.

DRIVING

When your Aussie is taking his flanking commands reliably, it is a good time to teach him how to drive the stock away from you. A driving Aussie will fall in behind the flock and move them. However, a heading Aussie may be reluctant to assume this position. It is important to note that the only thing that is going to change in driving is your position, *not* the Aussie's!

To teach the drive, send your Aussie to gather or bring the flock to you. As the stock gets near, walk toward your Aussie but off to one side. If your Aussie is acutely aware of your position, he may swing away to go to the head of the flock. If this happens, stop him by saying, "Come be-

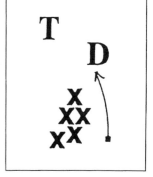
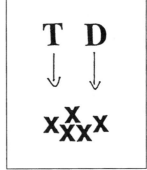

Above, left: Dog swings away toward the head of the stock.

Above, right: Trainer calls dog behind.

Left: In position to drive.

hind." When he responds, praise him. Then ask him to "Walk on." The Aussie with strong heading instincts may feel uneasy over leaving the head unguarded. He will veer away from you at the first opportunity. It is important to be calm with your dog. Call him behind again. Gradually,

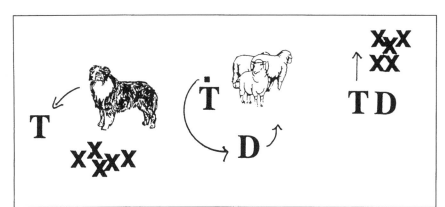

Far left: To change direction, the dog is called to the trainer.

Center: Dog is flanked to the head of the stock.

Right: Driving.

he will learn to do what you wish him to do. Ask him to drive several feet, then several yards. Always increase the distance gradually. Keep the sessions short and enjoyable. *Patience will yield rewarding results.*

During the first lessons on driving, it is helpful for you to walk beside your Aussie. This will give him confidence, and he won't be looking back constantly for directions. The driving Aussie will flourish with this segment of training. Occasionally, you can use a lightweight long line to check your Aussie as he flanks away. This helps him settle into driving. It can be beneficial with a fast Aussie that seems to move to the head before you can interpret the situation.

If your dog pushes the stock too fast, stop him and tell him "Steady." After your Aussie has driven the stock a short distance, change his direction and turn the stock. Tell him to come to you. When he reaches you, stop him and send him to the appropriate side as in flanking. This further instills in him the need to pick up and lift the stock in a controlled manner.

A fence or return alley can also be used with excellent results. Walk alongside your Aussie and the stock to cover the open flank. This will help the strong heading Aussie to relax. The stock is taken first one way around the field, then the other.

The supreme test: Las Rocosa Rogue OTD-C and Ch. Las Rocosa Leo 4-A, ATD-C team up to move a lone wild bison bull during an experimental project for the Department of Interior. Bison are the ultimate challenge because they are so difficult to herd and required a good team of Aussies to control them.

CROSS DRIVING

The next phase of training is a continuation of driving called the cross drive. Using the round pen is helpful in teaching this concept. When cross driving, the Aussie moves the stock in a parallel line in front of you from either the right or left side. First the Aussie moves the stock one way, then the other. The Aussie can keep you in view. Use the command "Come here" to pull the Aussie toward you. Out in the open, the Aussie can practice moving the stock in a circle around you.

In time, enlarge the circle to increase the distance. Ultimately, you must vary the length of the cross drive in both directions to expand your Aussie's flexibility. You can once again take advantage of a fenced field or arena to teach your Aussie to take the stock from the left to the right or from the right to the left in straight parallel lines from you. In both driving and cross driving, the flanking commands can be modified to "Come by" and "Come away."

PENNING

Now your Aussie must learn to pen the stock. Penning has many practical uses, such as moving livestock into or through a confined area (a stock trailer, across a narrow bridge, holding pens). Initially, only pens with generous openings are used so that the Aussie can get livestock in without a lot of intricate, tight maneuvers. It can put undesirable pressure on the Aussie when he must make precise movements in order to get the stock into a small pen. An Aussie should be well-versed on his flanking commands at this stage. Once he is flanking well, you can begin to add variety by incorporating different obstacles for him to negotiate with the stock.

Cross driving from left to right.

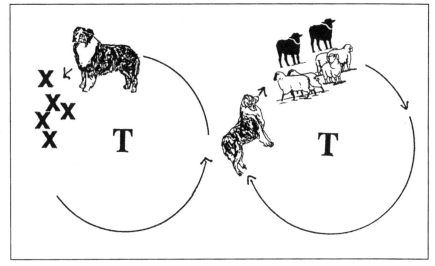

Cross driving in a round pen.

Sherry Baker handling WTCh. Twin Oaks The Bull in the 45 Ranch Trial. Photo by Cee's Pix.

As with all training, your Aussie must gain confidence by being successful. Then you can present him with new challenges. If he is not successful, go back to the basic exercises.

Penning requires that you be able to read the stock so that you can instruct your dog. If the livestock is panicked and the pen is too small, and you are in the wrong position or your dog is out of balance, you will not have much luck. You can, however, help improve your Aussie's balance by having him put three or four sheep in a corner of the field and hold them there. If he goes in too close or too tight, the stock will split in different directions. Then the Aussie must head them and put them back together.

When the Aussie exhibits good balance in the corner, you can practice the same exercise against a straight fence by having the Aussie take the stock to you and hold them there. The stock cannot be forced into a pen. They must be eased in. If one tries to break away, the Aussie must head it and bring it back. Once the Aussie has foiled the stock's attempts to escape, he should continue to exert enough pressure to keep them contained as he is easing them into the opening. The stock must be looking in the direction of the opening in order to go there. If necessary, one head of stock can be roped and tied inside the enclosure to help lure the others in.

Never place unreasonable or unfair demands on your Aussie during training. Remember that your dog will be unable to think clearly and function properly when he is tired or hot. The Aussie is also more prone to getting injured when he is tired.

Training is a team effort, and it is your job to help your Aussie learn how to succeed.

*Above: WTCh. Twin Oaks Kit Carson backing off a Scottish Highlander bull. Photo by Cee's Pix.
Below: WTCh. Southern Cross Blue Thunder CDX (Ch. Some Like It Hot of Adelaide ex Wildfire of Windermere CD, STD-sd). Courtesy Karla Michelson.*

SORTING (SHEDDING)

Being able to sort stock can be invaluable when you want to separate a group of individuals for veterinary attention, take them to market, sort your stock from the neighbors', and for many other reasons. This is called *shedding*. Shedding or sorting stock should only be attempted once the Aussie knows how to read and control livestock. If shedding is attempted too soon, an inexperienced Aussie will get into the bad habit of splitting stock. Sometimes a fence can be helpful in stringing the stock out to initiate the command, "Come here." When there is a slight gap or space, call your Aussie through to you.

The Aussie driving one group away from the other.

The Aussie fetching one group from another.

This is done only once or twice in a training session, and it is important to praise your Aussie when he does it correctly. It is especially helpful to use a larger group—perhaps a flock or herd of fifteen to thirty head. Even different groups or types of stock that naturally and easily go their own way can help the Aussie understand. When there is a sufficient gap after stringing out the stock, the Aussie comes through to you. Take whatever time is necessary to set up the correct situation. At first, the Aussie pulls one group away as he becomes successful at preventing the shedded stock from returning to the others. Then you can ask him to drive them away from the remaining flock or herd.

LOOK BACK

When your Aussie eagerly sheds and drives the sheep away, introduce the look back command. This teaches your Aussie how to leave one group of sheep, then turn back and look for the second bunch. This is begun by shedding a few sheep from the flock and having the Aussie drive them

"Ram Tough." This Dorsett ram is testing the ability of Las Rocosa Poco Sombra.

Las Rocosa Cornflower STD-C (Las Rocosa Lester ex Las Rocosa Lady In Blue) going in to low-heel a steer.

a short distance from the others. Then drop the Aussie with the lie down command. Walk up to him and say his name, and tell him, "Look back." You can pat your leg and encourage your Aussie to walk with you in the direction of the remaining stock. Send him out in an outrun. If he is overly worried about leaving his charges, take him by the collar and turn him in the direction of the other group. Give him the look back command, followed by the appropriate flanking command, to help him understand. Eventually, he will only have to be told to look back.

Whistle Commands

There are many times when you are working your Aussie at a distance or in adverse conditions, and

"Make my day!" WTCh. The Bear of Twin Oaks, CD, Hall of Fame sire, taking the challenge of a Barbado ram. Courtesy Sherry Baker.

he may have difficulty hearing your voice commands. This is when a shepherd's whistle is helpful. It makes the command understandable to the Aussie. To teach the whistle commands, blow the whistle and follow with the spoken command. Here are some suggested commands:

- One long blast, "WHEEOOO," is effective in telling the Aussie to "lie down."
- To call the Aussie to "come here," "WHEE WHO WHEET" should attract his attention.
- One short blast, "WHEET," might indicate "steady."
- Flanking commands are easily mastered by literally whistling the words. For example, "WHO WHEEOO" sounds close to "go by"; "WHEEOO WHEEOOO" sounds like "away to me."
- A couple of short blasts, "WHEET WHEET," can indicate "walk on."
- "WHEET WHEEOO" tells the Aussie to "look back."

If you are unsure of your commands, you can practice by playing them into a tape recorder to see how they sound. This way, you won't confuse yourself *and* your Aussie.

The shepherd's whistle allows the command to be carried over long distances. Blowing a shepherd's whistle takes practice, but it is not difficult to use. Place the solid edge of the whistle back against your tongue. Gently bite down on the whistle with the open side facing forward toward your lips. To give commands, blow air down and through the hole on the top side (whichever side happens to be facing up—it doesn't matter because both sides have holes). It produces the same effect as blowing air across a pop bottle. You can produce various tones by using your tongue to regulate the air flow across the whistle.

TEAM WORK

In real working situations, there are times when a team of Aussies is more effective than one Aussie alone, because it gives both Aussies more courage and power. It is helpful to use more than one dog when you are out on the range and when large herds need to be managed. And when difficult obstacles need to be negotiated, two Aussies can support one another. Finally,

WTCh. Twin Oaks Frederick Remington RTD-c teamed up with his sire, WTCh. Windsong's Falcon RTD-sc, to convince these steers that the grass is greener on the other side of the fence. Photo by Cee's Pix.

when working difficult stock, two Aussies are often necessary.

A good team consists of two Aussies that get along and that are willing to support one another—not compete with each other. It is also helpful to have individuals that complement each other in working styles. For example, one combination is a heading Aussie that can control the head of the herd and a driving Aussie that keeps the herd contained and moving along. Or a closer working Aussie can be used for immediate pressure, while a wider runner can counter the escape attempts by creating a second pressure point from farther away.

A young Aussie that has mastered the basic commands of "come here," "lie down," and "stay there" and that is beginning to take the flanking commands is ideal to start with an older, more experienced and dependable worker. An individual that is a willing worker but that is unable to take the pressure created by the demands of high-level training can still make an excellent backup Aussie in farm and ranch work.

To start working your Aussie in a team, he should be solid in controlling stock. Each Aussie must understand how to listen for his own commands. You accomplish this by practicing the basic commands with the team away from stock. For example, when practicing, you tell one Aussie to lie down and stay, while you call the other Aussie to you. With this method, it is beneficial to use each Aussie's name with the command. Soon each Aussie learns to respond only when he hears his name. When the second Aussie reaches you, alternate the roles.

Ideally, each Aussie should have his own set of commands. The whistle commands can also be used. One Aussie can be worked with whistle signals, while the other Aussie is given the verbal commands. When both Aussies respond favorably away from stock, they can be worked with stock in a controlled situation using the same exercises.

During each phase of training, whether it be working an individual or a team of Aussies, it is necessary to continue to improve and perfect the previous lessons. By working a variety of stock in many different situations, you will keep your Aussie keen and versatile. Not every individual will make a top trial Aussie, but with these ideas, you can develop your Aussie to his fullest potential and train an enjoyable, useful stock dog.

Both you and your Aussie must be flexible, because the stock are not always predictable or cooperative. Often in ranch work there are not controlled situations, and the techniques are not always as important as getting the job done effectively. The Aussie must be able to think for himself. A good ranch dog can take the place of several men.

For a complete educational experience, the *Herding I, II, and III* (Canine Training Systems) stock-dog training videos demonstrate all aspects of herding by the author from beginning training through advanced work.

HERDING/STOCK-DOG TRIALS

Herding trials are to preserve and develop the herding skills inherent in Australian Shepherds and to demonstrate that they can perform the useful functions for which they were originally bred. Another purpose of herding trials is to stimulate interest in the working ability of Aussies.

In ASCA, Aussies can gain titles in four levels of competition—Started Trial Dog (STD), Open Trial Dog (OTD), Advanced Trial Dog (ATD), and Post Advanced Trial Dog (PATD). Each division offers different classes of livestock—ducks, sheep (goats), and cattle. Titles reflect the class of stock under which the title was earned; for example, ATDC indicates an advanced title earned by working cattle. A Working Trial Champion (WTCh.) is awarded to an Aussie that earns Advanced titles in all three classes of stock.

ASCA offers Ranch Trials, where an Aussie can earn a Ranch Trial Dog (RTD) for competing in sheep (goats) or cattle. In addition, ASCA offers a Ranch Dog program in which actual working farm and ranch dogs can be recognized with a Ranch Dog (RD), Ranch Dog Good (RDG), or a Ranch Dog Excellent (RDX).

Herding tests offered by the AKC are on a pass-or-fail system to give inexperienced Aussies stock and trial exposure and to determine tht the Aussie being tested is under reasonable handler control. Herding tests allow an Aussie to demonstrate his ability to move and control livestock by fetching or driving. They show that he is sufficiently trained to work at the proper balance point in order to move the stock on the course. Once certified by two different judges, the Aussie receives a Herding Tested (HT).

A Pre-Trial test is an entry-level class to demonstrate that while the Aussie is not fully refined in training for regular competition, he exhibits sufficient training and herding experience just below the started level. When an Aussie gains certification under three different AKC Herding judges, he is awarded a Pre-Trial Tested (PT) title. An Aussie can earn titles in three levels of difficulty—Herding Started (HS), Herding Intermediate (HI), and Herding Excellent (HX). Herding Championships are earned by Advanced-titled Aussies for acquiring fifteen points while competing in the Advanced Division in cattle or sheep. Points awarded are determined by the total number of dogs defeated in the Advanced competition.

Rockin' Ray and Jumping Jane. Courtesy Ray Masal.

Chapter 20

PERFORMANCE CONDITIONING

STAMINA IS THE RESULT OF CONDITIONING. Conditioning for performance, whether it be for stock work, Frisbee, Agility, or any other dog sport, requires consideration on your part. Participation in the sport is not always adequate in preparing the individual for the rigors of competition or for farm and ranch work. A proper conditioning program should include exercise to promote necessary endurance and strength. It should concentrate on working all of the muscle groups and keeping the pads properly toughened.

Before you begin conditioning, consider your Aussie's present physical condition and age. A complete physical exam by your vet is necessary if your dog is overweight or advancing in age. Do not force a young Aussie into strenuous exercise, because his growth plates are not yet fully closed. Forced exercise can affect the later development of puppies. If a dog is overweight and out of shape, there is a decreased tolerance for heat and strenuous exercise. Working out in warm weather can cause exhaustion. Exercise needs to be gradual until the dog's condition is built up. In the city or the suburbs, once or twice around the block once or twice a day (during cooler times of the day in summer and warmer times of the day in winter) may be safe for starters. Stress is increased by extreme weather conditions.

If your Aussie lies around the house throughout the work week and is exercised too much on weekends, it is only natural that he will experience aches and pains on Monday mornings.

HOW TO CONDITION YOUR DOG

Conditioning through Training

Training is one method of conditioning. It is preferable to begin with short sessions and gradually build toward the desired physical condition. Exercise through training utilizes muscles necessary to perform the specific tasks the dog is being trained for.

Water Conditioning

Running your Australian Shepherd in shallow water helps get him into shape during the summer while keeping him as cool as possible. A workout in shallow water also decreases the stress of pounding on concrete pavement. Swimming increases stamina. Unless he is conditioned, an Aussie can tire quickly and even drown in deep water, so take caution and use good judgment with water exercise.

Retrieving

A tennis racket can be used to bat tennis balls to encourage your Aussie to run, jump, and retrieve for exercise and mental stimulation. Frisbee and flyball are both fun ways to get your Aussie into shape. Retrieving in shallow water can provide hours of healthy entertainment.

Bicycling, Jogging, and Using a Treadmill

Jogging and bicycling are excellent ways for both you and your Aussie to get exercise. Constant pounding on pavement (both asphalt and concrete) can cause bruising and strain. Be sure to watch for signs of pain or discomfort. Walking on a treadmill can be excellent but strenuous. Exercise on the treadmill must be carefully monitored so that no one suffers from injury or overexertion.

Practical Agility

Noncompetitive Agility training is excellent for teaching an Aussie how to negotiate all types of obstacles, and it promotes athletic ability. Agility builds muscles, increases strength and stamina, and

Courtesy Ann Martin.

Mahan's Red Bandit, CDX, AD, going over the A-frame at the 1992 Grand Prix of Dog Agility National Championships with owner/trainer Kent Mahan. Photo by Dan Presby.

develops confidence. Practical Agility training promotes athletic development for all types of Aussie activities (performance events and real working situations). Agility training is flexible and adaptable to any situation. The obstacles can be anything (barrels, tires, ladders, see-saws, slides, tunnels, hurdles, or A-frame) that teach Aussies to run, jump, and climb, and to crawl on, over, under, or through. Many local playgrounds offer excellent equipment.

OVERTRAINING AND INJURY

Aussies are not invincible machines, and they can become overworked. Overtraining can wear a dog out before he even gets into competition. The Aussie has so much heart that he will often continue to perform even though he is injured. Stop any training or exercise at the first sign of discomfort or lameness. When nutrients and energy are constantly depleted and the muscles are pushed continually, sufficient rest is critical to build and restore tired muscles and repair injured feet. Proper conditioning can help eliminate the possibility of injury. A tired Aussie is more likely to get injured or develop foot problems.

When your Aussie exhibits lameness, examine him thoroughly. Gently flex all joints (working

Negotiating a tunnel in Agility. Courtesy Ann Martin.

from the foot up), beginning with the obviously affected foot or leg. If it appears as though the injury is more than muscle strain, X-rays may be necessary to isolate the problem.

Exhaustion is generally manifested in the Aussie by a sagging body posture. If your Aussie becomes exhausted, stop the session immediately and get him into shade or out of the cold. Give him a small amount of water. When a dog is overtired from work or training, no amount of discipline, affection, or drugs is going to alleviate fatigue. Only rest will help. Your Aussie's attitude will be greatly altered with adequate rest.

STRESS AND YOUR AUSSIE

Stress is any physical or emotional strain on the body or mind. Stress results from a variety of situations—extreme heat or cold, overwork, strenuous athletic performance, injuries, illness, malnutrition, breeding, competing, confinement, pestering by rowdy kids, moving from the country to a life in the city, travel, and even deprivation of accustomed affection. General health and individual personality contribute to the way in which each Aussie reacts to disappointment and daily aggravations. A certain degree of stress is important for survival. Stress is necessary and useful as a motivating factor to keep your Aussie alert and attentive to his environment.

The metabolic response of the body to physical or emotional stress is to produce more adrenal hormones. When these hormones are released into the blood, breathing and heartbeat increase to prepare the body to face or flee (fight or flight) a challenge. When there is no outlet, the body reacts to stress by channeling the body's responses inward, affecting various nervous, circulatory, and digestive functions. When it occurs in excess, stress increases anxiety and results in premature aging, susceptibility to illness, and behavioral problems. An overload of stress, when your Aussie is continually "on alert," tends to dull the senses and decreases intellectual responses and his ability to react quickly. Chronic stress damages your Aussie's physical and emotional health by overworking his body's defensive response mechanisms to the point of exhaustion.

When your Aussie experiences stress, protein is mobilized from tissue reserves to produce antibodies and new blood cells. Extra energy is required. Diet plays an integral role in combating the effects of stress (see the chapter on Nutrition). Your Aussie looks to you for security and leadership. Keep a reasonable schedule, provide a peaceful place to rest, fresh water, regular feedings, and adequate exercise. Even though you may be limited in the amount of time that you spend each day with your Aussie, make up for it by improving the quality of time that you spend together.

Moves like this require strength and conditioning.

CARE OF THE FEET

Care of your Aussie's feet is of primary importance in a working dog. Neglected feet can lead to poor performance, infection, and other complications. The pads of a young Aussie, and of an Aussie living in the house or backyard, are often tender and soft. As the Aussie matures, the pads will toughen with exposure. Short but frequent exposure to different surfaces (rocks, concrete) is beneficial. It is also important that the nails are trimmed.

Injuries to the pad and to the webbing between the toes, and problems of the toenail and nail bed, are common. Pad injuries are the easiest to recognize. They include cuts and wearing of the pad, often caused by sharp or jagged objects like ice and rocks. Gravel and rocks on road surfaces often wear the pads thin. Dogs that are kept on gravel generally will have tougher feet than those kept on soft dirt, grass, or carpeting. In some parts of the country, thorns cause sore pads by creating small puncture wounds.

Disorders to the web are harder to recognize. They include splits in the skin deep between the toes and friction burns or blisters between the toes. To discover those injuries, you must examine between the toes in a bright light. Windblown or granular snow is especially severe on the webs, as are booties with holes in them. Sharp objects, thorns, rocks, ice, and salt all compound the problem. Injuries to the webs of the feet require diligent care to heal, because once they begin to heal, the foot tends to become moist and swollen, aggravating the problem.

Nail-bed problems may be just as frustrating as web injuries. Swelling and redness of the tissue are usually associated with serum or pus around the base of the toenail. This is easily overlooked on long-haired dogs. Conditions where the dog's feet break through the snow or ice, as well as rugged terrain, can cause the toenails to be torn away. These types of injuries can be reduced by routinely trimming the toenails.

Basic treatment includes cleaning the affected wound with a mild betadine solution and using systemic antibiotics for feet that are swollen or infected. A wide variety of foot ointments can be used with varying degrees of success depending on the conditions. Deep cuts should be sutured as soon as possible to aid in healing. Super Glue (T) or surgical glue has been used on cuts and on the nail, and to attach protective pieces of material to pads sliced or worn. All foot disorders heal more rapidly if the dog is kept clean and dry.

Most foot ailments may be prevented by recognizing potential problems and by properly using pad-toughening agents such as tincture of benzoine or protective booties. Be sure that you don't put booties on so tight that they cut off circulation. When booties are too tight, they hamper normal, natural movements. Booties should be removed during rest periods to restore normal circulation.

Booties lend effective protection and are effective in minimizing further trauma to an injured foot during the healing process. Cold temperatures also delay healing, so it is wise, whenever possible, to keep your dog warm.

WATER AND FOOD

Proper conditioning, involving appropriate training, good nutrition, and adequate care during critical periods in your Aussie's life, will produce a healthy herding Aussie. An Aussie fed an adequate diet can better withstand extreme cold and hot days and physical exertion. Aussies are trained to work for long periods of time outdoors in all weather, in what seems like perpetual motion. Actual working Aussies have different needs than nonperforming breeds. As the exercise program increases, feeding should also increase.

When training or working during the summer months, give small amounts of water every fifteen minutes or so to cool your Aussie's tongue and mouth. A squirt from a canteen or athlete's

Ch. Sakonnet Charlie Hustle CD taking the plunge. Photo by Linda Gray.

bottle works well. If necessary, apply water to your Aussie's head, legs, belly, and groin.

Avoid giving too much water or food immediately after exercise. A small amount of water and a small, light snack fed at least thirty minutes after exercise will help avoid hypoglycemia and provide a reward for hard work.

Avoid exercising your dog immediately after a meal. It is healthier for your Aussie to be able to digest his food in a nonstressful situation, preferably several hours prior to being worked. If he is trained early in the morning, then night feedings might be ideal.

SUMMER EXERCISE FOR YOUR AUSSIE

Avoid prolonged exposure to hot surfaces, especially asphalt, concrete, and sand that can burn your dog's feet. Once the pads are burned, it could take several weeks for them to fully heal.

Too much sun can also burn your dog's coat, nose, and eye rims (especially in lightly pigmented Aussies).

When the temperature is soaring, avoid strenuous exercise and training except during the cooler parts of the day. Provide a wading pool to keep your dog cooler during hot summer days, or turn the garden hose on him. Always protect your dog against heat stress (see Chapter 13). Dogs perspire through their tongue and foot pads. Always have clean, fresh water available to drink and stand in.

WINTER EXERCISE FOR YOUR AUSSIE

Whether your Aussie is an outdoor, indoor, or an indoor/outdoor dog, he needs exercise in the winter just as he does in the summer. Winter exercise and training may be more challenging. This helps to expend energy built up from too

Swimming is a fun way to tone up muscles and release pent-up energy. Photo by Wayne Rogers.

much time spent confined indoors. This time will also strengthen the bond between you and your Aussie.

It takes practice to learn how to walk on icy surfaces. Gradually introduce your dog to freezing temperatures. Avoid putting him outdoors in frigid air for long periods of time until he has adjusted to it. Vigorous exercise in subzero temperatures can increase the chance of respiratory problems and pneumonia unless your dog is accustomed to these conditions.

Wash and dry his feet to remove ice, salt, and caked mud from paws. This will reduce the risk of infection. Beware of frostbite. Frostbitten skin may turn reddish, white, or gray, and it may be scaly or sloughing (see Chapter 13, Emergency First Aid).

When temperatures drop, your Aussie needs to drink plenty of water, especially after a workout in cold weather, to avoid dehydration. If your Aussie doesn't seem to be thirsty, bait the water and make a broth by mixing in a tiny amount of canned food. Staying warm also demands extra calories.

Aussies often have a look of questioning curiosity in their eyes.

Ch. Yankee Clipper of Wingmont (Ch. Robinson's Bonnie Blue Yankee CD ex Ch. Moonshine of Windermere) Hall of Fame sire. Photo by L. M. Gray.

Chapter 21

THE DOG SHOW GAME

THE AMERICAN KENNEL CLUB (AKC), the Australian Shepherd Club of America (ASCA), the United Kennel Club (UKC), and the Canadian Kennel Club (CKC) all sponsor Breed or Conformation classes, Junior Showmanship, and Obedience competition.

The United States Australian Shepherd Association (USASA), as the parent club under AKC auspices, sponsors an annual National Breed Specialty show and may also host regional shows.

CONFORMATION

Conformation shows are based on the process of elimination. The procedure, although seemingly complicated, is quite orderly. Each individual is evaluated against the Australian Shepherd Breed Standard and then compared to other entries within each class. This is a place where the newcomer can view the Australian Shepherd and gain knowledge about the breed.

Types of Shows

Matches

Matches are generally informal shows for the purpose of training and providing experience for handlers, Aussies, and judges. Matches are generally entered on the day of the show. Championship points or Obedience legs may not be garnered at a match.

Point Shows

These are shows in which Aussies can gain Championship points and Obedience legs.

Conformation Dog Show Classes

The ASCA, the AKC, and the CKC are almost identical in show procedure and in classes offered. Specific show rules and regulations should be obtained and read carefully.

Regular Classes

Regular classes in both the ASCA and the AKC are first divided by sex (males and females) and are then judged consecutively, beginning with Puppy classes and proceeding through the Open classes. Puppies must be at least six months of age to compete in Regular competition. Males, or "Dogs," are judged first, followed by the female, or "Bitch," classes. Age is determined up to and including the day of the show. All regular classes except Best of Breed exclude Champions of Record.

Six to Twelve Months: This class is generally divided into two different age categories of six to nine months and nine to twelve months.

Twelve to Eighteen Months: This class is for Aussies twelve months to eighteen months of age.

Novice: To be eligible to compete in the Novice class, individuals must not have garnered three first-place wins in any one of the following Regular classes (excluding the aged Puppy classes): Bred By Exhibitor, American Bred, or any Open class. Nor can the individual have earned either one or more points toward a Championship.

Bred By Exhibitor: In this class, the Aussie (male or female) must be owned and handled by a breeder of record or by an immediate family member, including a spouse (husband or wife), father, mother, son, daughter, brother, or sister, or by an immediate household member of a breeder of record.

American Bred: This category includes all Aussies bred and whelped in the United States (which includes all territories and possessions of the United States and vessels sailing under the American flag).

Canadian Bred: This category includes all Aussies whelped in Canada.

Open: These classes are usually divided into four categories: Open Black, Open Red, Open

Gaiting on a relaxed leash.

Ch. Gun River's She's So Fine. Courtesy Brenda Olger.

Blue Merle, and Open Red Merle. This gives equal consideration to all of the acceptable color combinations; however, the Open class may be offered in any combination.

Winners Class: Only undefeated Aussies (dogs or bitches) of the same sex that are first-place winners from any of the Regular classes the same day are eligible to compete in the Winners class at any given show. No separate entry fee is charged. After the Winners (Dog or Bitch) has been awarded in either of the sex divisions (male or female classes), the individual placing second to the Winners Dog (or Bitch) shall compete with the other eligible individuals for Reserve Winners Dog (or Reserve Winners Bitch).

Right:
Old stuff by now. Meg Kimbler pictured winning a Pee Wee Junior Showmanship competition with Ch. Potter's Whiteoak Razzle Dazzle CDX, STD-dc (George's Red Rustler ex Dakota Blue Tassativio). Courtesy Potter.

Best of Breed: Both the Winners Dog and the Winners Bitch become eligible to compete for Best of Breed along with the "Specials," Champions of Record, and winner of the Veterans class. If either the Winners Dog or Winners Bitch garners Best of Breed, then he or she automatically assumes the Best of Winners award. If a Champion (Special) wins Best of Breed, the judge will award Best of Winners following the Best of Breed placement and prior to awarding Best of Opposite Sex (opposite of the sex chosen for Breed).

Best in Group: In the AKC, the Best of Breed winner is eligible to compete for the Best in his or her Group at all-breed shows. Aussies are assigned to the Herding Group along with Australian Cattle Dogs, Bearded Collies, Belgian Malinois, Belgian Sheepdogs, Belgian Tervuren, Bouviers Des Flandres, Briards, Collies (Rough and Smooth), German Shepherd Dogs, Old English Sheepdogs, Puliks, Shetland Sheepdogs, and Welsh Corgis (Cardigan and Pembroke).

Best In Show: The process of elimination narrows the competition to the first-place winner in each of the following seven groups: Sporting

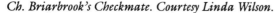

Ch. Briarbrook's Checkmate. Courtesy Linda Wilson.

The beautiful champion Leata.

Dogs, Hounds, Working Dogs, Terriers, Toys, Non-Sporting Dogs, and Herding Dogs. Each first-place winner will represent his or her group and compete for Best In Show.

What Class Is Best?

The Age classes are ideal for developing youngsters. This lets the judge know that the individual is in a stage of development. The judge can make a truer evaluation against other Aussies in the same stage of development. It is difficult for a young, developing Aussie to compete against older, mature Aussies.

Novice classes are often a good choice for the newcomer to the breed and to the sport of dog showing. Generally speaking, many beginning handlers and "green" dogs are competing, but Novice is not limited to the newcomer. Often handlers with several dogs may enter Novice. Newcomers should never feel compelled or limited to compete in Novice. There are usually fewer entries in Novice, which means that you may have a better opportunity of getting noticed.

If your Aussie is in optimum condition, it may be better to enter him (or her) in either the American Bred class or Open class. American Bred also gives the handler of several dogs an option of another class in which to compete. This may be a good class for the young dog just out of the Age classes. It also may be a good class for the puppy that has matured more quickly than other

UCD T Bar K Avant-Garde placing in the top ten at the Top Gun Obedience Competition with owner/handler Margarete A. Tim. Courtesy UKC.

Four- to Six-Month Puppy class. Nonregular Puppy classes may be divided by color. The winners of this class shall compete for Best of Breed Puppy, Best of Opposite Sex Puppy, or Best Puppy Dog (male) and Best Puppy Bitch (female).

Stud Dog and Brood Bitch Class: Each sire (or brood bitch) entered in the Stud Dog (or Brood Bitch) class must be accompanied by two to four of his (or her) offspring.

Brace Class: The Brace class comprises two individuals that look similar in markings, coloration, type, and size.

State Bred: The State Bred class comprises individuals that are either bred and/or whelped in any given state.

Veterans Class: To be eligible for the Veterans class, competing individuals must have attained their seventh birthday. This class is generally divided by sex. Veterans ideally exhibit the desired longevity of the Australian Shepherd breed.

individuals of his own age but that may not be quite as mature as the entries in the Open class.

Bred by Exhibitor is a class designed specifically for the breeder. It is certainly an honor to be eligible to compete with a home-bred individual.

Open classes are generally for individuals in optimum condition and usually contain the more mature and Championship-pointed individuals; however, Open is not limited to these entries.

Nonregular Classes

Nonregular classes are generally more commonly seen at Specialties but may be offered at any Member or Licensed show. No Championship points can be garnered or awarded for Nonregular classes.

Two- to Six-Month-Old Puppy Class: This is divided into Two- to Four-Month Puppy class and

High in Trial win. Photo by L. M. Gray.

ASCA's Supreme Versatility WTCh., Ch. Apache Tears of Timberline UD, during the Scent Discrimination exercise in Utility obedience. Courtesy Nick Davis.

Champions may compete. Winner of the Veterans class is an exception that may compete for Best of Breed. What an honor to garner Best of Breed with a Veteran!

Futurities: The requirements for eligibility in a Futurity can vary with the type of competition offered, but generally speaking, Futurities are for puppies that are nominated at or prior to birth. Nomination fees are renewed at designated dates before the actual competition. By entering a Futurity, the breeder of the litter is projecting that the puppies will develop as predicted.

How Championships Are Attained

To attain a Championship in the ASCA, each Aussie must win a total of fifteen points. Nine or more of these points must be attained at three separate shows with each major win (between three to five points) garnered under three different judges. The remaining points may be attained in any combination, including minor wins (one to two points).

In the AKC, any Aussie having won fifteen points shall become a Champion of Record, if six or more of said points shall have been won at two shows with three or more championship (three to five) points each and under two different judges.

Championship points recorded for both Winners Dog and Winners Bitch are determined by the number of eligible entries competing in the Regular classes for each sex. The points awarded are predetermined by a point schedule that varies from region to region. Points for any individual that is excused, disqualified, or dismissed, or from which any award is withheld by the judge, are not counted. Only the Winners Dog and Winners Bitch receive Championship points.

Once the requirements are met and officially confirmed, then a Championship Certificate is issued for the individual.

Junior Showmanship

Junior Showmanship is a competition designed for handlers, breeders, and judges of the future. It teaches the art of fine handling as well as sportsmanship (the art of winning and losing). Ideally, it teaches youth to be competent handlers and fair competitors.

Neutered and spayed Aussies may compete in Junior Showmanship. Although the actual quality of the dog is never considered by the judge,

The Dog Show Game

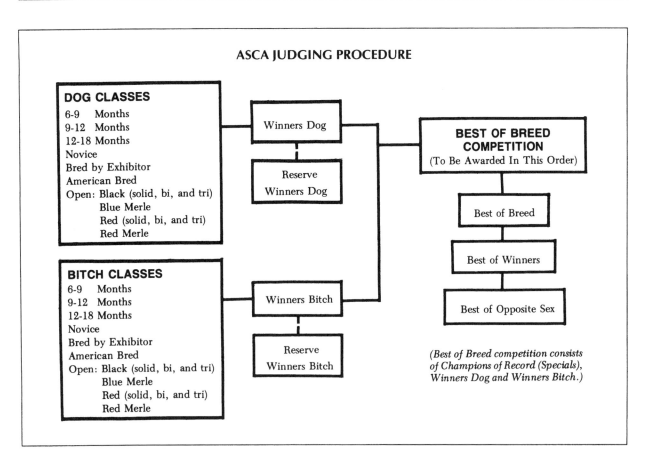

Although markings vary slightly, this pair of females makes an attractive brace. Left: Ch. Kline's Blue Heather of Coppertone CD (Heard's Salt of Flintridge ex Ch. Shank's Ginks CD); Right: Ch. Shank's Ginger Blue of Coppertone (The Herdsman of Flintridge ex Ch. Shank's Ginks CD). Courtesy Kline.

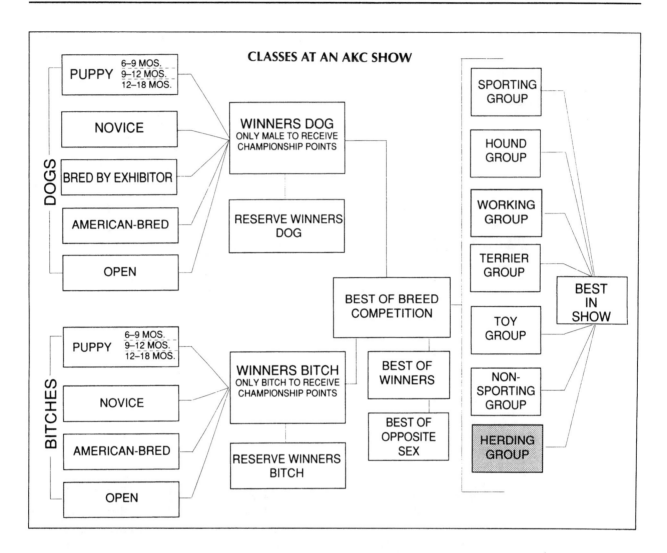

each handler's ability to "present" his Aussie is considered. Junior Showmanship is a team effort between each youth and his Aussie; therefore, there must be a rapport between them. Although the Aussie that is used for Showmanship need not be of top quality, he must possess the typical Aussie appearance.

There are certain differences between Showmanship and the regular Breed Ring. In Showmanship, the handler's ability is judged, with only the dog's cooperation. In Breed Competition, the quality and soundness of the dog are judged, and the only role that the handler plays is his ability to make the best presentation. Ring procedure is the same and the patterns are identical, but the Junior Showman must learn to execute them slightly dif-

ferently. In showing, there is a golden rule that a handler must keep his dog between himself and the judge at all times. Some judges "overwork" this aspect, causing junior handlers to frantically move from side to side and hand to hand. In an odd sense, it defeats the purpose. Nevertheless, each handler will develop his own style. Regardless of how elaborate or basic the style, the finest handlers master an economy of motion.

Junior Showmanship Class

Showmanship classes are divided into Novice and Open Competition. Classes may be further divided into Junior and Senior divisions.

THE DOG SHOW GAME

Ch. Copper Canyon's Caligari (George's Red Rustler ex Quaglino's Miss Pooh), National Specialty winner. Photo by Dai.

Novice: Novice is for boys and girls who at the time entries are taken and/or closed have not earned three first places at Sanctioned events.

Open: Open is for boys and girls who have garnered three or more first-place wins at Sanctioned events.

Junior and Senior Classes: Boys and girls must be at least ten years of age but less than thirteen (less than fourteen in the AKC) years of age for the Junior class. The Senior class is for boys and girls at least thirteen years old, but less than seventeen (less than eighteen in the AKC) years of age.

Best Junior Handler: Best Junior Handler is awarded to each first-place winner from the Novice and Open classes in the Junior and Senior divisions.

OBEDIENCE TRIALS

All breed clubs and all-breed kennel clubs host licensed Obedience trials where dogs compete on three levels: Novice, Open, and Utility. The levels vary in difficulty, and once the highest title, Utility Dog, is earned, your Aussie can continue to compete toward an Obedience Championship. Write to the AKC, ASCA, UKC, or the CKC for rules and further information on Obedience competitions.

Obedience trials are often held in conjunction with Conformation shows. Like many forms of horsemanship, Obedience was created for war and stemmed from the battlefields. The purpose of Obedience trials is not only to demonstrate the dog's ability to follow specified routines, but also his usefulness as a companion of man. Obedience is a sport where the participants are bound by the principles of good sportsmanship.

In order to earn Obedience titles, each team (the Aussie and his handler) must qualify in three Obedience trials under three different judges. In order to qualify, they must receive at least 50 percent of the points available for each exercise, with a minimum of 170 points out of a possible 200.

ENTERING A SHOW

To find out about when and where shows are going to be held, contact or join a local kennel club and an area affiliate club. Training classes where trainers and breeders often gather are good sources of information and guidance. Subscribe to *The Aussie Times*, the official publication of the ASCA, and to *The American Kennel Gazette* to gain specific information on area activities.

Get on good mailing lists for show, clinic, and seminar information. Contact the ASCA, the CKC, or the AKC for current show rules and regulations, and become familiar with them. See the Appendix for addresses.

Surefire of Windermere CD, OTD-S, STD-DC (WTCh. Las Rocosa Kublia Khan ex Ch. Christmas Wishes of Windermere CD, OTD-d, STD-c) shown winning a Record of Merit Versatility Award for excellence in Conformation, Herding, and Obedience competition.
Courtesy Karla Michelson.

Chapter 22

SHOW BUSINESS

DOG SHOWING IS AN ART THAT must be learned, practiced regularly, and perfected year after year. In addition to having a good specimen of the breed, winning and losing depends upon a number of other factors, including your own performance.

LOOK LIKE A WINNER

Your personal appearance will play a big role in your attitude, which in turn will set your dog off and make a statement about you and your self-confidence. Choose sporty and comfortable clothes, but don't dress so casually that it looks as if you just came in from cleaning kennels. Take pride in your appearance, because it reflects the entire sport of dog showing.

You need a pair of comfortable shoes in which you can run. Keep them polished, clean, and in good repair. You don't need to invest a lot of money in elaborate show outfits. A wise selection of a few well-made outfits can take you anywhere in style. Choose items that may be blended together to give the impression of different outfits made out of fabrics that will wash and wear well. Coordinate pieces and colors that are especially becoming to you and that complement your Aussie. The best-dressed people are those who stay away from "trendy" items and who stick with the basics. Study videos and show photos to view different presentations. Show pictures often reveal common mistakes that handlers make, like wearing a print or pattern that camouflages a merled Aussie rather than setting him apart for the judge to see.

Above all, be neat, clean, and well groomed. If you have only one or two good outfits, do not feel apprehensive about being seen in them time and again. Some of the top handlers have an outfit that complements so well that they wear it almost every time they enter the show ring.

Once you look like a winner, it will be easier for you to assume the role of positive handling when you enter the ring. Just don't forget to top off your appearance with a courteous manner.

Grooming To Win

The Aussie is a utilitarian and should be exhibited in a near to natural state. A certain amount of trimming is necessary, however. Preparing for the show should begin at least the week prior to the show. Trim the toenails and the hair around the feet and pads. The friction created during movement naturally wears down toenails and hair from around pads, showing off a tight, compact foot. Therefore, trimming is justified to enhance an outline that would be worn away naturally if each individual were in a situation to do so. Trim stray hair away from and around pads with a pair of blunt-nose scissors.

Some exhibitors believe that trimming is a tool to create illusions that camouflage faults. Such tricks will never make a poor Aussie into a good one, fool the eye of a knowledgeable judge, or alter genetic makeup. However, judicious trimming can aid in making a neater presentation.

Authoritative brushing and blow-drying techniques can intensify the most complementary lines for each individual. Brushing techniques can also make a slight difference between two Aussies of similar quality. They can create visual impact without altering the coat.

To accentuate stifle angulation or minimize a weak topline, brush hair against the grain. Proper brushing can also prevent the coat from indicat-

Carol Madsen winning top honors with her stunning champion, Las Rocosa Ashley (Taylor's Escalante ex McKinnley's Mandy). Photo by Wayne Rogers.

ing a fault that does not exist. For example, profuse hair on the back of the croup can make the rear look too high. Mist the hair with water or a light conditioner (humectant), brush, and place a cloth over the croup to flatten down the hair. Hair (feathers) sticking out on the elbow can give the impression of "elbowing out" when no such fault exists. This time, a cloth can be wrapped around the elbow to lay the hair inward.

Some Aussie exhibitors work "chalk" into damp hair on the legs and feet. Chalk on the legs and feet is brushed up and out against the growth. Chalk is a texturizer that whitens the white areas and stiffens the hair to create the appearance of heavier bone. Be aware that such foreign substances are *not allowed* in the show ring because they alter the natural texture of the coat.

Sparse, stray, and straggly hairs should be removed to neaten the overall appearance. Trim the backs of the hocks and pasterns. The long, straggly hairs that grow on the outside of the ears can be moderately thinned from the outside of the ear leather. The long hairs that sometimes grow on docked and natural bobtails may be removed. The feathering on a female can be thinned for purposes of cleanliness. Excessive trimming (scissoring) of the coat leaves the Aussie more susceptible to skin injuries.

Scissoring should never be used to shape or sculpt the body. Sculpting the head and ears is not only unnatural, but it also leaves the Aussie's head vulnerable to insect bites and trauma. If an Aussie requires such extensive preparation, then perhaps he is lacking in merit.

Whiskers may or may not be trimmed, depending on personal preference. However, whiskers should never be trimmed on an Aussie that is used to work rough stock. The whiskers are "feelers" to gauge distance when the dog is in close contact with the stock. To trim the whiskers on a stock dog would risk serious injury to him.

Bathe your Aussie anywhere from one day to one week ahead of the show so that his coat texture can benefit from natural oil distribution. To maintain the natural texture of your Aussie's coat, it is important to choose a shampoo that has a nearly neutral pH (slightly alkaline) like Johnson's No More Tears Baby Shampoo. Some exhibitors add a few drops of bluing (just enough to turn the water sky blue) to the rinse water to bring out the sparkle in white trim. Bluing removes yellow stains.

On the day of the show, you may want to rewash the feet and legs or other areas that have white trim. Lightly mist the hair coat with water and brush. Rub a tiny dab of petroleum jelly on the nose leather to keep it soft and shiny. *In the Ribbons, The Dog Show Game: Australian Shepherds*, a video on exhibiting Australian Shepherds, will give you additional information that may help you prepare your Aussie for show.

BE PREPARED

If the show is pre-entry, then you will want to take along your receipt of entry. You will need to take a copy of the registration papers for each Aussie. Take appropriate collars and leads, including one for Obedience and one for Conformation. Grooming tools, including a brush and a pair of scissors, may be needed for preshow preparations. A damp washcloth (or moist towelettes) and a dry towel may be necessary for emergency cleanup. Also bring bait (liver, hot dogs, or Special Cuts) or a squeaky toy that you may want to use in the show ring to get "animation." A travel crate is handy for confining your Aussie safely in the midst of activity and confusion. Take plenty of newspapers to line the bottom of the crate. If the show is held outdoors, you will want to provide some type of shade if it is not readily available for your dog. Nursery net (for ventilated shade) or a tarp can provide shade or protection from rain. Take along cleanup equipment to pick up after your dog. Include some smaller plastic sacks and a trash sack. Take along beverages and a snack for yourself. A blanket is another handy item. You may welcome the relief of an umbrella for rain or shine. Some sort of folding or lawn chairs are nice when none are provided at the show site.

You will want to arrive at the show site at least an hour prior to the listed judging time. At licensed or sanctioned events, the judging takes place on or shortly after the advertised time, not before. Verify the ring in which you are scheduled to show. After checking in, make any last-minute preparations before entering the ring. Take your Aussie out for exercise. This will let you relax before entering the ring.

IN THE RING

Here is where all your previous handling and training will pay off. Your Aussie has been taught to lead by your side and to stand while being groomed and handled on a regular basis. The show ring may bring out foreign reactions, but remember that you are in a new environment. If your Aussie's behavior is less than becoming, it is a sure sign that you need to get him out more and handle him in many new situations and unfamiliar surroundings. It takes a lot of effort to develop a confident attitude in your Aussie, espe-

Once around the ring.

cially if you are unsure. This nervousness transfers easily to your Aussie. However, practice makes perfect, so don't give up. Just make it a point to "haul" your Aussie more.

Generally, all movement in the ring will be viewed by the judge with the Aussies at a trot. You will need to teach your Aussie to gait in a trot at your side, while you learn to step in time with his stride.

Once Around the Ring

When you enter the ring, you will be identified by an entry number that is to be placed on your left arm. In North America, handlers enter the ring counterclockwise with their dogs on their left side. Generally, most judges will first view the entire class while the dogs are in a single line together stacked in a natural four-square stance. Often he will then ask the exhibitors to take their dogs around the ring in catalog order, which is the specific order in which each entry is accepted and listed in the catalog, or the steward will allow them to enter as they choose. At the judge's request, the steward will direct the exhibitors to either line up and stack their Aussies or to proceed gaiting around the ring. At this point, the judge will take over and command his ring.

Free-stacking by walking the dog into a natural four-square stance. Photo by Darcy Boyd.

Stacking (Posing)

Aussies can either be hand-stacked or free-stacked. Free-stacking means that you position your Aussie by walking him into a show pose—a natural four-square stance—and manually positioning his legs and feet. Free-stacking is commonly seen because the balance and symmetry typical of the Aussie also enable the dog to easily assume the natural four-square stance without a lot of assistance from his handler.

Handlers can either stand or kneel down by their Aussie's side during the individual examination. On occasion, some judges will ask each handler to move to the center of the ring and set up his Aussie. Remember—if you are hand-stacking, first set up the front legs, beginning with the one closest to the judge, and then set up the hind legs. Do not nitpick—it will only make your dog nervous. Draw positive attention to your entry by being efficient and ready. Don't let the judge catch you off guard. The individual examination is your time to show off your Aussie. Use it wisely. When the judge is going over the group as a whole, be alert. Keep an eye on the judge.

Speed Stacking

Speed stacking is an acquired skill. It is the ability of the handler to determine with a glance exactly which legs are out of position—and when to leave well enough alone. Speed stacking means being ready when the judge is making a final selection.

If a leg is out of position, you will want to first place the legs in the front. Begin with the leg in the judge's line of vision, because the greatest percentage of weight is carried by the forequarters. Then place the hind legs, beginning with the leg that is in the judge's line of vision. Sometimes speed stacking means that only one foot needs to be placed before you quickly resume "showing" your Aussie.

Gaiting

In gaiting around, it is more desirable to show on a loose lead rather than a tight one. When the lead is loose, it means that you are not placing any unnecessary strain on the lead that may interfere with your Aussie's ability to move freely. A tight lead can interfere with your dog's natural gait. A tight lead can also make a correct Aussie move like he has a structural fault.

Individual Examination

Each judge has a slightly different approach to going over the dogs. Most often, a judge will methodically begin at the head and work his way down. A look at the eye will reveal the size, shape, placement, and color as called for in the Breed Standard. Sometimes the judge will gently lift the ear forward toward the inside corner of the eye to check relativity of size. Sometimes the judge will lift the lips back to view the bite and teeth. However, the most accepted practice, and one that is appreciated by the judge, is when the handler shows the bite and teeth for the judge due to the possibility of transmission of disease.

If your Aussie appears to be unsteady, it is best that you kneel by his side during the entire exami-

Individual gaiting is designed to allow each entry an opportunity to be viewed without the distraction of the other entries. This is the time to really "show your dog."

You may talk to your dog in quiet tones, but do not try to strike up a conversation with the judge. Be polite and courteous. If you are unable to understand or hear a particular directive of the judge, ask him to repeat or explain it. Other than that, ask the ring steward to relay the information to the judge. It is acceptable to present the judge with a copy of a verification certificate from your veterinarian documenting accidental missing or broken teeth when the judge examines the mouth.

Individual Gaiting

After the individual examination, while each dog is fresh in the judge's mind, he will want to see the dog move. Playful young Aussies may want to frolic and show off even more while gaiting than during the individual examination. They may want to play tug-of-war or may balk or slink along at your side. Be positive in your attitude. Plan on putting in a few more hours of homework for future shows. At any time during your Aussie's life, he may act totally opposite to what is normal. However, with proper handling and socialization, this will remedy itself.

There are several familiar standard ring patterns that a judge will use to assess each individual's side gait and front and hind movement. Be sure to move your Aussie at a steady, consistent speed and in straight lines in the pattern requested. The judge will choose whichever pattern allows him the best angles for viewing gait (rear, front, and side). Usually you will be asked to move straight away from and back to the judge, followed by moving in a circle or "O" pattern around the judge. The judge may instead request a triangle, or an "L"-shaped pattern. Rarely will a judge ask to see an Aussie exhibited in the "T" pattern, except perhaps in Junior Showmanship competition.

Remember to keep your Aussie between yourself and the judge, but use an economy of motion while showing. Too often, handlers franti-

nation. Never scold or hit your Aussie in the ring. If necessary, be firm but never ruthless. You want to create a positive response in your Aussie. Too often, handlers expect perfection from their dog without doing the necessary homework. Stay out of the judge's road, but be there to assist by taking hold of your dog's head or collar to steady him.

The judge will proceed from the head down the neck to check lay-back (see The Standard of Excellence). The judge's hands will reveal muscle tone, depth and spring of rib cage, width of loin, presence of testicles (for males), etc. A good judge will never prod and poke, but will smoothly and effectively go from one point to another.

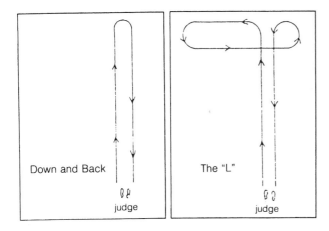

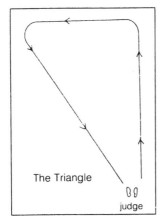

Gaiting patterns.

cally switch from side to side, causing the dog to break gait and interfering with the judge's view. When moving back toward the judge, try to stop approximately five or six feet away (the estimated height of your judge) to allow a full view of your Aussie. Sometimes, when the judge instructs a handler to take his dog straight down and straight back, the handler will try to hide a poor or faulty front by stopping off to one side instead of squarely in front of the judge. This only draws attention to the fault. As you move back toward the judge, adjust your pace until your dog is into the desired stance. You can use bait (food or a toy) to get your Aussie to put his head up and ears at attention to show expression.

If you drop food in the ring, make it a point to pick up after yourself. Use toys judiciously so that you don't distract another Aussie when the judge is examining the other dogs. Use these items while the judge is comparing your Aussie to another or while he is viewing the entire group as a whole.

Be as courteous to others as you would have them be to you. Occasionally, another handler (either very innocently or quite deliberately) will run up on your heels, possibly block the judge's full view of your dog, or crowd you in a tight space. In this case, firmly but politely request the other handler to either give you more room, or distance yourself. If this occurs several times with the same handler and you feel that the situation is deliberate, notify the ring steward. Do not involve the judge, because this is part of the steward's responsibility.

The judge may compare several individuals together and ask each handler to move his Aussie several times, but a decision will be made. You may or may not agree with the judge on any given day, but remember that this is just another day at the show.

THE ART OF WINNING AND LOSING

As a contestant, you must learn that there are honest differences of opinion. You must learn to take all wins and losses in stride. Try to be objective about yourself, about the performance of your Aussie, and about your competition. Graciously accept losses, and be able to win without boasting. It takes a good loser to be a good winner. Take each accomplishment with a sense of modesty. Congratulate the winners and allow them their own time to shine, because you, too, will have your day in the barrel.

By reducing the depth of field, the viewer's eye is drawn immediately to the handsome Ch. Touchstone's Deal Me In (Las Rocosa Joseph ex Ch. Touchstone Pear-Tree's Sheza Riot). Courtesy Lisa Cameron.

Chapter 23

PICTURE PERFECT

YOU DON'T HAVE TO BE A PROFESSIONAL photographer to be able to take dynamic photographs of Australian Shepherds. The basic elements necessary in shooting professional-quality photographs are: a knowledge of the Australian Shepherd breed, an Aussie, patience, the right light, correct film, and a camera.

CAMERAS

For the average person wanting to take their own photographs, 35mm cameras are the most practical. They are portable and are relatively easy to use. Film is readily available and does not require a custom lab for processing.

Lens and Depth of Field

Different lenses used on the same camera can create distinctly different shots of the same scene. The normal (fifty-millimeter) lens focuses on the Aussie while retaining a sense of his surroundings. A wide-angle lens will reproduce a greater portion in front of and behind the point of focus. This is desirable if you wish to capture your Aussie in the context of his environment or when he is standing in front of an interesting view. The shorter the focal length of the lens, the greater the depth of field. A long lens provides a smaller range in sharp detail, making it easier to throw the background out of focus. A long focal length allows you to get a close-up study of your Aussie by deemphasizing or blurring the background.

Select a normal lens for all-around situations (ringside, for example). Use a telephoto lens for portraits and for working shots at a distance. A medium-range telephoto lens offers a more natural look with no distortions.

Aperture

The depth of field increases as the size of the aperture decreases; therefore, the smaller the aperture, the greater the depth of field. The f-stop is the number assigned to describe each opening. A larger number, such as f/22 or f/16, indicates a small opening, while f/2 indicates a much wider opening. When the Aussie is positioned at a medium or close distance, a smaller aperture will generally give sharpness throughout the picture. A large opening will focus on or accent only the Aussie, while the background and foreground will be reduced to soft patterns.

When shooting an Aussie working livestock, a smaller aperture (larger f-stop) will increase the in-focus area, making it easier to bring both the dog and the livestock into focus. The larger the opening, the more difficult it will be to keep the Aussie and all of the livestock in focus.

Film

All film is rated with ASA numbers according to light sensitivity. Medium-speed film (ASA 100 to ASA 200) is a general-purpose film that is suitable for most situations. Medium-speed film offers good color reproduction and a good latitude for exposure (slightly over or underexposing) while still producing a usable print. It also reproduces good detail when enlarged. Fast film (400 ASA) is ideal for action and low-light situations. Four-hundred film offers a good latitude for exposure, color, and very little grain when enlarged. The speed of the film combined with the lighting conditions will determine which shutter speeds and f-stops will correctly expose each frame.

Light and Exposure

Light is an important element in your photos. The ideal time to shoot outdoor photographs is during the late afternoon and early morning when the light is longest. Light can play a major role in creating a photograph. Shady, hazy, or slightly overcast days produce appealing color. Shadows that are present in bright sunlight are often eliminated. The correct lighting can contribute greatly to a memorable photograph.

Light meters are a guide, offering a point of reference. However, you must learn how to meter the subject for the right exposure. When you are shooting the subject in even lighting conditions—where the dog and background are lighted equally—the automatic reading on the camera's meter will produce desirable results. When the subject is in the shade and the background is in the sun, you must move in close to take a reading from the dog to ensure proper exposure, because the background will appear brighter. When the subject is side-lit, you can take two readings, one from the sunny side and one from the shaded side. If in doubt, choose the area you think needs more exposure for detail.

Certain circumstances will dictate that you need to outthink the light meter, such as when you are shooting a subject in a backdrop of snow, or when the subject is backlit. If you want to properly expose your Aussie, it is important that you meter off of the dark side (the side nearest camera) of the dog and let the background go overexposed. If you take the reading from the

This photo freezes the action while WTCh. Twin Oaks Kit Carson RD puts the brakes on an uncooperative bovine. Photo by Cee's Pix.

background, the dog will be underexposed and will appear as a silhouette, and you will miss the subtle detail in dark- and solid-colored Aussies. A dark-colored dog, especially a solid black Aussie, will absorb the light. If the silhouette is an effect that you want, then meter off of the background. Your exposure will depend on whether the subject is back-lit or front-lit, or if the light source is on the side. A back-lit subject requires more exposure than a front-lit subject but not quite as much as when the subject is side-lit.

Whenever you are in doubt about a particular exposure, or when you are shooting in uncertain lighting conditions, take two additional photographs (insurance shots) of the same scene. After shooting at what seems like the correct exposure, shoot an extra frame at one or two f-stops lower, and another at one or two f-stops higher.

The lighting, pose, and angle of this photo contribute to an excellent Conformation shot of Hall of Fame sire and Working Trial Ch. Las Rocosa Bonny Kyle Ranch Dog Excellent. Photo by Cee's Pix.

Flash

Even during a bright, sunny day, flash may be desirable. Flash can enhance the subject by boosting the light level or highlighting back-lit subjects. In these situations, flash will balance the shadowed side of the subject and will bring out more detail, "life," and luster in your Aussie's coat and eyes. You can also keep your Aussie from squinting because you will not need the direct sun hitting him in the face. Flash is especially useful when you want a photo of a light red merle alongside a solid black dog. Flash can also eliminate undesired or distracting shadows.

You can prevent the "red or green eye" that happens when the direct light from the flash reflects off of the Aussie's eyes by angling the direct light slightly away from the dog. You also can use a diffuser cap over the flash unit to soften and distribute the light across the subject.

Before Shooting

Familiarize yourself with the particular features and controls of your camera. Practice loading film and quick focusing until you are completely confident. Whenever in doubt, refer to the owner's manual.

Many companies such as Pentax, Nikon, and Canon offer weekend schools for photography. Community colleges and recreational centers also offer a variety of photography courses. These classes teach you how to get the most out of your camera and offer tips on taking better pictures. Local camera shops can often provide sources for these classes.

Make sure that your camera batteries have ample power. Is the camera loaded? Check the automatic frame counter if you are in doubt, or test the film advance for a slight resistance. Many good frames have been lost when the unsuspecting user opens the back to put in a new roll.

Before loading new film, dust way any particles on the back of the lens that would blur or spot the negative. Dirt or film chips will also scratch the film. Use a blower brush or lint-free cloth. Load film in the shade. Once the camera is loaded, be sure that the film leader is properly inserted in the take-up spool and that the spool is turning. Advance the film a frame while the back is still open to ensure that the film sprockets stay engaged in the holes. When the film is advancing properly, the rewind knob will revolve. Make sure that the camera back is closed securely. Don't forget to set the correct ASA on the camera and the shutter speed that you plan to use.

Blow away any dust from the surface of the lens, or clean the lens with a photographic lens cleaner and tissue. Cameras with single-lens reflex won't display a picture in the viewfinder if the lens cap is left on, but other cameras will. Make sure that you have removed the lens cover.

Common Errors

Mediocre photographs often result from failing to focus on the primary elements of the scene (the Aussie, the Aussie and stock, the dog and handler). Cluttered and distracting backgrounds often spoil what otherwise could have been a dynamic picture. A lighter or brighter object or a white piece of paper on the ground will be the first object that your eye will catch rather than your Aussie. This is what you wish to avoid.

Be careful not to chop off important physical features, such as the feet or nose. The appearance of a tree or pole growing out of the subject can be easily avoided and a better shot achieved by changing camera angles.

Blurring, if undesired, can be avoided by using shutter speeds fast enough to stop the action. Agility, Frisbee, herding, Fyball, Obedience, and gaiting require a fast shutter speed to stop the action. When you are working with a camera speed lower than 1/125, a tripod is beneficial. When you are shooting performance events, a speed of 1/250 will usually stop action

The winter setting in front of the historic Mary Martha Church contribute to a memorable image of Ch. Wildhagen's Dutchman CDX and Wildhagen's Thistle of Flintridge. Courtesy Phillip Wildhagen.

coming toward or away from the camera, and 1/500 will freeze horizontal action. If desired, blurring (of the dog or background) can be effective to display Aussies in action. To get this effect, you can shoot at a slower shutter speed and pan with the dog in the same direction of his motion.

Taking Better Photos

Wherever possible, exclude anything from the composition that doesn't enhance the subject matter. You can try shooting from different angles or move closer to the subject. If necessary, expand or reduce the depth of field or switch lenses. Make

The angle at which the photo was shot gives the wrong impression that this Best of Breed Winner is short and squatty.

sure that when you are viewing the photograph, your eye is drawn to the main subject.

What the eye sees and what the film records are not always the same. When you are shooting static or posed scenes, touch your thumbs together and then hold your hands up to form a frame. Close one eye and look at the scene with the other. This two-dimensional view is similar to the way the camera views the scene. One rule of thumb for composing interesting shots is to divide the frame of your camera into four straight lines—two horizontal and two vertical. Each line intersects at four points (each slightly off-center). Capturing the subject at any one of the four points will create a more intriguing picture.

Before shooting, locate a pleasing background, but don't allow the background to take up too much of the picture and detract from the Aussie. A more dynamic picture can be created by taking a tighter shot of the subject so that the dog, not the background, is the main subject of the picture.

When you are doing your Aussie's portrait, shoot the picture either horizontally or vertically. The horizontal format works well for Conformation shots, especially when you are illustrating the longer proportions. When you are shooting a head study, a vertical layout seems to work well.

Try to approach the photo shoot in a relaxed manner. Your attitude will be conveyed to your Aussie as well. A nervous dog won't display his true personality. The Aussie that is trained to bait to food, a ball, or a squeaky toy will be easiest to photograph. It is beneficial to have an assistant on hand if he cooperates with you and takes your direction.

Always take a second shot. It is good insurance, and professionals will tell you that it can improve your chances of success.

ADVERTISING SHOTS

When you are trying to attract future clients, you want to create memorable photographs. True is the old saying: a picture is worth a thousand words. Look through current magazines and see which photos stand out from the rest. Standard win photographs with the handler, the Aussie, and the judge are fine for advertising a win; however, rarely will such a photograph be remembered for years to come.

When you wish to capture a Breed Standard Ideal, there are some small tricks that can create illusions of the perfect canine specimen. If the feet or pasterns are faulty or weak, pose the dog in the grass. If the Aussie's topline looks weak or his body is too long, then maybe you should shoot at a three-quarter angle. By the same token, just because you photograph your Aussie standing in the grass or in a three-quarter view does not mean that he is faulty. An individual with a correct front and an attractive head and expression might best be shown off in a three-quarter angle.

Hold the camera at the body level of the Aussie. This means that you will have to be kneeling or lying down (especially with puppies). An individual with short legs may benefit from a shot angled slightly upward with the camera positioned at ground level, while you can shorten the legs of a long-legged Aussie by raising the camera to a higher level. Do not shoot down or up at the dog or you will create an unnatural, distorted image. A high camera angle can make the Aussie appear short and dumpy, and a lower camera angle can make the Aussie look long and lanky. For the most part, when you are taking photos of a well-balanced Aussie, aim the camera at the dog's level toward the area underneath the withers. In a three-quarter view, aim at the shoulder.

No matter how you pose your Aussie, be sure that the camera angle enables you to see all four legs. Occasionally, you will see a beautiful photograph of a dog that appears to have only two or three legs.

An Aussie with a beautiful head and expression may be shown off best by a portrait of the head and chest. You can shoot the head from either the front, at a three-quarter view, or in profile, depending on which angle enhances the features best. When the Aussie is lying down, use a three-quarter view with the camera on an even plane with the Aussie's head. Focus on the eyes when you are trying to capture his expression. The eyes are the window to the soul. A squeaky toy, ball, whistle, baby rattle, cat, a bird in a cage, or bubbles are all effective tools to get expressions out of an Aussie. Any type of noise (rattling, rustling, crinkling, whistling, ringing, squeaking) can also produce the desired results.

Be creative, and be patient. Puppies do not have a long attention span, but they are playful and inquisitive. The moment the shot looks good, snap the picture. Don't be afraid to take several rolls of film to get a desired shot. Don't expect a puppy to stay in any one position too long. You will be much more successful if you are willing to move around and try different angles.

Different props are beneficial when you are shooting puppies. They can create a point of interest in the photograph as well as capture the puppy's attention. Children and Aussie puppies together can create a particular point of interest.

When you are shooting action, catch the Aussie in the peak of the action. Remember—what goes up must come down. This is where knowing your subject is beneficial in anticipating the perfect moment, whether it is capturing an Aussie in a flying trot, catching a ball or Frisbee in midair, or heeling cows. You must be a quick-draw artist with a trigger finger.

Practice makes perfect. The more practice you have at taking photos, the sooner you will develop a discriminating eye for recognizing the most complimentary shots.

Working Trial Ch. Zephyr's Kootenai Brown, one of Canada's leading sires. Courtesy Russell.

Chapter 24

GENETICS OF THE AUSTRALIAN SHEPHERD

GENETICS IS THE STUDY OF INHERITANCE. Inheritance is responsible for the form and function of the individual, although these can be modified to some extent by environmental and developmental factors. A basic understanding of genetics can be used to advantage not only by the breeder, who can apply genetic principles in selecting sires and dams in an effort to produce superior quality progeny, but also by the fancier when selecting a pet.

The general mechanisms by which traits are passed down from parents to offspring have been fairly well elucidated and appear to be rather constant in most living organisms. However, with regard to the inheritance patterns of specific traits within certain species and breeds of animals, much remains to be studied. This is particularly true of the Australian Shepherd because it is of fairly recent origin as a pure breed and is, therefore, without the benefit of many years' accumulation of breeders' records, nor have there been many genetic studies of the breed performed by the scientific community. Therefore, much of the information about the inheritance of traits in the Aussie is based on breeders' observations, accurate and complete record keeping, and cooperation among breeders. With more scientific studies, our knowledge of the genetics of the Australian Shepherd will be enhanced.

* This chapter was written by Lucia D. Kline, DVM.

Fundamental Principles of Genetics

Deoxyribonucleic Acid (DNA) is the chemical molecule that is the genetic material. It is in every nucleated cell of the body and carries coded specifications for growth, differentiation, and functioning of the organism. It can also replicate itself so that when a cell divides (*mitosis*), the two daughter cells contain exactly the same code (except for the egg and sperm cells, which will be discussed later).

Each molecule of DNA, along with other associated molecules, make up a *chromosome*. The number of chromosomes in each cell varies with the species of the animal. The dog has seventy-eight chromosomes that occur in pairs which are generally similar in size and shape (*homologous chromosomes*), one of each pair having come from the male parent and the other from the female parent. One pair of chromosomes—the sex chromosomes—determine the sex of the individual. The other thirty-eight pairs are called autosomes.

In the sexual organs, a special form of cell division (*meiosis*) occurs in which the homologous pairs of chromosomes are separated. The resulting egg and sperm cells contain only one chromosome of each pair. This is called *the principle of segregation*. Whether an egg or sperm cell receives a maternal or paternal chromosome of a given pair is strictly random.

Each pair of chromosomes divides independently of all other pairs so that the egg and sperm cell may each contain one of a great many possible combinations of maternal and paternal chromosomes. This is called *the principle of independent assortment*. These two principles form the basis of what is called Mendelian genetics, named after discoverer Gregor Mendel.

At fertilization, one sperm cell unites with the egg cell to restore the full number of chromosomes. One chromosome of each pair is contributed by the sperm cell, the other by the egg cell. Fertilization is also random such that any

Taylor's Buena (Sniff's Dandy Danny ex Petramala's Tate), a foundation matron of the breed owned by Joe D. Taylor of Moab, Utah.

one of many sperm cells containing a great many possible combinations of maternal and paternal chromosomes has an equal chance of fertilizing the egg cell. This randomness in the recombination of chromosomes already present in a breeding population explains much of the variation in the population. After fertilization, the egg cell goes through a complex series of mitotic cell divisions to produce the many thousands of cells of the body, and each of these cells contains exact copies of all the chromosomes of the original fertilized egg.

The DNA molecule is functionally subdivided into *genes*, which are considered to be the smallest units of inheritance. Each gene is a code for a specific protein or protein subunit. These proteins may serve either as structural proteins, which contribute to the form of the individual, or as enzymes, which catalyze cellular biochemical reactions that contribute to the functioning of the body. The same genes are present in all nucleated cells of the body, although different genes may be active in different cells—leading to the variation in the tissues of the body—or they may be active at different times during development. Each chromosome contains thousands of genes along its length and has been described as being similar to a string of beads, with each bead being a gene. All the genes on one chromosome have a linear order and tend to be inherited together; therefore, they are said to be *linked*.

A gene governing a given trait has a specific site, called a *locus*, on a specific chromosome. Homologous chromosomes contain genes that govern the same traits; therefore, an individual has two genes—one from its father and one from its mother—that govern the same trait. The gene governing the trait on one of the homologous chromosomes is in exactly the same locus as its partner on the other homologous chromosome. However, these paired genes may not be exactly alike even though they influence the same trait.

Alternate forms of paired genes are called *alleles*. These are the result of mutations and are responsible for the variations within the Australian Shepherd breed. There may be more than two alternate forms of a gene within a breed or species, called *multiple alleles*, but a given individual can only have one pair of these. When an individual has two identical alleles for a certain trait, he is said to be *homozygous* for that particular trait. When an individual has two different alleles as the pair, he is said to be *heterozygous* for the trait.

The kinds of alleles that an individual carries for each of the different gene pairs make up what is called the *genotype*, which is the actual genetic construction of the individual. The visible expression of these alleles, or what we observe, is called the *phenotype*. The phenotypic expression of any given allele depends on its interaction with its paired allele, and in some cases with other gene pairs and with the environment. The major form of interaction between alleles of a gene pair is called *dominance*. A dominant allele will be expressed regardless of whether it is paired with the same (*homozygous*) or a different (*heterozygous*) allele. If it is paired with a different allele, it will completely mask the effects of the other allele. In this instance, the other allele is called *recessive*. Recessive alleles for a trait are only expressed phenotypically when the individual is homozygous.

Which alleles for a given trait are recessive and which are dominant is determined by observing the frequency of the appearance of the phenotype dictated by the alleles in the offspring. Conversely, once the dominance pattern of the alleles is known, the probabilities of the appearance of phenotypes in the offspring of parents of known genotypes can be predicted on the basis of statistics. This is made simple by the use of a shorthand device in which a given trait or gene is assigned a letter. A capital letter is assigned to represent the *dominant* allele, while a lowercase letter represents the *recessive* allele. A geometrical device called the *Punnett Square* is used to visualize all of the possible combinations of alleles. As an example, in the Australian Shepherd, the basic coat color is determined by one pair of genes and is either red or black. The allele for black is dominant to the allele for red. The letter "B" has been assigned to this gene pair, and since black is dominant, it is represented by a capital "B" and red by a lowercase "b."

If an individual that is homozygous for black is bred to an individual that is homozygous for red, the Punnett Square can be utilized to determine the probabilities of the colors appearing in the offspring. The two alleles of one parent are placed across the top of the chart, with the two alleles of the other parent placed on the left side. Then all possible combinations of parental genes and their frequency of occurrence in the offspring can be predicted. Each allele of one parent has an equal chance of pairing up with either of the two alleles of the other parent. This pairing is represented by the boxes of the Punnett Square (Figure 1). Thus, it can be seen that all offspring of homozygous parents, one for red, the other for black, will themselves be black in phenotype but will carry the allele for red in their genotype and possess the potential to pass it to their offspring. Punnett Squares can be constructed for all the possible genotypes for the trait in the par-

Figure 1 Black parent homozygous for black

	B	B
b	Bb	Bb
b	Bb	Bb

Red parent homozygous for red

All progeny are heterozygous Bb and will be black in color.

Figure 2 Heterozygous black parent

	B	b
B	BB	Bb
b	Bb	bb

Heterozygous black parent

Genotypic frequency of the progeny:
25% BB
50% Bb
25% bb

Phenotypic frequency of the progeny:
75% black
25% red

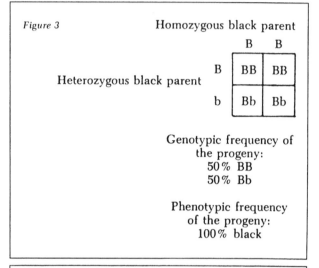

Figure 3 Homozygous black parent, Heterozygous black parent. Genotypic frequency of the progeny: 50% BB, 50% Bb. Phenotypic frequency of the progeny: 100% black.

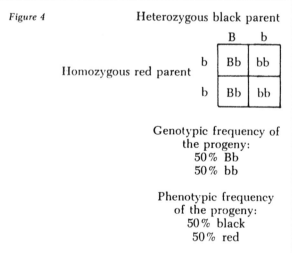

Figure 4 Heterozygous black parent, Homozygous red parent. Genotypic frequency of the progeny: 50% Bb, 50% bb. Phenotypic frequency of the progeny: 50% black, 50% red.

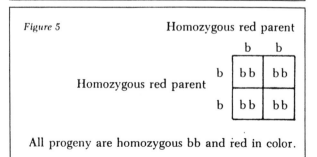

Figure 5 Homozygous red parent, Homozygous red parent. All progeny are homozygous bb and red in color.

ents and for the probabilities of the genotypes and phenotypes of the offspring determined (Figures 2, 3, 4, and 5).

This device can also be used when more than one trait is being considered, as long as the gene pairs for each trait are found on different sets of homologous chromosomes and are therefore inherited independently of each other. It must be remembered that these are statistical probabilities based on random recombination at fertilization. The statistical probabilities are reflected when large numbers of breedings produce large numbers of offspring. In a given litter, however, where only a relatively small number of offspring are produced, the probable statistical distribution of genotypic and phenotypic frequencies may not be reflected. Nevertheless, the chances of their occurrence at the time of breeding follow the laws of statistical probability.

Unfortunately, genetics is made much more complex by the fact that not every trait is determined by only one pair of genes whose alleles follow strict dominance-recessive relationships. As was stated earlier, the phenotypic expression of a trait may depend not only on the interaction between alleles, but also on the interaction with other gene pairs and the interaction of the individual with the environment. For example, it has been determined that at least ten gene pairs, with each pair on a different set of homologous chromosomes, influence coat color in the dog. The nine other pairs of genes have altering effects on coat color (black or red) to produce the wide variety seen in the canine species. The inheritance of the coat color patterns seen in the Australian Shepherd will be described in more detail later. The more important types of interactions that affect the phenotypic expression of the individual are as follows.

Codominance

This action occurs when both alleles of a pair are expressed and each allele *produces an independent effect in the offspring*. The phenotype of the heterozygote is *qualitatively different* in character from either homozygote, and the effects of both dominant and recessive alleles are expressed in the individual that carries both. Matings between heterozygotes for a given trait produce a phenotypic ratio in the offspring of 1:2:1 for that trait instead of 3:1.

Semi- or Incomplete Dominance

There are many genes whose alleles do not have strongly dominant or recessive relationships. Therefore, when these alleles come together in one individual in the heterozygous condition, they produce an *intermediate, but similar effect*. Semidominant alleles often code for the same genetic product, but in unequal quantity, leading to a heterozygote phenotype that is intermediate between that of the two homozygous parents. When two heterozygotes are mated, the alleles segregate and resort independently so that homozygous offspring for each allele resemble the extremes of the grandparents homozygous for the same alleles. Heterozygous offspring are intermediate like their parents.

Ch. Las Rocosa Leslie CSD (Ch. Las Rocosa Shiloh ex Hartnagle's Fritzie Taylor), a product of the famous Fritzie X Shiloh cross pictured against the image of her renowned son Ch. Chulo Rojo (sired by Taylor's Whiskey). Chulo is the foundation sire of the Fairoaks line. Courtesy Cornwell.

Above: Peas in a pod. Ch. Sweet Seasons of Heatherhill (Ch. Wildhagen's Dutchman of Flintridge, CDX ex McCorkle's Blue Tule Fog) on the left with progeny sired by one half-brother Ch. Windermere's Sunshine of Bonnie-Blu CDX. Left to right: "Seasons," Sunsweet of Heatherhill, Heavenly Sunshine of Heatherhill, Sweet 'n Sassy of Heatherhill, and Heaven Sent of Heatherhill. Photo by Dai.

Below: George's Red Rustler (Ginther's Rusty ex Ginther's Red Velvet), recipient of "Dog World" Award of Canine Distinction. "Red Rustler" is the foundation of Copper Canyon and one of the main contributing sires of the modern Aussie. Photo by Thom Carter.

Complementary Genes

These are genes belonging to different gene pairs that are similar in phenotypic effect when present separately in individuals. However, when present together in the same individual, they interact to produce a different trait. If two such genes are complementary for a dominant effect, the phenotypic ratio in the offspring resulting from two individuals heterozygous for both traits is 9:1; if complementary for a recessive effect, a phenotypic ratio of 15:1 results.

Modifier Genes

These are genes that act as enhancers or inhibitors of a trait determined by another gene pair. They cause a range of expression of the trait but seldom entirely obliterate it, and their effects are only evident in a suitable genotype. They are considered to be multiple factors whose members are generally unknown but that are amenable to selection in either direction by their visible effects on traits.

Epistasis

In this type of interaction, a gene or gene pair masks the expression of another non-allelic gene pair. The gene pair that is suppressed is said to be *hypostatic*. The *epistatic* pair blocks the biochemical reactions determined by the hypostatic pair to mask the effect. Epistasis is distinguished from dominance in which the masking effect occurs between genes of an allelic pair. Through epistatic effects and other gene interactions, traits may remain hidden for generations. This is called *atavism*.

Pleiotrophy

This is a situation in which a gene influences the expression of more than one trait. A gene has only one function—coding for the production of a single protein. However, this protein may play several different roles in the body, giving rise to the expressions of several traits at the phenotypic level. Certain pleiotropic genes may influence both qualitative and quantitative traits.

Penetrance and Expressivity

Some traits are manifested in varying degrees in different individuals possessing the genotype for expression of the trait. Certain individuals, although possessing the genotype, fail to exhibit the characteristic at all. *Penetrance* is a measure of the population that both possesses the genotype and expresses the trait. When a trait is not expressed in all individuals that possess the proper genotype, the trait is said to have incomplete penetrance. *Expressivity* is the range of expression of a gene in different individuals. The reason for incomplete penetrance and variable expressivity is not completely understood but is usually explained on the basis of modifiers that influence the action of a given gene or environmental variation. In such cases, breeding tests are used to prove genotype.

Polygenes

This concept was developed to explain the variation along a continuous range of quantitative traits such as size, conformation, viability, rate of growth, and time to reach maturity. Most traits of domestic animals are thought to be quantitative. Traits that segregate into distinct forms, such as with dominant/recessive gene interactions, are called qualitative traits and are said to have discontinuous variation. The concept of polygenes implies that quantitative traits are governed by a number of genes at different loci on many chromosomes. An individual gene exerts a slight effect on phenotype, but in conjunction with a few or many other genes, a gradual series extends from one parental extreme to the other. The greater the number of genes involved, the more continuous the variation. The contribution of a particular gene varies in accordance with the rest of the genotype—the effects of the various genes involved are not simply additive or equal, but are influenced by other types of gene interactions (linkage, epistasis, modifiers, etc.). One feature of polygenic traits is that their degree of expression can usually be influenced by the environment. Therefore, it is important to distinguish the genetic component from environmental effects. The degree to which a given trait is controlled by inheritance is called *heritability*. It is possible through selective breeding to manipulate traits influenced by polygenic inheritance to produce relatively pure breeding lines. However, at this time it is not possible to individually recognize the genes involved.

Phenocopies

These are alterations in a phenotypic trait induced by the environment but that resemble those caused by genetic factors. To distinguish hereditary traits from those caused by the environment, appropriate test matings are sometimes conducted. Traits of a hereditary nature will be passed to the progeny, while those caused by the environment will not.

Sex Linkage

This is the association of a hereditary trait with the sex of the individual because the gene for the trait is located on a sex chromosome. Females are homozygous for the X chromosome. Males are heterozygous, carrying both X and Y chromosomes. Unlike the somatic homologous chromosome pairs, the X and Y chromosomes do not have completely corresponding pairs of genes. A portion of the X chromosome has no corresponding counterpart on the Y chromosome, although most but not all of the genes of the Y chromosome do have corresponding genes on the X chromosome. A recessive allele occurring on the nonhomologous part of the X chromosome can therefore come to expression in a male because there is no corresponding dominant allele to suppress it. A female must be homozygous for the recessive allele in order for it to be expressed phenotypically. Sex of the offspring is determined by the chromosomes of the father. The mother can only pass an X chromosome to the offspring; however, the father can pass an X chromosome—in which case the offspring will be female—or a Y chromosome—in which case the offspring will be male. If the father is expressing a sex-linked trait, he can only pass the trait to his daughters, who will all be carriers of the trait. The daughters may or may not pass the trait down to be expressed in their sons depending on whether they are homozygous or heterozygous for the trait. If they are homozygous, having received an identical allele from their mother, all their sons will be affected, and all their daughters will be carriers of the trait. If they are heterozygous, half their sons will express the trait and half their daughters will be carriers.

Sex-Limited Gene Expression

This is the expression of a trait carried on autosomal chromosomes by only one sex. Although an individual of the other sex may carry homozygous alleles for the trait, it cannot be expressed in the individual because the individual's sex does not allow it. Sex hormones interact to limit the expression of the trait to a given sex.

USING GENETICS IN A BREEDING PROGRAM

From the above discussion, it may appear impossible to master enough genetics in order to plan matings that will result in offspring with the desired characteristics. It may seem even more futile in light of the fact that our knowledge of the

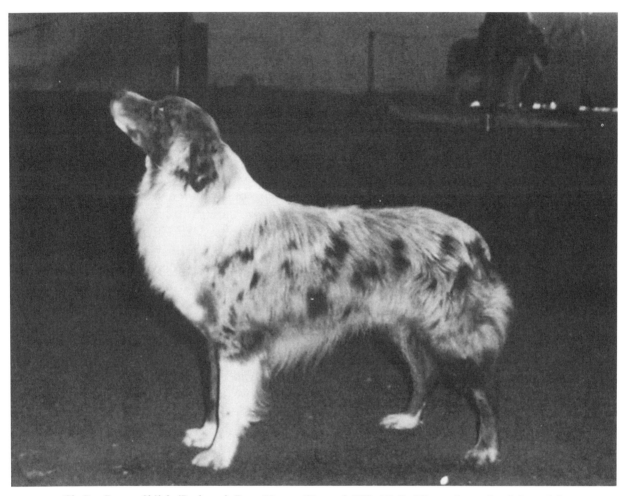

Ch. Las Rocosa Shiloh (Boehmer's Four Man ex Hosmer's Jill), Hall of Fame sire and recipient of the Dog World Magazine's *Award of Canine Distinction for his outstanding record as a sire.*

inheritance patterns of many traits is limited. However, the knowledge of Mendel's laws and a recognition of the complexity of the behavior of genes are prerequisites to the intelligent breeding of dogs. With an understanding of these, you can also understand methods of selection and systems of breeding that can make the planning of matings much simpler. It must be emphasized, however, that success in breeding also requires you to be a good judge—to be able to recognize traits of soundness as well as faults. Any application of scientific knowledge involves a certain amount of individual judgment, leading some to describe the breeding of animals as an art. Breeding is the process of choosing the genes most likely to produce the ideal Aussie.

The selection process is a major tool available to the animal breeder. Basically, it is an attempt to shift the traits of the population in a desired direction by retaining desirable individuals and excluding those with less desirable characteristics. Selection does not create new traits, but merely changes the proportion of desired and undesired phenotypes. Three basic methods of selection are available to the breeder on a practical basis:

(1) Phenotypic Selection
(2) Pedigree Selection
(3) Selection on the Basis of Progeny

The simplest method of selection is *phenotypic* or *individual selection*. This is the systematic choosing of sires and dams in which the desired traits are most strongly visible in the hope that their traits will be passed on to the offspring. The effectiveness of selecting an individual on phenotype is influenced by the relative importance of heredity or environment in the development of the trait. Heritability is a measure of the extent to which a trait is influenced by heredity—the higher the heritability, the more the agreement between phenotype and genotype. Obviously, phenotypic selection is most effective when heritability is high. It is also most effective for simple dominant and recessive traits, which limit its use.

Pedigree selection requires detailed knowledge of the traits possessed by the ancestors of the individual under consideration. Knowledge of the phenotypes of the ancestors provides information as to what traits are genetically available in the descendant. The closer the relationship, the more useful the information; therefore, usually only the first four generations are considered. Pedigree selection is based on the principle that the average phenotypic value for the family is a good indication of the mean genotypic value. It is useful for quantitative traits. If desired traits are seen consistently down through the generations, presumably the descendant will have the genes needed for the trait and have them in greater numbers. Study of the pedigree can also give some indication of the mode of inheritance of the trait, particularly if information on the phenotypes of the siblings (indirect relatives) to the ancestors in the pedigree (direct relatives) is also known.

Selection on the basis of progeny, called progeny testing, is based on the principle that progeny reveal the genotypes of their sires and dams. With this method, you examine the phenotypes of the offspring produced by the individual in question to determine if the expected desired traits are being expressed in the offspring with minimal undesirable traits. Validity of the progeny test increases directly with the number of offspring available for examination. It must be remembered that traits of offspring are the result of the combined effect of the genes of both parents. Progeny testing can be useful to determine if the parents carry recessive genes for either desirable or undesirable traits. If traits not revealed by the phenotype of the parents show up in the offspring, and if these traits are influenced by heredity rather than the environment, it can be assumed that the parents carry the genes for these traits. On the basis of this new information as to the genotypes of the parents, the breeder can decide whether to continue to use these animals in his breeding program, depending on whether he wishes to perpetuate or extinguish these particular traits.

The wise breeder will apply all three of these methods of selection whenever possible. Selection is not simply a one-time matter, but rather an ongoing process of analysis and evaluation. The most common difficulty is that you must select for many traits at the same time, including physical attributes, behavior, fertility, and vitality. The results of selection depend on the heritability of the trait, its mode of inheritance, and the intensity of selection. Obviously, traits of higher heritability are more responsive to selection than those governed by many genes with complex interactions. Selection for a trait produced by a single recessive allele can produce maximum effects in one generation. The intensity of selection, called the *selection pressure*, is measured by the difference in phenotype of the individuals chosen for mating from that of the average of the entire population—in other words—the degree of superiority of those selected. It also implies that fewer individuals of one generation are used to produce the next, because as you move farther from the mean, the individuals available with the desired traits become fewer in number. The greater the selection pressure, the greater the response to selection.

To be a successful breeder, it is not enough to be able to select superior individuals capable of passing the desired characteristics down to their offspring. You must also understand the genetic principles underlying the various systems of breeding and apply these systems in planned matings. With purebred animals, three systems of breeding are used:

(1) Inbreeding
(2) Linebreeding
(3) Outbreeding

Inbreeding is the production of offspring by mating individuals more closely related to each other than the average population. It has been used, together with principles of selection, to produce almost every valuable breed of domestic animal and to develop recognizable strains within breeds. Genetically, inbreeding increases the homozygosity of individuals for the genes that they carry. Since related individuals are more likely to carry the same alleles for a given trait by descent from a common ancestor, the chances of an offspring acquiring identical alleles of a gene pair are increased. As succeeding generations become more homozygous for various traits, the probability that all offspring will receive the same inheritance from their inbred parents is increased, and the population becomes more uniform. Statistics have been used to quantify the degree of genetic relationships and the effect that these relationships have on increasing homozygosity. Homozygosity increases with more intense inbreeding regardless of how the genes interact and express themselves phenotypically. Inbreeding is the method that most easily and rapidly establishes a population that breeds true to type.

Increased homozygosity occurs for defective traits as well as for desirable ones. Therefore, it is imperative that the foundation sires and dams in inbreeding programs be *superior* individuals, as free from faults as possible, and that inbreeding be accompanied by ongoing selection. Many defects affecting the vitality and functioning of the animal are recessive, since defects due to dominant genes are expressed phenotypically and carriers of the defect then are more easily recognized and eliminated. The increased homozygosity from inbreeding can result in the expression of these recessives, leading some to criticize inbreed-

Blue Heather of Windermere (George's Red Rustler ex Wilson's Little Annie UD), the foundation dam of Windermere, produced numerous breed greats. Courtesy Williams.

ing for creating defects. However, inbreeding does not create any traits, either good or bad. It merely allows them to appear if they were carried in the original breeding stock. This fact can be used to advantage in breed improvement, because once the presence of recessive genes for a defect is known, selection can take place to eliminate them from the gene pool. Conversely, if after several generations of close inbreeding, no recessive defects appear, it is unlikely that these recessives were present in the original breeding stock. Individuals from the line can then be utilized in the breeding programs of those wishing to avoid those traits. (It must be emphasized here that not all recessive alleles result in a defective trait, and not all defective traits are the result of recessive alleles.) Inbreeding involves some risk and does require you to understand the traits of your line. But it enables the breeder to identify and sort the desirable and undesirable traits in order to produce animals of consistent quality.

Linebreeding is a breeding system that is actually a form of inbreeding. It is the selection of sires and dams both related to some unusually desirable individual in order to keep the relationship of individuals in the kennel as close as possible to the desired ancestor. Ordinarily inbreeding is the mating of relatives, but there is no attempt to keep a high relationship to any particular individual. Linebreeding is indicated when some truly outstanding individual has been identified on both the basis of phenotype and progeny testing and has the objectives of perpetuating this individual's qualities and concentrating them as much as possible. Father X daughter, half-brother X half-sister, and grandson X grandmother crosses are examples of linebreeding.

Outbreeding, or outcrossing, is the mating of unrelated dogs, or at least dogs that are not related in the most recent four or five generations. It tends to produce effects opposite those of inbreeding and linebreeding, namely, it increases heterozygosity and tends to camouflage recessive traits. It does not eliminate them, however, and they may reappear in later generations. Because of increased heterozygosity, the resulting progeny do not tend to produce as true in perpetuating their own characteristics as consistently as inbred animals.

Outbreeding is useful, however, as a means of introducing new genetic material into a population. It allows the breeder to manipulate genes in new combinations, then repeat those matings which appear most successful in producing the most desirable traits. It is probably most effective when you wish to improve your line with regard to only one or a few traits, and the sires and dams chosen for the outcross matings are from inbred lines very similar to each other in all respects other than the traits to be changed. This type of outcrossing, between inbred lines that possess similar traits, is termed *positive assortative mating*. It increases the chances that genes for these similar traits will be preserved in the homozygous state, while introducing new genes for the trait to be changed. In this way, the advances made by inbreeding are less likely to be lost.

The use of the above tools will depend upon the objectives and resources of each breeder. With them, the breeder can modify the frequency of expression of traits in all sorts of combinations within the limits of the genetic material available, except those incompatible with life and reproduction. The complexity, manifested by the various forms of gene interaction and the interaction of the genotype with the environment, works to slow the breeder's attempt to shift gene frequency and produce animals most nearly approximating his view of the ideal Australian Shepherd. But it also increases the challenge of breeding improved dogs to perform major services, which, when successful, is very rewarding.

ELIMINATING HERITABLE DEFECTS

Heritable defects occur in every breed and species of animal. The abnormalities can be either structural alterations or defects in metabolism resulting from alterations in biochemical pathways. Part of the process of selection in breeding programs is eliminating genes with the desirable effects. The heritability of many abnormalities has not been demonstrated, nor has the mode of inheritance for many of them. Complicating the issue is the fact that defects resulting from external or environmental conditions often mimic those of genetic origin. Toxins, chemicals, and trauma can disrupt structural development and biochemical pathways in much the same way that faulty gene products do. However, the high recurring incidence of an abnormality within certain breeds or strains is strong evidence for its heritability.

Defects may be *congenital* (meaning present at birth) or *acquired* (meaning that they are not manifested until later in life). Congenital defects result from arrested or defective prenatal development and may be either genetic in origin or the result of external factors that cross the placental barrier. If the defect is incompatible with life, it may be manifested only as reduced litter size. In an attempt to differentiate whether the defect could be the result of genetic or environmental factors, the following should be determined: (1) if any puppies from previous litters of the same parents were affected with the trait; (2) if any ancestors of the litter were affected with a similar condition; (3) the number of affected individuals in the current or previous litters or in the pedigree; and (4) the possibility of exposure of the dam to diseases, drugs, toxins, or chemicals during pregnancy. Acquired defects may likewise be genetic in origin or the result of external factors, and a similar line of questioning can help to distinguish between the two. The heritability of acquired defects is often more difficult to determine because information on siblings and ancestors may be more difficult to obtain. Another disturbing feature of some acquired heritable defects is that they may not become evident until after the individual has reached breeding age and his genes for the defective trait have already been distributed among his offspring. Most breeders find it desirable to consult a geneticist if they suspect a heritable problem.

The method of genetic management of a given defect depends on its mode of inheritance, the frequency with which it occurs, its effect of viability and fertility, and its relative importance to the breeder. All forms of gene interaction have been found to occur among the various heritable defects. The control of any hereditary abnormality is enhanced by accurate detection of the defect as early in the animal's life as possible, and especially prior to breeding age, so that the individual exhibiting the defect can be selected against inbreeding. In addition, family studies and breeding tests are necessary to identify normal-appearing individuals carrying the genes for the trait.

Defects due to simple dominant genes are usually acquired and often do not become evident until after the individual has reached breeding age. Presumably, this is because defects due to a dominant gene are quite evident when expressed early in life, so breeders are more likely to eliminate such individuals from their breeding programs, thus extinguishing the trait. Eliminating a dominant gene is simple: merely do not use individuals who exhibit that trait for breeding. For abnormalities that are not grossly evident until after an individual is old enough to breed, studies are underway to develop techniques for detecting biochemical markers that could identify the susceptible individuals at an earlier age. Two other alternatives may not be acceptable to many breeders. The first is to delay breeding the questionable individual until after the age at which the defect becomes apparent. The second is to eliminate any offspring of an individual who later develops the trait. This method results in considerable wastage, however, because if the affected parent is heterozygous for the trait, only half of its offspring will receive the gene for the trait, while the other half will be normal.

The majority of documented hereditary abnormalities are autosomal recessive, resulting in homozygous, genetically normal individuals, normal-appearing heterozygous carriers, and homozygous recessive, affected individuals. The latter group, while capable of distributing the deleterious gene to all their offspring, are obviously affected and easily eliminated from breeding programs. In addition, both parents of an affected animal, while normal themselves in appearance, are carriers of the trait, and they, too, can be eliminated for breeding purposes. The problem is in distinguishing normal-appearing, homozygous dominant animals from the normal-appearing, heterozygous carriers when the genotype is unknown. *Test crosses* are used in an attempt to determine the genotype. This is progeny testing in its simplest form. With any of the methods of test-crossing, the production of a single affected offspring is evidence that the suspect individual carries the trait. The production of no affected offspring is *not* absolute evidence that the individual does not carry the trait but merely increases the *probability* that he doesn't, and the greater the number of unaffected offspring produced, the greater the likelihood that the suspect individual is not a carrier. Statistics have been applied by geneticists to calculate the probabilities associated with the number of unaffected offspring in the various types of test crosses.

The simplest method for detecting a normal heterozygous carrier of a recessive trait is to breed the suspect animal to one affected with the trait and whose genotype is therefore known to be homozygous for the defective recessive gene. The production of a single affected offspring proves that the suspect animal is a carrier. The chance that the suspect could be a carrier, even though no affected offspring result, is reduced to 3 in 100 when five normal progeny are produced; 1 in 100 with seven normal progeny; and 1 in 1,000 with ten normal progeny. It must be recognized, however, that all resulting progeny will themselves be carriers for the defect, so the breeder must be prepared to eliminate these from future breeding programs. Other methods of test-crossing for unknown carriers are to mate the unknown with known heterozygous carriers or to mate the unknown with its own progeny. The latter method requires crossing the unknown with multiple mates and producing large numbers of offspring and is therefore somewhat impractical. The resulting probabilities of the various methods are outlined in the table as illustrated below.

The genes for some abnormalities are found on the sex chromosomes, most commonly the X chromosome, although these traits may have nothing to do with sex determination. They are termed sex-linked. Sex-linked dominant defects are rare because they are grossly evident in both sexes and are easily eliminated. The problem arises with sex-linked recessives because they can be perpetuated by generations of females in the heterozygous state. All males who receive the allele for the trait on the X chromosome from their mothers will be affected because there is no corresponding allele on the Y chromosome to mask its effect. Fortunately, the detection of carrier females is relatively simple. If a female produces any affected progeny, she must be a carrier. There are two methods of test-crossing to detect carrier females: (1) breeding the suspect female to a known affected male; or (2) breeding the suspect female to an unaffected male. How these test crosses function is best illustrated by the use of Punnett Squares.

The mode of inheritance of some abnormalities is thought to involve multiple sets of genes in complex interactions. These traits are generally those relating to conformation and tend to be expressed in a range of types from worse to better rather than segregated into groups of distinctly normal and distinctly abnormal. These polygenic traits to not respond to selection as rapidly as do simple dominant and recessive ones and are further complicated by the fact that their degree of expression is more subject to environmental influences. The genetic management of multiple-factor defects is basically an attempt to accumulate in the progeny more effective genes by selecting those from the upper range of the distribution for mating. Conversely, it is avoiding the use of those individuals at the poorer end of the range in the hope of decreasing the frequency of those genes leading to the less functional forms of the trait. With polygenic traits, it is usually impossible to identify all of the genes

Methods of Test-Crossing to Detect Heterozygous Carriers of a Simple Autosomal Recessive Trait

Method	Number of Normal Progeny with None Affected	Probability of Carrier State	Comments
Unknown and Known Homozygous Recessive	5 7 10	3 in 100 1 in 100 1 in 1000	All of the progeny will be carriers of the trait.
Unknown and Known Heterozygous Carriers	11 16	5 in 100 1 in 100	Fifty percent will be carriers of the trait.
Unknown Parent and Five Unselected Unknown Progeny	11 per cross	5 in 100	The probability of the trait existing in the entire family is reduced to some extent by successful test-crossing of this type.
Unknown Parent and Seven Unselected Unknown Progeny	16 per cross	1 in 100	The probability of the trait existing in the entire family is reduced to some extent by successful test-crossing of this type.

involved and the nature of all of their interactions. Thus, the usefulness of test crosses to determine genotypes is limited. The basic principles, then, are to breed the best individuals available and those from lines in which the defect rarely appears.

Because polygenically influenced traits tend to fall along a gradient for better or worse rather than into distinct groups, it is often necessary for the breeder or breed clubs to arbitrarily assign a point in the gradient to be used as a cutoff for distinguishing acceptable versus unacceptable ranges of expression. Once this decision is made, the following recommendations for genetic management can be applied: (1) select for breeding only those individuals who fall into the acceptable range; (2) do not use for breeding those individuals who themselves are acceptable but whose parents or siblings or progeny exhibit unacceptable expressions of the trait; or (3) give preference to those acceptable individuals from pedigrees with several generations of acceptable ancestors. Through the use of these guidelines, the incidence of certain polygenically influenced defects has been greatly reduced in certain species of animals. It logically follows that for continued improvement, once the incidence of the defective range has been reduced, the standards for determining acceptable expression of the trait should be raised.

Another tool useful in the management of traits susceptible to environmental influence is to test the individuals under conditions of stress. It has been suggested that some individuals inherit a genetic predisposition to develop an abnormality, but that the trait will not come to full expression in the individual without conducive environmental influences. Environment may determine whether the individual is acceptable or unacceptable if that individual falls in the midrange of expression of a polygenic trait. Testing under stressful conditions requires the influencing environmental factors to be identified. Once this is done, the breeder must be willing to provide the environment conducive to expression of the trait. Individuals who do not exhibit the trait under adverse conditions are considered less likely to possess the genes for the trait, and presumably their selection for breeding purposes will lead to an even greater decreased incidence of the trait

> *UNKNOWN FEMALE X AFFECTED MALE: Punnett Squares illustrating test crosses for a sex-linked recessive trait.*
>
> If dam is a heterozygous carrier
>
> | | X^+ | $X^=$ |
> |---|---|---|
> | X^+ | X^+X^+ | $X^+X^=$ |
> | Y | X^+Y | $X^=Y$ |
>
> Affected Sire
>
> Progeny: Half the daughters affected (X^+X^+), half unaffected but carriers ($X^+X^=$). Half the sons affected (X^+Y), half unaffected ($X^=Y$).
>
> If dam is homozygous noncarrier
>
> | | $X^=$ | $X^=$ |
> |---|---|---|
> | X^+ | $X^+X^=$ | $X^+X^=$ |
> | Y | $X^=Y$ | $X^=Y$ |
>
> Affected Sire
>
> Progeny: All daughters unaffected by carriers. ($X^+X^=$). All sons unaffected ($X^=Y$).
>
> *The statistical probabilities, that an unknown female bred to an affected male is a carrier of the defect, are measured by the number of unaffected sons produced and are similar to those for crosses between an individual of unknown genotype and a known homozygous recessive for autosomal recessive defects.*
>
> *UNKNOWN FEMALE X UNAFFECTED MALE*
>
> If dam is a heterozygous carrier
>
> | | X^+ | $X^=$ |
> |---|---|---|
> | $X^=$ | $X^+X^=$ | $X^=X^=$ |
> | Y | X^+Y | $X^=Y$ |
>
> Unaffected Sire
>
> Progeny: All daughters unaffected, but half will be carriers (½ $X^=X^=$ ½ $X^+X^=$). Half of sons affected (X^+Y), half unaffected ($X^=Y$).
>
> If dam is a homozygous noncarrier
>
> | | $X^=$ | $X^=$ |
> |---|---|---|
> | $X^=$ | $X^=X^=$ | $X^=X^=$ |
> | Y | $X^=Y$ | $X^=Y$ |
>
> Unaffected Sire
>
> Progeny: All are unaffected and none of the daughters are carriers.
>
> *The probabilities that the dam is a carrier are based on the number of unaffected sons produced and are similar to those for crosses between an individual of unknown genotype and a known heterozygous carrier for autosomal recessive defects.*

under desirable conditions. Unfortunately, many breeders attempt to provide the environment that will least cause the trait to be expressed. This is understandable but leads to the defect being masked and, therefore, the genes for it to be retained in the population.

SOME TRAITS OF KNOWN OR PROBABLE INHERITANCE

For many traits—often those of most concern to the breeder—the heritability and mode of inheritance have not been determined. Many, including refinements of conformation, fertility, vitality, size, and maturity, are thought to involve so many gene pairs in such complex interactions that it is virtually beyond our present state of knowledge to identify all of the factors involved. The challenge, then, is to intelligently apply basic genetic principles in breeding programs in an effort to achieve the desired results. Other traits of relatively simple inheritance or those having a drastic impact on a species have been sufficiently studied. Described below are a few traits that may be of interest to the breeder or fancier of the Australian Shepherd.

Coat Color

Ten different loci have been identified as determiners of coat color in canines. These loci are believed to reside on different pairs of homologous

Punnett Square illustrating the probabilities associated with merle X merle matings.

	Merled parent	
	M	m
Merled Parent M	MM	Mm
m	Mm	mm

Progeny:

¼ homozygous nonmerles (mm): These individuals are solid in base coat color and have normal eyes.

½ heterozygous merles (Mm): These individuals are of the typical merle pattern and have normal eyes.

¼ homozygous merles (MM): These individuals are excessively white and express the ocular dysgenesis complex.

Punnett Square illustrating the probabilities associated with merle X solid matings.

	Merled parent	
	M	m
Solid parent m	Mm	mm
m	Mm	mm

Progeny: 50% heterozygous merles (Mm), 50% homozygous nonmerles (mm). None of the progeny express the ocular dysgenesis complex.

Punnett Square illustrating the probabilities associated with solid X solid matings.

	Solid parent	
	m	m
Solid parent m	mm	mm
m	mm	mm

Progeny: 100% homozygous nonmerled (solid) individuals with none of the progeny expressing or carrying the gene for the ocular dysgenesis complex.

chromosomes and are therefore inherited independently. Multiple alleles have been identified for each locus, and the expression of many alleles over certain ranges suggests the existence of as yet unidentified modifiers. The ten loci for coat color are believed to be constant between all the breeds of the canine species, with selection pressure having resulted in the concentration of certain alleles within breeds to produce consistent color characteristics.

Eye Color

The mode of inheritance of eye color has not been clearly elucidated. It probably involves interaction between coat color and eye color genes. An allelic series of genes for eye color has been postulated. Some authors suggest that the series contains three alleles; others, two. Whether dominance is partial or complete among the alleles is a matter of debate, although most agree that darker eyes tend to be more dominant. Most believe that dogs of liver base coat color will express their genotype for the eye color locus as a lighter shade than their black counterparts, even though they may have identical genotypes at the eye color locus. The interaction of genes for eye and coat color is a reasonable assumption, because the pigments for both are similar in embryologic tissue origin and are produced by the same metabolic pathways. The scientific community is in agreement that the partially or completely blue eyes seen in merled breeds relates in some way to the coat color gene for merling, as it is not normally seen in the solid body color pattern for these breeds. The varying shades of blue and combinations with brown or amber are explained on the basis of unknown modifiers affecting the penetrance of the blue trait. In fact, it is not uncommon for merles to have eyes that are completely brown or amber, although ophthalmic examination of portions of the eye other than the iris usually reveals a decrease in pigmentation brought on by the merle gene.

Tail Length

The mode of inheritance for bobtails has not been established, although most geneticists have concluded that it is due to multiple factors. Breeding tests and family studies among various breeds suggest that shorter tails tend to be dominant over longer tails, although usually not completely so. There is also evidence that the factors affecting tail length are probably polygenic, because tails of varying lengths have been observed in single litters among matings of sires and dams born with various phenotypes. It is worthy of mention that among other breeds of dogs and species of animals, selection for naturally occurring bobtails has been accompanied by an increased incidence of malformation of the posterior vertebrae and spinal cord, resulting in neurologic deficits such as fecal and urinary incontinence and abnormalities of gait or stance in the rear limbs. It should be noted that the ASCA Breed Standard accepts either naturally occurring bobtails or docked tails with no order of preference. Its only stipulation is that tails are to be four inches or under in length regardless of whether this length is achieved naturally or by surgical intervention.

Genetics of Coat Color in Australian Shepherds

Much of what is known about the genetics of canine coat color is based on the work of Clarence Little and other geneticists. None of the work, however, contained DNA studies. Molecular studies are showing that Little was often correct, but not always.

According to Sheila M. Schmutz, Ph.D, geneticist at the University of Saskatchewan in the Department of Animal and Poultry Science, *"The studies were based on hypothesized alleles at hypothesized loci to fit data obtained from coat colors and patterns of dogs from various breeds and litters. DNA research has shown that there are more genes involved than originally hypothesized."*

Dr. Schmutz also cautions, no gene acts in isolation. As a rule of thumb, the more coat colors that occur in the breed, the more genes will be needed to explain the genotype and phenotype of the Australian Shepherd.

Moreover, to diffuse further confusion, it is important to understand the nomenclature 'red' is used by the scientific community to describe reddish body color accompanied by black noses. 'Brown' is used by geneticists to describe the type of reddish brown color (with liver nose, lips and eye rims) *without* black which occurs in Australian Shepherds.

Skin and hair color in dogs is due to the presence of melanin (pigment), which is formed by cells called melanocytes. Melanocytes manufacture dark eumelanin (black/brown) and light phaeomelanin (yellow/tan/reddish) pigment. Different genes alter the number, shape, arrangement, position and type of melanin.

What has been confirmed by DNA studies is that several genes determine the basic coat color in Australian Shepherds. The interaction of additional genes influence the exact hue or shade.

Agouti Signal Peptide (ASIP), commonly referred to as the A Locus, competes with melanocyte stimulating hormone (MSH) that produces dark pigmentation (eumelanin) and governs the distribution of eumelanin synthesized in the hair follicle.

Practically speaking, Agouti changes hair color along the length (banding) or over parts of the body by restricting their full production to produce tan. Therefore, the black/brown-and tan or tricolor pattern is caused by the Agouti Gene. Most Aussies are an a^t/a^t.

A mutation in the Agouti Signal Peptide gene renders it in capable of producing phaeomelanin resulting in black coat color. A few Aussies carry this 'recessive black' (another allele instead of 'a') allele, although the lack of tan points on most Aussies is caused by another gene overriding the a^t/a^t genotype.

Melacortin Receptor 1 (MCR1) also called Melanocyte Stimulating Hormone Receptor Gene (MSHr), a HSH receptor, governs the type and distribution of base pigment (eumelanin or phaeomelanin). The gene, referred to as the E or Extension Locus has three common alleles, but virtually all Aussies are E/E which means that black/brown eumelanin pigment can be expressed over the whole body. The brown or liver red color is produced when the dog has any two copies of the three recessive brown alleles at the B or TYRP1 Locus.

Tyrosinase Related Protein 1 (TRP1) works within the melanocytes, affects the synthesis of eumelanin (black/brown), and changes eumelanin only. Phaeomelanin is unaffected. The mutations of what is also referred to as the Brown or 'B' Locus 'instruct' or modify the basic color to produce various shades of coat color observed in the breed and result in brown (liver red) instead of black eumelanin production of skin (nose, lips, eye rims, pads) and hair coat.

Black or 'K' Locus allows only eumelanin pigment to be produced (if an E is present) and k/k Aussies can produce both pigments. Bi-color Aussies have a K, while tricolors are k/k.

Genes that Distrupt the Pigment Pathway of the Migrating Melanocytes

The pattern genes affect the pathway of the migration cells intended to form melanocytes. Melanocytes are derived from a group of cells called the neural crest cells. These cells shape important parts of the nervous system of the inner ear and eye. These genes can have a huge affect on neurological/immunological function. To view a picture of migrating pigment cells you can go to: http://skyway.usask.ca/~schmutz/pathway.html

These genes affect eumelanin synthesis in the base coat color. This gene affects the distribution of pigmented cells (phaeomelanin and eumelanin) in canines.

In the heterozygous state results in irregular patches of the base coat. In the homozygous state produces excessive loss of pigmentation (defective white), resulting in nearly complete white appearing individuals accompanied by hearing, vision and brain abnormalities, because these genes are associated with nerve development. The homozygous m/m Aussie does not have random white markings on its body.

Phantom or cryptic (hidden) merles are individuals whose phenotype (observable traits) does not reveal merle patterns or the pattern is concealed. Rarely, but it can happen that a hardly noticeable merle pattern may be present somewhere on the body at birth, maybe even observable on a small portion of the tail that was removed when docked.

Genes that Restrict Pigmentation

'White Trim'. The gene that causes the acceptable white trim patterns (not to be confused with the white color produced from the merle gene) in Aussies is not known. Since many Aussies exhibit the phenotype for the white trim, the genotype is 'fixed' in our breed. Aussies without pigmentation (color) on the areas around the eyes and ears have a higher probability of hearing and vision problems.

Cream and Sable Colored Aussies

For the most part, the sable gene was eliminated through selective breeding. However, occasionally breeders produce a purebred Australian Shepherd that results in a sable puppy (black tipped reddish hair) with black nose. This sable is an $a^y/-$ dog and so should not be bred since this allele is dominant to the a^t allele, which is the 'desired' allele in typical Aussies. The only way that it could be hidden is in a bi-color parent.

The phenotype (observable trait) of the merle factored sable does not indicate the presence of a merle gene. When bred to a merle the cross can produce homozygous white offspring (defective white), consequently the early breeders and framers of the 1977 ASCA Breed Standard felt it was best to eradicate it. For the most part, the sable gene was eliminated from the breed through years of selective breeding. Since the a^y sable is dominant to a^t, the sable color puppy shouldn't resurface from two tri-color parents.

Brindle

Brindle markings were unknown to breeders of early foundation Aussies.

In summary, the main genes involved in coat color variation in Aussies are 'K,' 'B,' and 'M.' The K causes the difference between bicolor and tricolor. The B causes the difference between black or liver red coloration. The M causes the presence or absence of merle.

For more information on the genetics of canine coat color please visit http://skyway.usask.ca/~schmutz/dogcolors.html.

Hall of Fame Sire, Ch. Fieldmaster of Flintridge CD, one of the greatest influences on the modern Australian Shepherd, handled by Marcia Hall winning Best of Breed in 1971 at the IASA Specialty. Courtesy Dr. Heard.

RELATIONSHIP OF THE JAWS

The attention paid to the relationship between the upper and lower jaws, or "bite" as it is termed, by the breed standards of many breeds, including the Aussie, reflects the importance of this trait to the well-being and functioning of the animal. Under many breed standards, abnormality in the relationship is cause for disqualification of the animal from the show ring. Much to the frustration of the conscientious breeder, the number of genes involved and their mode of inheritance are by no means completely understood. There is general agreement that multiple factors are involved and that they are inherited independently for each jaw. The common abnormalities—"overshot" and "undershot" bites—are the result of disproportionate growth between the upper and lower jaws due to their genetic independence. Different factors may act at different stages of growth, resulting in abnormal bites appearing at various ages during the growth period. Due to their vulnerable position on the body, the jaws and teeth are highly susceptible to trauma. A traumatic accident in the growing individual may result in a defect in the relationship of the teeth, which mimics a genetic abnormality of the jaw assembly. It is of utmost importance in selecting individuals for breeding to be able to distinguish between abnormalities of genetic origin and those due to external factors. The incisor teeth, by virtue of their position and less secure attachment by a single root, are most susceptible to modifications in direction to growth as the result of injury. Thus, the common practice of determining bite by the relationship of the upper and lower incisors is less than reliable. (This relationship in the "scissors" bite is one of the upper incisors overlapping the lower incisors, with their opposing surfaces touching.) Evaluation of bite is more accurately accomplished by examining the relationship of the canine and premolar teeth. The correct bite requires the lower canine tooth to interlock between the outermost upper incisor and the upper canine, and for the premolars to intermesh with each other, with the lower premolars in front of their upper counterparts. Once individuals have been properly evaluated for correct jaw assembly, selection for this trait can take place as for any trait of polygenic inheritance.

Hip Dysplasia

Hip dysplasia is a defect in the conformation of the hip joint and is known to occur in most breeds of dogs. It is of concern to the breeder and fancier alike because it can result in severe pain and crippling of the dog. It is an inherited trait with a polygenic mode of inheritance. The basic defect appears to be an acetabulum (hip socket) that is more shallow than normal. This results in excessive laxity in the hip joint, which over time produces secondary changes in the shapes of the bones composing the joint in the body's effort to compensate. Diagnosis of hip dysplasia is made by radiographs which are best taken between two and five years of age. In a younger animal, the secondary bony changes may not yet be evident, and defects in the acetabulum may be so slight as to be difficult to detect. Normal wear and tear of aging may make it difficult to distinguish such changes from those due to the heritable defect in aged individuals. There is often poor correlation between the occurrence of hip dysplasia and outward symptoms in individual animals, so freedom from pain and lameness is no guarantee that the animal is free of the defect.

The Orthopedic Foundation for Animals (OFA) was established to encourage breeders to have their dogs' hips radiographed and evaluated by providing a program in which dogs proven phenotypically free of hip dysplasia can be certified as such. In addition, the OFA established guidelines for rating the quality of hip joint conformation in normal animals and the severity of hip dysplasia in affected ones. Like all polygenic traits, hip dysplasia is manifested by a range of

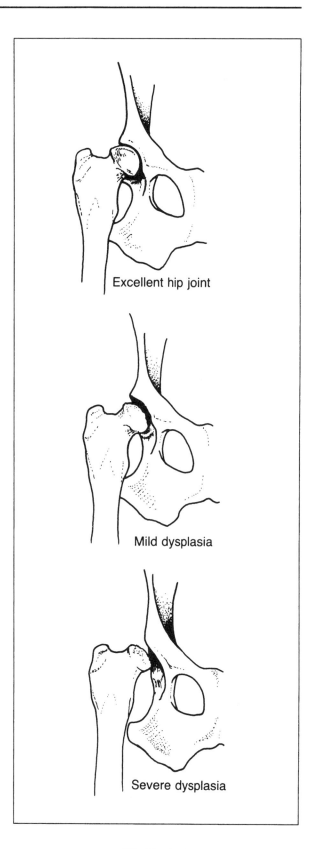

Hip Dysplasia

expression which is partially influenced by environmental factors. Diet, growth rate, and level of activity in growing puppies have been implicated. Some misguided breeders have attempted to lower the incidence and severity of dysplasia in their kennels by providing an artificially favorable environment. However, it must be remembered that this does not alter the basic genotype and only serves to perpetuate the genes for dysplasia. Breeding recommendations for decreasing the genetic incidence of hip dysplasia are the same as for any trait of suspected polygenic origin. Breeding studies, using only nondysplastic individuals from dysplasia-free families, have proven the effectiveness of this method in lowering the incidence of hip dysplasia. There is no evidence proving that "*excellent*" hip joint conformation ratings are significantly better in lowering the incidence of development of hip dysplasia in subsequent progeny than "*good*" ratings. Perhaps this is because differences in conformation at this refined level are due to factors other than those influencing hip dysplasia or to environmental influences. For the purposes of decreasing the incidence of hip dysplasia, selection simply on the basis of freedom from dysplasia without regard to hip joint conformation ratings appears to be sufficient.

Ocular Dysgenesis with Variable Deafness

A complex of eye defects accompanied by variable degrees of deafness is seen in excessively white Australian Shepherds believed to be homozygous for the merling gene. These defects occur in varying degrees and combinations and include the following: (1) reduced size of the entire eye (microphthalmia); (2) incomplete development, fissuring, and outpocketing of tissues in various parts of the eye; (3) detachment of the retina (the layer of tissue in the back of the eye responsible for receiving and transmitting light impulses to the brain) from underlying supporting structures; (4) abnormal shape and position of the pupils; and (5) incomplete development of the optic nerve and blood vessels supplying the eye. This complex is inherited as an autosomal recessive trait with incomplete penetrance, and whether it is the result of pleiotropic effects of the merle gene or of a separate gene positioned on the same chromosome (linked) at a locus close to the merle gene has not been definitely established. However, breeding studies tend to support the former. Pigments are thought to play an essential role in the embryologic development of vital structures in the eye and ear. Apparently, a certain threshold level of pigments is required for the normal and complete development of these structures. It has been theorized that the merle gene, when present in the homozygous state, inhibits pigment production to a quantity below the threshold level required for normal development. Because these are defects in embryologic development, this complex is considered a congenital abnormality detectable grossly or by ophthalmic examination in early life.

Merling is valued as a unique contributor to the characteristics of the Australian Shepherd breed. The retention of this trait in heterozygous individuals will probably prevent the ocular dysgenesis complex from ever being completely eliminated. However, genetic principles of selection and a willingness on the part of breeders to destroy affected individuals at a young age can greatly reduce its significance. When *normal merled* individuals are mated, approximately 25 percent of the resulting progeny can be expected to be of solid base coat color (mm), 50 percent merles of heterozygous constitution (Mm), and 25 percent excessively white homozygous merles (MM). Recognizing the association of the homozygous condition for merling with the ocular dysgenesis complex while desiring to retain the merle trait, conscientious breeders have adopted the practice of euthanatizing excessively white puppies at birth. Others, seeking to avoid this necessary task, have preferred to avoid merle matings. Matings of merles to solid individuals or solids to solids should produce no excessively-white homozygous puppies, providing the phenotypes of the mates accurately represent their genotypes. It is important to distinguish the excessive white of the homozygous merle condition from white occurring as the result of other independently inherited genes, such as those for white markings.

Ocular defects, other than the ocular dysgenesis complex, have also been reported in the Australian Shepherd. Some of these defects are believed to be genetically influenced, but their modes of inheritance have not been definitely established. The defects reported include retinal dysplasia and cataracts. Retinal dysplasia is abnormal development of the retina, resulting in its folding and detachment. Detachment may sometimes progress with the age of the animal and result in complete blindness. Retinal dysplasia is a congenital defect and can be detected by ophthalmic examination early in life. A cataract is any opacity of the lens. Cataracts can be congenital or acquired, and either form may be the result of either hereditary or environmental factors. Family studies and a detailed history of the potential exposure of an affected individual to inducing environmental factors may be necessary to determine whether a cataract is the result of inheritance of extrinsic factors in a given individual.

The Canine Eye Registration Foundation (CERF) has been established to study the incidence and inheritance patterns of eye defects in dogs. Like the OFA with hip dysplasia, CERF has developed a certification program for animals ophthalmically examined and determined to be phenotypically free of inheritable ocular defects. It has been recommended that puppies be examined at eight weeks of age to detect congenital heritable defects. In all domestic species, the eye undergoes some further maturation in the first few weeks of life. By eight weeks of age in the dog, congenital eye defects have usually reached fuller expression, resulting in more accurate detection. Because other inherited ocular abnormalities are acquired and, therefore, may not be detectable until late in life, CERF recommends annual reexamination of apparently normal animals, especially through five years of age. Since the modes of inheritance of many heritable ocular defects have not been established, specific breeding recommendations cannot be provided. However, it is generally advised not to breed any animals that are affected with potentially heritable ocular defects nor their close relatives.

Behavior

Dogs, like human beings, exhibit different personalities. Genetic mechanisms associated with structural characteristics have been studied much more thoroughly and successfully than those of behavior. This is due to the complexity of behavior and to the fact that behavior is developed under the combined influences of both heredity and the environment. Detailed breeding studies have shown that different genes become active at different developmental stages and that their expression during periods of activity may be modified by earlier environmental experience. The modes of inheritance of some behavioral traits, however, have been found to be rather simple, depending on only a few genes. These traits are modifiable only by experience within a limited range. These traits include differences in emotional reactions, such as gregariousness versus shyness, inquisitiveness versus reticence, and passiveness versus aggression, and the differences in social responses to man—trainability. On the other hand, the inheritance of such traits as the ability to perform well in particular situations and problem-solving capabilities tends to be very complex, mediated by numerous independent genetic factors. As a result, these traits exhibit broader ranges of expression that are more susceptible to the influences of environment. It is of interest to note that no correlation was found between behavioral patterns and conformational "type" within breeds, except where the expression of a behavioral trait was limited by physical capacities. Despite the complex nature of behavior, it is possible to alter behavioral traits, within certain ranges, by the process of selection. By identifying individuals that exhibit the most favorable behavioral traits and selecting them for

Ch. Shank's Ginks CD (Heard's Proud Buck of Flintridge ex Lacovetta's Shasta), foundation bitch of the Coppertone line. "Ginks" is pictured with Lucia Kline, DVM, author of this chapter, and breeder/judge Walter Lamar.

use in breeding programs, the genetic factors responsible for the desired traits will tend to be concentrated in succeeding generations. In this way, individuals capable of providing major services to man, probably the most important of which is companionship, are more likely to be consistently produced.

The list of traits described above is far from exhaustive. Readers are encouraged to consult the various texts available on canine genetics for information on other traits. As stated previously, the information on heritability and modes of inheritance for traits specific to the Australian Shepherd is limited. The genetics of certain, but not all, traits is similar among breeds. However, for other traits, different modes of inheritance have been determined for different breeds.

Therefore, you must not be too hasty in drawing conclusions from other breeds with regard to the inheritance of traits in the Australian Shepherd. Likewise, it is important to try to differentiate whether a trait is governed more by genetics or by the environment. This is sometimes difficult because some traits, resulting mainly from the animal's genetic constitution, can appear similar or even identical to ones caused mainly by extrinsic factors. Only extensive family studies and breeding trials can prove the tendency for a trait to be inherited, and even then the results may be inconclusive. By increasing the scope of scientific inquiry and applying good judgment and basic genetic principles, our understanding of the Australian Shepherd and progress in breed development can be greatly enhanced.

Taylor's Whiskey (Mansker's [Lamar's] Turk ex Mansker's Anna Lee), a foundation sire known for his working progeny, owned by Joe D. Taylor of Moab, Utah.

Hall of Fame progeny of Las Rocosa Katy Did It. WTCh. LasRocosa Whispers Success, WTCh. Western Legends, and Ch Las Rocosa Take This Chance OTD-s, STD-dc, are the result of a breeding program developed through years of careful selection based on the yardstick of performance to produce a bloodline of distinction. Glo Photo, by Gayle Oxford.

Chapter 25

THE MATING GAME

BREEDING CONCEPTS

Breeding Australian Shepherds is not quite as simple as breeding a flock of sheep or dairy and beef cattle. In the latter, you are breeding for a known, concrete factor: mutton or wool, beef or butterfat. Unlike breeding livestock, in which you are reproducing a visible, concrete factor, breeding Aussies entails trying to reproduce and improve a less tangible quality: performance. Performance stems from physical ability and "want to" and is closely tied to general conformation. No matter how much "want to" an Aussie may possess, it is of little value if he does not have the physical ability to allow him to perform. On the other hand, if an Aussie is extremely capable of performing and does not "want to," it is of equally little value.

The capable breeder aims not simply for type and conformation, but also for style, temperament, and "heart" or endurance, because those are the qualities that determine superior performance. It is clear that breeding for qualities such as desire, style, and temperament is not an easy task, especially when those qualities must be accompanied by the ability to perform.

An Aussie's temperament is an essential ingredient for performance. The need for disposition is equal to that for conformation. Temperament is closely associated with "trainability" and with the desire to execute tasks when called on. "Heart" is endurance. It is the ability to work when tired and to give that extra effort. Conformation is the freedom of movement that makes the task easier to accomplish.

PEDIGREES

A pedigree is a key to your dog's background and helps indicate consistency for certain traits that have been passed on through the generations. The pedigree is a family tree. It is the record of each Aussie's sire and dam by name and reflects performance of the ancestry as far back as permits.

To some, the pedigree is a myriad of names with little or no meaning. The pedigree is no guarantee that the subject of the pedigree is any better or worse for having the document. For the future breeder, it is an indispensable point of reference. It establishes the strain (or strains) from which the individual has descended, and in this way, you may be able to determine the possible and probable tendencies of the sire and dam. It also gives you the opportunity to delve into the history of your Aussie and to help you find suitable, appropriate mates for the future.

BREED STANDARD

The Breed Standard will help you determine an ideal specimen. (See the chapter The Standard of Excellence). The Breed Standard must be utmost and unaltered in your mind.

SETTING GOALS

A breeding program must have the proper correlation of conformation, bloodlines, and performance as represented by individuals which, when crossed, will produce an ideal with as much consistency as possible. The program can, will, and should vary if results are not forthcoming, but the ideal or goal cannot be altered if permanent improvement is to be achieved. Only failure awaits you if you do not know what you desire, because every breeder has the option to vary his program. Every successful breeder is always constant in his goals.

Breeders need to study family characteristics—the good points as well as the undesirable ones. Being aware of any possible weakness as well as the strengths leads to an intelligent breeding program.

Any progressive breeder must have an ideal in mind. The constructive breeder should always try to be an impartial judge of his own Aussies and of the Aussies of other lines. If you lose the ability to look with an impartial eye and an open mind at both the virtues and faults of your own Aussies, your chances of realizing your goals and of improving the breed are very slim.

THE BROOD BITCH

The value of a good brood bitch is considerable, and the value of a great one is incalculable. Not only does 50 percent of all hereditary material go into the offspring from the bitch, but according to her desirable matronly qualities, she is largely responsible for getting the puppies off to a good start. The bitch's behavior greatly influences the actions of her puppies. The early training that she gives her litter will establish the foundation for human handling and relationships with other dogs in later life.

The brood bitch is the cornerstone of a bloodline for generations. Care in selecting a foundation female will influence the strength of your bloodline and the future of the Australian Shepherd breed. If you are someday fortunate enough or wise enough to possess a truly great brood bitch, one that is a pleasure to work and a joy to be around, that possesses ideal characteristics, and that also has the ability to transmit them—

Taylor's Lola (Taylor's Whiskey ex Taylor's Buena) with a litter sired by Ch. Stonehenge Justin Case of Las Rocosa, a blue merle. The resulting litter from a merle to a solid (with or without white and/or copper trim) can consist of both merle and solid progeny.

do not part with her! If she transmits those great qualities, you will someday develop pleasing uniformity of type, disposition, soundness, and working qualities that can establish a bloodline and make breed improvement possible.

If you are trying to establish a breeding program, it is best to acquire a proven brood bitch. Her progeny serve as a valuable evaluation for consistency in type and quality. Although most breeders cannot and/or will not part with a bitch of this caliber, sometimes circumstances make a foundation bitch available to discriminating buyers. A good, proven bitch also has unlimited access to good studs.

If a proven bitch is not available, try to obtain a top-quality daughter of the bitch. The visible characteristics possessed by the bitch, also known as the phenotype, play an important role in choosing future breeding stock. The ancestry must be carefully evaluated as well, because a top-winning Champion-titled bitch does not always have the ability to throw "top-winning" puppies if those traits are not present in the pedigree.

When you are judging the quality of a breeding bitch, also evaluate the progeny. However, if the progeny do not measure up, consider the sire's quality, because he contributes the other 50 percent. There should be overall consistency within a litter. If a certain cross does not produce a greater portion of offspring that are at least as good (if not better) than the dam, then she should be bred to a different stud. After breeding her to three or more studs with no luck, then it is wise to eliminate her from the breeding program as a brood bitch. A bitch of this nature, however, can still make a good performance animal or companion.

A strong ancestry of top-producing bitches is exceptional to a lineage with a solid background of top-producing sires. A superior stud can be found or can appear in a greater number of pedigrees because he can be bred to a larger number of females in a lifetime. For example, if a sire breeds to a different female for each month in a year, he is capable of siring twelve litters. If the average litter consists of six puppies, then he has sired seventy-two offspring. By comparison, the offspring of a superior foundation bitch is limited to the litters that she may have in the same lifetime. A female that is bred twice in one year is capable of having two litters. With the average litter size being six puppies, then this bitch has produced twelve puppies in the same given period.

However, it must not be misinterpreted that the sire is of less importance, because consistency in quality of any individual is equally dependent on both the sire and the dam, who each contribute 50 percent.

The general health and reproductive soundness of the ancestors are especially important in the brood bitch. Any reproductive weakness or ill health harbored in a bitch will carry through to the offspring. Before you have control over it, you have instilled a weakness that makes breeding sound reproducers next to impossible. This also limits the gene pool. It is not only expensive to "baby" such inadequacy, but detrimental to the health and soundness of the Australian Shepherd breed in general.

In the wild, reproductive problems are unaided by man's devices and are therefore eliminated. Usually, if a bitch has a difficult time during mating, she may have a problem whelping. It is nature's way of preventing a fault from passing on.

For all practical purposes, it is of little value to place a great deal of emphasis on ancestry beyond the fourth generation. The greatest genetic contribution is attained from the sire, the dam, the grandparents, and the great-grandparents. A bloodline is well established with the stability of fifty-two ancestors in the fifth generation.

THE STUD DOG

The selection of a potential sire is a grave responsibility. Any sire offered "at stud" can serve many bitches and therefore have a large number of offspring. Because of this, his quality, either good or bad, leaves his mark on the breed.

A sire must have all-around excellence through his ancestry. A male himself should have a strong constitution combined with charisma, desire, trainability, temperament, and heart packaged in a well-balanced, sound structure. He must, beyond question, be able to transmit his phenotype to his progeny.

The criteria for choosing a sire are exactly the same as for choosing a brood bitch. Keep in mind that you are breeding the entire inheritance of a sire, not just his phenotype (what you see), regardless of how superior he himself may be. If

*Ch. Hemi's Regal Request CD, STD, OTD, ASCA Hall of Fame sire.
Courtesy Gary and Mary Hawley.*

you are unsure about a young or unproven male that looks exceptional, you may want to go back to the fountainhead and breed to his sire, which would give you at least half brothers with which to continue.

Breeding is not an exact science. There is no one formula that will ensure success to every breeder, and no two Aussies are alike. It is often said that serious breeding is an art. The combined instincts of the breeder to cross certain individu-

Strong family traits, a consistency of type passed through the sire line. Left to right, all sired by George's Red Rustler: Maggie of Copper Canyon (out of Faxon's Jamie), Ch. Bright Future of Windermere (out of Wilson's Little Annie UD), "George's Red Rustler" (Ginter's Rusty ex Ginthers Red Velvet), Ch. Copper Canyon Caligari CD (out of Quaglino's Miss Pooh), De Rose's Blue Velvet (out of De Rose's Sally), Hoyt's Dago Moreno UD (out of Faxon's Donnagal).

als, lines, and types become subject, knowingly or unknowingly, to a medium of genetics. Genetics is correctly defined as an unexacting science.

What You Should Know Before You Breed Aussies

Registration papers do not indicate quality. Many Aussies should not be bred together, and some Aussies should not be bred at all! Breeding should consider structure, disposition, and working ability with the goal of improving the Australian Shepherd breed. The Australian Shepherd has been determined by years of selective breeding. Many genetic factors contribute to the litter, and the puppies may not inherit their parents' temperament or structure. Aussies used for breeding must be sound. Genetic defects can plague the puppies if the parents are not screened prior to the mating. Unless you are willing to check for hereditary defects in order to perpetuate sound and correct Aussies, you should not breed.

Genetic Defects

Aussies should be checked prior to breeding and determined to be free of heritable eye and hip defects.

Eye Defects

The Aussie's eye consists of an iris (the colored section) that dilates and contracts to increase and decrease the incoming light, similar to the shutter on a camera. The pupil is the opening through the iris that constricts in bright light and opens in dim light. The retina is composed of cells in the back of the eye that convert light to nerve impulses, thus creating images and reflecting and intensifying light for better night vision. Ocular diseases can alter these functions, resulting in impaired vision. Aussies used for breeding should have their eyes checked annually by a board-certified ophthalmologist. Eye checks can be made as early as six weeks of age.

Cataracts

Opacities of the lens, inside the eye, obstruct the passage of light to the retina, causing clouded or blurred vision and blindness. Acquired cataracts resulting from injury (caused by trauma to the head or eye) or senile cataracts that develop in aging Aussies are not hereditary. Generally, a tiny opacity of the lens that remains unchanged over a six- to twelve-month period is not inherited.

On the other hand, juvenile cataracts that develop bilaterally (in both eyes) by the time an Aussie is two years of age is an inherited disease and should be eliminated from a breeding program.

Anopthalmia

The absence of a true eyeball caused by absent ocular tissue is a dominant trait associated with homozygous merles.

Collie Eye Anomaly (CEA)

CEA is a recessive inherited ocular disease. The basic defect is an underdeveloped area in the vascular layer (blood vessels) underlying the retina. Retinal dysplasia or detachments (with or without bleeding), and the presence of colobomas can affect one or both eyes. The onset occurs between three and eight weeks of age.

Colobomas

Colobomas are notchlike defects in or adjacent to the optic nerve, or are absent or defective ocular tissue. A coloboma affecting the iris is a relatively minor defect, providing the hole or abnormal opening is small enough that it allows the eye to contract sufficiently, enabling it to still control the amount of light that enters the eye.

Microphthalmia

Abnormally small eyes is a dominant trait associated with the dominant state of homozygous merles.

Persistent Pupillary Membrane (PPM)

PPM is a congenital disorder originating in the iris and occurs when the normal fetal covering is not completely reabsorbed by the body within six weeks of age. PPM is not believed to be inherited when it is the sole abnormality.

Retinal Dysplasia

Retinal dysplasia (detached or folded retinas) is abnormal development or maturation of the retina. This defect may be caused by prenatal viral infections (herpes virus or parvovirus) in the dam or puppies, or it is inherited through a recessive gene and surfaces between three and eight weeks of age.

Progressive Retinal Atrophy (PRA)

Also known as night blindness, PRA is a retinal degeneration. Dogs with PRA exhibit impaired vision or blindness at night or in dim light. PRA is one of a group of devastating recessive inherited diseases that eventually cause blindness in many breeds. Fortunately, this is not a hereditary problem in Australian Shepherds. PRA is included because retinal atrophy can result from disease, although it is not progressive or genetic in nature.

Hip Dysplasia

Hip dysplasia is poor hip-joint conformation (phenotype) that can cause lameness and premature arthritis. Hip dysplasia is a polygenic disorder that may be significantly affected by environmental factors. The Orthopedic Foundation for Animals (OFA) reviews hip-joint conformation through pelvic radiographs by three independent veterinary radiologists. If a dog is at least twenty-four months of age and is determined by the OFA to have normal hips, he is assigned an OFA breed number. Dogs rated as OFA–Excellent, OFA–Good, and OFA–Fair are sound and within normal limits and can be used for breeding. If the hips are evaluated as Borderline, they are not eligible for an OFA breed number, and a repeat study is recommended six to eight months later.

Ch. Copper Canyon's Caligari "Jimmie."
Photo by A. T. Carter.

FUNDAMENTAL GENETICS, AUSSIES COLOR BREEDING, AND WHITE

Recognized colors by the Breed Standard are blue merle, red merle, solid black, and solid red, all of which can be with or without white markings and/or copper (tan) points. The white trim that is allowable for Australian Shepherds clearly appears on the muzzle, the top skull, the foreface, the neck, the chest, the stomach, the feet, and the legs. Acceptable white trim can vary from small amounts on the tips of the toes to full blazes, collars, and stockings (see Chapter e, The Standard of Excellence).

Breeding Solid Black Aussies

An Australian Shepherd that appears black may have either two black genes (black/black) or one black gene and one red gene (black/red). The black Australian Shepherd that has two black genes (black/black) can only pass on black genes, which means that all of the puppies will be black. The other black Aussie (black/red) with one black gene and one red gene, commonly known as red factored (or a red carrier), will produce black puppies unless the other parent is a red Aussie with two red genes or a red-factored black Aussie.

Breeding Solid Red Aussies

A red Australian Shepherd when bred to another red Australian Shepherd will produce an entire litter of red puppies. If a red Aussie is bred to a black Aussie that has only black genes, the puppies will be black, but those black puppies will now carry one red gene. When they are bred to a red-factored Aussie, both black and red puppies may appear in the litter.

Merle Pattern

Merling is a pattern, not a color. As previously pointed out, there are two colors in which this pattern may appear—the red merle and the blue merle. When a merle is bred to a solid Aussie, the puppies inherit the colors (as described above) from their parents in addition to the pattern in which the color is expressed. Although there are many other factors that influence coat color, this discussion is basic to keep it understandable. Also, in order to explain the merling gene, assume that the parents are without any white trim.

Mating a Solid, Nonmerled Aussie to Another Solid, Nonmerled Aussie

When a solid red or black individual is mated to another solid Aussie, the parents can pass on only

Two very attractive brothers, Ch. McDugg of Windermere ATD-D, OTD-S, STC-C, and Surefire of Windermere CD, OTD-S, STD-DC (WTCh. Las Rocosa Kublia Khan RDX ex Ch. Christmas Wishes of Windermere CD, OTD-D, STD-SC).

The only blue merle pattern Ch. Fieldmaster of Flintridge CD exhibited in his glossy black coat was the small patch of merle on his face. Courtesy Dr. Heard.

solid, nonmerling genes, resulting in solid red or black puppies.

Mating a Solid, Nonmerled Aussie to a Merled Aussie

When a solid, nonmerled Aussie is mated to a merled Aussie, the solid, nonmerled Aussie can provide only a nonmerled gene, while the merled parent with one merled gene and one nonmerled gene can pass on either a nonmerled gene or a merled gene to his offspring. When a puppy inherits two solid genes (one from each parent), the result will be a solid, nonmerled puppy. When a puppy inherits a solid, nonmerled gene and a merled gene, the puppy will be a merled individual.

Mating a Merle to a Merle

When two merled Aussies are mated together, the puppies will inherit either merled genes or nonmerled genes from their parents. Some puppies will inherit a nonmerled gene from each parent, resulting in a solid-colored puppy. Other puppies will receive a nonmerled gene from one parent and a merled gene from the other parent, resulting in merled puppies. The remaining 25 percent of the litter (one out of four puppies) will receive two merled genes, one from each parent. When Aussie puppies inherit two merled genes, the result is a double (defective) merled white. These puppies are almost white in appearance and may or may not have a few merling spots or diluted speckles. These individuals can have defective organs, and their hearing and sight are almost always impaired. In some cases, the eyes are not completely formed or the puppies have no eyes. The eye rims, lips, nose, and pads are without pigment except where some merling is present. The defective merled whites occur in approximately 25 percent of the litter.

Defective puppies have no effect on normal-colored puppies in the litter. The remaining puppies (approximately 75 percent) that are solids and merles are totally normal because they have inherited either two nonmerled genes or one nonmerled gene and one merled gene. The *only* time when defective (double) merled whites, known also as homozygous whites, occur is when there is a concentration of the merling genes by mating two merled individuals together. It can be totally avoided by breeding solid-colored individuals to merled individuals. Whenever you cross two merled Aussies, it is necessary to cull the defective whites, which are identified by the appearance of white and diluted coloring.

Patterned White Aussies

Too often, novice or inexperienced breeders confuse the defective merled whites with "mismarked" or patterned white Australian Shepherds. These individuals can appear in a litter in which two solid Aussies or a solid and a merled Aussie, or two merles, are bred together. These "white" puppies are not defective like the double merled whites, nor are they a product of the merling gene. These Aussies may have solid-colored bodies with white spots (not to be confused with merling spots), or they may have white bodies with colored spots, or more than half of their bodies may be white. The head is always colored, and the ears and eyes are surrounded by full pigment other than white.

Irish Pattern (White Trim)

The distribution of acceptable white trim on Australian Shepherds is due to what is known as the Irish spotting pattern. The Irish pattern governs white markings that appear on the muzzle, the foreface, and the top skull. The Irish pattern is also responsible for producing white collars, white socks on the feet, and white on the tip of the tail (in Aussies born with a tail).

Piebald

Piebald genes often express themselves by extending white markings up along the stifles and connecting the white hair under the body. The piebald gene produces irregular, nonsymmetrical patterns of white. For example, a patterned white Australian Shepherd may have a fully colored body with a white splash, or he may have a fully colored head with a white body and only a few colored spots.

Defective Double Merled Whites (Homozygous Whites)

Novice or inexperienced breeders mistakenly identify the defective double merled whites (homozygous whites) for patterned whites and sell them to unsuspecting buyers. It is often difficult to determine impaired vision or blindness until the puppies are toddling. The handicap usually goes unnoticed until the puppy is in an unfamiliar environment and away from his littermates, which is why the Australian Shepherd Breed Standard disallows individuals that are not correctly marked.

BREEDING FOR THE WRONG REASONS

If your goal is to raise a litter of puppies to educate you children and allow them to experience the miracle of birth, think again! As a breeder, you are liable for the care and welfare of each puppy for a lifetime. It is up to you to see that each puppy is placed in a suitable home where he will receive a lifetime of proper care. Without deposits paid in advance, there is no guarantee that the puppies will sell by weaning age. Unless the puppies have potential homes, there is always the chance that they may not sell for months. Until then, it is your responsibility and expense to house, train, feed, provide medical care, and socialization for them. When puppies are no longer cute, they chew, bark, defecate, and require room to run and play. Even if the puppies are sold at an early age, they are sometimes returned to the breeder for various reasons.

Puppies are not always born at a convenient time. In the event of emergency labor in which a cesarean may have to be performed at 3 A.M., the children will miss out entirely. In addition, there is always the risk that they may lose a beloved friend if the bitch has serious problems and dies while in labor or delivery.

Breeding Aussies is not a money-making venture. One of the worst reasons to breed Aussies is to recoup your purchase price and expenses. Planning a litter takes time and money. The veterinary care, inoculations, food, stud service fees, and advertising can be expensive even if you *don't* have emergencies or other unexpected expenses.

Pedigree of:

Ch Stonehenge Justin Case of Las Rocosa CD Blue C/W RF F=4.38%
M
B2743 A18977-73X5
12/16/1974

Parents	Grandparents	Great-Grandparents	2xGreat-Grandparents	3xGreat-Grandparents
Ch Las Rocosa Shiloh CD Red Merle C F=7.18% A79 (3)A108-77270 4/8/1970	Boehmers Four Man Blue W RF F=0.00% A451 A3939-612156	Taylors Rusty A3139-6396	Lamars Turk	Manskers Smokey
				Manskers Duchess
			Manskers Freckles	Sislers Shorty
				Vassars Fanny
		Porters Gillian A2795-612135	Harpers Old Smokey	Tucsons Joe
				Tucsons Sis
			Gwen Fre Ho Genie	Davidsons Blue Boy
				Millers Shorty
	Hosmers Jill Red Merle C/W F=1.37% B1735 (2)A282-7220 11/20/1967	Taylors Whiskey A733 (1)A113-66279	Lamars Turk	Manskers Smokey
				Manskers Duchess
			Manskers Anna Lee	Manskers Kim
				Manskers Freckles
		Taylors Buena A732 A3141-6396	Sniffs Dandy Danny	Sislers Joker
				Smiths Trixie
			Petralamas Tate	Basque Dog 3
				Basque Bitch 3
Ch Shanahans Phantom CD Blue C/W F=0.15% A111 7/28/1971	Ch Deines Spark Black C/W F=0.00% A41 9/22/1969	Hartnagles Hud A74 (2)A75-66279	Taylors Whiskey	Lamars Turk
				Manskers Anna Lee
			Taylors Buena	Sniffs Dandy Danny
				Petralamas Tate
		Townsends Miss Dixie	Wyoming Ranch Dog	
			Wyoming Ranch Bitch	
	Deines Lady Lucky Blue W F=3.13% A64 3/8/1963	Deines Blue Dingo	Montgomerys Blue	Hartnagles Badger
				Jill
			Bodens Dolly	Hartnagles Badger
				Jill
		Deines Toby	Deines Jess	
			Deines Jinx	Elys Feo
				Elys Blue

DEVELOPING A BLOODLINE OF DISTINCTION

The goal of inbreeding (the practice of breeding two dogs that have close-up ancestors in common (daughter to father, mother to son, and brother to sister matings) is to get the progeny as predictable and consistent (homozygous) as possible. Line breeding is a type of inbreeding, but not as intense (cousin to cousin, niece to uncle, nephew to aunt matings).

Both inbreeding and line breeding tend to cut down variability (heterozygosity) in the offspring, while fixing (setting) type by increasing uniformity (homozygosity). The type being fixed is selected by the breeder and governed by the traits exhibited in the ancestors. If the breeder 'selects' Aussies with genes for a specific working style or character, then by inbreeding, it is possible to get these genes in homozygous condition to reinforce them in the family line involved. This breeding system (staying in the family) should only be practiced when intensifying the good qualities through line breeding and *weeding out the poor and inferior genes.*

Let me make it very clear. Inbreeding or line breeding should **ONLY** be practiced if the ancestors and individuals involved are healthy and free from genetic disorders, intelligent, structurally sound, and possess proven working ability of the desired type. If so, then inbreeding can be constructive. Inbreeding does not cause the offspring to be more liable to manifest a disorder, be less hardy, or cause a decrease in size, unless those characteristics are already present in the genetic makeup.

It is correct that inbreeding and line breeding intensify a strong constitution, good bone, vigor, and working ability OR a weak constitution, lack of vigor, delicate bone, or lack of working ability, if these traits have been well developed in the bloodline.

Out-crossing (mating unrelated pairs) is a better breeding system for inexperienced breeders because unrelated dogs would not be as likely to double up on the same harmful genes. However, two different bloodlines can carry the same recessive detrimental gene.

In developing a bloodline it is also *necessary* to out-cross to maintain strong, healthy immune systems, which are dependent on genetic diversity. As a breeder you always have to keep your eye towards the future. It is important to find bloodstock that is compatible to yours without compromising any of the qualities that it took years to establish, improve and perfect.

We started our bloodlines with Hartnagle's Badger (Ely's Blue and Christensen's Buster) and Hartnagle's Goody (Ely's Feo and Ely's Blue). Ely's Feo was brought to the United States by a herder from the Basque country in Andorra. The herder was employed by the Warren Livestock Company at the time.

Juanita Ely, a rancher, was one of the oldest documented breeders in the country. She had acquired her first Aussie in the 20s with two bands of sheep she bought in Idaho. As a livestock person, she knew the value of recording the lineage of the dogs, to preserve and establish them. Juanita recognized the need to register the ancestry of 'Blue Australian Shepherds' and was largely responsible for contacting Ed Emanuel at the National Stock Dog Registry (a division of the IESR) to use their services to register the breed.

Juanita Ely used her dogs to herd their cattle and several bands (each band consisting of 1,000 to 1,500 head) of sheep on the range in the harsh working conditions (thick cactus, heavy crusted snow, heavy underbrush), rain or shine in the real world. Ely's Blue, the dam of both Goody and Badger had been proven on the ranch, day in and day out.

The Badger line had courage, longevity, and staying power. We admired those characteristics and continued to breed for them. Once when working a single Brahman bull, Badger got tromped pretty hard. Dad thought the bull had killed him. He sadly picked up Badger's limp body and laid him aside, so he could bury him beneath the lilac bushes at the house. Apparently, the bull had just knocked him out cold. After a few minutes, he came to and shook his head. The next thing we knew Badger went back to work and put that bull in its place.

The years progressed and Badger (1954-1969) entered his twilight years. Mom and Dad traveled many, many miles all across the country looking for a suitable replacement for Badger. It was no easy task. Finally, Hartnagle's Hud came into our lives. He filled the bill beyond our wildest expectations. He was everything we had hoped for and more, and he proved it time after time. Hud was intelligent, athletic and fun to have around. He never held a grudge. Hud was a clown, but when it came down to business, you could trust him with your life. If a mad mother cow or a grizzly bear had you pinned to the ground, Hud would protect you even if it cost him his life. He was dependable. As tough as he was with rough stock, he was equally as gentle with babies.

We were so pleased with Hud we decided we had to have a female of the same cross. Hartnagle's Fritzie Taylor, and Hud were by Taylor's Whiskey and out of Taylor's Buena. Whiskey and Buena also were proven by hard, continuous ranch work in real working situations where they proved they could handle themselves in all types of terrain and under varied conditions.

Las Rocosa Lester was the product of a mating that crossed Champion Las Rocosa Leslie CSD (out of Hartnagle's Fritzie Taylor) back to her sire, Champion Las Rocosa Shiloh CD (out of Hosmer's Jill). Leslie had also been proven on the Taylor Ranch.

Shiloh's dam was a full sister to both Hud and Fritzie Taylor, who were all of the same family lineage. These dogs were sound, athletic, had stock savvy, were able to face a stubborn ram with authority, and who were undaunted by cattle.

Not only did Shiloh have heart, trainability, stock savvy, power and endurance, he had a style all his own. He was the Champion of Champions. Shiloh worked like a cat on the hunt. He could handle anything and without even asking, he would gather the stock and bring them to us. If something tried to break away from the bunch and tried to escape, it did so only once before Shiloh put it back in its place. He had the uncanny ability to read and rate whatever was being handled. Shiloh was prepotent (having the capacity to transmit those qualities back to the offspring) for reproducing his natural style (the distinctive performance which is a combination of intelligence, working attitude; concentration and force), Consequently today, you'll see many Aussies exhibiting a stylish blend of eye and a natural fetching style, with balance.

Both Leslie and Shiloh were sound, athletic, dependable, and could head and heel with equal ease. We felt the cross between Shiloh and Leslie would be a cornerstone for the future of our bloodline. The cross was made and produced Las Rocosa Lester. Lester was bred to only a few of our very select bitches and for our own use. His record is unsurpassed. He went on to sire some very prominent working dogs who (by virtue of line breeding) were able to transmit the qualities of their ancestry. Lester was one of our most prepotent sires whose offspring have stood the test of time, and have gone on to make their own mark on the breed, many of which are recorded in the ASCA Hall of Fame.

As we developed the Las Rocosa bloodline, we knew we also wanted to maintain the traits we highly admired in the Badger line. We were able to do that with Champion Stonehenge Justin Case of Las Rocosa CD. Justin Case was by Champion Las Rocosa Shiloh and out of Champion Shanahan's Phantom CDX. 'Fanny,' was a descendant of Hartnagle's Jinx who was later registered as Deines' Jinx in the Stock Dog Registry.

Justin measured up in every way. He embodied the type of temperament (trainability and intelligence), working style, stock savvy, soundness and athletic ability we demanded in our dogs. He proved his value as a sire, by passing on those same characteristics.

We have always recognized it is vital to evaluate every generation to determine the qualities and characteristics that are being perpetuated. A successful breeding program has to be based on more than blue ribbons, it has to be built upon a strong foundation that is tested from one generation to the next, proven by the yardstick of performance.

Chapter 26

THE BIRDS AND THE BEES

THE SCIENCE OF REPRODUCTION IS directly responsible for the development of all breeds including the Australian Shepherd. Reproductive cells with inheritable factors are passed down through the generations. The female produces eggs (ova), which, when united with the male's reproductive cells (sperm) and fertilized, initiate another generation to carry on the inherited genetic makeup.

THE BROOD BITCH

The bitch has to be in peak condition, and this occurs only through continual effort. She must be free from parasitic agents and current on all inoculations prior to breeding, and she must be maintained on a high-quality diet.

Your Aussie bitch should be given an annual health checkup. Prior to breeding, she should be given a reproductive soundness examination. Her overall condition needs to be checked, including her temperature, respiration, urinary functions, weight, skin (hydration/condition), and dental condition. She should be at optimum weight before breeding. If she is too heavy, she may have problems producing milk for the puppies once they are whelped. Vaginal cultures must be obtained to identify the presence of bacteria or infections such as brucellosis. A vaginal examination will detect possible vaginal strictures.

Sterility is a condition of infertility. Whatever the cause, there are no "cure-alls" for the condition. Rather, each case requires careful diagnosis and specific treatment.

Thyroid imbalances such as hyperthyroidism (an overactive thyroid) and hypothyroidism (deficient thyroid secretions) can totally alter the metabolism. Discharges and infections within the reproductive tract, usually in the cervix, uterus, or fallopian tubes, and some types of physiological imbalances, such as cystic ovaries, failure to ovulate, retained afterbirth, neonatal death, abortions, resorptions, genetic faults, obesity, and specific diseases, can all lead to reproductive failure. If sterility is suspected, then blood work should be done to check the thyroid levels. Never breed a bitch when an infection is present, because the condition could spread.

The reproductive tract in the female consists of two ovaries (which are the source of estrogen, the hormone responsible for female characteristics), two oviducts, and two uterine horns (the womb, a "Y"-shaped structure), which form a muscular ring called the cervix. The cervix is tightly closed except during estrus and whelping. The cervix at the neck of the uterus separates the uterus from the vagina. The vagina is the passage that leads from the uterus to the vulva.

The Aussie female reaches sexual maturity generally between six and fourteen months of age. The female is monestrus, meaning that she will have only one heat cycle per breeding season. She may cycle at any time during the year, usually twice a year. The reproductive cycle is broken into four distinct phases: proestrus, estrus, metestrus, and anestrus. These stages vary slightly between individuals.

THE ESTROUS CYCLE

Proestrus

The ovaries are the essential reproductive organs in the female. The ova are contained within tiny sacs called follicles. While under the influence of follicular stimulation hormone (FSH), the follicles develop on the ovaries. The ova are minute, but as they reach maturity, they increase in size. Maturing ova produce the estrogen hormone, which induces a blood-tinged discharge (uterine lining) and swelling of the external genitalia (vulva). This marks the beginning of the heat cycle. The female will usually drink more water during proestrus and will therefore urinate more frequently. Males are attracted to the female through the scent of pheromone in the vaginal secretions and urine. The odor creates hormonal stimulation in the male.

Hartnagle's Fritzie Taylor (Taylor's Whiskey ex Taylor's Buena), one of the great foundation dams of the breed. One of the most successful crosses occurred between Fritzie Taylor and Ch. Las Rocosa Shiloh. The cross was repeated on several occasions and invariably produced excellent results.

Ely's Blue (1950, Heavron's Bob ex Young's Bitchie), the Legendary "Ghost Dog" on the old gold National Stock Dog Registration (IESR) Certificates. "Old Blue" was a full sister to Sisler's Queen and a major contributor to many foundation offspring, including Hartnagle's Badger. Sisler's Panda, one of Jay Sisler's trick dogs, was a daughter of Ely's Blue. Courtesy Juanita Ely.

The bitch will be playful with dogs of both sexes, but when the male tests her receptivity by trying to mount her, she will swing away, snap, and growl at him. During the courtship, the female becomes aloof and coquettish, while the male becomes a show-off and sometimes a clown. He will usually parade around and try to impress her. The female will not allow copulation until she reaches estrus.

Estrus

As the female approaches estrus, the period of receptivity (when she is in a "standing" heat), you will observe a pronounced genital swelling due to the high levels of estrogen. The pink, blood-tinged discharge will begin to "clear," or you may notice a yellowish, straw color.

When she is ready to be bred, the female's attitude toward the male will change drastically from hostile to receptive. She will "flag" her tail and lift it toward the side. She will arch her back and swing her hindquarters toward the male. When the male mounts her, she will stand to be bred. The swelling of the external genitals may be less pronounced than on the previous day. It is generally agreed that the first day of estrus occurs when the bitch will accept the male for copulation. The duration of estrus is generally between six and fourteen days, with the average being around nine or ten days.

The female will shed her eggs one to three days from the first point of estrus (receptivity). The female may continue to accept mating for close to a week.

Metestrus

Metestrus is the short period between three to five days after the ova are released. During

WTCh. Parrish's Illusion CD, Hall of Fame dam. Courtesy Marti Parrish.

Like father, like son. The strong family resemblance is evident between this father and son. Courtesy Joel Finch.

metestrus, the follicular cavities in the ovaries secrete progesterone, the pregnancy hormone.

Diestrus

Diestrus is the fourth stage of the reproductive cycle and can occur about six days after ovulation. It marks the end of the heat cycle. It varies with each individual, but most bitches will be completely out of heat between the eighteenth and twenty-third days, with the average being twenty-one days.

During the next two months, the progesterone level will remain high in her system, whether or not she has been bred. Diestrus is characterized by a refusal to mate. The outward signs of proestrus, such as flirting, are more or less absent. Physical signs, such as swelling of the external genitals, are diminished, and there is a decline in the vaginal discharge. The female may display hostility toward an advancing male.

Anestrus

Anestrus is the resting stage for the reproductive cycle, and hormonal secretions are very low. Anestrus may last from three to nine months, depending upon the individual, her age, and the environment.

FALSE PREGNANCY (PSEUDO-PREGNANCY)

When the ova do not become fertilized, the body may behave as though the female is bred. The breasts start to develop and secrete milk. You may see all the signs of a normal pregnancy. In rare cases, the bitch may also exhibit symptoms of labor. Pseudo-pregnancy is the period when the body will function as though it were actually pregnant, although in reality it is not.

VAGINAL SMEARS TO DETERMINE WHEN TO BREED

Vaginal smears are microscopic examinations of the cell formations within the vaginal tract. The smear will map out hormonal patterns for bitches with "silent heats" (estrus cycles with few visible signs) and will indicate optimum breeding times for artificial insemination.

A small quantity of vaginal material is collected from the vaginal wall and then swabbed onto a slide. The slide is treated with a stain solution and a distilled water bath. When the slide is dry, the contents are examined under a micro-

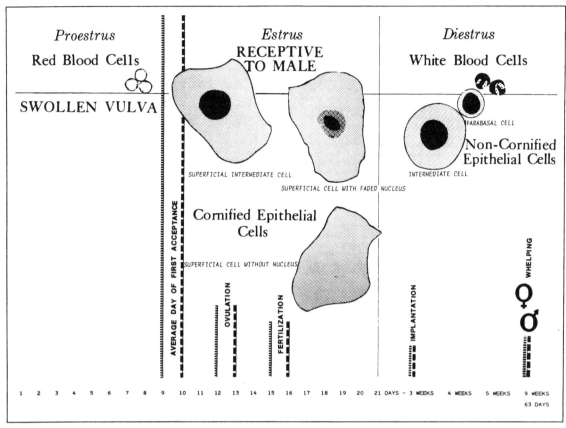

Behavioral events and physiologic changes that occur during the canine estrus cycle.

scope to reveal cell formations and to record the changes as hormonal activity progresses.

During proestrus, there is an accumulation of red blood cells with an insignificant amount of white blood cells. An abnormally high percentage of white blood cells indicates that an infection is present. As the cycle progresses and estrogen levels rise, the vaginal lining (epithelium tissue) increases in density. The cells are then shed from the surface of the lining and discarded in the discharge. Epithelial cells are easily distinguished from blood cells. They are larger, and the nucleus of the cell structure is enveloped in a translucent rim.

The number of blood cells will decrease as the heat cycle progresses. The epithelial cells continue to transform toward what is known as the "cornified" stage, at which point they change from a regular to an irregular shape. In the cornified stage, the nucleus (yolk) will be barely visible, if present at all. The rim of the cell will begin to curl up. When all cells are in the cornified stage, actual estrus begins, accompanied by the visible signs during the acceptance period. Ovulation will occur three days later. The ova will take approximately three days to mature, at which point the eggs will be fertilized (about six days following the first incidence of the fully cornified stage). The cells should remain cornified from ten to fourteen days. At the beginning of diestrus, the cells sharply progress back to the noncornified state.

When you examine vaginal smears over an entire cycle period, the cells may never become cornified. This means that ovulation has not occurred. Even if she is bred, the female may not conceive.

MAMMARY GLANDS

The mammary glands are not directly involved in the reproductive process, but they are dependent upon the ovaries for their growth and functioning. These glands are made up of milk-secreting tissues that communicate with the exterior by a teat. The milk secreted by one gland cannot transfer to another, but the milk from each may be reabsorbed and pass into the blood.

THE STUD DOG

The Aussie stud must be in optimum condition. He must be kept free from parasitic agents and be current on all inoculations. He should be maintained on a regular exercise program and a top-quality diet. Have him checked periodically for brucellosis and other infections. Have his sperm evaluated when the reproductive soundness examination is performed. At this time, your veterinarian can also determine which problems may or may not be hereditary.

Once the tissues of the body reach a certain stage of growth and body development begins to decrease, the reproductive cells (sperm in the male) begin to ripen. Normal sexual activities of the male generally occur when the Aussie is eight months old.

When the male reaches sexual maturity, the testicles are descended into the scrotum. They are present around weaning age. The scrotum is a double sac situated outside the body itself, under the tail and anus. The testes are responsible for producing semen, which is composed of spermatozoa and other fluid secretions. Spermatozoa originate in the seminiferous tubules. The testes not only produce the reproductive or germ cells, but they also contain Leydig's cells from which testosterone—the male hormone—is secreted. Testosterone is also necessary for spermatozoa to mature and become fertile.

The testicles are subdivided into coiled seminiferous tubules that straighten out at the top of

The foundation sire and dam for Southern Cross. Top: Surefire of Windermere CD, OTD-s, STD-cd (WTCh. Las Rocosa Kublia Khan Crown Pt. ex Ch. Christmas Wishes of Windermere CD, OTD-d, STD-c). Bottom: Wildfire of Windermere CD, STD-ds (Ch. Las Rocosa Little Wolf STD-cd ex Ch. Christmas Wishes of Windermere CD, OTD-d, STD-c). Courtesy Karla Michelson.

the testes and join to form a combined tract, or one tubule, known as the epididymis. After leaving the testicles, the spermatozoa travel through the epididymis, where the sperm become motile and fertile.

The remainder of the semen is produced by fluid secretions from the prostate gland, located at the beginning of the urethra. It surrounds the neck of the bladder. Semen is passed in three fractions. It is during the transferring of the last, or third fraction, that the actual "tie" occurs.

The first fraction contains a minute amount of fluid secreted from the urethral glands. It is devoid of spermatozoa. The second phase is the sperm-bearing fraction. During this sperm-rich stage, conception can take place. The third and final stage is comprised of prostatic secretions that are free from sperm.

The penis is made up of the urethra and muscle tissue called the glans penis. Together, they

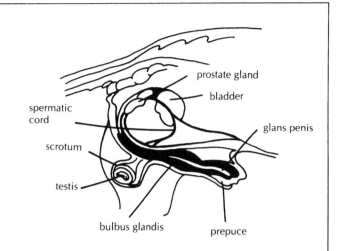

The male reproductive system of the dog is unique in that the bulbus glandis enlarges after intromission. The swelling of this gland locks the dog and bitch together until ejaculation has taken place. This "tie" may last anywhere from five to thirty minutes or more.

The male reproductive system.

facilitate entry into the female's vaginal opening without full erection. The female's "muscular ring," which contracts, causes a thrusting reflex. As soon as the bulbus glandis swells, completing the penile erection, ejaculation occurs. The full swelling of the bulbus glandis "locks" the male's penis within the female's vagina. When the male rotates his body backward and dismounts, the penis is reflected backward 180 degrees. The penis is bent back behind the bulbus glandis, which will constrict the veins so that the blood does not return to the body. The erection remains while ejaculation continues to drive the sperm into the oviduct, where fertilization takes place, during the third fraction of ejaculate. The breeding "tie" may last anywhere from five minutes to an hour but generally will last between fifteen to thirty minutes. It should be noted, however, that conception may take place without a tie.

The prepuce (the fold of skin that covers the head of the penis) should be checked for inflammation, lacerations, and persistent frenulum (a condition in which a fold or membrane restricts the mobility of the prepuce). The penis should be checked for abnormal discharge or inflammation, lacerations, and tumors.

The testicles should be carefully palpated and evaluated for size and consistency. Palpation should also reveal abnormalities (if present) and pain, tumors, or hernias. One testis may be slightly larger than the other, but a great degree in size variation is not normal. Testes lacking a moderate amount of firmness may indicate testicular degeneration and atrophy. Swollen or enlarged testes may indicate infections.

Until the testes descend into the scrotum, the stud will remain infertile, because while the testes are retained in the abdomen—their position in fetal life—the sperm, being very susceptible to high temperatures, cannot develop. The scrotum, then, is a device for keeping the testes at a lower-than-body temperature.

It sometimes happens that only one testis will descend into the scrotum. This condition is known as monorchidism. In other cases, neither testis descends, a condition known as cryptorchidism. In cases where just one descends, the male may be fully fertile but should never be bred, because this condition is a serious hereditary fault. Failure of the testes to descend may be due to improper functioning of the anterior pituitary gland.

The prostate should be palpated for size and shape, which should help reveal any prostatic diseases or tumors. These conditions can greatly alter semen and reduce fertility.

A true champion of champions, Hall of Fame sire, Ch. Las Rocosa Shiloh was without a doubt one of the greatest foundation sires of the modern Australian Shepherd. Many famous Aussies trace their ancestry back to Shiloh.

Decreased concentrations of testosterone may occur in a male if there is a hormonal cause for lack of sex drive (libido). Males with a history of previous inflammatory diseases may have temporary infertility secondary to elevated body temperatures during the febrile episodes.

Diseases of the epididymis can also cause infertility in the stud dog. A direct cause of infertility can be due to the thyroid function, which can totally alter the state of metabolism.

Following a period of inactivity as a stud, a male should be bred twice to a bitch to ensure live sperm in the semen.

If there is a question regarding fertility, thyroid activity should be checked by a blood test. Immunosuppressive drugs and X-rays can temporarily alter the male's ability to produce live sperm, so be sure to guard against this when breeding. Consult your veterinarian.

Semen Evaluation

It is imperative for the semen to be collected and handled properly in order to give an accurate evaluation. Temperature shocks, contamination, and urine can give inaccurate results.

Several factors are considered in such an evaluation. Sperm are observed for motility (locomotion), which indicates the ability of the sperm to travel swiftly in direct lines to fertilize an ovum. The genetic material is contained in the head of the sperm, while the tail enables the sperm to reach the ova. Morphology is observed to determine if normalities exceed abnormalities of sperm formation. Abnormalities can include misshapen heads, kinked or bent midpieces, coiled tails, detached heads, and so forth.

All of this information is used to determine the fertility or lack of it in a stud dog. In cases where infertility is suspected, information such as protoplasmic droplets and bent tails can be directed toward improper maturation in the epididymis (possibly an indication of disease or infection of the epididymis).

If poor results are attained on one evaluation, especially if the male has not been bred recently, then the evaluation should be repeated.

REPRODUCTIVE SOUNDNESS

Nutrition, genetics, general management, and health all play primary roles in breeding soundness. Many factors determine reproductive soundness in both the male (stud) and the female (bitch). Sterility in either is defined as unproductiveness, or the inability to reproduce. In other words, it is a condition in which normal mating of apparently healthy dogs is not followed by conception. Sterility may result from any one or more of a large number of conditions including age, environment, stress, diet, disease, lack of proper exercise, overwork, irregular work and/or exercise, underfeeding, or nutritional deficiencies. Some of these factors result in permanent sterility, while others are more temporary. Reproduction cannot take place if the genitals are diseased. For example, to subject a female with an abnormal discharge to repeated services (matings) in hope that she will settle is basing expectations on false premises. Healthy puppies cannot be incubated within, or produced from, sexually diseased parents.

Breeding unsoundness is always a cause for rejection of Aussies intended to be included in a breeding program, although this unsoundness may not impair the individual's ability to function in other capacities. Breeding unsoundness includes malformation of the genitals and of the birth passageway, cryptorchidism, monorchidism, scrotal rupture, and other abnormalities.

Hereditary unsoundness is the most serious because of the possibility of transmission to the offspring. Mechanical injuries (such as a broken pelvis) do not pass to the offspring but may cause death in the female. When either an injury or hereditary unsoundness is subjected to the strain of reproduction, especially labor while whelping, the female may die.

Exercise

Every Australian Shepherd should receive proper exercise throughout his life. A regular exercise program is especially important for breeding animals. Regular exercise stimulates circulation, which is responsible for supplying oxygen and vital nutrients to the tissue cells. It is imperative to build and maintain the cardiovascular system. It is too often forgotten that the heart is a muscle that must be maintained to withstand stress and shock. Exercise is the natural aphrodisiac for stud dogs. It maintains a healthy appetite, helps alleviate boredom, and keeps the mind active and alert.

Swimming, daily walks, retrieving games (Frisbee, Flyball), Agility, and herding work are all ways to keep your Aussie physically fit. It is important that you use good judgment regarding

Hall of Fame sire Ch. Fieldmaster's Three Ring Circus (Ch. Fieldmaster of Flintridge ex Whispering Pines of Flintridge) is one of the best known "Fieldmaster" sons. Courtesy Wilson.

the age and physical capabilities and limitations of your Aussie. Consistency and regularity are important. Irregular spurts of activity may result in muscle strain and exertion and lend a susceptibility toward injury. A walk around the house or kennel is not sufficient exercise to maintain an Aussie in adequate muscle tone.

Diet

There is no single factor more responsible for excellent health than diet. Poor nutrition is a big factor in reproductive failure.

WHEN TO BREED

Excessive breeding demands placed upon sires and dams should be avoided before the dog reaches maturity. The vigor from a certain degree of maturity is essential for the highest reproductive efficiency.

This, however, is often in conflict with man's desire for early and late financial returns from his breeding animals. Though young animals are frequently violated in breeding practices, it is not uncommon for a dog to be bred almost to the point of senility. The results are often unsatisfactory, such as the stud's inability to settle the bitch or the bitch's inability to conceive. Abortion, retained afterbirth, and weak offspring are not uncommon under these circumstances.

Ideally, the sire should not be used before two years of age, although he is generally capable of reproduction at eight months of age. The bitch may come into estrus as young as six months of age and be capable of reproduction. Even though she can conceive, she will not be physically mature enough until she is nearly two years old. By this time, the individuals have developed mentally and physically, which enables them to deal with the excessive demands of reproduction. When bred younger than this, the individual may be robbed of the chance to attain the mental and physical development that is so important for a solid foundation.

The Mating

Generally speaking, it is ideal to breed an inexperienced male to a proven, cooperative bitch, especially the first time. However, some maiden bitches, if receptive toward the young stud, are a wiser choice than a veteran bitch with an alligator-type of response. This inexperienced bitch should be bred ultimately to an experienced veteran stud, if possible.

Prior to the actual time of mating, it is assumed that both the stud dog and brood bitch have been checked by a veterinarian for reproductive soundness. All contracts and financial arrangements should be agreed upon before the actual mating takes place.

The external areas surrounding both the female's vulva and the male's sheath should be cleansed to prevent contamination. Take great caution to use a mild shampoo. Avoid any soap or shampoo that may be harsh and cause irritation. Rinse the areas well with clear water. Never apply any agent (especially ones with spermicidal characteristics) to the genitals, primarily to the internal folds, unless advised to do so by your veterinarian.

The actual mating can be best accomplished in an area devoid of outside distractions. No more than two people should be present to lessen possible confusion.

The ground or floor surfaces should have good footing, such as broom-finished concrete, rubber matting, carpeting, or grass. Avoid slick flooring.

When the stud and bitch are first introduced, there will generally be a period of courtship before copulation. Mating can often take place without direct assistance, but someone should always be present to help if necessary.

When the timing is correct, it is quite obvious (especially with a cooperative female). Occasionally, the bitch will allow the stud to mount her, but when the penis touches her vulva, she may yelp and pull away. If this occurs several times, you may need to wait until the following day. The experienced stud dog, however, is a better judge of such matters than any chart, especially if the bitch is going through an unusual heat cycle.

The bitch in a standing heat during the period of receptivity will swing her hindquarters toward the stud and "flag" her tail. The bitch's vulva may contract when the male's nose or tongue touches it. When the male mounts, he will grasp the female's flanks with his forelegs. The stud will thrust his pelvis several times before he gains entrance to the vaginal opening. He will step on alternate hind legs and increase the pelvic thrusting to seek intromission to the vaginal opening. Once intromission occurs, the bulbus glandis passes through a muscular ring, which then contracts, and the bulbus glandis engorges with blood to initiate the "tie." The male may then pause and attempt to swing one hind leg over to one or the other side and turn 180 degrees around after dismounting. The pair will then remain in a tail-to-tail position for the duration of the tie.

The female reproductive system consists of the ovaries, uterine tubes, uterus, vagina, and vulva, as illustrated.

The ovaries are responsible for egg production, and are also the source of certain hormones. The ovaries of the newborn bitch contain her lifetime supply of eggs—hundreds of thousands.

After ovulation the eggs pass through the tubes into the uterus. Each tube is about the size of a two-inch section of spaghetti. Unlike most mammals, in the dog fertilization takes place in the uterine tubes, and the fertilized eggs remain there for about six days before moving to the uterine horn.

The uterus is "Y" shaped, and during pregnancy the developing fetuses are distributed between the two horns. The uterus is divided into three areas: the horns, the body, and the cervix. The horns lead to the body of the uterus, which is the passageway to the vagina. The cervix, lying at the base of the uterus, is the doorway. On one side of it lies the uterus, the ideal environment for the incubation of the fertilized eggs. On the other side lies the vagina, the opening to the outside.

The vulva is the external genitalia of the female. The lips of the vulva swell and become puffy during estrus.

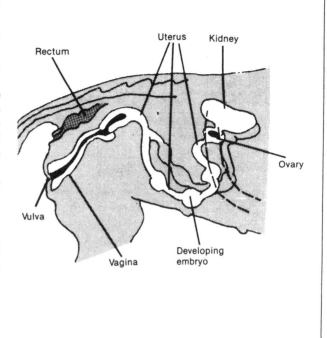

The female reproductive system.

The legendary Ch. Las Rocosa Rojo Hombre CD (Ch. Las Rocosa Shiloh ex Hartnagle's Fritzie Taylor). Courtesy Watts.

The male may need assistance in swinging his hind leg over the female's back. Some females will act aggressive toward the stud even though they are in a period of receptivity. A vaginal smear can be taken to confirm the stage of her heat cycle. One assistant should take charge of the female's head if she acts aggressive toward the male or tries to bite him. If she tires to bite him, apply an emergency muzzle (described in Chapter 13, Emergency First Aid). If a bitch becomes frightened, she may snap at anything, including you.

If the bitch tries to jump around or lie down, especially during the tie, you must intervene. Place your arm under her stomach to keep her on her feet. Do not allow her to drag the male around once they are tied. Steady her by speaking in calm tones. The other assistant should hold the male's collar if necessary to prevent him from dragging the female around.

One tie appropriately timed is sufficient to produce a nice litter. It is a common practice to breed on the first or second day of estrus, then to skip a day and breed again on the third or fourth day (approximately forty-eight hours apart). The period of receptivity for each female is different. One female will stand for a stud on the tenth day of her cycle, while another will not be ready until the fourteenth day.

The stud should not be bred every day. It takes forty-eight hours for the spermatozoa to regenerate for maximum fertility. There is no advantage whatsoever to breeding a female every day even though she will accept the stud. In fact, overuse can be detrimental to the stud.

Dual Mating

Cases have been reported in which a female has been bred by more than one male. During the receptivity period, a female may permit one or more males to mount and copulate with her. Once each ovum has been fertilized by a sperm, it becomes impenetrable. Therefore, while each puppy can have only one sire, a litter may be comprised of one or more sires.

If the female is bred to a specific stud and accidentally becomes bred to another male, it is possible that some of the ova will be fertilized by one male, and one or more of the ova will be fertilized by another male.

The litter sired by more than one male will have half-brothers and sisters. If both sires are purebred Aussies, then the puppies are purebred Aussies. If one sire is a purebred Aussie and the other sire is of a different breed or is a mongrel (mutt), then only the portion sired by the purebred male will be purebred.

When paternity is questionable, DNA testing is necessary to determine parentage. It is your responsibility to safeguard your female in heat from being exposed to any male other than the one to whom she is bred. If you plan not to breed her, then keep her away from *all* males (including relatives) that are not neutered.

DNA Paternity Testing

DNA is a biomolecule containing each individual Aussie's genetic information or fingerprint. DNA is extracted from blood samples. It is cut into fragments that are then separated into bands. The bands are transferred to a nylon membrane, and the DNA sequences are identified. Once the nylon membrane is processed, the DNA fingerprint becomes visible to the naked eye, resembling a UPC bar code used on grocery store items.

Approximately 50 percent of the bands are inherited from the dam, and the other half from the sire. Paternity is established by first eliminating those bands in a puppy's sample that match the dam's sample, then determining which sire's bands match the puppy's remaining bands. The process may be especially complicated in cases where close relationships are shared between Aussies due to inbreeding and linebreeding practices.

Certain registries may accept the results of a DNA paternity test as a positive identification for registration purposes with prior approval.

Artificial Insemination

Artificial insemination is a process of artificial breeding. It refers to the manual introduction of the sperm (through the use of fresh or frozen semen) into the female's genitals. It is, therefore, distinguished from a natural mating. Artificial insemination is not intended to replace natural breeding, but it is an effective measure to help prevent the transmission of venereal diseases and infections that may on occasion occur from natural breeding.

Artificial insemination with either fresh or frozen semen can offer a supplemental method for a breeding program. Artificial insemination with fresh semen is a very effective step toward breeding a female to a superior stud that may be temporarily incapable of naturally covering the bitch due to an acquired injury, such as a broken leg.

Frozen semen helps cut prohibitive shipping expenses, possibilities of loss, and exposure to injury, death, disease, infection, or trauma that may occur during shipment. Artificial insemination is a step toward preventing the overuse of a prominent sire. Frozen semen banks offer a solid foundation toward maintaining genetic material from superior sires, especially if a stud was lost prematurely due to disease or disaster.

Each species or breed can only progress through the progeny of great sires and dams, and then through their offspring. However, it is important to not lose sight of the future and overlook the *present* great individuals while trying to recreate the past.

The Bitch

The bitch must be in the correct stage of her estrus cycle, which can be diagnosed and confirmed by examining a vaginal smear microscopically and/or by observing her reactions while in the presence of a "teaser" male. Ovulation usually occurs between twenty-four and seventy-two hours after the onset of estrus.

Due to the longevity of the male's sperm in the reproductive tract, it is suggested that insemination within the first few days of estrus would allow sperm to be present in the oviduct to fertilize the ova as they mature.

It is essential that only sterile equipment be used and that it be maintained at body temperature. Insemination is best handled by a veterinarian or by an experienced vet technician due to the danger of incorrectly inserting the pipette. The techniques of insemination are as essential as the methods employed for collecting and handling semen.

The one great disadvantage to artificially inseminating bitches that are unable to breed naturally is that a hereditary weakness or reproductive complication may be introduced into a line that otherwise would have been eliminated if left up to nature.

The Stud

The techniques of artificial insemination include collecting semen from the male and examining it microscopically for the absence of foreign material. Volume is measured, pH (ranging from 5.5 to 6.5, averaging 6.0) determined, the color noted, and motility, density, and morphology observed.

Semen must be collected and handled properly if good results are to be obtained. The quality of semen can be adversely affected if it is exposed to cold or heat shock (incorrect temperatures) or contaminated by chemical agents, disinfectants, soaps, alcohol, spermicides, urine, or excessive quantities of water.

Conception

Fertilization, or conception, takes place when live sperm are present in the oviduct and the ova are ripe (mature). Fertilization cannot take place until the ova have matured, even though both sperm and ova may be present in the oviduct for several days.

Fertilized ova will leave the oviduct and enter the uterine horn between eight and twelve days after conception. Implantation—when the ova

Silvertone's foundation sire Ch. Las Rocosa Ricky Taylor (Ch. Las Rocosa Shiloh ex Hartnagle's Fritzie Taylor). Courtesy Allee.

become attached to the uterine wall—occurs about eighteen days after ovulation. After implantation, placental tissue will form around the fetus. These fetal membranes nourish the puppies with nutrients from the dam's maternal blood and then circulate fetal waste back to the dam for removal through her own excretory system.

DISEASES OF THE REPRODUCTIVE TRACT

Genital Infections

Brucellosis

Brucellosis, a bacterial infection caused by *Brucella canis* and first discovered in 1966 by researchers at Cornell University, is a major cause of reproductive failure. The disease can be identified by positive cultural or serologic results.

The most prominent symptom of brucellosis in a female is abortion after the thirtieth day of gestation (usually between the forty-fifth and fifty-fifth days). To a lesser degree, "orchitis," infections of the accessory sex glands, and other systemic malfunctions, occur in both males and females. Infertility is prevalent in both sexes. The organism is present in the blood, urine, milk, and semen of infected Aussies.

Whenever reproductive failure occurs, the dog or bitch should be evaluated for canine brucellosis. Infected Aussies appear perfectly healthy even though they are carriers and spreaders of the disease.

Even if the infection can be eliminated, fertility will be permanently impaired. Isolating or eliminating diseased individuals is imperative. Because treatment is uncertain and often unsuccessful, the emphasis must be on prevention. Test all Aussies prior to breeding.

To prevent the possibility of further contamination, it is imperative to disinfect all areas that an infected individual has inhabited.

Herpes Virus

Herpes virus is responsible for fetal resorption (a process in which embryos die in the womb, dehydrate, and are expelled through the vagina), runted and stillborn puppies, abortion, and neonatal deaths. Bitches acquire immunity through prior exposure to affected adults.

Vaginitis

Vaginitis is an inflammation of the vagina. The condition is often characterized by a discharge. Before reaching sexual maturity, "adolescent" bitches may develop a type of vaginitis. Males seem to be excited by the odor of the discharge. This will generally disappear with the first estrus.

Inflammations and infections of the vagina or vulva may result from an injury or trauma during the breeding or whelping (parturition). Contamination of the perineal area (the area in front of the anus extending to the external margin of the vulva) may result in an ascending infection. Foreign bodies and bacteria are the most common causes.

Spayed females and older bitches can be affected by vaginitis. Bladder infections sometimes can accompany the condition. Vaginitis that often affects older bitches is noted by a heavier discharge that causes them to clean the vulva constantly unless they are too ill to tend to themselves properly. The mucous membranes may be irritated and reddened.

It is best to seek the professional assistance of your veterinarian if you notice a discharge. A visual examination does not always determine the actual source of infection. Blood-tinged and/or pus-filled discharge may develop into a far more serious condition such as metritis or pyometra. Both require professional care.

Proper hygiene, such as bathing the perineal area with a mild, nonirritating germicide and clipping the hair away from the perineal area, will alleviate the chances of contamination.

Postpartum Disease (Acute Metritis)

Metritis is an inflammation of the uterus. It commonly results from a bacterial infection acquired during whelping (parturition), sometimes during estrus, or during breeding. Dead fetuses, retained placenta, and trauma to the mucous membranes of the uterus and vagina all provide a suitable environment for bacteria to gain entry into the uterus through the open cervix. Abortion greatly magnifies the chances for a bitch to acquire metritis.

Infections can occur by the careless use of artificial insemination instruments that contaminate and/or injure the uterine wall or vagina. They may also be introduced by the stud dog or through careless attempts to dilate a smaller vagina (which should never be attempted).

Bitches affected with acute metritis are depressed. There is a brownish or blood-stained, foul-smelling discharge. Fever, loss of appetite, vomiting, tenderness in the uterine region, and a swelling and congestion of the vulva occur. If the bitch has a litter, she may be negligent. The condition requires antibiotics with immediate veterinary attention. Treatment may also necessitate surgery. The mortality rate increases with advanced stages of the disease.

Pyometra (Hyperplastic Endometritis)

Pyometra is an accumulation of pus in the uterus. It is extremely serious and can prove fatal unless treated immediately. It appears more frequently in females older than five years of age. While metritis is more commonly associated with a bacterial infection, pyometra appears to be more of an endocrine (hormonal) problem. It is attributed to an ovarian dysfunction with an increased secretion of progesterone. When the cervix contracts under the influence of progesterone, pus fills the infected uterus with no outlet for drainage. A lack of appetite (anorexia) is usually followed by depression. The respiratory rate increases and the temperature falls, then elevates again. As the condition progresses, the temperature falls and becomes subnormal. There is generally a continuous, purulent discharge accompanied by a sickly sweet odor. The vulva may be enlarged, and occasionally, persistent diarrhea may accompany the disease. The abdomen is enlarged, and pain may be present upon touch. Other symptoms include progressive weakness and extreme thinness. The bitch may vomit following the intake of water. Due to an elevated temperature, the female will want to drink large amounts of water.

The problem becomes obvious three to six weeks following estrus, when the glandular secretions provide a foundation for the multiplication of organisms. The bitch will become extremely ill if she is not treated. Professional help must be sought immediately, or death will soon follow. Because this disease does not respond well to drugs, surgical removal of the uterus may be imperative unless it can be treated by cleaning under the influence of certain hormones in coordination with antibiotics. The latter is successful only in selected cases.

Playing peek-a-boo.
Photo by Hubert Green.

Chapter 27

MATERNITY WARD

PUPPIES ARE BORN APPROXIMATELY nine weeks, or sixty-three days, from the time of conception. A variation of a few days is not uncommon. Pregnancy can be diagnosed by feeling puppies through the abdominal wall. It is also possible to diagnose pregnancy as early as twenty-nine days with the use of an instrument that can detect heartbeats.

About the third week of pregnancy, it may be possible to feel the whelps in the uterus, which has naturally become enlarged. The whelp may feel like a lump the size of a ping-pong ball. You can gently palpate (feel) the external area along the abdomen down toward the rib cage. Careless probing, however, will only cause irritation and discomfort to your bitch. There is no way to determine how many fetuses the bitch is carrying, because some of the embryos will be located higher up in the uterine horn. Around the fifth week (thirty-fourth to thirty-sixth day), the embryos will be engulfed by fluids, and it may be more difficult to discern their presence.

No noticeable outward physical signs of pregnancy will occur in the bitch until the fifth week after conception. At that time, you may notice an enlargement of the abdomen and loin area, high up behind the ribs. The teats may be enlarged with a pinkish coloration.

Management

During the first five weeks of gestation, feed your bitch the same quality diet, and maintain the same routine to which she was accustomed prior to conception. You must employ common sense. She can continue the type of play and exercise to which she is accustomed as long as she feels up to it and is not forced to do strenuous activities. Lack of exercise and obesity can cause whelping problems. Controlled exercise should always be part of the daily routine.

It is wise to keep the bitch away from flying hooves and horns in the middle to later stages of her pregnancy to avoid possible injury to the abdominal area. During the later stages of pregnancy, she may not feel like getting a great deal of exercise. Encourage her, however, to take daily walks, which will help her keep fit. This is especially important for the house companion that may or may not be used to a great deal of exercise. During the hot summer months, walks during the cool mornings and evenings are more pleasant than ones during the heat of the day. It is unwise to let her play with overly rough companions, but a familiar playmate will encourage free exercise.

During the last four weeks of gestation, your bitch will require an increased food intake. Her body will demand more nutrients balanced by appropriate levels of energy. Water should be available at all times. Self-feeding programs are well suited, because they allow the bitch to take in nutrients as her body requires them. If you feed predetermined portions, then feed your bitch according to her body weight. You must constantly keep track of her daily weight change and feed her accordingly. Feed your bitch the same amount of ration per pound of body weight. From the time of conception to the time of whelping, she will be eating 15 to 20 percent more food. The predetermined portions should then be divided into two or three feedings throughout each day. This will avoid undue pressure from the intestinal tract on the enlarged uterus.

A diet designed specifically for lactation is ideal for the bitch during gestation. The diet should contain at least 25 percent protein on a dry-matter basis. If the protein content of the ration is below that, feed a "complete" all-meat supplemental commercial canned ration as 15 to 25 percent of the total. However, do not oversupplement with any one ingredient. Oversupplementing vitamins, minerals, or fats can lead to serious imbalances that are highly detrimental. All ingredients must be balanced or the diet becomes deficient and the mortality rate of your puppies increases. It is far more beneficial and less expensive over the long run to invest in a quality diet designed to meet the nutritional needs of your bitch. A cheap diet may require fifty dollars in supplements to be adequate.

Due to increasing pressure on her bladder from growing puppies, your bitch might accidentally urinate on the floor. Do not punish her, because this is unavoidable. Take her outside more frequently during this time.

Any signs of illness, abnormal odorous discharges (bloody, greenish, or blackish), elevated temperature, vomiting diarrhea, or listlessness should be immediately reported to your veterinarian. Infections indicate that complications may occur.

From a week to several days before whelping (parturition), the bitch may have a sagging appearance in her loin. She will have shortness of breath due to the whelps pressing upon her vital organs. The sunken-in look is acquired due to the puppies "dropping down." Her breasts will turn pink to reddish in color and become enlarged.

During the entire gestation period, the bitch's body undergoes elaborate preparations for the final event. The placenta has generated enough surplus hormones to prepare the breasts. The breasts contain a treelike structure of milk ducts, with the nipples representing the tree trunks. Under pressure of increased hormonal production, these structures become enlarged, shooting out thousands of new branches and twigs.

Everything is in a state of readiness to provide food for the new life. Actual milk production, however, will not start until the pituitary gland at the base of the bitch's brain gives the word.

WHELPING CHART

Date bred (January)	Date due to whelp (March)	Date bred (February)	Date due to whelp (April)	Date bred (March)	Date due to whelp (May)	Date bred (April)	Date due to whelp (June)	Date bred (May)	Date due to whelp (July)	Date bred (June)	Date due to whelp (August)	Date bred (July)	Date due to whelp (September)	Date bred (August)	Date due to whelp (October)	Date bred (September)	Date due to whelp (November)	Date bred (October)	Date due to whelp (December)	Date bred (November)	Date due to whelp (January)	Date bred (December)	Date due to whelp (February)
1	5	1	5	1	3	1	3	1	3	1	3	1	2	1	3	1	3	1	3	1	3	1	2
2	6	2	6	2	4	2	4	2	4	2	4	2	3	2	4	2	4	2	4	2	4	2	3
3	7	3	7	3	5	3	5	3	5	3	5	3	4	3	5	3	5	3	5	3	5	3	4
4	8	4	8	4	6	4	6	4	6	4	6	4	5	4	6	4	6	4	6	4	6	4	5
5	9	5	9	5	7	5	7	5	7	5	7	5	6	5	7	5	7	5	7	5	7	5	6
6	10	6	10	6	8	6	8	6	8	6	8	6	7	6	8	6	8	6	8	6	8	6	7
7	11	7	11	7	9	7	9	7	9	7	9	7	8	7	9	7	9	7	9	7	9	7	8
8	12	8	12	8	10	8	10	8	10	8	10	8	9	8	10	8	10	8	10	8	10	8	9
9	13	9	13	9	11	9	11	9	11	9	11	9	10	9	11	9	11	9	11	9	11	9	10
10	14	10	14	10	12	10	12	10	12	10	12	10	11	10	12	10	12	10	12	10	12	10	11
11	15	11	15	11	13	11	13	11	13	11	13	11	12	11	13	11	13	11	13	11	13	11	12
12	16	12	16	12	14	12	14	12	14	12	14	12	13	12	14	12	14	12	14	12	14	12	13
13	17	13	17	13	15	13	15	13	15	13	15	13	14	13	15	13	15	13	15	13	15	13	14
14	18	14	18	14	16	14	16	14	16	14	16	14	15	14	16	14	16	14	16	14	16	14	15
15	19	15	19	15	17	15	17	15	17	15	17	15	16	15	17	15	17	15	17	15	17	15	16
16	20	16	20	16	18	16	18	16	18	16	18	16	17	16	18	16	18	16	18	16	18	16	17
17	21	17	21	17	19	17	19	17	19	17	19	17	18	17	19	17	19	17	19	17	19	17	18
18	22	18	22	18	20	18	20	18	20	18	20	18	19	18	20	18	20	18	20	18	20	18	19
19	23	19	23	19	21	19	21	19	21	19	21	19	20	19	21	19	21	19	21	19	21	19	20
20	24	20	24	20	22	20	22	20	22	20	22	20	21	20	22	20	22	20	22	20	22	20	21
21	25	21	25	21	23	21	23	21	23	21	23	21	22	21	23	21	23	21	23	21	23	21	22
22	26	22	26	22	24	22	24	22	24	22	24	22	23	22	24	22	24	22	24	22	24	22	23
23	27	23	27	23	25	23	25	23	25	23	25	23	24	23	25	23	25	23	25	23	25	23	24
24	28	24	28	24	26	24	26	24	26	24	26	24	25	24	26	24	26	24	26	24	26	24	25
25	29	25	29	25	27	25	27	25	27	25	27	25	26	25	27	25	27	25	27	25	27	25	26
26	30	26	30	26	28	26	28	26	28	26	28	26	27	26	28	26	28	26	28	26	28	26	27
27	31	27	May 1	27	29	27	29	27	29	27	29	27	28	27	29	27	29	27	29	27	29	27	28
28	Apr. 1	28	2	28	30	28	30	28	30	28	30	28	29	28	30	28	30	28	30	28	30	28	Mar. 1
29	2			29	31	29	July 1	29	31	29	31	29	30	29	31	29	Dec. 1	29	31	29	31	29	2
30	3			30	June 1	30	2	30	Aug. 1	30	Sep. 1	30	Oct. 1	30	Nov. 1	30	2	30	Jan. 1	30	Feb. 1	30	3
31	4			31	2			31	2			31	2	31	2			31	2			31	4

Courtesy of Gaines.

WHELPING BOX

At least one week prior to whelping, move the bitch to her whelping box. This will accustom her to new surroundings. If the litter arrives a few days early, then you will be prepared.

The whelping box (or house) should be large enough to accommodate the bitch with her rapidly growing puppies and, if necessary, provide adequate shelter until the litter is weaned. If the whelping box has high sides, like a house with a roof or lid, the top should be removable or built with hinges to allow easy access. The box should be constructed of material that can be cleaned and disinfected easily to discourage viral, bacterial, and parasitic infections. Children's wading pools are popular with many breeders because they are easily disinfected.

The box should be well ventilated but never drafty, so that the bitch and puppies do not become overheated. The box can be built slightly off the ground (one to three inches) to prevent dampness and cold from seeping inside. Some designs include a railing that is placed three to four inches from the floor bottom and the same distance from each side. This margin may help prevent the bitch from pinning and crushing the newborns against the side walls. Whether indoors or outdoors, the box should have one side lower or an opening that enables the bitch to get away from the puppies when necessary.

The bedding can consist of large carpet pieces. Indoor-outdoor carpeting is excellent because it can be cleaned and disinfected easily. Never use loose, deep, or flimsy material that can suffocate or bury the puppies.

During the actual whelping, black-and-white newspaper is ideal, because it can be disposed of when soiled and dampened. After the puppies are born, other types of bedding can be used.

Courtesy Lisa Cameron.

Preparing for the Birth

Supplies that should be on hand when you are preparing for the whelping include several paper sacks or plastic garbage bags, towels, dental floss, sterilized scissors, germicide, iodine, calcium (or oxytocin), brandy, milk, eggs, honey, a heating pad, a hair dryer, and, in an emergency, a good hot water bottle. Keep an emergency number for your veterinarian on hand. Also have the bitch's milk replacer, a ten- to fifty-milliliter (preferably plastic) syringe, a #5 or #10 French feeding tube, adhesive tape, disinfectant, a pencil, and a pad of paper.

Signs of Oncoming Labor

Several days before the onset of labor, your bitch may begin nesting. She may try to locate a place other than the one that you have designated for her, which is why it is important to choose a secluded place away from traffic and activity. She will probably decrease her food intake, but the most reliable clue of approaching labor is the drop in body temperature. Several days prior to whelping, her temperature may drop several degrees from the normal temperature of 101.2°F to 102°F down to 100°F. She will probably be panting more heavily because of her discomfort. The bitch may lie first on one side and then on the other. She may even squat. She may appear to be more restless and may pant more frequently for several days, especially if this is her first litter. The older, more experienced brood bitches may have better developed mammary glands than the young bitches, but this varies with each individual.

Your bitch may begin "nesting" by vigorously shredding up her bedding and scratching and digging around her bedding and at the carpet to prepare a comfortable whelping spot. This may occur intermittently for twenty-four to thirty-six hours, or for as little as two hours. She may even try desperately to find a new location under the house, in the barn, or in some favorite secluded resting spot around the yard under the shrubs and bushes. Keep an eye on her, especially during the cold months, in case she begins to whelp. She could possibly drop one on the ground or escape to some secluded spot at the last minute to give birth. When she goes out for her daily exercise or to relieve herself, supervise and restrain her activities.

Her natural instincts are to seek solitude in which to protect herself and her puppies. Other animals (even her playmates) and people may be a threat. It is wise to keep all other animals away, even her constant companions. This is not the time to invite the children and neighbors in for a look. Your bitch may go into a state of hysterical excitement, delay the whelping, try to hide, or even become aggressive toward them, and rightfully so! If your bitch feels threatened, she may injure the puppies while whelping or try to hide them once they have been whelped.

Bathing Your Bitch

In preparation for the upcoming labor, you will need to cleanse your bitch's hindquarters, stomach, and teats with a mild antibacterial soap. If you bathe her entirely, do it a week prior to the due date (especially in case the bitch may be early in whelping) before her temperature drops. Use lukewarm water to avoid any drastic temperature shock that could upset her system. You can use a mild baby shampoo. Be sure to rinse her well and dry her completely to avoid chilling. If there is excessive feathering that could become entangled with the birthing of the litter, thin it out and clip it away from the area around the vulva. This will help the bitch keep herself cleaner during the following weeks. Comb or clip away excessive hair from the bitch's nipples. This makes sucking easier and cleaner for the puppies.

Parturition

Imminent Labor

During this stage, the bitch may appear more restless than during the previous few days. She will pant continually and will lick her hindquarters intermittently. Periodically, she may fall asleep in her whelping box awaiting the time of delivery.

Contractions will begin lightly during this period but will eventually increase in both frequency and severity. The first-time expectant mother may appear extremely curious about the activity taking place within her body. She may be a little more nervous than an experienced female, but if everything is progressing normally, her instincts will guide her through the entire process.

Take notice when prelabor begins. If the bitch does not begin whelping during the next twenty-four to thirty-six hours, something may be wrong that will require veterinary service. Extreme pain, trembling, shivering, vulvar bleeding, collapse, vomiting, foul and odorous discharges, and straining for more than two to three hours are all reasons to get her to your veterinarian. Consult the vet if the female does not whelp by the sixty-fifth day and immediately if any of the above symptoms occur.

Australian Shepherds for the most part are sound and healthy with minimal whelping complications. This is due to the fact that the majority of foundation bitches used in early breeding programs were healthy and sound breeders, and this was passed down through the generations.

What Begins Labor?

One theory is that the vastly enlarged uterus has been stretched beyond its limit, and that the uterine horn expresses itself by contracting in an effort to expel the irritant—the puppies. The most accepted theory is that just before the whelping process begins, there is a dramatically sharp decline in the amount of sex hormones circulating in the bloodstream. The placenta has become senile and is no longer able to produce the hormones that have made the uterus lie quiet for months. In any case, this rapid decline of hormones in the bloodstream is a signal that labor is about to begin. The uterus, which is made up almost entirely of muscular tissue, starts to contract.

Just prior to the onset of actual labor, the bitch's temperature will drop sharply to 97°F or 98°F. You may notice that the mucous membranes have become pale. There may be a thick mucous discharge from the vulva that should be free from color and foul odors. The bitch will clean her external genitals because the contractions will cause a vaginal discharge.

Internally, the whelping process has already begun. The cervix will begin to "relax." It dilates during the first stage of labor, and the puppies rotate so that they are in the correct position for their journey down the uterine horn. Canine fetuses lie in two tubes, the uterine horns, which are shaped like a short-stemmed "Y." Puppies are generally carried on both sides but may be all in one horn or the other. The puppies are packed in tightly at the time of birth. Each puppy born has a 50 percent chance of being presented for breech delivery (hind end first). If the head is born first, the birth is easier because the shape of the head is more suited for forcing its passage through the pelvis. A tail or foot does not bear enough pressure to open the passageway. There is no way to turn a puppy inside the mother, because the area is too cramped after the uterus has contracted around the fetus during labor.

Each puppy is propelled by contractions of the uterus and by the fluid pressure in its own bag. The fluid is the dilating and distending medium when the uterus relaxes in front of it and contracts behind it. The bitch may have contractions that will make her hind legs stiffen and push. Take note of when the bitch exhibits the first straining pain. This may be violent enough to cause her to grunt or to cry out. Most people think that dogs deliver their young in short order, without pain or trouble. This is far from the truth. The bitch does not always exhibit or vocalize pain.

The Whelping

The actual whelping usually begins with this pain. The bitch may rest a few moments. Involuntary

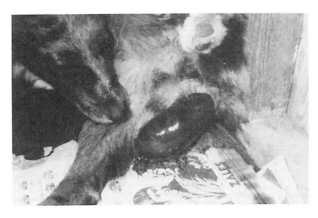

A black water-filled sac containing the puppy will appear at the vulva. The wet spots on the papers in the whelping box are from fluids called "water" that lubricate the birth canal. Photo by Jerry Rowe. Courtesy Sharon Rowe & Sue Dennis, authors of "Pups 'N Stuff"

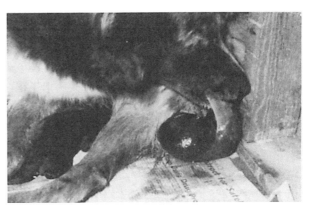

The bitch will tear the sac (a thick grayish, membranous bag) away from the puppy so that he may breathe. She will lick it away from the face, nostrils, and mouth. Photo by Jerry Rowe. Courtesy Sharon Rowe & Sue Dennis

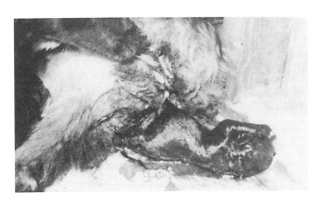

Rather than waiting for her contractions to expel the placenta, the bitch is pulling it out on her own. Photo by Jerry Rowe. Courtesy Sharon Rowe & Sue Dennis.

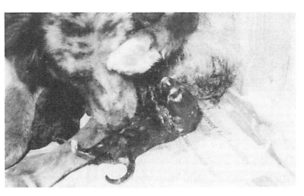

The mother will detach the puppies from the placenta by "cutting the cord." Photo by Jerr Rowe. Courtesy Sharon Rowe & Sue Dennis.

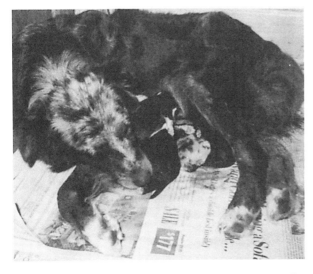

After the bitch has whelped the litter, she requires sufficient time to rest while the puppies nurse quietly. Photo by Jerry Rowe. Courtesy Sharon Rowe & Sue Dennis.

Some mothers will pick up their puppies to move them from one place to another. Photo by Charles Anderson. Courtesy Sharon Rowe & Sue Dennis.

contractions of the uterus combined with voluntary abdominal muscles push upon the whelp. The final labor period lasts from the time the bitch has regular contractions until the birth of the first puppy and should not last any longer than an hour. The bitch may walk around and drink water between labor pains. If she needs to go outside, she may squat and strain a little after relieving herself. Just bring her calmly back to her whelping box.

A gush of water should follow the first straining pain or major contraction. As the sac containing the placenta becomes dislodged, it releases the surrounding fluids, which flush out the birth canal and serve as a lubricant. You may notice wet spots or wet papers in the whelping box. A black, water-filled sac will appear at the vulva. This is the bag of amniotic fluid that precedes the birth of each puppy.

Sometimes the sac breaks during the course of delivery, in which case you may only see a rush of greenish-black fluid. Normally the bitch will tear the sac by licking or biting at it. In the case of a maiden bitch, the sac may appear and retract once or twice at the entrance to the vulva. The puppy should soon be expelled. If it is not after several times, you may need to assist. The bitch may be crouching or lying and sometimes even standing for the final expulsion. Some bitches like to brace themselves against the side of the whelping box to get better leverage.

Each puppy is completely enclosed in a sac, which is a thick, grayish, membranous bag filled with liquid. The puppy gets his oxygen (and nutrition) before birth from the bitch. The placenta (afterbirth) is attached to the mother's uterus. The whelp in the sac is connected to the placenta by the umbilical cord. At the time of birth, the uterus begins to contract, pushing the puppy downward for his entrance into the world. At that time, the placenta detaches from the uterine wall, leaving the puppy "on his own."

There is still enough oxygen left in the blood of the placenta to supply the puppy during the birth process, but if the birth is delayed too long, the puppy will suffocate. The bitch should turn to tear the sac away by licking it away from the puppy's face. She will bite the umbilical cord, crushing it with her teeth to keep it from bleeding.

Be a nonobvious observer. Do not interfere if the bitch appears to be in control. Your interference may cause her to be nervous, in which case

Ch. Pear Tree's Blast of Sass (Ch. Beauwoods A Shot of Pear Tree ex Ch. Blue Isle Sassy Lookin') basking in the sun with her son. Photo courtesy Marti Parrish.

she may react in an irrational manner. She may even resort to cannibalism if she feels threatened and may try to eat the "endangered" puppies. It is best to resist your impulse to help unless there is an immediate danger to the bitch or to the puppies. A normal, healthy Aussie female is capable of whelping her puppies easily with no assistance unless a complication arises. Your job as the observer is to be there in the event a problem does occur.

The bitch washes and tumbles each puppy about very vigorously as soon as each is born, for several reasons. The hard washing makes the puppy complain loudly, which gets air into his lungs. It also stimulates circulation and dries the wet coat. If necessary, you can accomplish the same thing by rubbing the puppy briskly, with his head held down (to allow any fluids to drain), using a terrycloth towel.

Maiden Bitches (First-Time Mothers)

Once the first puppy is born, wait for a minute to see if the bitch will remove the sack from the puppy's face. If she does not do this quickly, do it yourself by tearing the membrane away from the face, nostrils, and mouth, then wipe the puppy's face with a cloth. Use a baby's nose aspirator to clear the mouth. If the puppy remains in the bag, he could get amniotic fluid into his lungs, causing pneumonia or suffocation. Give the puppy back to his mother. Some maiden bitches are frightened of their newborn pups, and the maternal instincts may not be very evident until the delivery of a few puppies.

Removing Fluid From the Lungs

A puppy may need to have fluid removed from his lungs. Hold the puppy in your hand with his back and the back of his head and neck against the palm of one hand. Place his face down lower than the rest of his body between the first two fingers of your other hand. Hold the puppy's head, neck, and body firmly. Place your thumb and fingers around the tiny body. Then, in a sharp motion, swing your hands downward. Never swing the puppy by his legs. The puppy should gasp, taking in air, and gravity should help pull the fluid and mucus out of his lungs. Wipe it off as it appears. Repeat the shaking process until the puppy's breathing is free of fluid. Hold the puppy close to your ear and listen for rasping or rattling noises, which mean that fluid is present. Check the tongue to see if the puppy is getting enough oxygen (a blue tongue indicates that the puppy is not receiving enough oxygen).

The shaking and brisk rubbing with a towel can be alternated and repeated to get a weak puppy breathing normally. Get the puppy dry, and keep him warm.

Severing the Cord

The bitch severs the cord by crushing it so that it does not continue to bleed. She will crush the cord either before or after expelling the placenta. The cord seals adequately when the bitch cuts it with her teeth, and there is little need to worry about bleeding. She will then clean the puppy, while the puppy makes his way to nurse. Healthy, strong puppies will begin sucking vigorously.

If the bitch does not cut the cord, you must do so. Grasp the cord several inches away from the puppy's body between your thumb and forefinger. Gently milk the remaining nutriment into the puppy once or twice. Make sure that you do not place any pressure on the cord. With the cord pinched between your fingers, tie a piece of dental floss about two inches from the puppy's body (loop it around twice and knot). Clip the cord with a pair of sterile scissors (the duller the better), and swab it with iodine. Never pull the cord from the puppy. The pressure placed on the navel could cause a hernia. When the cord dries up, the excess will drop off. For the moment, however, it is best only to clip away any thread ends that the bitch may be able to rip away, because this could also cause a hernia.

Eating the Placenta

A bitch's purpose in eating the placenta is to provide her with nourishment and liquid complete with the protein, vitamins, and hormonal substances that her body needs. In the wild state, a bitch would be unable to hunt for food, and the placental nourishment would sustain her during the first few days after whelping. Keep track of the number of placentas expelled. If there wasn't one for each puppy, you will need to contact your veterinarian. A retained placenta can cause serious complications, such as uterine infections, pyometra, or metritis. Sometimes the placenta will not be expelled directly after each birth, but it should be expelled with the birth of the following puppy.

Breech Births

When a puppy is whelped breech, the hind legs appear first, or the buttocks may come first with the hind legs folded back. The puppy could even be presented upside down. When this occurs, the hind legs will appear first, or the buttocks may come first with the hind legs folded back. Very often during a breech presentation, the puppy will arrive safely and easily. But occasionally a problem may arise. If the puppy remains stuck, or if he appears and then disappears several times, you may need to step in and help.

Grasp the puppy gently with a sterile terrycloth. Use a gentle, steady, firm pull timed with the bitch's own effort to expel the whelp. If you jerk or roughly grasp the head, tail (never grasp the tail), or legs, you may cause permanent damage. A lubricant such as petroleum jelly may help. Never pull straight out or upward. Always pull firmly and slightly down toward the bitch's stomach as she is naturally trying to push the puppy out. You may need to pull gently to one side and then to the other. If the puppy is upside down, you may try to gently rotate the body so that his own backbone is parallel to that of the bitch. If during a breech presentation only one leg is out, you will need to use a sterile, gloved finger to locate the other leg and guide it out. If after several attempts you have no success, call your veterinarian. Too long of a delay may put the bitch and other puppies in immediate danger.

Unlike normal puppies that cry out when the mother begins washing them, puppies that have been placed under stress during the whelping procedure may be limp and quiet. These puppies require immediate assistance, because it is possible that the oxygen supply has been cut off. These puppies may lack the strong reddish-pink tones of good circulation and may appear blue. Even the lifeless-appearing puppy may be able to be saved if you begin supportive measures at once. If the puppy is bloodstained or stained with a green fluid, you can be sure that he is in a critical state.

Make sure that all of the membrane is removed from the puppy's mouth and nostrils. If the puppy fails to breathe immediately, give artificial respiration. First suck any contents from the nose. Place your lips over the puppy's nose and mouth and blow. Use tiny, short breaths so that you don't rupture his lungs.

Use a towel to briskly rub the body as the mother would when she cleans the puppies. You may even have to use your index finger and lightly tap the puppy's back, which should make the puppy gasp for breath. Once the puppy begins breathing normally and his color is normal, you can attend to the umbilical cord. Make sure to keep the puppy warm.

Now place the puppy on one of his mother's teats so that he may intake some colostrum. It is imperative for the puppy to receive milk within the first twenty-four hours of life. Colostrum contains antibiotic properties that give the puppies temporary immunity against infectious diseases. Colostrum helps get the puppy off to a healthy start in life.

You may have to gently open the puppy's mouth and place him on one of his mother's teats. The puppy should start sucking. If not,

Left: A normal birth; the puppy is head first. Note the way the birth canal curves over the pelvic bone. If you need to assist, always pull down, toward the bitch's stomach.
Far Right: A breech birth. The puppy's rear is first. Breech births are sometimes more difficult. If possible, keep the bitch from breaking the sac until the puppy's head is out.

Normal versus breech birth.

gently roll the bitch's nipple between the ball of your thumb and forefinger to express milk. Now apply enough gently pressure on the puppy's lower jaw to open his mouth and encourage him to "latch on."

Hard Labor

When the bitch has been in hard labor for two hours with no puppies arriving, or the labor has completely ceased and you think that there may be more puppies inside, either call your vet or take the bitch there yourself. She probably needs professional help. If you are in doubt, consult your vet about the situation immediately.

The uterus of some females does not have the required "tone," or push power, to expel the puppies. This may be the result of improper exercise, of a lengthy labor, or of the birth of a large litter. The bitch generally becomes weary, a condition called uterine inertia. She is incapable of having contractions sufficient to move the puppies downward and out.

You may offer the female a bowl of vanilla ice cream, or milk and honey (or sugar) with an egg yolk or two. The calcium may be beneficial, combined with a short rest, to help revive her strength. Take the bitch out on lead during intervals of whelping to relieve herself. Make sure that you carry a towel in case she whelps while on "break." The short walks will introduce fresh air into her lungs and help improve her circulation.

Your veterinarian may recommend a hormonal injection (oxytocin). Due to the nature of oxytocin, a dose can be given intramuscularly to stimulate contractions of the smooth muscle of the uterus. This type of injection may be repeated at intervals. Directions must be followed explicitly, and oxytocin must never be given until the cervix and birth canal are completely dilated. Oxytocin is usually given after whelping, or at least after the whelping of one pup. It is also used to "clean out" any remaining uterine contents or retained placentas. Consult your veterinarian. He may prescribe a limited amount of oxytocin to keep on hand if he feels that you have the ability to use it exactly as recommended.

WHELPING PROBLEMS

Sometimes the head or the puppy himself may be too large to pass through the pelvis. If professional assistance is not rendered in time, the puppy will die along with the others of the litter. A dead puppy is a source of possible infection to the bitch. If untreated, she may die or be unable to have any more litters. Never wait for your bitch to collapse. More than two hours after delivering a puppy or three hours after the onset of labor is a signal to respond.

If the bitch is in labor a long time trying to deliver a dead puppy, and surgery is required, she may be too weak from the pain and effort to survive the anesthetic. Furthermore, if the bitch has become poisoned from the presence of one or more dead puppies in the uterus, she is an extremely poor risk for surgery.

There are two possible solutions to problem whelping—forceps or cesarean section. Your vet's primary concern is for the life and well-being of the bitch, which should be your concern, too.

Forceps

If the puppy is dead, the veterinarian may remove the puppy with forceps. He will have to carefully extract him little by little. Puppies usually cannot survive a forceps delivery. This method is seldom used if more than two puppies are present in the uterus.

Cesarean Section

A cesarean section can be performed and is always indicated if any of the puppies have a chance of being alive (that is, if you have taken adequate care and have not waited too long) and if the bitch is in good condition.

This type of surgery is necessary if the pelvic bone and muscular structure are too rigid to permit sufficient separation to allow the passage of a puppy. Some females have a male-type pelvic construction. This can also happen if a female is too old before having her first litter. Whelping complications can also occur from injuries such as fractured pelvic bones. An experienced vet can help diagnose this continuing complication when the first cesarean is performed. It is not advisable to breed a female if she is unable to whelp a litter naturally.

The female that has had an anesthetic for delivery is not herself until at least a half day to an entire day after delivery. Provisions must be made for the feeding and care of the puppies. If you place the puppies with her before she has completely recovered from the anesthetic, they might hurt her and she might bite them, not fully realizing what is going on.

A side, or flank, incision for a cesarean is more satisfactory. The bitch can lie comfortably on one side and not have a sore spot near any one nipple. Offer the bitch a drink of warm milk, beef or chicken broth, or plain water. Allow her a few hours of rest, then give the puppies an opportunity to nurse.

CARE OF THE NEW MOTHER

Only after the mother has had sufficient time to clean the puppies and to regain her strength will you want to go over the puppies. Note identifying markings, and weigh each puppy. Examine each puppy for defects or unsoundness.

Make sure that the bitch gets a chance to exercise. Initially, she will be reluctant to leave her puppies. Make sure that no other animals or people will make her feel threatened for her litter. Allow the bitch to take short breaks to relieve herself. After the first three days, she should not be as reluctant to leave her puppies. The bitch will not be very hungry, but you should have food and water available at all times.

You will probably notice a discharge for several weeks after the whelping. A darker red discharge clearing to a pinkish color is a healthy sign, because it usually means that all afterbirths have been expelled. A bright red discharge can indicate hemorrhage that requires immediate professional attention. A greenish-colored or

Kiddie wading pools make excellent whelping boxes. Courtesy Lisa Cameron.

purulent discharge often occurring within forty-eight to seventy-two hours after whelping generally indicates an infection, which will require immediate attention from your veterinarian.

The female's temperature will return to normal if all is well. If her temperature rises above 102.5°F, it is a signal for concern. Any unusual or odorous discharges or obvious bleeding should be reason enough to consult your veterinarian.

You will want to call your veterinarian as a courtesy to let him know that all is well, at which time it is a good idea to schedule a visit for the following day. Within twelve hours, and no later than twenty-four hours, the bitch should receive a general checkup and oxytocin to ensure proper "clean-out."

MILK SUPPLY

The breasts should feel full to the touch when milk is sufficient. Sometimes a bitch's milk doesn't "come down" normally. If the puppies appear restless and if, after nursing, the puppies lack a full, well-rounded appearance, insufficient milk may be the cause. Gently press the nipple between the ball of your thumb and forefinger. A drop of milk should form readily. Warm washcloths placed on the breasts followed by very gentle massage are beneficial in getting the milk ducts to flow. Make sure that the bitch has plenty of water to drink. Water is necessary for adequate milk production. If the milk still doesn't flow, it will be necessary to get the bitch to the veterinarian. Occasionally, an injection of oxytocin during the first twenty-four hours following whelping helps to induce the milk flow. This also helps to rid the uterus of any possible retained debris. If this is not taken care of, the puppies will not receive the colostrum that they need.

If the bitch is ill or has had a lengthy whelping, you may need to assist her with her duties and care for the puppies temporarily until her milk comes down.

ECLAMPSIA

Eclampsia (puerperal tetany) is a disease of nursing bitches and is occasionally observed during the final stages of pregnancy. If not treated immediately, it can cause death. The condition is due to the bitch's inability to utilize the calcium and phosphorus in her system. It is also caused by strain placed on the bitch while nursing a large litter. The disease is marked by nervousness, convulsions, excitability, stiffness, and staggering.

The attacks appear suddenly and can resemble heat prostration. The affected bitch may be unable to stand. She may stagger around, her muscles may become rigid, and she may exhibit a stilted gait. Her temperature rises, her respiration is rapid, and her pulse is accelerated. You will

Pretty as a picture. Mistretta's Misty Shadow (Ch. Mistretta's Ballou Pirate ex Van-B's Misty Blue) with her litter sired by Ch. Hilltop Apollo L. R. (Ch. Sharp's Ragnar ex Robertson's Cindy). Courtesy Mistretta.

probably notice panting, excitement, and restlessness followed by convulsive spasms; the bitch will fall to her side and kick violently. The muscles are tense, the mucous membranes are congested, and there is an increased flow of saliva. The bitch will remain conscious during an attack. The duration and severity of an attack vary, but affected bitches should receive immediate treatment. This is an emergency situation, and veterinary care is imperative for the survival of the bitch.

Some breeders will supply a calcium and phosphorus supplement in a ratio balance of 1.2:1. Bone meal is natural and probably one of the safer calcium/phosphorus supplements available. If you are feeding a professional diet designed for the lactating bitch, then it probably won't be necessary to consult your veterinarian.

MASTITIS

Sometimes a litter, especially a large one, will place undue stress on the bitch while she is nursing. The strain traumatizes the mammary glands. The needle-sharp nails of the puppies can scratch and bruise the bitch's breasts, creating further trauma.

Mastitis is inflammation of the breasts. It is a condition that results principally from infection with microorganisms. A wide variety of bacteria, as well as some yeasts, are capable of producing mastitis.

The affected breast may be hot, hard, tense, and tender. The milk may be watery and straw-colored and on occasion blood-tinged and may be stringy. The milk secretion is greatly or completely suspended. There is a general systemic disturbance, such as depression, and a rise in temperature accompanied by a loss of appetite.

The breast must be protected from injury as much as possible. Once the bacteria enter the opening in the teat, they may establish themselves in the milk cistern.

If the condition progresses, mastitis may be noticed when the affected breast abscesses and "bursts," which may look as if the breast has ripped, forming a jagged and gaping wound.

Warm and cold compresses and antibiotic treatment are imperative. Call your veterinarian for diagnosis and treatment. This condition may be complicated with other problems, such as metritis.

Chronic mastitis is not easily recognized. Although inflammation occurs, only small areas of tissue are involved, and the milk will appear normal. However, the chemical properties of the milk change from the inflammation, and bacterial activity increases. Occasionally, chronic mastitis will develop into acute mastitis. When this occurs, the milk will have clots and a watery appearance.

If the puppies seem ill, or if they cry, it may be due to a colicky condition caused from "bad milk." Depending upon the severity of the condition, the puppies may have to be weaned entirely and hand fed. If not weaned and hand fed, the sucklings may die from the affected milk. Regardless of the form of mastitis, the bitch will undergo antibiotic treatment and will require veterinary care. If the bitch's condition is not toxic, the puppies may continue to nurse. The affected breast should be isolated and protected. Your veterinarian may be able to tape the affected teat with gauze. Keep the puppies' nails trimmed to minimize injury to the breasts.

THE BITCH'S TEMPERAMENT

It is natural for a nursing bitch to become protective of her puppies in the presence of strangers, family, friends, and neighbors. Recent reports indicate that 500 milligrams of vitamin C may help alleviate a disgruntled attitude, although it will not alter her protective instincts.

Proud parents. Left to right: Beauwood's Whispering Pine (Ch. Yankee Clipper of Wingmont ex Beauwood's Paprika), Sakonnet Times, and Sakonnet's American CD (Sorensen's Red Man ex Taylor's Blue Prissy). Photo by L. M. Gray.

*During the first twenty-one days, the puppy is dependent upon his mother and littermates for nourishment, warmth, and security. Human handling should be careful and restricted during this time.
Photo by Trish Thornwald.*

Chapter 28

THE NURSERY

CARING FOR THE NEWBORN

THE FIRST TWENTY-FOUR HOURS ARE CRUCIAL to the newborn puppy. Puppies must be able to nurse within this time to obtain the bitch's colostrum—the milk that is secreted by the bitch just after parturition. Colostrum is more concentrated than ordinary milk, and it contains higher levels of protein and vitamin A. Through the colostrum, the puppies are able to gain initial passive immunity against disease.

Regular bowel movements in puppies are very important. Two common problems are constipation and diarrhea. Impaction of meconium—the excrement accumulated prior to birth—may prove fatal. Meconium is passed naturally when the mother licks the newborn puppies for stimulation. The blackish substance is passed with the first bowel movement. The puppy depends upon the cleaning and licking to pass bladder and bowel wastes, which the bitch will clean up and consume.

VITAL SIGNS

The average suckling's temperature during the first two weeks is 94°F to 97°F and rises to 99°F. By the fifth week, the temperature should be nearing the adult body temperature, which is between 101°F and 102.5°F.

During the first twenty-four hours of life, healthy newborn sucklings have a cardiac rate that accelerates from 120 to 150 heartbeats per minute up to 220 beats per minute through the first five weeks. The respiratory rate is eight to eighteen breaths per minute during the first twenty-four hours and fifteen to thirty-five breaths per minute during the following five weeks. The adult Australian Shepherd has an average respiration rate of seventeen to twenty-two breaths per minute, but this can vary from ten to thirty breaths per minute. The adult's heartrate is seventy to one hundred and forty beats per minute.

The first few weeks of life are devoted to eating and sleeping. During this period of "activated sleep," the puppies develop muscles through twitching and involuntary body movements. Newborn puppies make a sort of contented humming sound when everything is all right. Crying, moaning, wailing, or restlessness (crawling) are danger signals. Chilling, overheating, hunger, and disease can all cause discomfort and even death to sucklings. Handling should be kept to a minimum during this time.

Newborn sucklings do not have a shivering reflex (thermoregulatory mechanism) until after the sixth day of life, nor do they have the ability to maintain their own body temperature. They depend on their mother's warmth, or they get warmth from an external source such as heating lamps. During cool weather, puppies are susceptible to getting chilled, which can lead to hypothermia or to bacterial and viral infections that cause Fading Puppy Syndrome.

When the puppies near the eighteenth day, they will begin to walk, further stimulating their ability to maintain their own body heat.

The puppies should be identified by recording specific and unique markings or by painting the toenails with different brilliant colors of poodle nail polish. They should be weighed daily for the first week of life and then every two to three days until they are four weeks old. A consistent weight gain and normal stools will give you the most accurate reflection of the puppies' state of health. The newborns should gain weight from the first day of life and should gain steadily until they reach adulthood.

The sucklings should gain one to two grams per day, per pound of approximated adult weight. For example, a puppy expected to weigh forty pounds at maturity should gain forty to eighty grams, which also can be computed to one and one-half to two and one-half ounces (1 ounce = 28 grams) per day during the first six months. Most Aussies continue to grow at a steady rate until they are approximately six to nine months of age, at which time they will begin to slow down. If there is not a constant growth pattern (which can be confirmed by weighing every week), then you will need to adjust and/or supplement the puppies accordingly.

EXAMINATION OF THE LITTER

The Australian Shepherd is primarily a sound breed. Only a few defects that can occur will be of immediate interest to the breeder. Abnormalities such as cleft palate, spina bifida, and umbilical hernia may be due to an unknown genetic factor or can be congenital, caused by a foreign substance that crossed the placental barrier. These substances may include medications, vaccines, bacteria, or viruses that interfere with the proper development of the embryo.

Excessive White Coat Color

Due to the inherited disorders associated with the defective white factor (homozygous dominant state of the merle gene), such as complete or partial deafness and/or blindness, it is recommended that puppies born with excessive white coat color be culled at birth. (See the Australian Shepherd Breed Standard for acceptable color patterns.)

Cleft Palate

A cleft palate is evidenced by the presence of milk bubbling from the nostrils. A cleft palate occurs when there is a gap or opening in the roof of the mouth that leads directly to the sinus. This defect interferes with a puppy's ability to nurse.

Spina Bifida

Spina bifida occurs when the tissue across the lumbar and sacral areas does not properly knit together prior to birth, leaving the open spinal column vulnerable to infection. Spina bifida causes poor bladder and bowel control.

Hernia

An umbilical hernia occurs when the walls of the stomach do not fuse together properly in the embryo. An umbilical hernia can be caused by trauma placed on the navel during the severing of the umbilical cord, leading to a protrusion at the umbilicus. It can be corrected through minor surgery.

CULLING

Culling is not a pleasant subject, but it is one of the grave responsibilities of breeding Australian Shepherds. Culling takes place when some factor becomes apparent that could affect the mental and physical welfare of the prospective owner, the Australian Shepherd breed, and the individual Aussie. Euthanasia (humane death) can be arranged when you take your bitch in for her postwhelping examination.

TAIL DOCKING AND DEWCLAWS

Tail docking is traditional with the Australian Shepherd. Herding or driving dogs were exempt

The natural bobtail.

from taxes, and the tails were docked to prove their status and occupation.

Tails and dewclaws can be painlessly removed during the first seven days before the nervous system develops. Because the dewclaws are not attached at this time, they can be snipped off easily without complication. Docking and dewclaw removal should be done between the third and fourth day. Some breeders will dock within the first twenty-four or forty-eight hours after birth. An extra twenty-four hours, however, gives the puppy an opportunity to stabilize his system through the first three days of nursing.

There are many methods of removing tails, and it is wise to have an experienced breeder or your veterinarian show you the correct way. For minor surgical procedures such as tail docking and dewclaw removal, you'll need a scalpel with sterile blades, surgical scissors, Betadine Scrub, gauze, a tourniquet (dental floss), and a tissue bond such as Super Glue.

Although scissors work effectively in the removal of dewclaws, a scalpel is recommended over tail-docking scissors and similar devices for tail removal. The blade cleanly severs the joints without twisting or placing strain on the spinal column. Scissors can crush and pinch the discs, causing permanent spinal damage. *In any case, the docked tail should cover the anus.* It has also been expressed by some breeders that cutting too close may damage certain nerve endings and affect the mobility of the hindquarter. The specific purpose of the tail is to show expression, but most important, it is to whisk away debris and to provide a balancing factor. In specific cases, it is more difficult for an individual to maintain cleanliness without at least one or more joints.

Each joint can be estimated as approximately an inch in length at adulthood. The Breed Standard allows up to four inches in length to accommodate the natural bobtail, *an identifying characteristic of the Australian Shepherd.* However, it is more widely accepted for show dogs to be docked between the first and second joint.

Back dewclaws are not always present in the Australian Shepherd, but the front ones are. Occasionally, there may be one hind dewclaw. These should always be removed, and this can be done easily when the tail is docked. Even after removal, regrowth may occur. The front dewclaws may or may not be removed, according to your personal preference. Removal lends a clean appearance to the foreleg and eliminates the possibility of the dewclaw getting hung up and ripped on dense thicket. Because the front dewclaws are more tightly attached to the bones of the leg, removal is a bit more crucial. Your veterinarian or an experienced breeder can show you how, but *never* use any type of hot iron to sear or cauterize. The intense degree of heat has been known to stunt the bone, causing improper development of the toes.

TOENAILS

Within a few days after birth, your puppies will need to have the tiny hooks trimmed from their razor-sharp toenails. Scissors designed to trim cat claws work best. This practice keeps the puppies from tearing up their dam's breasts, which can make her reluctant to feed her litter. It also begins to establish early minimal socialization and handling.

RAISING ORPHAN AND FOSTER PUPPIES

If you have orphan puppies, try to find another mother that will take them. Survival is greatly increased with a canine foster mother. Many females will accept an orphan if you rub the scent of her own puppies on the newcomer. Always offer the puppy bottom first—rarely will a bitch with strong mothering instincts ignore a bottom to clean. If no substitute bitch is available, if the bitch will not accept the puppy, or if she does not have an adequate supply of milk for her own litter, then you must take over the job. If another animal around the house wants to be a "foster" parent, do not discourage it. The attention and warmth will be beneficial.

The main need of newborn puppies is to be dried thoroughly and to be kept at a constant temperature. A temperature-maintenance pad, or a whelping nest with a thermostatic control that can be adjusted between 85°F and 95°F, is necessary to maintain a constant temperature as the needs of the litter change.

During the first seven days, puppies should be maintained at 95°F. The temperature can then be decreased to 85°F. In the case of an emergency, put the puppies inside clean socks or sweater sleeves. Keep the heads and noses out. A heating pad covered with a waterproof material and set on a very low temperature can also be used. Place one-half of the pad on the floor of the box, and the other half up to the side wall. This way, the puppies can get close to the warmth if they are cold, or they can get away if they are too warm. If a hot water bottle is used, continually check for constant temperature to prevent the bottle from cooling. A drop in temperature can initiate hypothermia by chilling the puppies. Hot-water bottles should probably be covered with a blanket or towel to prevent them from burning the neonatal puppies. Keep orphan puppies in a sturdy box large enough to accommodate the puppies but small enough for them to maintain their own body heat. Use material in which the puppies' nails cannot get caught. Newspaper is unsuitable for maintaining the puppies' temperature.

Keep the box in a draft-free area in your house. Do not leave the puppies in the sun or on the damp ground. Keeping them in the house will allow you easy access and observation. If something is wrong, you will be alarmed by their crying or by the feel of their body temperature.

Orphan puppies can either be bottle fed or tube fed. The latter is the most efficient method if there are more than a couple of orphans, but due to the possibility of accidentally placing the feeding tube into the lungs, tube feeding is only recommended under the supervision of a veterinarian. Bottle feeding is preferred and imperative in developing the natural sucking reflexes.

Many puppies have been lost from overanxious feeding. A tiny puppy is unable to pass urine or move his bowels without stimulus. This occurs naturally when the bitch licks and cleans her puppies during the first two weeks. This stimulus must now be done with a damp, warm cloth or a piece of damp, warm gauze or cotton. Gently massage the stomach and the urinary and anal orifices with the damp material after each feeding. Keep stroking until elimination discontinues.

Bottle Feeding

Bottle feeding is beneficial to orphans in that it allows the puppies to redevelop their natural sucking reflexes. When the puppies are newly whelped, instincts direct the neonatals to their mother's teats, which they grasp with their tongue and mouth. The strong suction induces the milk to flow. The puppies use their paws to "knead" their mother's breasts, further stimulating milk production. It is also important to give the puppies a natural nursing position—lying on the stomach with the head raised slightly. Never feed puppies on their backs, as they will choke easily.

The proper formula is designed specifically to simulate the characteristics of the bitch's milk.

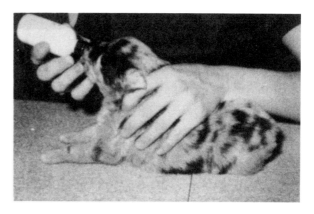

The correct feeding position. Photo by Jerry Rowe. Courtesy Sharon Rowe, "Pups 'N Stuff."

EMERGENCY MILK REPLACER

Dennis F. Lawyer, DVM (Purina Labs) recommends a laboratory-tested emergency home-formulated milk replacer: One cup of milk (eight ounces), three egg yolks (no albumin), one tablespoon corn oil, one drop high-quality oral multiple vitamin (preferably baby vitamins), and a tiny pinch of salt. This should be blended uniformly and warmed to 95°F to 100°F. When tested on the human wrist, the temperature should be very near your own (it should feel warm, not hot).

These fall under several brand names, such as Esbilac and Vetalac.

Use a baby bottle (i.e., Playtex Nurser) with a firm nipple. If the milk will not readily form droplets on your wrist, you will have to use the tip of a heated needle to prick the tip. Test it again. The milk shouldn't flow out, but seep. Too much milk flow could choke the puppy. Squeeze a small amount of milk into the tip of the nipple and place it in the puppy's mouth.

Feed the puppy five to six evenly spaced intervals throughout the day and night during the first week, four to five intervals throughout the second and third weeks, and three to four intervals during the fourth and fifth weeks. A regular schedule should be kept to avoid the possibility of colic. Pepto Bismol may help relieve digestive disturbances. Some breeders will occasionally use a drop or two of whiskey mixed with warm water. If this does not seem to do the trick, then you will want to feed at more frequent intervals and possibly adjust the amount of formula. The puppies will indicate their needs by the amounts of food that they accept and by their level of contentment after consuming it. Hand-fed puppies must be burped in the same manner as a human baby after feeding.

Mix only enough formula for immediate feedings. The bottles and nipples should be thoroughly disinfected between feedings to prevent contamination.

By twenty-one days, a gruel can be made by mixing a weaning formula and small amounts of quality canned food. Milk replacer can also be mixed with one part of either boiled ground meat (hamburger, chicken) or cottage cheese with four parts boiled rice. A shallow baking dish such as a pie tin allows the puppies easy access to the food.

Keep a supply of fresh water available in a shallow dish as well. Continue to supplement the formula until the puppies are at least four or five weeks old.

Tube Feeding

Tube feeding employs a method of "injecting" the formula into the puppy's stomach. This is a valuable aid in supplying nutrients to neonatal puppies, and it can be done with ease, because the puppies do not develop the gag reflex until about the twelfth day. Tube feeding can help to get puppies off to a good start, but once the puppies seem to "pick up," you should switch to bottle feeding.

Tube feeding involves considerably less time as compared to bottle feeding. If the chore of caring for orphan puppies becomes too great with a larger litter, perhaps a friend will share the burden.

For tube feeding, you will need a ten- to fifty-milliliter plastic syringe. The tubing should consist of some sort of semi-rigid rubber that can be passed down into the puppies' stomachs. A #10 French feeding tube is ideal for the newborn puppy.

To determine the correct length for the tube, hold the puppy so that his head will be extended forward (not up). Place a tube along the side of each puppy. The tip of the tube should *not* extend past the last rib, from the tip of the nose. Mark the tube. This will allow the tube to extend into each puppy's stomach. It must not go beyond the mark, because it could cause pressure or perforate the stomach. Constantly recheck this length, and remark it as each puppy grows. Boil the syringe and tube before using them, and after each use disinfect them to prevent contamination.

Heat the formula to 95°F or 100°F, near your own body temperature. Double-check the puppy's position and, if necessary, readjust it. Your veterinarian can demonstrate the correct methods of tube feeding.

Fill the syringe with the already warmed bitch's milk replacer, then attach the premeasured feeding tube. Expel the air from within the syringe by injecting the plunger just until the formula begins to drip from the tip of the tube. Place each puppy (one at a time) horizontally in the natural nursing position. While he is lying on his stomach on either a flat surface or in the palm of one of your hands, gently extend the puppy's head forward, neither up nor down. Lubricate the tube with several drops of formula. Open the mouth partially, and carefully slip the tube over the tongue. The puppy should begin to swallow the tube. As this happens, gently insert the tube no farther than the predetermined mark (identified with adhesive tape). If there is any resistance, withdraw the catheter. Any difficulty may indicate a danger signal.

Once you are confident that the tube is in the stomach and not the lungs, inject the fluid slowly. The administration should gradually take

When the puppies begin walking, it is time to gradually introduce solid food. Courtesy Marti Parrish.

place over a period of two to two and one-half minutes. When the puppy has been fed the correct amount, the stomach should appear round and full, but not hard and distended.

After you have fed the puppies, you will need to clean them to stimulate excretion. This must be done during the first few weeks of life. You will be able to recognize when the puppies are capable of eliminating on their own without the need of external stimulus. However, you will still need to keep the puppies cleaned meticulously as the mother would.

Generally, you can administer two ounces of bitch's milk replacer per pound of body weight in a twenty-four-hour period during the first weeks. This will yield sixty to seventy calories per pound of body weight every twenty-four hours. The second week, the puppy will require approximately two and one-half ounces of bitch's milk replacer per pound of body weight every twenty-four hours. Three ounces of the formula given during the third week should provide an estimated eighty to ninety calories per pound of body weight every twenty-four hours. During the third week, you will begin to introduce the litter to a gruel. The puppy's system may now require 100 to 110 calories per pound of body weight each day.

CARE OF THE EYES

Puppies' eyes begin to open between the seventh and the fourteenth days. The lids first open at the inner corner and gradually extend toward the outside. The tissue around the eyes may become swollen when the eyes begin to open. Soak a gauze or cotton pad in a solution of one teaspoon salt in eight ounces of lukewarm water, and gently swab the eyes clean. Pus may secrete from the slightest pressure. Keep the eyes cleaned with each scheduled feeding.

Consult your veterinarian, because any infection can spread and cause complications. Neglect or improper handling may result in loss or impairment of the eyes for life. Also, the infection may respond best to the application of certain ophthalmic ointments that your veterinarian may want to prescribe.

If eyes become puffy or swollen before they are open, you will need the assistance of your veterinarian. Do not attempt to pry open the tissue. The eyes are very sensitive, and you could cause permanent damage.

Bowel Movements and Urine

The puppy should have three to six bowel movements during a twenty-four-hour period. The stool should be of a firm consistency and yellowish in color. If diarrhea occurs, administer a few drops of Kaopectate, or Pepto Bismol. If the excretia appears curdled or watery, the pup is being overfed. The urine should be light colored—a pale yellow. Deep yellow urine signals dehydration, requiring more frequent feedings.

Give plenty of TLC.

Puppy Ailments

Healthy neonatal sucklings feel warm to the touch. They nurse vigorously, and when stimulated by their mother, they should demonstrate vitality. Many factors can affect the newborn puppy, and the puppy in return has a very limited ability to react to the environment and to disease.

Dehydration

Besides lacking the shivering reflex for the first six days, newborns have a minute amount of subcutaneous fat (fat lying directly beneath the skin). Until the puppy's main energy supply is replenished through several days of nursing, his energy source—glycogen blood sugar that is stored in the liver before birth—becomes depleted rapidly. Dehydration is apparent when the skin looks loose and nonelastic. It will remain "pinched" rather than immediately springing back to its original state. This is an extremely serious condition. Generally, puppies require sixty-five to ninety milliliters of water per pound of body weight every day. If the puppy appears to be only mildly dehydrated but is nursing vigorously, then keep an eye on him. However, it is best to consult your veterinarian, because what may look like a milk case of dehydration could be accompanied by complications.

If the puppies are being kept in a warm environment, the chances for your puppies' survival are very good.

Chilling and Hypothermia

Chilling results in hypothermia, which becomes complicated by hypoglycemia. The vicious cycle may begin when the mother refuses to nurse the puppy and pushes him away from the others, or when a puppy is accidentally removed from the whelping box.

A hypothermic puppy will feel cool to the touch. Care must be taken not to raise the body temperature too quickly, inducing shock. Bring circulation to the puppy by gently rubbing him between your hands or with a towel. Place the puppy underneath your armpit or your shirt, jacket, or coat. A severely chilled puppy may be revived by immersing him up to his neck in a pan of lukewarm water, then thoroughly drying him to prevent chilling. Heating pads set at low temperatures are used *only* after the puppy has regained normal body temperature.

Do not feed any formulas until the puppy's body temperature normalizes. Administer glucose only for the first feeding, and this only when the puppy feels warm again. The digestive system is unable to sufficiently digest formula until the body temperature is normal. Gatorade or Pedialyte has been used under emergency circumstances as a fluid replacer until veterinary assistance can be sought. One teaspoon of honey or corn syrup (forms of glucose) in an ounce of warm water can also be substituted. You can administer it with an eye dropper every fifteen to thirty minutes. If necessary, minute amounts can be administered with a tube. Do not introduce milk-replacer formulas if the body temperature is below 94°F.

The Healthy Puppy	The Sick Puppy
gains weight	doesn't gain weight
sleek, smooth coat	rough, dull coat
cries infrequently	cries frequently
good muscle and skin tone	limp, wrinkled skin
round, plump, firm body	flat, tucked up appearance
pink mucous membranes	pot-bellied
activated sleep	reddish-purple or blue mucous membranes
yawns frequently	scattered around the nest
nurses strongly	cries or mews
	diarrhea
	can't or won't suck

Careful observation will warn you of any complication. If your bitch seems abnormally depressed, anxious, or upset, it would be wise to have her checked. It is in whelping and caring for puppies and their mother, more than at any other time, that you and your vet will need to work as a team. Be sure to have a veterinarian you can trust and work with; then consult him regularly.

The healthy puppy versus the sick puppy: what to look for.

Diarrhea

Diarrhea is a common occurrence in puppies and may be caused by any one of several conditions, including bad milk from the mother, parasites, infections, varying formula preparations, overfeeding and overheating, and colic. Diarrhea can easily lead to dehydration.

Two to four drops (up to eight) of Kaopectate or Pepto Bismol every few hours may help correct the situation. Rice water has been known to be an effective remedy against diarrhea in certain circumstances. If the situation is not corrected within the first twelve hours, consult your veterinarian. Administer all forms of glucose at only one-half teaspoon to one ounce of water, and feed only small amounts. Hand-fed puppies should temporarily be taken off formula. If the puppy volunteers to nurse the mother, then allow him to do so. Saline solutions, some containing electrolytes, can be administered subcutaneously in the case of dehydration caused by diarrhea.

Overheating

Overheating can occur during summer months when temperatures are soaring and the whelping box is not properly ventilated or when heating lamps are placed too close.

Because newborn puppies cannot pant or drink water to help regulate body temperature, they can become overheated, which will be symptomized by crying, whimpering, and general restlessness. Immediately remove the puppy from the heat source and use a cool, damp washcloth to wipe the puppy down. Dehydration may also accompany the condition. Water can be administered by placing drops on the tongue with an eye dropper.

Constipation

Constipation causes toxemia. The puppy may appear normal in general appearance, but he will not nurse or demonstrate vitality. The puppy may squeal and

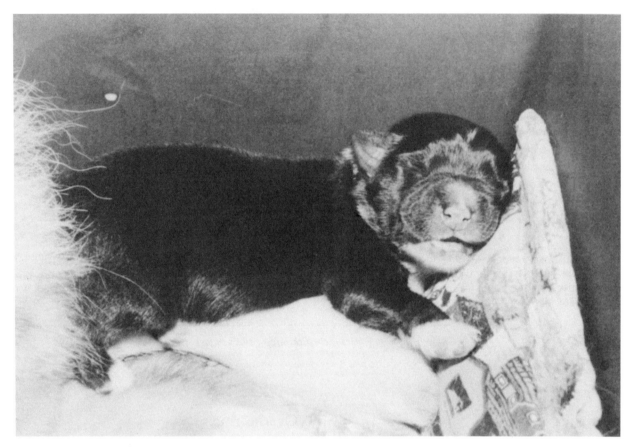

Touchstone's Sockeye Sally just before the eyes have opened during the first twenty-one days after birth. Courtesy Lisa Cameron.

whimper. Use a damp, warm cloth to gently massage his stomach. If this does not produce results and relief for the puppy, take him to the veterinarian.

Canine Herpes Virus (CHV)

Herpes virus is a fatal infection that causes sudden death. It is acquired between the time of whelping to one month of age, generally between three days to three weeks of age. The incubation period is three to eight days.

CHV is responsible for vaginitis in adult bitches. It may be manifested in adults by a nasal discharge or an upper-respiratory-tract infection. CHV growth is greatly inhibited at 102.2°F. The virus flourishes between 95°F and 98.6°F, which is the average temperature range of puppies through the first month of life. At about five weeks of age, puppies are nearing their adult temperature, which is why the virus does not develop to an acute degree in adult dogs.

Bitches that have been infected with CHV develop immunity. Subsequently, puppies whelped after an infected litter generally will not be overtaken by the virus.

Cases of tracheobronchitis, commonly called "kennel cough" (a respiratory-tract infection), may be an adult expression of herpes virus. Individuals with the symptoms should be isolated. Presently, there is no vaccine for CHV. The initial symptoms are similar to those found in distemper, hepatitis, and viral pneumonia. The puppies can become hypothermic, they stop nursing, they are listless, and they have runny noses, labored respiration, and congestion. Cyanosis (blue skin coloration) of the nose leather, lips, feet, and tongue is due to unoxygenated blood. Agonized crying and screaming lasts for hours until death. The lungs are generally affected with pneumonia. Death usually occurs within twenty-four hours after the onset of symptoms.

If you suspect any of the above symptoms, get to the veterinarian. You may be unable to save the litter, but a diagnosis is imperative to correctly determine if the virus is present.

PUPPY SEPTICEMIA AND PERITONITIS

Peritonitis and Septicemia infections may start off from a bacteria (E. coli, staphylococci, and or streptococci) that gains entry via the umbilical cord. Septicemia can also be caused from wounds from tail docking, dewclaw removal or from infections from the dam, and can result in an infection that spreads throughout the bloodstream.

Crying, bloating, refusing to eat, swelling of the naval, lethargy are all symptoms of a serious problem. Diarrhea is not a indication of Septicemia.

When the bacterial infection localizes in the abdomen, toxins paralyze the intestines, the abdomen bloats, and in addition to crying, bloating, refusal to eat, you may notice dark discoloration in the groin area.

In both cases, good supportive care and antibiotics are required. These infections can be greatly reduced with good hygiene.

RECOMMENDED VACCINATION AND WORMING SCHEDULES

Because the maternal antibodies are inadequate or nonexistent in orphans, the puppies should be vaccinated as early as two weeks of age, or according to your veterinarian's recommendations.

At three weeks of age, the litter can be wormed with pyrantel pamoate to kill the intestinal stages of roundworms and hookworms. (See the chapter on Health Care.)

HANDLING DURING THE FIRST TWENTY-ONE DAYS

During the first fourteen days, handling should be kept to a minimum. It is important to trim the toenails and to weigh the puppies for daily weight gain and health, but too much handling will interfere with the sleeping and eating that are necessary for proper development.

During the third week, when the puppies are between fifteen and twenty-one days old, the mild stress of careful handling can be beneficial as long as it is gentle and brief. Massage between each puppy's toes, his ears, the area along the neck, the back, and the legs with a gentle circular motion for no more than two to three minutes.

By the fourth week, the puppy is less dependent on his mother. The puppy learns to eat, play, and bark. Gentle socialization is important, as is play among littermates. Photo by Cee's Pix.

——— Chapter 29 ———

RAISING PUPPIES

DURING THE FIRST TWO WEEKS, the puppies spend approximately 90 percent of their time sleeping and are totally dependent upon their mother to meet all of their needs. Between the third and fourth weeks, solid food can be introduced by making a gruel with a high-quality dog food and boiled rice with meat or vegetable broth designed to meet the needs of growth. Keep shallow dishes with fresh water available at all times.

At approximately three to four weeks, the puppies' temporary canine teeth erupt. By the fourth week, the puppies can see, hear, smell, and walk.

The fourth week is an extremely critical stage. Human imprinting can begin during the fourth week, but the puppies need to remain in a stable environment with the security of their mother and littermates. The puppies are increasingly aware of their environment. All human interactions should be regulated carefully so that the puppies do not become overly stimulated by sights and sounds.

At five weeks, the puppies have all of their senses (hearing, sight, and scent). The central nervous system and the brain are in the final stages of growth, although they are not fully developed.

Five-week-old puppies express a great deal of curiosity and are not inhibited by fear. This is a good time to introduce them to ducks to stimulate their herding instinct. The different sights, scents, and sounds will also enhance the senses. Brief playtime away from their kennel is

SEE HOW THEY GROW

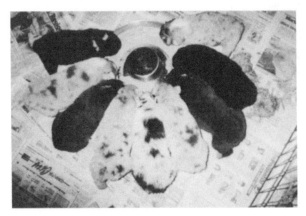

Twenty-one days. Courtesy Marti Parrish.

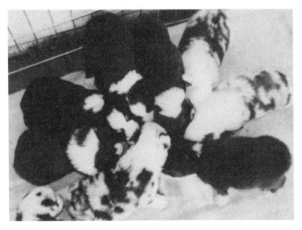

Four weeks. Courtesy Karla Michelson.

important to broaden their horizon, but because the puppies are not emotionally mature, too much handling or stimulation can overwhelm them and do more harm than good. Important canine skills are learned through the mother's discipline and teaching and through interaction and play with littermates. This also sets the foundation for human handling at a later time. At about five weeks of age, the weaning process begins. The puppies venture away from their mother and littermates to explore.

By the sixth week, most of the twenty-eight temporary or "milk teeth" have emerged. The first in a series of temporary inoculations can be given during this time.

The sixth week is an excellent time to continue or initiate exposure to ducks. Exposure to many friendly people and places other than the puppy's own kennel and littermates several times a week will help build confidence and broaden his environment. Otherwise, the puppy may have difficulty adjusting to new situations and surroundings.

Puppies can be removed from the litter and mother at seven weeks, but each puppy needs a "new" mother image. This is an ideal time to begin leash and house training. The seventh week is the optimum time for puppies to go to their new home.

During the eighth week, puppies do not bounce back or recover from being startled or scared as easily as they did at five and six weeks. They are more cautious and hesitant. Human interaction is highly important, but negative or adverse conditioning and unnecessary stress, such as shipping by air, should be avoided between the eighth and tenth weeks. The puppy requires continued socialization with kind handling and gentle discipline.

At nine weeks, the puppies are extremely receptive to learning by association, but they have a short attention span. Kindergarten obedience can be introduced by using positive reinforcement.

By ten weeks, the puppies are growing out of the cautious stage. Puppies are more trustworthy with house training. Between ten and twelve weeks of age, the pack instincts surface for dominance, and the pecking order is being established. It is important for the owner to establish himself as pack leader at this time. It is also important to separate the litter, or the puppies will become more interested in dogs and not as interested in people.

Between twelve and sixteen weeks of age, puppies can still be socialized and taught, but it will be more challenging if the puppies have not received special handling until now. The puppy is still being influenced by his environment.

By sixteen weeks, the mental capacity is fully intact, but the puppy requires much experience. It is important for the puppy to continue to explore friendly places and have confidence-building experiences. Play training is ideal, because puppies still have a short attention span. Adult teeth begin erupting at this time.

Above: Ch. Oak Ridge Miss Judy Bea as a puppy. Photo by Bobbie Myrick.
Above, Left: Seven weeks old — the ideal time for a puppy to go to his new home.
Above, Right: Photo by Trish Thornwald.

Right: Courtesy Karla Michelson.

Left: Hiltop's Hilton of Las Rocosa at six weeks of age. Courtesy Wanda Robertson.

Below: A bundle of joy. A six-week-old litter of Glacier-Crest puppies.

From sixteen weeks on, the adolescent puppy is ready for a world filled with adventure. Hormonal changes can affect personality. Additional confidence building is important during this time. Although not as obvious as the first time, Aussies will go through another cautious, hesitant period between five and ten months of age.

Males begin to assert their dominance between six and eight months of age, and teething subsides between eight and twelve months.

Between eight to twelve weeks of age, each puppy should look like he will as an adult but in miniature. Puppies that trot as their main gait are said to be in balance with themselves. Testicles should be present in males at this age.

During rapid growth, the hindquarters may appear to be higher than the forequarters. The topline may appear to sag, while the legs go in different directions. In evaluating puppies during this adolescent stage, breeders prefer to see different traits. In some lines, a puppy that "toes out" slightly is more likely to correct himself even as late as three or four years of age when the dog has filled out and is fully matured. Certain developmental stages are more bloodline specific, and the experienced breeder will be able to guide you through these periods.

The ears will usually go through a variety of changes during teething. One ear may stand straight up while the other hangs down on the other side. If the ears are small in size and stand "pricked" or semipricked during this stage, some breeders will "weight" the ears to cosmetically correct them for show purposes. They will roll up wetproof adhesive tape placed on the inside tops of the ears and then "set" the ears to fold at one-fourth to one-half above the base. In cold weather, these ears may stand up more than during warm weather. You can gently massage ear leather to make ears more pliable and willing to lie down. Products such as vitamin ointments, bag balms, and neatsfoot oil will also soften ear leather. Be cautious during cold weather to prevent frostbite damage caused by restricted circulation to the ears when they are taped or glued.

Between twelve weeks and twenty weeks, the puppy coat will shed out, and the adult guard hairs will begin growing in. They will first appear down the back and across the shoulders. The feathers and ruff will become more profuse. It is also during this period that the bite may "shift" as the muzzle lengthens and the jaw grows into adult proportions.

Dispositions are entirely individual. Most Australian Shepherds will go through an insecure adolescent period between six and nine months of age. This is a very critical mental developmental stage. Socialization and handling are imperative to build confidence.

Pigmentation on the nose leather is a concern for many Aussie owners. Pink spots on the nose, especially those that are surrounded by pigment, will usually fill in with age. Pink spots on the nose should not cause concern. The dudley nose (one without pigmentation) is a concern due to direct sun exposure. The sun can cause irritation to the unpigmented area; therefore, it is more susceptible to sunburn and solar dermatitis. Although the butterfly nose is faulted after one year of age, some Aussies may take two to three years for the nose to become fully pigmented. This is due to the breed's tendency for coat coloring to darken with age. Some deep-colored merles will appear almost solid in color as these individuals approach their twilight years.

MATURITY

Some bloodlines are quick to mature. In early developing lines, individuals may appear fully mature by twelve months of age. By two and one-half to three years of age, these individuals may appear to be "overdone," thereby lacking athletic ability.

Early maturity has given youngsters the disadvantage of being "pushed" to finish their Championships, Obedience titles, Stock Dog titles, and so forth, before they have reached the mental maturity to accept the pressures of competitive preparation and training.

SUGGESTED IMMUNIZATION SCHEDULE

Age	Interval	Type of Vaccine
6 to 6 1/2 weeks	first shots	Distempter and Parvovirus (plus other vaccines in combination if recommended by your veterinarian).
10 to 12 weeks	4 weeks	DA2PL+CPV+CV (Distemper, Hepatitis [Adenovirus Type II], Parainfluenza, Leptospirosis, Canine Parvovirus, Corona Virus (These are given in various combinations or all in one. Follow recommendation of your vet.) Bordatella. Lyme disease when available in your state
14 to 16 weeks	4 weeks	Booster shot of all above DA2PL+CPV+CV, Bordatella, Lyme disease. First Rabies vaccination.
1 year	8 months	Booster all vaccines.
Annually as adult	1 year	Booster Distemper, Hepatitis, Lepto, Parainfluenza, Parvo and Corona Virus, Bordatella vaccines.
1 year	1 to 3 years	Rabies booster (Varies according to state and local laws. Vaccine is good for 3 years after initial booster at 1 year.)

SUGGESTED DE-WORMING SCHEDULE

8 weeks	Fecal check and worm for round or hookworm if present.
16 weeks	Re-worm for above and check feces to make sure dog is clear.
16-20 weeks	Blood test for heartworm if recommended. Start on heartworm preventative.
Every 6 months	Fecal recheck and treat if necessary.
Any time	Fecal check if puppy or dog has persistent diarrhea, vomiting, pot belly, and poor condition, or if roundworms or tapeworm segments are visible.

In slower maturing lines, individuals will be physically "balanced" but still not fully "blossomed" or "filled out" until two and one-half to three or even four years of age. These individuals often look exceptional at six and seven years of age. The Australian Shepherd possesses longevity because of slow maturation. Maturity is a quality that must be observed to fully understand the changes manifest during growth. When your dog reaches this point, he will look more like the individual that you pictured when you acquired him.

Due to the varying degrees of developmental differences between bloodlines, it is wise to observe not only the parents, grandparents, brothers, and sisters, but also the progeny of the aforementioned to gain a keener insight about the pattern of development in related individuals.

The feminine features of the Casa Blanca female on the left are distinctly different from the masculine features of her litter brother on the right (Ch. Winchester's Rollin Rapids ex Rocky Oaks Blazing Star). Courtesy Judy Chard.

This should tell you a lot about your puppy. Remember, however, that each dog is an individual. There are many physiological changes that take place from puppyhood into adulthood. Generally speaking, all individuals will go through stages where they are not "together" and in certain instances will appear to "fall apart" during the teenage stage. This, of course, will also vary with each individual. They will begin to regain physical balance somewhere between nine and eighteen months.

SELECTING THE PERFECT PUPPY

At seven to twelve weeks of age, you will want to begin "culling" or "grading" the litter and deciding which puppies to keep and which to sell, and for what purpose. When you are choosing a puppy that does not yet have his own records, certain puppy tests are a valuable guide for finding a stable, responsive, intelligent Aussie. Other factors enter the picture when you are evaluating for specific jobs, such as for herding. Certain traits, such as aggression, may be necessary in a hard-driving stock dog, whereas this would not be desirable in a companion for small children. The breeder will serve as a valuable source of information because he has experience with the bloodline, knows the characteristics of the puppy's ancestors, and has viewed the puppies on many occasions in different situations.

Puppy Tests

Inherited traits are modified through environmental factors. Early handling and training will play a tremendous role in developing each Aussie's potential. As Dr. Michael Fox points out in his book, *Understanding Your Dog*, basic temperamental characteristics of young puppies will remain with them throughout their life.

Testing a litter during the seventh week (between the forty-third and forty-ninth days) reveals the raw Aussie without a lot of outside influences. While the general temperament of the puppy can be clearly assessed during this time, remember that the dog is not fully mature until he is close to eighteen months of age.

It is important that the puppies be separated from their littermates by ten weeks of age to prevent one from being bullied by the other one.

Nervous responses (noise and touch sensitivity) can have a big effect in training and handling Australian Shepherds. Ideally, working dogs have a balance of inherited traits. A dog lacking sensitivity to touch and/or noise will require more stimulus in training. On the other hand, a highly sensitive Aussie can become overly stimulated and set off his defense reflexes. Body sensitivity increases dramatically between eight and ten weeks of age.

Noise Sensitivity

In this test, confidence and stability can be observed. This test can be conducted during the seventh week of age, before the fear-imprinting period (eight to ten weeks) but not before six weeks, when the neurological system is still developing. Place the puppy in a large or open area. Bang on the bottom of an empty pan several times with a metal spoon (out of the puppy's view).

The ideal Aussie will be alert to the noise and will try to find where the sound is coming from. Ultrasensitive Aussies spooked by the unexpected noise will require a much gentler approach in training and quieter handling. Sensitive Aussies may become intimidated by loud, harsh commands, the crack of a bullwhip, the clanging of chute gates, and other loud noises. Most important, however, is the Aussie's ability to recover quickly from such a shock. On the other hand, Aussie puppies that are insensitive to the noise will hardly take any notice and are not going to be as responsive and alert in training.

Touch Sensitivity

In their book *Working Dogs*, Elliott Humphrey and Lucien Waner introduce a test to determine how sensitive a dog is to touch. I have modified the following test somewhat from that test.

To test for touch sensitivity, the tester gently presses between the puppy's toes (on the webbing) with his thumb and forefinger, getting firmer until

Between ten and twelve weeks of age, it is vitally important for the owner to give each puppy individual attention away from the other puppies. Otherwise, the puppies will develop a bond with each other rather than with the owner. This is also an ideal time for the owner to establish himself as the pack leader and define basic rules for the puppy.

the puppy responds. A highly sensitive puppy will react immediately. A responsive, balanced puppy will react after a few seconds. The insensitive puppy won't readily react within ten seconds. The puppy that complains after receiving a momentary pinch, but readily bounces back and forgives the tester (demonstrated by seeking his attention, licking him, and wagging his tail), is ideal.

The Aussie sensitive to touch requires milder physical corrections. A hefty jerk on the collar can cause him to flee or behave aggressively. On the other hand, less sensitive Aussies will require a heavier, firmer approach. A heavy jerk on the training collar yields little response in stubborn or insensitive Aussies.

Information gathered in puppy testing conducted during the 1930s in Switzerland at Fortunate Fields (the original Guide Dog School) was

DEVELOPMENTAL STAGES OF A PUPPY

Age	Basic Needs	Behavior and Training
1-14 days (1st & 2nd week)	Warmth • Food Sleep • Mother	Not responsive to humans • Sleeps 90% of time Needs stimulation for urination & defecation
15-21 days (3rd & 4th week)	Warmth • Food Sleep • Mother	Eyes open • Begins to walk Should be handled carefully • Needs mother and littermates • First worming
22-35 days (4th & 5th week)	Socialization with canines and humans • Rest • Play	Begins to eat, bark, and play • Begins to respond to human voice Needs play and socialization outside the puppy pen
36-49 days (6th & 7th week)	Weaning • Separation from littermates • Human socialization	Strong dominant/subordinate relationships are developing • Motor skills improved • Temporary immunizations given • Capable of learning simple commands and being leash broken • May go to new home during seventh week
49-56 days (8th week)	Security • Love	Often termed the "fear period" • Puppy should not be frightened or unnecessarily stressed during this period
50-63 days (9-12 weeks)	Bonds to human • Learns to accept human as pack leader Socialization	Totally removed from dam and littermates • Capable of learning Come-Sit-Stay Needs confidence instilled • Begin housebreaking • Exposure to variety of environments important
64-112 days (12-16 weeks)	Security • Discipline Socialization • Attention	Learns by association • Goes through "avoidance period" Needs continued low-key socialization and exposure
113-168 days (16-24 weeks)	Socialization • Love • Consistent Discipline • Basic Training	Fully developed mentally; needs experience • Will attempt to establish dominance • Adapts a negative or positive attitude toward training at this time Praise lavishly for correct behavior
25-32 weeks (6-8 months)	Basic Training • Consistent discipline • Continued attention and socialization	Ready for beginning show or obedience classes • Attention span is lengthening • Needs continuing exposure to new situations • Males begin to assert dominance
33-56 weeks (8-12 months)	Continued socialization, reassurance and training • Affection and reassurance necessary	Show pups often in "puppy bloom" but should not be pushed too fast • Teething period ends • Puberty (period of sexual maturation) begins • May go through a second avoidance period • Neutering can be performed.
12-18 months (1-1½ years)	More disciplined and structured training • Love	Training can be more intense

*Play is necessary for developing inherited traits.
Photo by Trish Thornwald.*

*Ch. Aristocrat's Hell on Wheels
(Ch. Fieldmaster's Cast the Die ex
Ch. Silvertone's Easy Money).
Above: at eight weeks of age.
Below: as a finished champion.
Courtesy Magazinne.*

further developed in Bar Harbor, Maine, by Dr. John Paul Scott and his associate, Dr. John L. Fuller. In their work, *Genetics and the Social Behavior of Dogs*, research indicates that between the twenty-first and twenty-eighth days, puppies experience a critical developmental period (fear imprint period). If the puppy is emotionally upset, it can have a lasting effect on his sociability. Social attachments are formed between the fourth and sixteenth weeks (the socialization period). By the sixteenth week, the dog's character is basically formed. This research contributed to the work of Clarence Pfaffenberger, who put the information to the acid test in his Guide Dogs for the Blind program. Aptitude tests were developed for the selection of dogs for training and breeding, and concepts about raising and training puppies are also translated in his book, *The New Knowledge of Dog Behavior*.

The results of these tests weed out the dogs that are too dull or too sensitive for noise or correction, that lack stability and spirit, and that are fearful or stubborn. The tests are conducted once a week over a five-week period (from eight to twelve weeks of age) to gain a more accurate picture of the overall puppy. Curiosity toward the introduction of new experiences (investigating an object dragged along at the end of a string, a flashlight being shined toward them) is a sign of intelligence. Puppies that try to locate the source of a loud whistle or car horn out of the puppies'

The same male at different stages of development. Top left: twelve weeks old. Top right: four months old. Bottom left: at one year old, the individual is skeletally proportioned, but the muscles have yet to fill out. At this stage the adult guard hair and undercoat have fully replaced the puppy coat. Bottom right: two and a half years old.

view is highly desirable. Any puppy that startles at the sounds will be too sound sensitive. It has been discovered that natural retrieving is significant in predicting willingness to please. Puppies that show no interest in balls often retrieve a duck or pheasant wing. Furthermore, early socialization is important in later training.

As pointed out by behavioral specialist William Campbell, author of *Behavior Problems in Dogs*, personality profiles are beneficial, but puppy selection is not a scientific experiment. The breeder has observed the litter since birth and has had the opportunity to see the puppies in many different situations, both apart and in the company of their siblings. The manner in which each puppy responds to his littermates may be totally opposite to the way in which he reacts with humans.

In all of the tests, each puppy should be evaluated apart from his littermates and in an environment new to the litter. It is important to see the puppy under the mild stress of the new place, because this will give a clearer indication of the character and confidence level of the individual.

The first part of the first test evaluates how eagerly and readily the puppy seeks human attention. The tester should kneel down several feet away from the puppy. Without saying anything to the puppy, the tester should clap his hands to attract the puppy's attention. Observe if the puppy comes eagerly, slowly but willingly, hesitantly, or not at all. A puppy that comes willingly indicates his desire for human companionship.

The second part of the test evaluates the puppy's willingness to follow a person who is walking away from him. The tester should once again clap his hands to attract the puppy's atten-

At four months of age (left), the puppy appears squatty with short legs and a long body. The ears are beginning to go through a variety of changes. The beautiful, fluffy puppy coat looks rough while undergoing drastic changes. At five months of age (below left), the head becomes distorted looking. This is the beginning of the ugly duckling stage. It appears as if each anatomical feature is developing independently. The ears go whichever way they please during the teething stages.

Ch. Las Rocosa Little Wolf during the awkward puppy stages of four and five months.

tion, then walk away. The puppy's enthusiasm to follow without being coaxed predicts his future willingness to please his owner.

The next test is a two-part test to assess the dominance of the puppy. To evaluate the puppy's reaction to physical restraint, roll the puppy over on his back and hold him in this position for approximately thirty seconds. The puppy should struggle to get up, or struggle, then settle, but should not become frantic or overly aggressive.

The second part of the test involves cradling the puppy with your hands interlaced under the puppy's chest, then gently lifting him off of the ground, which places the tester in control. The middle-of-the-road puppy will struggle, then settle, but will not behave aggressively. After thirty seconds, gently set the puppy back down on the ground.

One of the best indicators of the puppy's desire to please is his willingness to retrieve an object (ball, toy, a knotted sock, a crumpled piece of paper). If the puppy readily and repeatedly will chase the object and bring it back or chase it and carry it off, he has good drives or desire.

A correct, beautiful head type as portrayed by BIS Rarities MASCA and NAMASCUSA Champion Wigglebutt Elektra Blu. Photo by Bill Ogle.

Chapter 30

ABOUT MINIATURE AUSSIES

HISTORY

THE HISTORY OF MINIATURE AUSSIES began with the Australian Shepherd breed. Doris Cordova, a horsewoman in Norco, California, started a breeding program to concentrate on small sized or "miniature" Australian Shepherds. She based her line on a small, 15 inch blue merle male named Cordova's Spike (born 4-1-78). He was the first Aussie registered as a Miniature Aussie with the National Stock Dog Registry (NSDR).

Cordova asserted that the Miniature had all the attributes of the larger breed but in a more compact form. She believed that the breed's desire to work, coupled with their intelligence, made them an excellent choice for the gentleman rancher on a country estate, especially around horses. She particularly felt their small size was most practical in the house or to take along in a vehicle. She wrote, "On the road the advantages of the small Aussie become obvious—truly a fine traveling companion."

LITTLE BLUE DOGS

While there have always been "little blue dogs" in Australian Shepherds, the majority of them were 18 to 19 inches tall. In 1975, when we were drafting the ASCA Breed Standard, we did a statistical study on the breed. We measured several hundred individuals from the foundation bloodlines. Ninety-five percent (95%) of the dogs were in a normal bell-curved distribution. The greater number of Aussies emerged in the middle, between 18 inches and 23 inches at the withers. The remaining five (5%) were either slightly smaller (17 3/4 inches) or slightly larger (just over 23 inches).

The ASCA and AKC Breed Standards for Australian Shepherds list a preferred size, but no disqualification exists, because *quality must never be sacrificed in favor of size*. The original foundation dogs were selected for hardiness and for their ability to handle livestock in the western ranch country, and not for size.

CHARACTER AND TEMPERAMENT

Miniature Aussies are intelligent and loving companions. They excel in obedience and agility. They have a strong sense of boundary and an uncanny ability to sense danger. Like their larger counterpart, they should bark to warn, but not just for recreation, which makes them a good watch dog and companion.

Minis require adequate exercise and even more importantly—mental stimulation. They were founded on working dogs with strong herding and guarding instincts. The correct temperament for the Mini should exhibit the intelligence of a breed that was developed to think and act independently, with willingness to please and listen to their master. Individuals with the appropri-

Tony Hoard and Sandy Oaks Wigglebutt Q, a lively duo performing crowd pleasing antics with the Purina Incredible Dog Team. Photo by Bill Ogle.

ate herding instincts should demonstrate the self-assurance to handle a stubborn ram, and yet be gentle with lambs.

The personality of the Miniature Aussie may be somewhat reserved. However, reserved must not be confused with the type of timidity caused from being fearful, which would be a severe fault. They may treat strangers with restraint until they figure out if they are friend or foe. Even though they may be small, they are not content to be confined in a small area away from people. Above all else, they want to be part of a family.

BUYER BEWARE!

In an increasingly urban world, miniature breeds continue to rise in popularity. The Mini Aussie is no exception. There seems to be a growing interest in undersized Aussies that excel in performance events and yet are small enough to enjoy in smaller spaces.

A sudden rise in status, however, is seldom ever good for the breed concerned. With the recognition, it is not unusual for unprincipled breeders to bend to the temptation to satisfy the ever-increasing demand for extremely small Aussies at the expense of pure breeding.

In some cases, dishonest individuals have infused toy breeds to speed up the "miniaturization" process in order to establish abnormally small Aussies.

Due to the fraudulent and unethical breeding practices of some unscrupulous breeders, little dogs are appearing that look like Australian Shepherds to some extent, but in fact are crossbred. Consequently, Miniature Aussies are held in disapproval by many Aussie fanciers. A pedigree representing a purebred ancestry can be only validated through DNA testing.

Even though Minis may have purebred Australian Shepherd ancestry and are promoted as a variety of the breed, they are not considered Australian Shepherds by the Australian Shepherd Club of America (ASCA) and the United States Australian Shepherd Association (USASA). Please see their official statements regarding Miniature Aussies at the end of the chapter.

Destined for greatness, BISS Ch. Wigglebutt Seven of Nine as an alert, attentive puppy. Photo Courtesy Angela Ogle.

FINDING THE PERFECT INDIVIDUAL

Finding the right dog starts with doing your homework thoroughly. The best place to start searching for a puppy is at the Mini Aussie breed clubs: Miniature Australian Shepherd Club of America (MASCA) and North American Miniature Australian Shepherd Club of the USA (NAMASCUSA). Both clubs are working together to promote the breed and protect breed integrity. They are a good source of information and can help you locate dedicated breeders that use health clearances for blood stock. Each parent club also provides an avenue for club-related activities at regional and national levels. Aussies registered through the parent clubs MASCA and NAMASCUSA are eligible to participate in the programs and gain titles these clubs offer.

While pet stores are a convenient source of supply, they are not going to have the breed's best interest at heart. Nor are they well versed or qualified to help the new owner evaluate correct type and structural soundness. They are usually

BISS Ch. Wigglebutt Seven of Nine CGC, HIC, UAGI, RL1, RL2, CL1, MASCA V1 in the winners circle with the late Wanda Robertson, one of ASCA's earliest breeder judges. Photo by Paw Print Pet Photography.

unaware of health problems more common to certain bloodlines, such as epilepsy, which can be emotionally and financially devastating to the owner. To avoid this pitfall you need to locate a responsible breeder who is producing sound, healthy dogs whether for performance, a companion, or show prospect.

JUDGING THE BREED

Though small, Mini Aussies with the heart, intelligence, athletic ability and drive for performance events cannot be fragile. The Miniature Aussie Breed Standards describe a perfect replica of the Australian Shepherd. They should be judged as if they were Australian Shepherds, only proportionately smaller.

The preferred ideal size is between 14 and 18 inches. Even though the NAMASCUSA breed standard states that over 18 inches is a severe fault, quality must never be sacrificed in favor of size. This precludes that size would not dictate excellence. Soundness and athletic ability *cannot* be compromised in order for the breed to function in serious performance events. This is significant, considering that Australian Shepherds were chosen for their ability to herd sheep and cattle across the western ranch country, and not for size.

When judging the Mini Aussie, it is important to carefully study the head to make sure the head is balanced. The length of the muzzle should equal the length of the top skull (from the tip of the nose to the middle of the stop) and from the middle of the stop (depression between the muzzle and the top of the skull) to the occiput. It is not uncommon to see some Mini Aussies that exhibit a shorter muzzle than the topskull. While this may be considered attractive, there is more of a tendency of prognathism (undershot) bites.

When a short muzzle is selected for in a breeding program, there is a tendency for teeth to become crowded in the dental arch, which is evidenced by rotation of the third premolar. Shorter air passages can lead to inefficient temperature regulation and respiratory problems, leaving the Aussie more vulnerable to heat stress in hot and humid weather, which is harmful to a working breed.

Undershot bites are a class three malocclusion due to the relationship of the long mandible (lower jaw) and relatively shorter maxilla (upper jaw), and are therefore disqualified. Overshot bites—shorter mandible and relatively longer maxilla—are a bite defect and are *not normal* in any breed, therefore must be disqualified, according to the World Small Animal Veterinary Association World Congress 2001.

Serious faults to be disqualified in both varieties include any color that is not one of the four recognized colors, white body splashes, a Dudley nose (no pigment in nose leather), monorchidism and cryptorchidism. Severe faults of importance are a domed head and prominent (bulging) eyes, which can be signs of dwarfism or cross-breeding.

The domed head is not the faintly rounded topskull described in the AKC standard, but the abnormal type found in toy breeds in which bulged eyes are also common.

Eyes that are not adequately guarded in the eye socket by skeletal protection of the correct orbital depth can be easily injured and dislodged out of the socket by a bump to the head, which would disqualify the individual as a durable working dog.

Breeding Mini Aussies

In order to maintain true athletic ability and practical working aptitude in the Mini Aussie, it is important that they are performance tested at every generation to verify that those qualities are being passed from one generation to the next. Without testing, there is no guarantee.

It is very easy to breed undesireable traits, but difficult to eradicate one, and it can take generations of a selective and careful breeding program before the ideal is again achieved. Selective breed-

Maximum Miss Scarlett Shadow, a true working ranch dog of excellent ability and the foundation dam for Maximum Aussies. Scarlett as she is better known is pictured wearing behind a herd of cows on the Carver Ranch in Brenham Texas. Photo Courtesy Terri Carver.

Carla Sue, registered as Maximum Scarlett Dancer HSDs, HCCg, a daughter of Maximum Miss Scarlett Shadow, is following in the footsteps of her dam by demonstrating good, natural balance on stock.

ing will stabilize undesirable qualities as well as desirable ones. It is vitally important to cull, or weed out, any unwanted traits.

HEALTH ISSUES AND GENETIC DISORDERS CONCERNING MINIS

Miniature Aussies share the same genetic disorders Australian Shepherds do, plus those associated with extreme miniaturization (unnatural small size) when the normal occurring small size is deviated from and demeaned to the 'toy' department. With that being said, any feature that deviates from the correct type such as bug eyes or domed head are severe faults. The rapid reduction of skull size can cause bulging eyes that are prone to trauma, and a foreshortened face is predisposed to respiratory problems and over-crowding of teeth.

Artificially produced miniaturization or cross-breeding may also result in dramatic reproductive problems, females requiring Cesarean sections, and males unable to breed naturally.

Dwarfism is a disorder that can affect Mini Aussies. According to Dr. George Padgett, author of *Control of Canine Genetic Diseases*, skeletal dysplasias (dwarfism) are a varied group of inherited disorders that are not well defined.

In chondrodysplasia, a type of dwarfism, bowed legs can result from unequal growth rates on the double bones (tibia and fibula or the ulna and radius) and disproportionately small, stunted limbs (obvious signs of dwarfisim). The arrested development of the long bones result from the abnormal calcification process as cartilage is replaced by bone. Dwarfs are more predisposed to disc disease, a common neurological condition, and can suffer from premature aging as the intervertebral discs (nucleus of the disc) become calcified and loses necessary shock absorbing abilities for sufficient strength and flexibility of the spine.

Sparse hair (alopecia) and skin problems are commonly associated with pituitary dwarfism, an inherited metabolic irregularity of the thyroid gland.

Although luxated patellas (displaced kneecaps) can be trauma induced, when the patella slips towards the inside rather than to the outside, it is more often associated with the small sizes of the long bones of the legs of abnormally small dogs. According to some research, torsion and bending of the tibia may be a consequence of unusually small bones.

Champion Bluegrass Solo playing with Seven as a puppy, who is one of his offspring out of Eaglecreek's Texas Bluebonnet. Photo Courtesy Angela Ogle.

ASCA AND USASA OFFICIAL STANCE CONCERNING MINI AND TOY AUSSIES:

Australian Shepherd Club of America: The Miniature Australian Shepherd, North American Shepherd, North American Miniature Australian Shepherd, and/or Toy Australian Shepherd breeds are not recognized as a variety of Australian Shepherd by ASCA. The club considers such dogs to be a distinct and separate breed and will not accept them into its registry.

"Our bylaws state that ASCA's purpose is: 'To encourage members and breeders to accept one breed standard for the Australian Shepherd as approved by the Club as the only standard of excellence by which Australian Shepherds shall be judged.' It is the mission of this club ASCA and the mission of its members to preserve the breed rather than change it."

United States Australian Shepherd Association: Recently there has been a rise in the movement to breed miniature and toy versions of the Australian Shepherd. The Miniature Australian Shepherd and the Toy Australian Shepherd are not recognized or considered varieties of the Australian Shepherd by this organization, the United States Australian Shepherd Association, Inc. (USASA), or by the American Kennel Club (AKC). Since these dogs are not AKC registered, they cannot be verified by USASA as purebred, and therefore are not considered Australian Shepherds by this organization.

The USASA does not support the purposeful

The dynamic, multi-titled, BISS Ch. Wigglebutt Seven of Nine CGC, HIC, UAGI, RL1, RL2, CL1, MASCA V1 catching a disc in mid air, illustrating the type of action that earned her MVA, among numerous other awards and titles. Photo by Mike Waller.

Sandy Oaks Wigglebutt Jaxx JHD demonstrating correct gait as he trots towards the camera. Photo courtesy Raechelle Embry.

breeding of Miniature Australian Shepherds and Toy Australian Shepherds, and expects all members who have breeding programs to breed to the USASA/AKC recognized standard of excellence. The USASA further expects all members to be ever vigilant in the preservation and protection of the Australian Shepherd.

Miniature Aussie Registries

Miniature Australian Shepherd Club of America
PO Box 1692
Winter Park, FL. 32790-1692
E-mail: MASCA@mascaonline.net
Website: http://www.mascaonline.net

North American Miniature Australian Shepherd Club of the USA
PO Box 141097
Broken Arrow, OK 74014-1097
Phone/Fax 918-357-5844
Email: registrar@namascusa.com
Website: http://www.namascusa.co

Appendix A: Sources of Information

ASSOCIATIONS AND CLUBS

American Kennel Club (AKC)
Headquarters
260 Madison Avenue
New York, NY 10016
Telephone: 212-696-8200
Website: http://www.akc.org

AKC Operations Center
8051 Arco Corporate Drive, Suite 100
Raleigh, NC 27617-3390
Telephone: 919-233-9767

Australian Shepherd Club of America (ASCA)
6091 E. State Hwy 21
Bryan, TX 77808-9652
Telephone: 979-778-1082
Fax: 979 778-1898
E-mail: manager@asca.org
Website: http://www.asca.org

Canadian Kennel Club (CKC)
200 Ronson Drive, Suite 400
Etobicoke, Ontario
M9W 5Z9
Telephone: 416-675-5511
E-mail: information@ckc.ca
Website: http://www.ckc.ca/en/

Miniature Australian Shepherd Club of America
(MASCA)
PO Box 1692
Winter Park, FL. 32790-1692
E-mail: MASCA@mascaonline.net
Website: http://www.mascaonline.net

North American Miniature Australian Shepherd Club
of the USA
(NAMASCA)
PO Box 141097
Broken Arrow, OK 74014-1097
Telephone/ Fax: 918-357-5844
E-mail: registrar@namascusa.com
Website: http://www.namascusa.com

United Kennel Club (UKC)
100 E Kilgore Rd
Kalamazoo MI 49002-5584
Telephone: 269-343-9020
Fax: 269-343-7037
E-mail:registration@ukcdogs.com
Website: http://www.ukcdogs.com/

United States Australian Shepherd Association (USASA)
9330 N County Road 15
Ft. Collins, CO 80524
Telephone: 970-568-3806
E-mail: slfonta@msn.com
Website: http://www.australianshepherds.org

AUSSIE RESCUE

Aussie Rescue & Placement Helpline, Inc. (ARPH)
PO Box 5305
New Castle, PA 16105
Telephone: 877-ARPH-779
E-mail: arphinc@aol.com
Website: http://www.aussierescue.org

Mini Aussie Rescue & Support, Inc. (MARS)
PO Box 636
Hillsboro, NH 03244
E-mail: info@miniaussierescue.org
Website: http://www.miniaussierescue.org

Second Time Around Aussie Rescue, Inc. (STAAR)
7070 Rye Loop, Bryan, TX 77807
Toll-free number: 1-87-RESCUE US (1-877-372-8387)
Email: Rescue@staar.org
Website: http://www.staar.org

EDUCATION / INFORMATION

Alpine Publications (Dog Books)
38262 Linman Road
Crawford, CO 81415
Telephone: 800-777-7257
Fax: 970-921-5081
E-mail: alpinecsr@alpinepub.com
Website: http://www.alpinepub.com/

Australian Shepherd Blog
http://allaboutaussies.wordpress.com

Canine Training Systems (Training DVDs)
9325 E. St. Charles Rd.
Columbia, MO 65202
Telephone: 573-214-0900
Fax: 573-214-0909
E-mail: info@caninetrainingsystems.com
Website: http://www.caninetrainingsystems.com

Hartnagle's Las Rocosa (Aussie Books and Training DVDs)
32160 Private Road 55
Kiowa, CO 80117
303-621-2880
E-mail: Hartnagle@aol.com
Website: http://www.lasrocosa.com

Hoflin Publishing (Australian Shepherd Annual)
4401 Zephyr St.
Wheat Ridge, CO 80033

Telephone: 303-420-2222
Fax: 720-207-0382
Website: http://www.hoflin.com

GENEALOGY AND PEDIGREES

Aussie Pedigrees Online
Patrick MacRoberts
31560 Newcastle Road
Newcastle, CA 95658
Telephone: 916-663-9025
E-mail: macro@hrdndog.com
Website: http://www.hrdndog.com/pedigrees

Australian Shepherd Genealogy Chart
(Aussie Spider Web)
See Education / Information:
Hartnagle's Las Rocosa (Books and Videos)
Website: http://www.lasrocosa.com

HEALTH / GENETICS

AKC Canine Health Foundation (CHF)
PO Box 900061
Raleigh, NC 27675-9061
Telephone: 888-682-9696
Email: caninehealth@akcchf.org
Website: http://www.akcchf.org

Australian Shepherd Health and Genetics
Institute, Inc. (ASHGI)
730 E. Weldon Ave.
Fresno, CA 93704-6135
Telephone / Fax: 559-485-2136
E-mail: 51ca @ ashgi.org
Website: http://www.ashgi.org

Orthopedic Foundation for Animals (OFA)
2300 E Nifong Boulevard
Columbia, MO 65201-3806
Telephone: (573) 442-0418
Fax: (573) 875-5073
Email: ofa@offa.org
Website: http://www.offa.org

University of Pennsylvania Hip Improvement
Program (PennHip)
E-mail: pennhipinfo@pennhip.org
Website: http://www.pennhip.org

The Veterinary Medical DataBases-VMDB/CERF
1717 Philo Rd
P O Box 3007
Urbana, IL 61803-3007
Telephone: 217-693-4800
Fax: 217-693-4801
E-mail: CERF@vmdb.org
Website: http://www.vmdb.org

Washington State University
(Ivermectin Toxicity Test)
College of Veterinary Medicine
Veterinary Clinical Pharmacology Laboratory
PO Box 609
Pullman, WA 99163-0609
Telephone / Fax: 509-335-3745
E-mail: VCPL@vetmed.wsu.edu
Website: http://www.vetmed.wsu.edu/announce-ments/ivermectin

DOG SPORTS

Association of Pet Dog Trainers Rally Obedience
(APDT)
c/o Linda Sperco
31 Revere Avenue
Maplewood, NJ 07040
Telephone: 800-PET-DOGS
E-mail: rallyo@apdt.com
Website: http://www.apdt.com

American Herding Breed Association
c/o Linda Leek
E-mail: lbsiouis@hotmail.com
Website: http://www.ahba-herding.org/

Australian Shepherd Trial Association (ASTA)
c/o Tennley Dexter
P.O. Box 58
Gaylordsville, CT 06755
Telephone: 860-354-9069 CT / 270-378- 5910 KY
Website: http://www.a-s-t-a.org/

Dog Activities
Website: http://www.dogplay.com

North American Dog Agility Council (NADAC)
P.O. Box 1206
Colbert, OK 74733
E-mail: info@nadac.com
Website: http://www.nadac.com

North American Flyball Association, Inc. (NAFA)
1400 West Devon Avenue, #512
Chicago, IL 60660
Telephone / Fax: 800-318-6312
E-mail: flyball@flyball.org
Website: http://www.flyball.org

United States Dog Agility Association (USDAA)
PO Box 850955
Richardson, TX 75085
Telephone: 972-487-2200
Fax: 972-272-4404
E-mail: info@usdaa.com
Website: http://www.usdaa.com

Appendix B: Titles Your Dog Can Earn

ASCA (Australian Shepherd Club of America Titles)

ASCA CONFORMATION
CH - Champion

ASCA OBEDIENCE
CD - Companion Dog
CDX - Companion Dog Excellent
OTCH - Obedience Trial Champion
TD - Tracking Dog
TDX - Tracking Dog Excellent
UD - Utility Dog
UDX - Utility Dog Excellent
OTCH - Obedience Trial Champion

ASCA STOCK DOG
STD - Started Trial Dog
OTD - Open Trial Dog
ATD - Advanced Trial Dog
WTCh - Working Trial Champion
PATD - Post Advanced Trial Dog
RD - Ranch Dog
RTD - Ranch Trial Dog
RDX - Ranch Dog Excellent

AGILITY
E- Elite
GI - Gamblers / International
GJ - Gamblers / Junior
GS - Gamblers / Standard
GV - Gamblers / Veteran
JI - Jumpers / International

AKC (American Kennel Club) Titles

AKC CONFORMATION
CH

AKC OBEDIENCE
CD
CDX
OTCH
TD
TDX
UD
UDX
UDXTD - Utility Dog Excellent Tracking Dog
UDXVST Utility Dog Excellent Variable Surface Tracking
VST - Variable Surface Tracker

AKC HERDING
PT - Pre-Trial Tested
HT - Herding Tested
HS - Herding Started

HI - Herding Intermediate
HX - Herding Excellent
HC - Herding Champion (HCh)

AGILITY
NA - Novice Agility
NAJ - Novice Jumps with Weaves
OA - Open Agility
OAJ - Open Jumpers with Weaves
AX - Excellent Agility
AXJ - Agility Excellent with Weaves
MX - Master Agility Excellent
MXJ - Master Excellent Jumpers with Weaves

NADAC (North American Dog Agility Council)

NAC - Novice Agility Certificate
NJC - Novice Jumpers Certificate
NGC - Novice Gamblers Certificate
OAC - Open Agility Certificate
OJC - Open Jumpers Certificate
OGC - Open Gamblers Certificate
EAC - Elite Agility Certificate
EJC - Elite Jumpers Certificate
EGC - Elite Gamblers Certificate
NATCH - Agility Trial Champion
O - Outstanding - (prefix to any NADAC title)
S - Superior
V- Veterans (suffix to Novice, Open & Elite)
J- Juniors
JH - Junior Handler
TN-N - Novice Tunnelers Certificate
TN-O - Open
TN-E - Elite
WV-N - Novice Weavers Certificate
WV-O - Open
WE-E - Elite
TG-N - Novice Touch N Go Certificate
TG-O - Open
TG-E - Elite

USDAA (United States Dog Agility Association)

AD - Agility Dog
AAD - Advanced Agility Dog
MAD - Masters Agility Dog
JM - Jumpers Master
GM - Gamblers Master
SM - Snookers Master
RM - Relay Master
VAD - Veteran Agility
ADCH - Agility Dog Champion

359

NAFA (North American Flyball Association)

FD - Flyball Dog
FDX - Flyball Dog Excellent
FDCH - Flyball Dog Champion
FM - Master Flyball Dog
FMX - Master Flyball Dog Excellent
FMCH - Master Flyball Dog Champion

AHBA (American Herding Breed Association)

HCT - Herding Capable Tested
HRD - Herding Ranch Dog I, II or III (Beginning, Intermediate, Advanced Level)
HTD - Herding Trial Dog I, II, or III (same as above)
HTCh - Herding Trial Champion

UKC (United Kennel Club)

UKC Conformation and Obedience Titles are preceded by the letter 'U" ie U-CH = UKC -Champion, U-OCH -Obedience Champion, etc.

UKC AGILITY
U- AGI - Agility 1 (Novice)
U-AGII - Agility 2 (Open)
U-AGIII - Agility 3 (Advanced)
U-ATCH - Agility Trial Champion

CKC (Canadian Kennel Club)

CKC CONFORMATION
CH - Same as AKC/ASCA

CKC HERDING
HS - Herding Started
HI - Herding Intermediate
RX - Herding Excellent

CKC OBEDIENCE
Same as AKC/ASCA

CKC AGILITY
AGN - Novice
AGI - International
AGX - Excellent A
AGMX - Excellent B

Bibliography

Bailey, E. Murl, DVM., *Emergency and General Treatment of Poisonings*, College Station, Texas.

Bowen, R.A., DVM., *Breeding Soundness Examination of the Male; Outline of Reproductive Anatomy; Reproductive Diseases in the Male; Reproductive Physiology of the Dog; Seminal Evaluation*. Colorado State University, Animal Reproduction Laboratory, Fort Collins, Colorado, 1980.

Carmichael, L.E., DVM., Ph.D., *Canine Brucellosis: The Silent Threat*. James A. Baker Institute for Animal Health, Cornell University, 1984.

— "Herpes Virus, Canis: Aspect of Pathogenesis and Immune Response." *Journal of Veterinary Medicine*, Vol. 156, June 1970.

Evans, C.D., DVM., "Heat Stress: Warm Weather Hazard to Dogs." *Purina Kennel News*, Volume 3, Kansas City, Missouri, 1976.

Faulkner, L.C., DVM., *Reproduction in Dogs*, Colorado State University, Animal Reproduction Laboratory, Fort Collins, Colorado, 1980.

Haskins, Steve C., DVM, *Cardiopulmonary Resuscitation*. Volume 4, No. 2 (February), Continuing Education Article No. 6. Department of Surgery, School of Veterinary Medicine, University of California, Davis, California.

Holst, P.A., DVM., *Breeding Management; Vaginal Cytology*. Colorado State University, Animal Reproduction Laboratory, Fort Collins, Colorado, 1980.

Hoskins, John D., DVM., *Diarrhea*. Ralston Purina Company, 1975. Veterinary Clinic Sciences, Small Animal Hospital, Iowa State University, Ames, Iowa.

Huxsoll, David L., DVM., and Hemelt, Irene E., A.B., "Clinical Observations of Canine Herpes Virus". *Journal of Veterinary Medicine*, Volume 156, June 1970.

Lawler, Dennis F., DVM., *Tube-feeding Puppies*. Ralston Purina Company, St. Louis, Missouri, 1980.

Lewis, L.D., DVM., *Feeding and Care of the Dog*, Colorado State University, Animal Reproduction Laboratory, Fort Collins, Colorado, 1980.

Little, Clarence D., DVM., *The Inheritance of Coat Color in Dogs*, Third Edition. New York: Howell Book House, 1969.

Merck Veterinary Manual, Seventh Edition. Rahway, New Jersey: Merck and Company, 1991.

Olson, P.N., DVM., *A Method for Collection of Semen in the Dog; Artificial Insemination of the Bitch; Clinical Approach to Reproductive Failure in the Dog; Reproduction Patterns in the Bitch; Reproductive Patterns in the Male*. Colorado State University, Animal Reproduction Laboratory, Fort Collins, Colorado, 1980.

Osweicer, Gary D., DVM., *Common Poisonings in Small Animal Practice*. Columbia, Missouri.

Pickett, B.W., DVM., *Seminal Handling for Maximum Reproduction Efficiency*. Colorado State University, Animal Reproduction Laboratory, Fort Collins, Colorado, 1980.

Pollock, Roy V.H., DVM., and Carmichael, Leland E., DVM., *Newer Knowledge About Canine Parvovirus*. 30th Gaines Veterinary Symposium at the School of Medicine, Oregon State University, January 27, 1981.

Stockner, P.K., DVM., *Reproductive Diseases of the Female; Reproductive Soundness Examination*. Colorado State University, Animal Reproduction Laboratory, Fort Collins, Colorado, 1980.

Wallach, S.J.R., DVM., *Sexual Behavior of the Male and Female Dog*. Colorado State University, Animal Reproduction Laboratory, Fort Collins, Colorado, 1980.

Index

Acute Metritis, 307
advertising
    -photos, 252-253
aggression, 170-172
    -herding, 205
agility
    -commands, 186-187
    -competition, 9, 181
    -practical, 222-223
    -structural, 19, 27, 37-38, 45
    -training, 181-187
aging, 153-157
    -diet, 155-156
    -exercise, 156
    -process, 154
    -working, 156
Agoiti Signal Peptide (ASIP), 272
air kennel, 163
allergic reaction, 138
Altdeutscher Schaeferhund, 4
American Kennel Club (AKC), 6-7, 17, 73, 175-176, 229
anal glands, 100
Andorra, 291
angulation, 27, 30, 46-47
anopthalmia, 276, 285
anthelminitcs. See dewormers
arm,
    forearm (radius-ulna), 45
    upper (humers), 30, 44, 46
artificial insemination, 305
artificial respiration, 136
associations. See individual associations
Australia, 1
Australian Shepherd Club of America, 5-7, 17, 229, 355
    -Hall of Fame, 292
autoimmune problems, 122
balance, 19, 27, 29, 32, 37, 46
    -herding, stock work, 213
barking, 72-73, 173, 190
Basques, 1, 4, 291
Basque dogs. See Basques
bathing, 101-103
behavior, 66, 337-340
    -aggression, 170-172
    -breeding for, 277-278
    -problem, 170-173
biking, 13, 222
birth
    -Cesarean, 354
    -breech, 318
    -defects, 326-327
bitch. See also reproduction
    -brood bitch, 289, 293-294
    -care of new mother, 320-321
    -reproductive system, 294, 303
bite. See also grip and teeth
    -breeding for, 274-275
    -types of, 23-24
    -undershot, 23, 353

bites
    -animal, 138
    -insect, 145
    -snake, 149
bleeding, 122, 138-139
    -internal, 139
bloodlines, developing, 291-292
Blue Shadow, 5
boarding, 164-165
bobtail, natural, 19. See tails
bobtail shepherds, 3
bowel movement, 332
breed clubs, 6-7
    -See also individual associations
    -See Appendix
Breed Standard, 7, 17-39, 272-274, 282, 328
breeding, 281-289, 353-354 See also mating
    -inheritance, 270-272
    -program, 262-266
brindle, 274
brucellosis, 306
brushing, 101
burns, 140
camping, 161
Canadian Kennel Club, 7, 17, 229
Canine Eye Registry Foundation (CERF), 277
Canine Good Citizen Test (CGC), 175-176
Cardiopulmonary Resuscitation (CPR), 137
careers, canine, 14-15
castration. See neutering
casting, 207
cataracts, 277, 285
Champion
    -requirements of, 234
    -obedience, 12, 237
    -working, 219
character, 20 See also temperament
    -Miniature Australian Shepherd, 350, 351
chest, 27-28
chewing, 73, 173
children, 55, 66, 81-87, 172
choking, 140
cleft palate, 327
coat, 19, 34, 55, 96, 352. See also color
    -care of, 96, 101-103
    -shedding, 55, 96
coccidia. See coccidiosis.
coccidiosis, 69, 123
Collie Eye Anomaly (CEA), 285
colombomas, 285
color
    -acceptable, 35-36
    -breeding for, 270-271, 286-291
    -eyes, 25, 271
    -genetics of, 272-274
    -nose, 35, 340
commands
    -agility, 185-186
    -basic, 168-170

-directional, 207
-herding/stockdog, 192-199
-whistle, 216-217
conception, 305-306
concussion, 139
conditioning, 221-223
conformation
    -classes, 230, 234-236
    -entering, 234
    -handling, 241-245
    -judging, 18-49
    -preparation for, 239-241
    -selection, 58
    -shows, 10, 229, 230
constipation, 123, 140-141, 333-334
contracts, 59
convulsions. See seizures
coronavirus, 120
crates, 63. See also training
cross-driving, 212
croup, 27-29
cryptorchidism, 39, 299, 353
culling, 327
cuts, 141
deafness, 273, 276, 288
defects, 266-270, 285-286, 326-327
    -eliminating, 266-270
    -in miniature Aussies, 351, 353-355
defective white factor. See homozygous merle
dehydration, in puppies 332
dewclaws, 30-32
    -removal of, 327-328
dewormers, 125-127, 341
diarrhea, 122-123, 141
    -in puppies, 333
    -treatment of, 123
    -viral, 120
diet, 108-114
    -aging dogs, 116, 155-156
dislocations, 141-142
disposition, See temperament
disqualifications, 35, 39, 353
distemper, 120
distichiasis, 353
DNA, 256, 272, 351
    -see paternity testing
dog food. See diet
dog shows. See conformation and trial
dominance, 66
driving, 189, 206, 210-212
drowning, 145-146
drugs
    -common, 125
dudley nose. See nose
dwarfism, 354
dysplasia, 275-276, 286

ears, 26

-care of, 97
-conformation, 26
electrical shock, 142
Ely
    -Blue, 5, 291, 295
    -Feo, 5, 291
    -Juanita, 5, 291
Epilepsy, 352
    -See also seizures
eye, 25
    -care of, 97
    -defect, 273, 276-277, 285-286
    -herding, 190, 193
    -injury, 142, 209
    -puppies, 331-332
Farrington's Buster Ivory, 6
fear, 172
feeding, 114-117
    performance, 225-226
feet, 30-33, 37, 46
    -care of, 225
fetching, 203-204
first aid, 135-151
flanking, 207-208
fleas, 129-130
Flintridge, Heard's
    -Blue Spice of. See Heard's
    -Cactus of. See Heard's
    -Chilie of. See Heard's
    -Fieldmaster of, 6
    -Salt of. See Heard's
    -Wildhagen's Dutchman of, 6
flyball, 11
foreign objects, 142-143
forequarters, 30-31, 46-49
fractures, 143
Frisbee, 11, 176-179
frostbite, 143-144, 227
gait, 37-38, 41-49
gaiting, 243-245
genes
    -for behavior, 277-278
    -for coat colors, 272-274
genetic
    -disorders. See defects
George, Lois, 6
George's Red Rustler, 6,
German Coolies. see Koolies
German Tiger Dogs. See Altdeutscher Schaeferhund
gestation, 309-310
Ghost-eyed dogs, page 7 of color section
giardia, 124
grief, 157
grip, 23, 189
gripping, 21, 27, 208
grooming, 95-103, 156
guarantees, 58
Guide Dogs for the Blind, 15

Harper's Old Smokey, 6
Hartnagle's
   -Badger, 5, 291-292
   -Fritzie Taylor, 292
   -Goody, (Goodie), 5, 291
   -Hud, 292
   -Jinx, 291
head, 21-22, 352
heading, 189
Heard, Dr. Weldon T., 5-6
Heard's
   -Blue Spice, 3, 6-7
   -Cactus, 5
   -Chilie, 6-7
   -Salt, -6-7
hearing dogs, 15
heart massage, 136-137
heartworm, 126-127 See Ivermectin
heat stress, 144-145
hepatitis, 120
herding
   -commands, 192-199
   -instincts, 3, 189
   -trials, 11, 219
   -titles, 219
hernia, 317, 327
herpes virus, 306, 334-335
hiking, 13, 187
hindquarters, 32-33, 46-49
hip joint, 27-29, 32-33, 38, 46. See also dysplasia
hocks (metatarsi), 32-33, 46-49
homozygous merle, 273, 276, 289, 291, 326
hunting, 13
hypothermia, 145, 332
identification, 74, 163
illness
   -puppy ailments, 332-335
   -signs of, 122
immunization. See vaccinations
Imodium, 125, 133
inbreeding, 265, 291
injury
   -abdominal, 138
   -brain, 139
   -carrying an injured dog, 138
   -eye, 142
   -foot, 225
   -lung, 145
   -nose, 146
   -physical, 150
   -see also over training
   -throat, 149-150
   -traumatic, 150
instincts, 3, 189
International English Shepherd Registry (IESR) 7
Ivermectin, 125, 133
   -toxicity, 133
jaw, 274, 353

jogging, 12, 222
jumping up, 173
Junior Showmanship, 187, 234-237
kennel
   -cough, 120
   -dogs, 54
   -facilities, 90-93
Koolie, 4
labor, 313-314
Las Rocosa, Hartnagle's, 5-6
   -Leslie, 6, 292
   -Lester, 6, 292
   -Shiloh, 6, 292
   -Sydney, 6
   -Justin Case of, 290-291
laws, dog, 76-79
legs, 30-33, 37, 41-46
   -foreleg, 30-31
   -hind leg, 32-33
leptospirosis, 120
lice, 130-131
lifting, 205, 209
line breeding, 265-266, 291
livestock
   selecting, 202
loin, 27-29, 45
longevity, 291
look back, 215
lost dogs, 74-75, 164
lung, 28, 145
luxated patellas, 354
Lyme disease, 121-122. See also ticks
mange. See mites
mastitis, 322-323
matches
-show, 230
maturity, 340-342
medication
   -antibiotics, 123
   -common drugs, 125
   -dewormers, 125-129, 133, 341
Melacortin Receptor 1 (MCR1), 272-273
Merino Sheep. See Spanish Merino
merle, 273, 276, 287-289
   -cryptic, 273
   -phantom, 273
   -See also color
metatarsi (hock) 32-33
microphthalmia, 276
Miniature Australian Shepherd
   -benefits, 349, 351
   -breeding, 353
   -finding, 351
   -health issues, 354
   -history, 349
   -judging, 351
   -temperament, 350

Miniature Australian Shepherd Club of USA
   (MASCUSA) 351, 356
Mistretta, 6
mites, 131-132
monorchidism, 39, 301, 353
motion sickness, 164
muzzle, 21, 23-24, 47, 352
    -applying emergency, 136
    -use in stock training, 205
National Stock Dog Registry (NSDR), 7, 291
neck, 27-29
Nettesheim's Twinkles, 5
neutering, 58, 76
North American Miniature Australian Shepherd Club of USA
   (NAMACUSA), 351, 356
nose, 35-36, 47, 340
    -care of, 98
    -Dudley, 35-36, 353
    -injury, 146
nursing, 321
nutrition, 105-107
Obedience, 12
    -choosing the dog, 57
    -commands, 168
    -titles, 12, 237
    -trials, 12, 237
occiput. See head
Old German Shepherds. See Altdeutscher Schaeferhund
Orthopedic Foundation for Animals (OFA), 275-276, 286
outcross, 265-266, 291
outrun, 209, 215-216
overheating, 333. See also heat stress
over training, 223
paralysis, 146
parasites, 124-133
parvovirus, 120
pasterns, 30-31, 46
paternity testing, 304
patterned white, 273
pedigree, 59, 264, 282
pelvis, 29, 31-33
penning, 212-213
peritonitis, 335
persistent papillary membrane (PPM), 286
pigmentation, 273
play, 66, 192
point of shoulder, 30-31, 45
Poison Control Hotline, 146
poisoning, 146-148
porcupine quills, 148
Progressive Retinal Atrophy (PRA), 286
puppy
    -ailments, 332-335
    -development, 337-342
    -developmental stages, 344
    -evaluating, 190
    -handling, 335

    -hazards, 62, 89
    -orphans, 328-332
    -selection, 190-192, 342-343
    -socialization, 65-66, 340
    -testing, 342-347
    -weaning, 338
pyometra, 307
Pyrenees Mountains, 4,
Pyrenean Shepherd, 3-4, 72
rabies, 121
registry, 6, 291
registration, 7, 59
reproduction
    -artificial insemination, 305
    -controlling, 75
    -mating, 302-304
    -pregnancy, false, 296
    -problems, 294
    -soundness, 300-301
retinal dysplasia, 276-277, 286
retrieving, 222, 346
ribs, 27-29
roundworms, 128
sable, 273
sanitation, 77, 91
scent hurdle racing, 12
Schutzhund, 13
Search and Rescue, 15
seizures, 148-149
sensitivity, 343-344
septicemia, 335
shedding, 96
    -sorting stock, 215
sheep, 1-2, 4, 202
Sisler, Jay, xii, 5, 14, 369
    -Blue Star, 5
    -Keeno, 5
    -Shorty, 5,
    -Stub, 5
skunks, 149
sorting, 215
soundness
    -reproductive, 300-301
Spain, 1, 4-6
Spanish Merino, 4
spaying, 58, 75-76
spina bifida, 327
spirit dogs, see ghost eyed
sports (dog), 9-14
sprains, 149
stacking, 243
stock, methods of moving, 202, 206
stockdogs, 15
    -classes/divisions, 219
    -selecting, 57
    -titles, 219
    -training, 192-219
    -trials, 11, 219

Stonehenge,
    -Justin Case of, 290
stop. See headstifle, 32-33
stress, 224
    -heat, 144
stud dog, 284-285, 298-300
tail, 27
    -docking, 327-328
    -genetics of, 271-272
tapeworms, 128-129
Taylor's
    -Buena, 256, 290
    -Whiskey, 279, 290
teamwork, 217-219
teeth 23-24, 353
    -broken, 139
    -care of, 98-99
    -milk teeth, 337-338
temperament, 20, 53, 56, 281-282, 342 (dominance), 350
    -bitch's, 323
tests,
    -Canine Good Citizen, 7, 73, 175-176
    -herding, 219
    -personality, 56
    -puppy, 190-192, 342-347
    -tracking, 12
therapy dogs, 15, 187
thigh, 32-33
ticks, 132-133
toad poisoning, 150
toenails,
    -care of, 99-100
    -puppies, 328
topline, 27-29, 37, 45-49
toxic substances, 147
tracking
    -titles, 12, 179
    -training, 179-181
trainability, 190, 282
training
    -basic, 167-170
    -crate, 63
    -grooming table, 96-97
    -house, 64
    -leash, 67
    -over training, 223
    -puppy, 68, 338
    -rewards, 167-168
    -tools, 168
travel
    -aging dog, 157
    -air, 162-164
    -bus, 164
    -crates, 160, 163
    -ship, 164
    -train, 164
    -training, 159
    -vehicle, 161

trials. See herding, stockdog, Obedience
tricks, 14
tuck up, 27-28
Twin Oaks, 6
Tyrosinase Related Protein 1 (TRP1), 273
umbilical cord, 317
United Kennel Club (UKC) 5-7, 17, 229
United States Australian Shepherd Association (USASA), 6-7, 229, 351, 355-356
urination, 54
    -illness, 122
    -pregnancy, 310
    -newborn puppies, 332
vaccinations, 77
    -schedule, 341
vaginitis, 306-307
vital signs, 136-137
    -puppies, 325-326
vomiting, 122, 150-151
waste removal. See sanitation
Welsh
    -Old Welsh Bob Tail, 4
    -Sheepdog, 4
wheelchair assistant, 15
whelping, 313-319
    -breech birth, 318-319
    -box, 312
    -chart, 311
    -problems, 320
whipworms, 129
whistle commands, 216-217
white
    -pattern white, 289
    -See also color, homozygous merle
    -white trim, 273, 289
Wood, Fletcher, 5
Wood's
    -Blue Shadow. See Hartnagle's Goody
    -Dandy, 6
    -Jay, 5
worming schedule, 341
worms, 124
    -dewormers, 125
    -deworming, 335
    -types of, 126-129
wounds, 141

About the Author

Jeanne Joy Hartnagle-Taylor, author of *All About Aussies* and *Greasepaint Matadors: The Unsung Heroes of Rodeo* (Alpine Publications), is the third of four generations to enjoy a lifetime association with Australian Shepherds. From the time she was a small child, she saw and used the breed in the environment for which it was originally intended.

Jeanne Joy has done much for the promotion of Aussies by exhibiting at livestock events, fairs, and rodeos, and by writing various articles for publications such as *Western Horseman* and *Cattleman*. She also developed the highly acclaimed stock-dog training video series, *Herding I, II,* and *III* (Canine Training Systems). *All About Aussies* was nominated for a Dog Writer's Award.

Her experience has taken her on assignment with the Department of Interior to work wild bison with her Aussies as well as with the United States Department of Agriculture to gather livestock for inspections. She has presented training clinics and seminars all across North America and Europe. She performed at the Livestock Expo in Tepatitlán, Guadalajara, by special invitation from the governor of Jalisco, Mexico.

Jeanne Joy also has judged the European Championships at the Continental Sheepdog Trials. She is an accredited ASCA Conformation and Stock-Dog Judge (only one of six), and an AKC Herding Judge.

Jeanne Joy has titled Aussies in all areas of competition. She has been in the top ten at the National Stock Dog Finals with her Working Trial Champion, and she has entertained thousands of spectators with Agility and Flyball demonstrations at state fairs with the Superdog Agility Shows.

Jeanne Joy was the breeder of the winning entry at the First Stock Dog Futurity, and along with her family was the first kennel admitted into the Australian Shepherd Hall of Fame for breeding a standard of excellence.

Photo by Joe Bishop.

Jay Sisler performing his trademark act with Sisler's Shorty and Stub.

Order Your Copy Today!

Now in it's
3rd Edition
with 2009 Updates
on miniature Aussies.

ISBN 1-57779-074-X

List Price $49.95

___ YES! I want to order _____ copies of *All About Aussies 3rd Edition* @ U. S. $49.95 each. Foreign orders must be paid by money order, Visa, or MasterCard. Shipping in the U.S. is free; call or email for rates outside USA.

My ___check or money order for $_____ is enclosed.

___ Charge my Visa or MasterCard   Exp. Date_____

Card Number_____

Deliver to:

Name_____

Address_____

City_____State_____ Zip_____

Country_____

Phone_____ email_____

___Please send information on how I can earn FREE BOOKS by referring *ALL ABOUT AUSSIES* to others!

Mail to:
Alpine Publications, 38262 Linman Road, Crawford, CO 81415
CALL 1-800-777-7257 or 970-921-5005
Browse all our titles at: www.alpinepub.com

You might also enjoy...

Teach all levels of USDAA and AKC agility with the help of veteran exhibitor/trainer. ISBN 1-57779-091-4

All-time top handler Peter Green gives proven tips to winning in the conformation ring. ISBN 1-57779-020-0

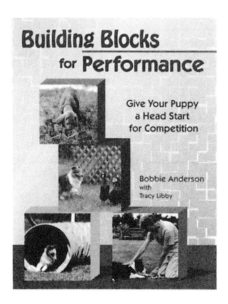

Make your dog a star in any type of performance events with these proven methods. ISBN 1-57779-037-5

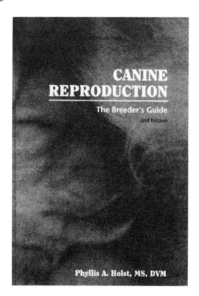

For some of the best information on breeding and raising puppies, choose this one. ISBN 1-57770-028-6